The Afro-Latino Memoir

The Afro-Latino Memoir

Race, Ethnicity, and Literary
Interculturalism

Trent Masiki

The University of North Carolina Press CHAPEL HILL

This book was published with the assistance of the Authors Fund of the University of North Carolina Press.

Set in Merope Basic by Westchester Publishing Services
Manufactured in the United States of America

Library of Congress Cataloging-in-Publication Data
Names: Masiki, Trent, author.
Title: The Afro-Latino memoir : race, ethnicity, and literary interculturalism / Trent Masiki.
Description: Chapel Hill : The University of North Carolina Press, [2023] | Includes bibliographical references and index.
Identifiers: LCCN 2023004226 | ISBN 9781469675268 (cloth ; alk. paper) | ISBN 9781469675275 (pbk. ; alk. paper) | ISBN 9781469675282 (ebook)
Subjects: LCSH: Thomas, Piri, 1928–2011—Criticism and interpretation. | Moore, Carlos—Criticism and interpretation. | Vega, Marta Moreno—Criticism and interpretation. | Chambers, Veronica—Criticism and interpretation. | Cepeda, Raquel—Criticism and interpretation. | American literature—Hispanic American authors—History and criticism. | American literature—African American authors—History and criticism. | Autobiography.
Classification: LCC PS153.H56 M38 2023 | DDC 810.9/8—dc23/eng/20230316
LC record available at https://lccn.loc.gov/2023004226

Cover illustration: Olga Albizu (1924–2005), *Radiante* (1967, oil on canvas, 172.7 × 157.5 cm). Smithsonian American Art Museum, Washington, D.C. (gift of JPMorgan Chase).

For Naima and Samara

Contents

Acknowledgments ix

Introduction 1
Between Cultures and Canons

CHAPTER ONE
Laughing the Demons Away 34
Piri Thomas and the Black Aesthetic

CHAPTER TWO
From Bohemian *Piolo* to Leftist *Jorocón* 61
The Pan-African Radicalization of Carlos Moore

CHAPTER THREE
Morenophilia/Morenophobia 79
Marta Moreno Vega, Afro-Caribbean Religion,
and Ethnic Intermarriage

CHAPTER FOUR
Post-Soul Latinidad 104
Black Nationalism in the Memoirs of
Veronica Chambers and Raquel Cepeda

Coda 130
Literary Nationalism, Postrace Aesthetics,
and Comparative Latino Literary Studies

Notes 139
Bibliography 179
Index 223

Acknowledgments

It was either during the process of applying to the program or during the first year of my doctoral studies that one of my professors said, "We know you can write, but do you have something to say?" That is when I knew that the W. E. B. Du Bois Department of Afro-American Studies at the University of Massachusetts-Amherst was the right place for me. *The Afro-Latino Memoir: Race, Ethnicity, and Literary Interculturalism* would not have been possible without the historical foundation, theoretical grounding, methodological training, and racial justice mission I received from the core and affiliate faculty members in my doctoral program. I am eternally grateful to them for modeling how to be a lifelong student, teacher, and scholar of Africana studies. I am especially thankful to James E. Smethurst, Steven C. Tracy, and Rachel L. Mordecai for continuing to read my work, provide professional guidance, and write letters of support.

The Afro-Latino Memoir exists because UNC Press and Lucas Church, my editor, believed it should. Thank you, Lucas, for having faith in my manuscript. Earnest thanks to the peer reviewers who recognized its merit as well; the scope and level of detail in your feedback were absolutely essential. For investing in my research, teaching, and scholarly potential, I am profoundly indebted to the Fulbright US Scholar program, the National Endowment for the Humanities (NEH), the Center for Humanistic Inquiry (CHI) at Amherst College, and the Kilachand Honors College (KHC) and African American Studies program at Boston University. Thanks to the generous support of the Fulbright program, I spent a year teaching expository writing and US literature in Panama. My year abroad enhanced my understanding of how race and ethnicity are constructed and lived in Latin America and the littoral Caribbean. My NEH Summer Stipend and CHI Fellowship provided me with the funding, resources, and time I needed to write the third chapter of this book, a chapter that was not originally conceived as part of this project. I am immensely appreciative of my CHI cohort; Darryl Harper, the CHI director; and his wife, Sonia Y. Clark. To my CHI cohort, thank you for helping me think through and articulate my ideas about the value of putting the post-soul in conversation with Afro-Latinidad. Darryl, thank you for being a steady and compassionate leader in the midst of the pandemic. To Sonia, thank you for your professional advice, impeccable culinary skills, and limitless wit and joy.

Prior to joining the CHI, I spent three transformative years at Boston University as a KHC postdoctoral scholar. The success of KHC's postdoctoral program is due to the phenomenal leadership of Carrie J. Preston and her executive team. Heartfelt thanks to you Carrie for being genuinely invested in the professional development and personal growth of the postdoctoral scholars. To Joanna Davidson, thank you for observing my class and for having me speak in the Walter Rodney Lecture series. To my dear friend Richard Tonetti, thank you for infusing KHC with your humor and good spirit. Thanks also to my fellow KHC postdocs, both near and far. The three years we spent codesigning syllabi, teaching seminars, developing cocurricular programming, discussing pedagogy, reading cultural theory, holding mock job talks, peer reviewing job materials, and crafting book proposals were an invaluable apprenticeship. Though our postdoc years are well behind us, John Frederick Bell and I keep the KHC fellowship aflame in Worcester. During my time at Boston University, I had the great pleasure of working with Louis Chude-Sokei, chair of the African American Studies program and editor of *The Black Scholar*. Louis, thank you for making it possible for me to teach my Afro-Latino Memoir course, guest-lecture in your Black Thought course, and discuss, in various forums, my research on Afro-Latino literature and culture. I am forever thankful to you for offering me the opportunity to conceive and guest edit *Post-Soul Afro-Latinidades*, a special issue of *The Black Scholar*. At this point, I would be remiss if I did not also express my appreciation to Boston University's Center for Antiracist Research, its Postdoctoral Association, and its Office of Professional Development and Postdoctoral Affairs. These three institutions provided op-ed writing workshops, hosted the postdoctoral seminar series, and conducted grant writing seminars, respectively.

Over the course of my intellectual journey in Afro-American and Latino studies, I have been humbled by the generosity of my colleagues. Many thanks to John H. Bracey Jr. and Randy Ontiveros for introducing me to book editors. I am much obliged to Agustin Laó-Montes, A Yẹmisi Jimoh, Ylce Irizzary, Antonio López, Lee Bebout, Elena Machado Sáez, Ricardo L. Ortíz, Michael Birenbaum Quintero, Esther Jones, and Ousmane Power-Greene for offering professional advice and support on a range of levels. For publishing my article on Black nationalism in the memoirs of Veronica Chambers and Raquel Cepeda, I am supremely thankful to Lourdes Torres and the editorial board of the journal *Latino Studies*. The fourth chapter of this book is an expanded version of that article.

Since 2016, I have been fortunate to work with several excellent journal editors and anonymous peer reviewers. I am grateful to these editors and peer reviewers for their candid and substantive feedback on my scholarly articles. The experience I gained publishing those articles prepared me for this book project. I am especially grateful to Emily J. Lordi, Médar Serrata, Jorge Santos, and Travis Franks for reading and commenting on drafts of my articles and book chapters. Sincere thanks to Flávia Santos de Araújo, Isabel Espinal, Angélica María Sánchez Barona, Maria Ximena Abello, Spencer Kuchle, Watufani M. Poe, Rose Lenehan, and Janice Yu for serving on and organizing conference panels and symposia with me. In addition to reading my work and serving on panels with me, Regina Marie Mills co-guest edited *Post-Soul Afro-Latinidades*. For that labor of love, I am truly beholden. Thanks are also due to Ayendy Bonifacio for anchoring *Post-Soul Afro-Latinidades* with his erudite and lyrical personal essay. Besides my colleagues, I would like to applaud the librarians at Boston University, Amherst College, and Worcester Polytechnic Institute for tracking down the various and varying sources I needed to complete this project. Distinct acknowledgments to the interlibrary loan team at Boston University for always going the extra mile, specifically during the pandemic.

To the village of friends and family members in Shreveport, Worcester, Woburn, and Arizona, thank you for being there for me and my family in ways both large and small. Special recognition to Lamont A. Slater for his moral support and intellectual camaraderie. Brother Slater, thank you for being an oasis of encouragement in the burning sands of doctoral and professional achievement.

For their remarkable patience, I am most grateful to my family. Naima and Samara, my wise and victorious daughters, are the sources of my inspiration. To my wife, Suzy, thank you for your boundless love and support. None of this would have been possible without you.

The Afro-Latino Memoir

Introduction

Between Cultures and Canons

In March 2002, Latinos displaced African Americans as the nation's largest ethnic minority group.[1] Since then, Latinos have steadily grown and maintained their demographic primacy. In the 2020 US Census, 18.7 percent of Americans identified as Hispanic or Latino, whereas only 12.4 percent of Americans identified as solely Black/African American.[2] The loss of African Americans' demographic distinction is one of several features that marks the end of the "post-soul" era (mid-1970s–2000),[3] an era in which integration and neoliberalism reshaped African American life, culture, and political activity. In 2005, Nelson George, the cultural critic who coined the term post-soul,[4] predicted that African Americans would build greater intercultural solidarities with Latinos by 2025 because so many Latinos were indeed Afro-Latinos.[5] As recently as 2016, Afro-Latinos constituted 25 percent of the ever-growing Hispanic population.[6] Currently, 2.4 million Americans identify as Black Hispanics.[7] George's prediction that African Americans would form cultural and political solidarities with the growing Afro-Latino population is based on the presumption of a linked racial fate.[8] The discourse of linked fate animates the Afro-Latino turn in Latino and Africana Studies.[9]

By popularizing the history of Afro-Hispanics in the US, Latin America, and the Caribbean, scholars Miriam Jiménez Román, Juan Flores, and Henry Louis Gates Jr. have done the important work of bridging the connection between Latino and Africana studies for a mass audience. In 2010, Jiménez Román and Flores published *The Afro-Latin@ Reader: History and Culture in the United States*. The following year, Gates released the PBS documentary *Black in Latin America*. These two works are emblematic of an increasing scholarly and public interest in global Afro-Latino history and culture, an interest that overlaps with the United Nation's International Year for People of African Descent (2011) and its International Decade for People of African Descent (2015–24). The accessibility of Jiménez Román and Flores's reader and of Gates's documentary enhance public awareness of the transnational circulation and transcultural history Afro-Latinidad in the Americas.[10] As Jiménez Román and Flores point out, Afro-Latino immigrants have been forming cultural and political solidarities with African Americans for over

150 years.[11] The first significant wave of Afro-Latino immigration from the Hispanic Caribbean was a consequence of the Cuban cigar industry establishing factories in Florida and New York to escape the upheaval of Cuba's Ten Years' War (1868–1878).[12] Although Cuban immigrants arrived in New York City and lived among free African Americans as early as 1823, relatively few of them were Afro-Cubans before 1868.[13] A second wave of Afro-Latino immigration to the US occurred after the conclusion of the short-lived Spanish-American War, in which the US acquired Cuba, Puerto Rico, Guam, and the Philippines in 1898.[14] Twentieth-century waves of Afro-Latino immigration include those that occurred in the postwar era as a consequence of Operation Boot Strap (1947) in Puerto Rico, the Cuban Revolution (1959), and the Dominican Republic's Civil War (1965).[15]

The long history of Afro-Latinos in the US not only raises questions about what constitutes Latino literature but also about what constitutes African American literature. Why does the *Oxford Companion to African American Literature* (1997) include a sizeable entry on Piri Thomas, the Puerto Rican author of the groundbreaking memoir *Down These Mean Streets* (1967)? Why does the *Norton Anthology of African American Literature* (2014) include entries on foreign Hispanophone writers like Nicolás Guillén, but not on Afro-Latino authors like Thomas, who was born in Harlem, became a member of the Harlem Writers Guild, and participated in the Black Arts Movement conferences of the 1960s and 1970s? Thomas was such a staple figure in the Black Arts Movement that major African American magazines like *The Crisis* and *Negro Digest* reviewed and sold his books.[16] They also kept readers abreast of the book banning cases that plagued *Down These Mean Streets* from 1971 to 1982.[17] Thomas's story illustrates the profound impact of African American culture on the constitution of Afro-Latino identity and literature. The understudied influence of African American literature, culture, and racial discourse on postsegregation Afro-Latino life writing is the subject of *The Afro-Latino Memoir: Race, Ethnicity, and Literary Interculturalism*.

The Afro-Latino Memoir opens the border between the canons of Latino and African American literature by centering a long, but often neglected, history of African American intercultural exchange and political solidarity in Latino autobiography and life writing. I argue that Afro-Latino coming of age memoirs written in the postsegregation era expand not only what it means and has meant to be Latino in the US, but also what it means and has meant to be African American. Six key questions outline the stakes of my argument. Are the African American experience and Afro-Latino identity mutually constitutive? If so, then what is Latino about African American literature? What is

African American about Latino literature? Should the Afro-Latino memoir be included in the African American as well as the Latino literary canon? What cohesiveness do both canons stand to gain or lose by such inclusion? What can the Afro-Latino memoir reveal about the relationship between Latinidad, Pan-Africanism, and Black nationalism? Using cultural poetics, life writing theory, and intertextual, intersectional, and close textual analysis,[18] I demonstrate that Afro-Latino memoir writers strategically use their affiliation with the African American condition to articulate and assert their sense of national and diasporic belonging. Analyzing how various modes of Black nationalism shape what it means to be and become Afro-Latino uncovers the intercultural and transnational nature of Afro-Latinidad. *The Afro-Latino Memoir* combines literary analysis and historical methods to reveal how African American nationalism, narrative strategies, cultural tropes, and political ideologies inform the conceptualization and performance of Afro-Latinidad in the US from the postwar to the post-soul era. *The Afro-Latino Memoir* makes a unique and significant contribution to the field of US multiethnic literary studies by shedding new light on how African American literary production, expressive culture, political ideology, and religiosity shaped the writers in this study. It challenges narratives of Latino American and African American cultural strife, promotes interdisciplinary engagement and collaboration among scholars, and provides a shared cultural history that Latino Americans and African Americans can use to build formidable political coalitions in the twenty-first century. Despite their literary, historical, and cultural significance, Afro-Latino memoirs are marginalized in both Latino and African American studies. *The Afro-Latino Memoir* remedies this problem by recovering Afro-Latino memoirs from their undeserved neglect.

The African American presence and influence in Afro-Latino memoirs are woefully understudied in US multiethnic literature. In *Afro-Latin@s in Movement: Critical Approaches to Blackness and Transnationalism in the Americas*, Petra R. Rivera-Rideau, Jennifer A. Jones, and Tianna S. Paschel argue that, until the 1970s, Latin American and Latino studies scholarship often marginalized Afro-Latino history, culture, and political organizing, limiting examinations "to particular areas: music, dance, food, physical strength, and sexual prowess."[19] Black studies fared no better, contend Rivera-Rideau, Jones, and Paschel: "African Diaspora Studies . . . have largely neglected to incorporate Afro-Latin Americans or Afro-Latinos into their analysis, a curious omission given the substantial black population in the region."[20] Transnationalism and transculturalism between Latino, Latin American, Caribbean, and African

American communities are not completely neglected by scholars working in Black and African American cultural studies, but historically the projects in these fields have been nationally focused and Anglophonecentric. However, when theorists and historians in literary and cultural studies do explore Latino and African American interculturalism, they tend to highlight a relatively small fraternity of writers: Arthur (Arturo) A. Schomburg, Nicolás Guillén, Piri Thomas, and more recently, Evelio Grillo.[21] Although two of these four Afro-descendant authors are memoirists, there has been little sustained critical attention given to the African American influences in Latino memoirs beyond Thomas's *Down These Mean Streets* (1967) and Grillo's *Black Cuban, Black American* (2000). What can be learned about Latino and African American interculturalism from studying the memoir rather than some other literary genre? Newspapers, magazines, public records, and archives contain evidence of the people, events, and narratives that populate memoirs. The memoir, therefore, is subject to historical analysis and public scrutiny in ways that other literary genres are not. The memoir allows literary and cultural studies scholars to develop narratives of Afro-Latino life that exceed what can be learned about ethnoracial identity formation from a mere close textual analysis of fictional characters, thematic concerns, and formal structures in novels, plays, poems, songs, or films.

The memoirists in my study include Piri Thomas, Carlos Moore, Marta Morena Vega, Veronica Chambers, and Raquel Cepeda.[22] These five writers have ethnonational roots in various parts of the Hispanic Caribbean: Puerto Rico, Cuba, Panama, and the Dominican Republic. Four of the five were born and raised in the continental US. The period of history covered in their memoirs ranges from 1928 to 2013. The majority of these writers established close personal and professional relationships with African American radicals and activists. For example, Piri Thomas was inspired and mentored by John Oliver Killens and Carlos Moore was ideologically groomed by Lewis H. Michaux and Maya Angelou. African American cultural icons and movements inspired Veronica Chambers and Raquel Cepeda. Chambers, for instance, alludes to Zora Neale Hurston, Toni Morrison, Audre Lorde, and W. E. B. Du Bois as literary ancestors while Cepeda finds spiritual salvation and Pan-African solidarity in hip-hop culture and the Afrocentric theosophy of the Five Percent Nation, a splinter sect of the Nation of Islam. The chapters in *The Afro-Latino Memoir* are sequenced according to the birth order of the writers. This chronological scheme provides a narrative arc that illuminates how the ethos of the Black Arts and post-soul eras respectively influenced conceptions and expressions of Afro-Latinidad.

Using cultural, intersectional, and intertextual analysis, I show how and why the writers in this study use African American narrative strategies, cultural tropes, and political ideologies to write themselves into the archive of US literary history. The narrative strategies I explore include the use of what Robert B. Stepto calls "symbolic geography." Symbolic geography is a literary concept that describes two defining features of African American autobiographical writing: ascent and immersion narratives. Both of these narrative strategies describe journeys of African American racial identity formation. The classical ascent narrative is a story about a slave's escape out of Southern bondage into Northern freedom. Ascent narratives focus on heroic self-transformation through, among other things, the attainment of education, financial security, political empowerment, and increased social mobility.[23] The immersion narrative is a "cultural immersion ritual" that involves travel to and prolonged residence in the Deep South by a subject who, typically, did not grow up there.[24] Usually, the journey is voluntary. In the immersion narrative, the South is prefigured as the taproot of African American identity and cultural authenticity. The South becomes the place where the immersion hero acquires the "balms of group identity" that ameliorate the alienation produced by living outside of the ancestral homeland.[25] The cultural tropes I examine in this study include racial initiation, literary ancestry, colorism, passing, tricksterism, and masking. These cultural tropes are common to each of the memoirs. I highlight them as they occur in each of the memoirs, allowing readers to trace the thread of recurrence from chapter to chapter. The ideological influences I investigate exist in the affiliations the writers in this study had with various African American organizations and cultural groups: the Harlem Writers Guild, literary conferences at Fisk University and Howard University, the National Memorial African Bookstore, the Cultural Association for Women of African Heritage, the Africology and African American Studies Doctoral Program at Temple University, and the Five Percent Nation, a splinter sect of the Nation of Islam. The genealogies of influence in my study reveal that the literary and cultural histories of Latinos and African Americans have been more intertwined and mutually informing than typically imagined.

In addition to their engagement with various forms of African American nationalism, all of the authors in this study published their memoirs in the postsegregation era. I call this era of cultural production the Afroethnic Renewal because it is coterminous with a radical demographic shift in the Black/African American population. As scholars Ira Berlin, Christina M. Greer, and Candis Watts Smith note, postsegregation era immigration re-Africanized the US.[26] Berlin calls this phenomenon the "fourth great migration." He defines the fourth great migration as the influx of immigrants of African descent who entered the US as a consequence of the 1965 Immigration and Nationality Act, the 1986 Immigration and Control Act, and the 1990 Diversity Immigrant Visa Program. The immigrants of the fourth great migration came from Africa, Latin America, and the Hispanic Caribbean.[27] Increasingly, both African and Afro-Latino immigrants are reshaping US culture in ways that interrogate and expand traditional conceptions of African American identity, politics, and expressive culture. As immigrants of African descent and their US-born children integrate themselves into the culture and politics of the US, they place pressure on popular and official conceptions of the term Black/African American, forcing it to expand its definitional scope. Heightened intercultural fusion and sociopolitical solidarity between African Americans and other communities of African descent in the US characterizes the literature and cultural production of the Afroethnic Renewal.

There is ample territory to cover at the intersection of Latino American and African American life writing studies. It is time to center marginalized memoirists like Carlos Moore, Marta Moreno Vega, Veronica Chambers, and Raquel Cepeda. Bringing renewed attention to Afro-Latino literary and cultural history in the US through the study of Afro-Latino memoirs provides Latino American and African American communities the common ground on which they can build lasting bridges of political solidarity rather than walls of exclusion in the era of Black Lives Matter. This is the much-needed cultural work performed by *The Afro-Latino Memoir*.

The Afro-Latino Memoir is the first scholarly monograph to focus on African American nationalism, narrative strategies, and cultural tropes in Afro-Latino memoirs. As a bridge text, it advances the theory that postsegregation Afro-Latino literary production not only challenges conventional notions of Latino subjectivity but also expands what it means to be and become African American. *The Afro-Latino Memoir* does this by employing conceptual tools and methods from African American, Latino, literary, and life writing studies. In addition to the aforementioned texts on Afroethnic immigration, this book is in conversation with new and established theories regarding the history and nature of African American literature and its relationship to literary nationalism. *The Afro-Latino Memoir* is inspired by established and recent studies that explore the nature and purpose of African American literature, studies by scholars ranging from Robert B. Stepto, John Ernest, and Gene Andrew Jarret to Kenneth W. Warren and Margo N. Crawford.[28]

It is equally inspired by Tommie Shelby, William L. Van Deburg, Wilson Jeremiah Moses, and John H. Bracey's histories and theories of Black nationalism.[29] As much as it relies on James E. Smethurst's examination of the Black Aesthetic and the Black Arts Movement,[30] *The Afro-Latino Memoir* is also engaged with the work of post-soul cultural critics, theorists, and their detractors: Greg Tate, Trey Ellis, Nelson George, Mark Anthony Neal, Thelma Golden, Debra Dickerson, Bertram D. Ashe, K. Merinda Simmons, Margo N. Crawford, and Emily J. Lordi, among others.[31]

In recent years, several books that examine Latino and African American sociopolitical entanglements have made significant contributions to Latino studies. *The Young Lords: A Radical History* (2020) by Johanna Fernández and *An African American and Latinx History of the United States* (2018) by Paul Ortiz are two representatives of this trend. *The Afro-Latino Memoir* relies heavily on the historical and cultural studies of Jesse Hoffnung Garskof, Vanessa Valdéz, Nancy R. Mirabal, Claudia Milian, Antonio López, Frank A. Guridy, Agustin Laó-Montes, Marta E. Sánchez, Anani Dzidzenyo and Suzanne Oboler, Lisa Brock and Digna Castañeda Fuertes, and Juan Flores, among others.[32] These scholars have produced important critical studies that examine Afro-Latino history, subjectivity, and transcultural engagement with African Americans, works that expand conventional notions of Latinidad and establish a cultural history of Afro-Latino Pan-African solidarity. However, *The Afro-Latino Memoir* goes further by applying their theories to African American narrative strategies and cultural tropes in Afro-Latino literature. To that end, *The Afro-Latino Memoir*, extends the current scholarship in Latino studies on intercultural affinities between Afro-Latinos and African Americans.

Ricardo L. Ortiz, Ralph E. Rodriquez, Jill Toliver Richardson, Ylce Irizarry, David J. Vázquez, Marta Caminero-Santangelo, Marta E. Sanchez, Raphael Dalleo, Elena Machado Saez, Ifeoma C. K. Nwankwo, Lisa Sánchez González, Eugene Mohr, Richard L. Jackson, William Luis, and Harold Augenbraum and Ilan Stavan have produced important studies that explore what constitutes Latinidad, what qualifies as a Latino literary text, and representations of panethnic and intraracial subjectivity in Latino literature.[33] The examination of Afro-Latino memoirs in the majority of their studies tends to be limited to an analysis of *Down These Means Streets* by Piri Thomas. *The Afro-Latino Memoir* intervenes in the field by simultaneously bringing attention to understudied Afro-Latino memoirists and by revealing new insights about *Down These Mean Streets* and its relationship to the Black Arts Movement.

Regarding memoir and life writing theory, *The Afro-Latino Memoir* relies on theoretical frameworks developed by Philippe Lejeune, G. Thomas Couser, Paul John Eakin, Ben Yagoda, Leigh Gilmore, James Olney, and Sidonie Smith and Julia Watson, among others.[34] In terms of Latino and African American life writing, this project is indebted to the work of Norma Cantú, Silvio Torres-Saillnt, Lourdes Torres, Kenneth Mostern, William L. Andrews, David L. Dudley, Joanne M. Braxton, and Stephen Butterfield.[35] It is also indebted to the literature on the bildungsroman, particularly to theories advanced by Alejandro Latinez, Stella Bolaki, Martin Japtok, Thomas L. Jeffers, Gunilla Theander Kester, and Geta LeSeur.[36] *The Afro-Latino Memoir* contributes to multiethnic life writing studies by revealing new insights about how African American nationalism mediates the intersection of race, ethnicity, and transculturation in Afro-Latino coming of age memoirs.

Memoir, the Bildungsroman, and Ethnoracial Apprenticeship

Why focus on the memoir? Is life writing or literary fiction the better medium for examining the relationship between Afro-Latino identity formation and the African American condition? Unlike forms of literature that are not bound by "the autobiographical pact,"[37] memoirs are committed to historical facticity and veracity.[38] This commitment speaks to life writing's exalted status in Latino studies. Literary scholar Silvio Torres-Saillant argues that "autobiography may be regarded as the most important form in Latino literature" because the genre dramatizes its community's perennial concern "with questions of identity, citizenship, and belonging."[39] The conventional wisdom about Latino autobiographical literature is that it has five defining features. One, it tends to represent a communal portrait of the author's ethnic group. Two, it favors the bildungsroman narrative arc. Three, it is often formally experimental. Four, its thematic content tends to be sociopolitical, addressing the intersectionality of class, culture, sexuality, citizenship status, and ethnoracial identity. Five, it tends to chronicle the author's incorporation into society and achievement of the American Dream even as it simultaneously critiques anti-Latino bigotry. These five pillars constitute the consensus view about the genre.[40] Although there are several scholarly articles, book chapters, and monographs on Latino autobiography, to my knowledge, there are no critical studies exclusively devoted to the Latino memoir. Furthermore, few of the books on Latino life writing fully address the politics of Afro-Latino passing, invisibility, triple consciousness, and

Pan-African solidarity with African Americans, suggesting the need for the intervention *The Afro-Latino Memoir* makes.

What is a memoir, what is a bildungsroman, and what is the relationship between the two? In *Memoir: An Introduction*, G. Thomas Couser defines a memoir as a nonfiction literary genre that "depicts the lives of real, not imagined, individuals."[41] Although the memoir "developed in tandem with the novel,"[42] Couser reminds us that it "is not supposed to require fiction's willing suspension of disbelief."[43] Relying on memory rather than research and depicting a portion of its subject's life rather than the entirety, "Memoir's commitment to the real," asserts Couser, "doesn't just limit its content (what it can be about), it also limits its narrative techniques (how the content can be presented)."[44] The memoir can also be written in the same narrative mode as a bildungsroman.

Novels that chronicle the psychological maturation and social integration of a protagonist from youth to adulthood fall into the literary category of the bildungsroman. A bildungsroman is a novel that narrates the cultural formation, psychological development, and bourgeois social integration of its protagonist from childhood to the point that he or she leaves home and attains independence. The bildungsroman's singular focus on the formative years of its protagonist's life explains its translation in English as a *novel of formation* or an *apprenticeship novel*. Johann Wolfgang von Goethe's novel *Wilhelm Meister's Apprenticeship* (1796) supplies the stylistic conventions and thematic concerns that define the bildungsroman genre, a genre that some theorists suggest does not exist.[45] The apprenticeship metaphor in Goethe's title is derived from the first of the three stages of professional development in the medieval European craft guilds: apprentice, journeyman, and master. *Wilhelm Meister's Journeyman Years, or the Renunciants* (1821), the sequel to *Wilhelm Meister's Apprenticeship*, confirms Goethe's intentional use of the guild system in his literary conceit.

The prospect of intellectual, social, and moral mastery is the key trope of bildung narratives, as seen in Patricia Alden's definition of the genre: "Central to the genre is the notion of individual selfhood achieved through growth and of social experience as an education which forms, and sometimes deforms, that self. The projected resolution of this process is some kind of adjustment to society. Wherever it appeared, the Bildungsroman was associated with bourgeois humanism, with faith in progress and with the value of the individual."[46] Thomas L. Jeffers writes that the bildungsroman's "crucial theme is precisely change: physical, psychological, and moral," and that the subjectivity of its protagonist is latent and becoming rather than manifest and perfected.[47] The development of the bildung hero is twofold, argues Gunilla Theander Kester: "*Bildung* embodies a double process of inner developing and outer developing, what the Germans call *Anbildung* and *Ausbildung*. On the one hand, the word *Bildung* describes how the strengths and talents of the individual emerge, a development of the individual; on the other hand, *Bildung* also describes how the individual's society uses well the individual's manifest strengths and talents, a social 'enveloping' of the individual."[48] The notion that social mobility and moral progress are inevitable for those in, and those who aspire to be in, the bourgeoisie typifies nonfiction bildung narratives like Ben Franklin's *Autobiography* (1791), the prototype for American autobiography and memoir. Franklinesque American autobiography and memoir promote, writes Stella Bolaki, "Exceptionalism, individualism, mobility, freedom, the American Dream, and transcendence," as well as "self-industry, commitment, and reason."[49] The Germanic bildungsroman, argues Kester, is associated with "positivism, white male superiority, and a sense of the self as a unified entity," and it "proposes the growth of a subject from one fixed state of mind to another: immaturity and maturity."[50]

The didactic, acculturative function of the bildungsroman is to groom a community of readers by helping them comprehend the practical benefits of the bildung hero's social and moral cultivation "in the context of vocation, courtship, and parent-child relations," contends Jeffers.[51] The bildungsroman is intrinsically conservative in that the typical resolution involves the protagonist's attainment of a job, a spouse, and domesticity. A bildungsroman's "primary function," contends Bolaki, "is to make integration into the existing social order legitimate by channeling individual energy into socially useful purposes."[52] This makes the bildungsroman an optimal vehicle for promoting the interests of the nation-state: education, workforce development, marriage, nuclear families, bourgeois morality, community engagement, and public and private sector employment, including military service. As is classically practiced, the post-Goethe bildungsroman intrinsically reproduces and perpetuates the status quo.

The secular moral philosophy in the European and American bildungsroman tradition implies a bijective relationship between aesthetic and moral refinement. To fully appreciate the import of the didactic function of bildung narratives and their use as social engineering tools, it is helpful to review the religious origins of the word *bildung* as a synonym for pious self-transformation. The word *bildung* took on its figurative meaning of moral development and social integration in medieval Germany under the influence of Christian mysticism, and in seventeenth- and eighteenth-century Germany under the influence of Neoplatonic pietism and classicism. Susan L. Cocalis traces this history in her essay "The Transformation of *Bildung* from an Image to an Ideal." Cocalis argues that in medieval Germanic mysticism "the verb *bilden* originally signified God's creation of human beings in His image (*Bild*), until Meister Eckhardt and later mystics appended Plotinus's philosophy of emanation and reintegration to it."[53] In other words, the verb *bilden* refers to the act of forming and process of formation. Eckhartian mystics were infatuated with Plotinus's metaphor of the individual as a sculptor and the individual's soul as a block of stone. They believed that individuals were responsible for sculpting their own souls into masterful works of art through reflective practice, and they called this process of introspective self-perfection *"bilden."*[54]

In the late 1600s, German Pietists "equated *bilden* with *lernen* [the verb for learn] and conceived of it [*bilden*] as both an aesthetic and organic process," contends Cocalis.[55] *Bilden* becomes linked to the noun *bildung* through the work of the German Pietists Johann Joachim Spalding and Friedrich Christoph Oetinger. When Spalding and Oetinger translated the Earl of Shaftesbury's *Characteristics of Men, Manners, Opinions, and Times* (1711) into German in the mid-1700s, they rendered Shaftesbury's principle moral tenets "inward form," "formation of genteel character," and "good breeding" as *"innere Bildung," "Bildung,"* and *"Selbstbildung,"* respectively.[56] The medieval conception of bildung as a religious process of personal perfection becomes secularized after the translation of Shaftesbury's *Characteristiks*. In Shaftesbury's secular moral philosophy, individual perfection is not sufficient. The bildung hero, the "moral artist," must contribute to the perfection of the "common good" by preserving "the civil liberties necessary for the cultivation of the moral arts" and "enlightening humanity through an aesthetic education."[57] The neoclassicist intellectuals Johann Joachim Winckelmann and Christoph Martin Wieland also played significant roles in secularizing the bildung concept among the German intelligentsia. "Both men," writes Cocalis, "equated Bildung with the Greek ideal of kalokagathia, i.e., with being beautifully formed, well-educated, and morally good. But whereas Winckelmann conceived of Bildung as an ideal state of being, such as that immortalized in classical art, Wieland interpreted it as a formative process."[58] As Joseph R. Slaughter's summation of Cocalis notes, bildung signifies "form and formation (both product and process)."[59]

In German, the individualist hero of the bildungsroman is the *bildungsheld*. The bildungsheld's story "is situated in the context of the lives of parents, siblings, relatives, and wider community, the plot often leading to the formation of a family of his or her own."[60] Traditionally, the bildungsheld is male. "The classical Bildungsroman," writes Kester, "charts the rite of spring of a young man who journeys from immaturity and *naiveté* to maturity and *savoir-faire*."[61] In Anglophone, Euroethnic bildungsromans, the male blidungshelden are often plagued with a father that is physically or emotionally absent. Jeffers calls this crisis of paternity an "imbalance, namely the modern age's problematic life-without-father."[62] Jeffers perceives this pattern in *David Copperfield* (1849), *The History of Pendennis* (1848), *The Ordeal of Richard Feverel* (1859), *Roderick Hudson* (1879), *The Princess Casamassima* (1886), *The Way of All Flesh* (1903), *The Longest Journey* (1907), *Sons and Lovers* (1913), *A Portrait of the Artist as a Young Man* (1916), and *The Last Puritan: A Memoir in the Form of a Novel* (1935). The protagonists in these novels are each literally or figuratively fatherless.[63] Jeffers sees the crisis of paternity as a moral "imbalance" of the modern age, but he fails to account for its presence in bildungsromans about ethnic minorities because of his decision to focus on texts about White bildungsheld, feeling that society has neglected "youthful white males."[64] Jeffer's artful dodge marginalizes bildungs narratives written by writers of Latino and African American descent. For obvious reasons, the crisis of paternity is particularly endemic in US slave escape narratives, the founding genre of African American autobiographical writing. Geta LeSeur, however, recognizes it in contemporary African American and Afro-Caribbean Anglophone bildungsromans: "Boys in the African American and West Indian novels, by contrast, are largely the concern of their mothers, since there is a pervasive and literal absence of fathers in their lives."[65]

The crisis of paternity has a parallel in the crisis of maternity in the bildungsroman of US female ethnic minority writers. Bolaki's study of the bildung narratives of Jamaica Kincaid, Sandra Cisneros, Maxine Hong Kingston, and Audre Lorde focuses on female protagonists and their maternal relationships. Bolaki examines Jamaica Kincaid's *Lucy* and *At The Bottom of the River* and Audre Lorde's *Zami: A New Spelling of My Name*, *The Cancer Journals*, and "A Burst of Light: Living with Cancer" as representative US Afro-Caribbean texts. "The traditional female Bildungsroman," writes Bolaki, "represses *Bildung* or quest, ending in marriage or culminates in death when the female heroine distorts the acceptable social scripts."[66] However, the writers in Bolaki's study depart from these classic forms of closure. The mother-daughter "clashes" in the bildungs Bolaki examines dispense with "the American myth of self-creation" and "individualism and unbounded mobility."[67] US ethnic bildungs, in general, argues Bolaki, highlight the lack of physical and social mobility. They "speak about domestic enclosure in houses and ghettos, one's responsibility towards their community, and the need for belonging."[68] In other words, they privilege the provincial rather than the cosmopolitan. Because of this cultural rootedness and proximity angst, the ethnic female bildungshelden in Bolaki's study, literally and figuratively, construct themselves "alongside their mothers . . . through either processes of mourning or translation."[69] The mother-daughter relationships in these narratives tackle "issues of colonialism and sexuality, as in Kincaid's and Lorde's work in which the mothers are either colonial agents or agents of 'passing.'"[70] The fraught mother-child relationships in these narratives constitute a crisis of maternity.

The crisis of maternity is essentially a crisis of a toxic presence in the Afro-Latino bildung memoirs of my study. Both the female and male protagonists I examine suffer a crisis of maternity, a dysfunctional mother-child relationship. With stunning regularity, most of the authors of these memoirs portray mothers as clownish, immature, ineffectual, aloof, neglectful, and/or abusive. In contrast, they portray surrogate mothers, when there are surrogate mothers, as mature, competent, wise, loving, and nurturing.[71] Two of the key conventions of bildung narratives—the confessional mode and the focus on the formative years—often compel the authors in this study to hold their parents up to public scrutiny like no other genre does.

Public scrutiny and incredulity are two of the occupational hazards of autobiographical writing declares Leigh Gilmore.[72] However, the threat of "unsympathetic scrutiny," I argue, might not always be perceived as a threat by some writers.[73] The opportunity to publicly expose the debilitating effects of racial trauma is a contributing factor in the autobiographical impulse that compels ethnic minority writers to meditate on the roles race and racism play in their identity development. Subaltern writers, notes Bolaki, employ bildung "to claim America for immigrants and ethnic groups, to expose the traumas of a colonial education by decolonizing the self, or to illustrate the process of coming to voice for marginalized individuals and larger groups."[74] Narratives of "trauma, illness, and death," and "marginality, enforced silence, and hampered movement," argues Bolaki, productively expand the thematic boundaries of conventional bildung narratives.[75] Jeffers might argue that Bolaki overlooks the presence of trauma in classical bildung narratives like *David Cooperfield*, as Cooperfield's formative years were a "neglected-and-abused-child nightmare."[76]

Returning to the topic of autobiography by people of African descent, Kenneth Mostern discusses the importance of the intersection of racial trauma,

African American autobiography, and identity politics. Mostern "accepts the category of the 'memory of slavery' conceived by Gilroy as a determinate trauma—a psychoanalytic category, here sociologized—as an explanation of the persistence of 'blackness' as a mechanism in US politics," and he uses "the category of autobiography, which is not 'personal experience,' but rather an articulation based on the determinate memory and recall of experience via the lens of traumatically constrained ideology, to describe the continuing racialization of politics."[77] From its inception in the Colonial era as a response to White supremacy, African American autobiography, Mostern reminds us, has always been more of a political process than an aesthetic object: "In particular, autobiography is that *process* which articulates the determined subject so as to actively produce a newly positive identity. To the extent that racial trauma is, precisely, what autobiography recalls, racial identity politics is determined, and a variety of other politics may, as hooks knows, be repressed."[78] African American autobiography is a political process and a political tool. Authors of African American bildung narratives craft a subjectivity that is "contingent, collective, and historical," posits Kester, because they ideologically relate "to what is lost, the absent African home continent, and to what still seems unavailable to many African Americans, a home on the American continent."[79] "The classical European paradigm set by Goethe," asserts Kester, "implies that chaos, anarchy, and rebellion spring from within the subject while a society, from without, implants order, rules, and stability. The general American literary tradition—of which the slave narrative is one outstanding example—reverses this distinction. Its main purpose is to uphold the innocence of the subject facing a cruel, unjust world."[80] I draw a similar distinction between Euro-American and Afro-Latino bildungs. The former views unassimilated people of African and/or Latino descent as a threat to the dominance and stability of American society, whereas the Afro-Latino bildung views American society as an institution that especially traumatizes individuals and communities of African heritage. Because of extant White privilege and structural racism, the social education and identity formation of Americans in general is inherently a racial apprenticeship. Americans of African descent experience ethnoracial apprenticeship differently than Euroethnic Americans. Because of their unique cultural subjectivities and transnational histories, Afro-Latino immigrants and their descendants may experience and process anti-African racism differently than their African American counterparts, but they still recognize that it is a mutual problem that requires a collaborative solution and Pan-African solidarity.

However, Afro-Latinos' transnational histories and heritages add another dimension of complexity to their bildung narratives, both fictional and non-fictional. According to Alejandro Latinez, "Latin American and Hispanic/Latino Bildungsroman paradoxically and creatively, reproduce a condition of permanent *becoming*, which define subjects' identity."[81] Latinez's study includes, among many others, analyses of *Bless Me, Ultima* by Rudolfo Anaya, *The House on Mango Street* by Sandra Cisneros, and *When I Was Puerto Rican* by Esmeralda Santiago. Latinez "focuses on the intersection of the ideological and narratological configuration of the Bildungsroman as a formative story and the social and economic development as a narrative of national formation."[82] The narrative of underdevelopment imposed on Latin American countries by the US, suggests Latinez, construes those countries as junior partners in the global community, junior partners who require the paternal guidance of the putatively more advanced nations of the world. The idea that Latin American and Hispanophone Caribbean countries are like undeveloped bildungsheld, contends Latinez, was initiated by President Truman's "1949 inaugural lecture and the 1951 classic United Nations document 'Measures for the Economic Development of Underdeveloped Countries.'"[83] In the eyes of the industrialized nations, the underdeveloped countries of Latin America and the Hispanophone Caribbean are at best immature and at worst infantilized. In *Cuba in the American Imagination: Metaphor and the Imperial Ethos*, Louis A. Pérez Jr.'s demonstrates that the narrative of Latin American and Hispanophone Caribbean infantilization antedates the Truman administration, going at least as far back as the Spanish American War of 1898. Pérez Jr. examines depictions of Cuba as a child in US political cartoons from the late nineteenth century and early twentieth century.[84] Tracing the trope of Hispanic Caribbean and Latin American infantilization back to the Spanish American War provides more context and support for Latinez's claim that the Latino bildung is a narrative of permanent becoming.[85] No matter how much moral, social, intellectual, or material progress the Latino bildungsheld makes, the dominant society in the US never fully embraces him or her. This social and cultural subordination of the Latino bildungsheld, concludes Latinez, intrinsically makes the US Latino bildungsroman a narrative of arrested development.

Latinez's arrested development thesis is not so much inaccurate as it is incomplete. It is no surprise that reading Latino experiences and literature through the lens of the dominant culture tends to produce distortions, omissions, and suppressions that yield narratives of underdevelopment, incompletion, incompatibility, disunion, alienation, and deracination. However, the Afro-Latino memoir, by and large, tends to conform to Couser's view of the bildung memoir. "Bildungsroman," writes Couser, "tells how an identity was formed through steady growth, or growth in stages, rather than a sudden abrupt reversal or illumination."[86] As I demonstrate in this study, examining the influence of African American literature, history, and culture in Afro-Latino bildung memoirs reveals discourses of growth, wholeness, and solidarity, discourses that call for conceptualizing contemporary Afro-Latino and African American literature as two mutually reinforcing domains in the literature of the Afroethnic Renewal.

What, if anything, is distinctive about the American bildungsroman? Literary scholar Sarah Graham's definition of bildungsroman as a narrative of a life in "flux" is consistent with the consensus view of the genre.[87] Graham's notion of flux resonates with Bakhtin, who famously describes the bildungsroman as a novel of emergence, a novel that focuses on "man in the process of becoming."[88] Bakhtin identifies five types of novels of emergence. The bildungsroman, he argues, displays properties of the novel of education and the novel of historical emergence. Both types of these novels depict life and lived experience as a school. The former, writes Bakhtin, "traces a typically repeating path of man's emergence from youthful idealism and fantasies to mature sobriety and practicality."[89] In the latter, "man's individual emergence inseparably is linked to historical emergence . . . He emerges *along with the world* and he reflects the historical emergence of the world itself."[90] The novel of education is structured on "cyclical time," whereas the novel of historical emergence is structure on "national-historical time."[91] This distinction between the nation and the cyclical self is significant when one considers that the bildungsroman, as Graham reminds us, is reflective of a nation's beliefs, values, and historical development. Graham identifies two strands of American bildungsroman. The celebratory strand "affirm[s] the nation's founding promises through the achievements of . . . protagonists . . . who overcome obstacles to achieve triumphant self-realization. Their victories affirm the validity of the 'American Dream,' which holds that all citizens can improve their circumstances, however deprived their origin."[92] The depreciatory strand "reveals that the nation's assurances do not hold for many young Americans."[93] Graham situates all ethnic and sexual minority American bildungsroman in the latter category. Graham's two-strand theory holds true for the bildung memoir, but its "horizon of expectations"[94] is different because of its commitment to "the autobiographical pact."[95]

Unlike the bildungsroman proper, the bildung memoir depicts the lives of real people, people who hail from particular ethnoracial communities. If we take life to be a school, as Bakhtin does, then autobiography and memoir can be thought of as primers, or better still, as manuals for personal or collective agency. Antonio Gramsci makes this case in "Justification for Autobiography." Gramsci contends that autobiography can be politically instrumentalized: "One justification is this: to help others develop in certain ways and towards certain openings. . . . By narrating [one's life], one creates this possibility, suggests the process, indicates the opening. Autobiography therefore replaces the 'political' or 'philosophical essay': it describes in action what otherwise is deduced logically."[96] The Afro-Latino bildung memoir, in its capacity as a tool of political organizing and consciousness raising, rhizomatically interlaces the celebratory and depreciatory. Like its African American counterpart, the Afro-Latino memoir critiques America's flaws as it celebrates Black resistance, endurance, and quotidian excellence. The sheer existence of the Afro-Latino bildung memoir, the fact that Afro-Latino authors had the time and support to write and publish a memoir, subtends the notion that the American Dream is achievable even if it is not equitably distributed.

What is an *ethnoracial apprenticeship* and how is it related to the Afro-Latino bildung memoir? Ethnoracial apprenticeship, as I define it, is the intersectional process of ethnic and racial socialization that we each experience as individuals as we come of age in our homelands. The ethnoracial apprenticeship is the coming-of-age story of our ethnoracial consciousness. In "'Qué assimilated, brother, yo soy asimilao': The Structuring of Puerto Rican Identity in the U.S.," Juan Flores contends that racism in the US prompts Nuyoricans (i.e., Puerto Ricans born and raised in New York) to rediscover their island heritage and politically embrace their Taíno and African backgrounds.[97] Flores uses the concept of apprenticeship to describe the three-stage development of ethnoracial consciousness among Nuyoricans: "That which begins as and appears on the surface to be no more than the nostalgic, metaphorical evocation typical of an immigrant sensibility is in the Puerto Rican case an apprenticeship in social consciousness, the reconstructed 'patria' serving as the relevant locus of cultural interaction and contention."[98] Ethnoracial apprenticeship is reexperienced by transnational migrants and immigrants as they come to learn their host country's ethnic and racial identity norms. In the spring of 2015, I left my home in Worcester, MA, to teach for a year in Chiriquí, an agricultural province in western Panama. I was there as a Fulbright US Scholar, teaching expository writing and US literature, in English, at the Universidad Autónoma de Chiriquí in David, Panama's second largest city. Although I taught in David, my family and I lived in a gated community in Boquete, a small town twenty-four miles outside of the city. As an emerging scholar of Africana studies, I cherished the year I spent in Panama. Learning to appreciate how Panamanians conceived and practiced ethnic and racial identity was one of the most instructive aspects of my time there. In many ways, Panamanian notions of Black, White, and Indigenous identity are similar to US constructions of race and ethnicity, but in other ways they are not. Living as African Americans with fair to moderate Spanish-speaking skills in Panama provided me and my family opportunities to experience understandings and performances of race and ethnicity that ranged from the new, to the salutary, to the objectionable. Some of these experiences were more challenging than others, but even the most challenging ones provided moments for teaching and learning, for professional and personal growth. In this respect, I consider my time in Panama as an ethnoracial apprenticeship.

The Afro-Latino coming-of-age memoirs I examine are rich sites of ethnoracial apprenticeship and literary interculturalism between Latinos and African Americans. The late Piri Thomas, the first memoirist in this study, came of age in the New York of the 1940s. Raquel Cepeda, the youngest and last memoirist in this study, came of age in 1980s New York. Although the experience of the writers who came of age in the Jim Crow era differ vastly from those who grew up in the wake of the Black Power Movement, there is a continuity in how they relate to the African American experience. The concept of ethnoracial apprenticeship is apt because it speaks to the African American models of racial consciousness that influenced these writers as they came of age. In acknowledging the historical reality of this influence, I do not intend to suggest that African Americans are the stewards of Black identity. Nor do I intend to suggest that the relationship between African Americans and other people of African descent is one of tutelage. As a person who is half African American and half Ugandan, I believe there are as many ways to be a person of African descent as there are people of African descent. Like other scholars in Latino and African American studies, I agree that the relationship between African American and Afro-Latinos should not be construed in a way that suggests that the former community tutors the latter on matters of racial consciousness and authenticity.

However, as I have discussed with colleagues at Latino studies conferences, the memoirists whom I study use the discourse of teaching and learning to describe how they variously came to embrace, modify, and reject US conceptions of racial identity. Examining the discourse of teaching and learning in these memoirs reveals that Afro-Latinos' use of African American cultural tropes and their participation in African American social organizations are varied, valued, and viable strategies of racial identity formation in the US. Ethnoracial apprenticeship speaks to the inspiration Afro-Latino communities derive from African American literary ancestors, aesthetic models, cultural traditions, and sociopolitical movements. Ethnoracial apprenticeship is a reciprocal process of identity formation, a process in which African Americans learn just as much from Afro-Latinos as Afro-Latinos learn from them about what it means, has meant, and can mean to be Black in America.

The Politics of Naming: Latinos, Afro-Latinos, Blacks, and the Afroethnic Renewal

The US Census added the "Spanish/Hispanic" identity category to its short-form survey in 1980. Twenty years later it added "Latino" to the survey.[99] In "What's in a Name? The History and Politics of Hispanic and Latino Panethnicities," Ramón A. Gutiérrez provides a through and meticulous history of the origin of "Latino" and "Hispanic" as ethnic identifiers, tracing their emergence to the mid-nineteenth century. Gutiérrez writes: "By the late 1850s, *californios* were writing in newspapers about their membership in *América latina* (Latin America) and *latinoamerica*, calling themselves *latinos* as the shortened name for their hemispheric membership in *la raza latina* (the Latin race). . . . *Hispano* and *latino*, as abbreviated versions of *Hispano-Americano* and *latinoamericano*, flourished in California's Spanish-language discourse during the second half of the nineteenth century but had virtually disappeared by the 1920s."[100] Whether they were capitalized or italicized, the terms Latino and Latina have been in circulation for more than 160 years among people of Latin American descent in the US.[101]

The *Oxford English Dictionary* lists the earliest uses of "Afro-Latin American" and "Afro-Latin" as 1900 and 1906, respectively.[102] Sociologist Laó-Montes confirms that terms for Afro-Latinidad gained currency in Latin American studies around the same time.[103] Motivated by the Civil Rights/Black Power movements, Black scholars living in the US began writing groundbreaking studies about Afro-Latin Americans as early as 1962, writes William Luis in his short biography of *The Afro-Hispanic Review* (*AHR*). The *AHR* is the academic journal founded "as a publication of the Afro-Hispanic Institute at Howard University in January of 1982."[104] Although Anani Dzidzienyo and Pierre-Michel Fontaine used the term "Afro-Latin America" in 1978 and 1980, respectively, in their research on race in Brazil,[105] the concept of Afro-Latinidad boomed in Latino studies in the years immediately following the ascendancy of Hispanics as the largest ethnic minority in the US.[106] How, if at all, do contemporary understandings of Latino and Afro-Latino differ from their initial conceptions? What does it mean to be Latino now? Who is and who is not Afro-Latino in the era of Black Lives Matter?

In *On Latinidad: US Latino Literature and the Construction of Ethnicity* (2007), literary scholar Marta Caminero-Santangelo makes significant contributions to the understanding of the relationship between Latinidad and Afro-Latinidad. In her introduction, "Who Are We?," Caminero-Santangelo explores her reservations about the nature and efficacy of Latino as panethnic critical category of analysis. After thoroughly charting the constructions and applications of Latino ethnicity in the scholarly literature, Caminero-Santangelo makes peace with the artificiality and imprecision of the term Latino as a panethnic identifier because it allows her to analyze and critique the linkages and ruptures between disparate communities of Americans of Hispanic descent as well as those linkages and ruptures between Latinos, Native Americans, and African Americans.[107] Caminero-Santangelo does not use the term Afro-Latinidad in her examination Latino panethnicity, but in her second chapter, "'Puerto Rican Negro': Defining Race in Piri Thomas's *Down These Mean Streets*," she explores the rifts and bonds between Latinidad, Afro-Latinidad, and African American identity. Laó-Montes, however, examines these rifts and bonds at hemispheric and world systems levels in his explorations of Afro-Latinidades.[108]

In his 2007 article "Afro-Latinidades: Bridging Blackness and Latinidad," Laó-Montes interprets Afro-Latinidad through the concept of the African diaspora. He defines the African diaspora as a condition of common global oppression, a process of cultural theory and expressive practice, and a coalitional, social justice project. He defines Afro-Latinidad as "the histories, memories, social locations, expressive cultures, social movements, political organizations, and lived experiences of peoples of African descent in Latino/America. Afro-Latinidad is a category of difference, in contrast to identity discourses based on hegemonic notions of nationality and race in Latino/America." Laó-Montes uses Afro-Latinidad to critique and redefine conventional and hegemonic discourses of "Africanity, Americanity, and Latinidad"; his concept of Afro-Latinidad challenges and expands standard conceptions and applications of national identity, geographic belonging, and ethnoraciality.[109]

In contradistinction to Laó-Montes and Caminero-Santangelo's examinations of Latinidad and Afro-Latinidad as theoretical concepts, Flores and Jiménez Román are concerned with the history of Afro-Latinos in the US.

According to Flores and Jiménez Román, the twenty-first-century popularization of the term Afro-Latino in America is a reaction to four phenomena: (1) the homogenizing function encoded in the panethnic term Latino, (2) Latino anti-Black racism, (3) the near exclusive use of the term "black" as a racial category for US Afro-descendants, and (4) the Eurocentric cultural hegemony that shapes popular consciousness in the Americas and the Caribbean.[110] Silvio Torres-Saillant argues that Dominicans who choose to identify as Black are rejecting the intellectually and morally suspect ways in which mixed-race concepts like *mestizaje* and *mulatez* (aka *mulataje* and *mulatería*) can be used to reinforce the Eurocentric discourse of White supremacy.[111] Additionally, Torres-Saillant contends that racially conscious Afro-Latinos have a coalitional, bridge-building role to play in the drama of US Black/White race relations.[112]

Like Hispanic and Latino, there are competing definitions of who and what constitutes an Afro-Latino subject. Flores and Jiménez Román posit a transnational definition of the term Afro-Latino in their 2009 article "Triple-Consciousness? Approaches to Afro-Latino Culture in the United States."[113] They clarify this hemispheric definition in *The Afro-Latin@ Reader*: "They are people of African descent in Mexico, Central and South America, and the Spanish-speaking Caribbean, and by extension those of African descent in the United States whose origins are in Latin America and the Caribbean."[114] William Luis, in "Afro-Latino/a Literature and Identity," uses graduated categories of Afro-Latino identification. These categories include Afro-Hispanics, Afro-Hispanic immigrants, and Afro-Latinos. Afro-Hispanic, as Luis defines the term, refers to people of African descent who are native-born citizens of Hispanophone countries in Latin America or the Caribbean. Luis applies the ethnolinguistic descriptor "Afro-Hispanic" to these individuals even when they migrate to and reside in the US. In contrast, he uses Afro-Latino to refer to the US-born offspring of Afro-Hispanic immigrants. Afro-Latinos are raised and educated in the US; they may, according to Luis, still have significant symbolic or real transnational relationships with the host countries of their initial immigrant progenitor(s). Afro-Hispanic immigrants in the US, through willful acculturation, Luis contends, can transform themselves into Afro-Latinos.[115] Like Luis, Flores, Jiménez Román, Caminero-Santangelo, and Torres-Saillant, I use the terms Latino, Afro-Latino, and their orthographic variants to refer to people of Latin American and/or Hispanic Caribbean descent living outside of Latin America and/or the Hispanic Caribbean.

Like Afro-Latinos, African Americans are no strangers to the politics of naming. As early as the 1780s, Americans of African descent used African, or some variation thereof, as their preferred collective identifier for the race.[116] However, in the 1830s, there was a sharp linguistic turn. African Americans began increasingly referring to themselves as "colored." They resorted to this metonymic racial identifier, and its variants, to emphasize their Americanity and deemphasize their Africanity. African Americans adopted his discursive strategy to confront the American Colonization Society's (ACS) campaign to expel them from the nation. Founded in 1816, the ACS advocated for the forced repatriation of free African Americans to Africa.[117] Since the linguistic turn of the 1830s, African Americans have variously called themselves colored, Negro, and Black.[118] In addition to debating which of these appellations is more desirable, African Americans have also debated whether capitalizing them fosters any meaningful sense of racial dignity and respect.[119] Like our eighteenth-century ancestors, I prefer panethnic identifiers that stress our historical connection to Africa, identifiers such as Afro-American and African American. While I am weary of coining gratuitous neologisms and mindful of the limitations of panethnic descriptors, Afroethnic renewal is the term I use to define how immigrants of African descent and their US-born children reshape African American demographics, culture, and literature. Afroethnic, unlike the metonymic terms colored, Negro, and Black, avoids the racialization of language and the reduction of peoples, histories, and cultures into homogenizing metaphors that disconnect them from the history and reality of Africa.[120] The additional benefit of the term Afroethnic is that it recognizes the ethnic diversity of Afrodescendants in the US. It acknowledges that people of African descent in the US have manifold national and cultural backgrounds. The term Afroethnic also reminds us that immigrants of African heritage have been renewing African American culture since the 1870s, if not before. This is particularly true of Afro-Latinos.

The post-1965 wave of Afro-Latino immigrants is part of the fourth great migration, the larger wave of Afro-diasporic immigration that redefined what it meant to be African American in the twenty-first century.[121] Like Berlin, the political scientist Christina M. Greer explores the relationship between African Americans and peoples of the fourth great migration. She uses the term "black ethnics" to categorize people of African descent living in the US. She disaggregates Black ethnics into "three categories: black American, Afro-Caribbean, and African."[122] Greer uses the term "black American" to denote descendants of Anglophone racial slavery in the US and to distinguish them from "foreign-born black ethnics" (i.e., African and Afro-Caribbean immigrants).[123] The value of the term "black American," argues Greer, is twofold:

(1) it diminishes the ambiguity of the term African American, and (2) it does not "presume" that Black Americans have "links to African identity."[124] Greer argues that African and Afro-Caribbean immigrants adopt a Pan-African identity that puts them in solidarity with Black Americans, yet they do so while simultaneously preserving the particular transnational ethnic identities with which they arrived. Interestingly, Greer excludes "black Latinos" from her "black ethnics" category because they come from Hispanophone countries. She writes, "Because Latino populations are more likely to separate themselves by nationality than by skin color, a cohesive black Latino identity is less likely to be formed from within the Hispanic community."[125] Conversely, I do not believe that Latinidad trumps race when it comes to Black solidarity in the US. I argue that many "black Latinos" do adopt a Pan-African politics of cultural and political solidarity not only within the Hispanic community but also with other non-Hispanic "black ethnics." This adoption is manifestly evident in contemporary Afro-Latino memoirs, the work of Afro-Latina theorists,[126] organizations like the Afrolatin@ Forum,[127] and in the small, but meaningful, presence of Afro-Latinos in the African American literary canon.

Latinities, African American Literature, and the Post-Soul Aesthetic

In the mid-1990s Vera M. Kutzinski and William Luis endeavored to explain the increased scholarly and popular interest in "Afro-Hispanic American literature" and US Hispanic Caribbean literature, respectively. Focusing on writers in Latin America, Kutzinski argued that although "the specific parameters of Afro-Hispanic literature" have not been set, "the authenticating rhetoric adopted by Afro-Hispanist criticism largely reflects the legacy of the Black Power and Black Arts movements of the immediate North American past, as well as the ideology of the Francophone Négritude groups."[128] Luis reached a similar conclusion about the Black Power movement's role in bringing attention to, if not shaping, US Hispanic Caribbean literature. Defining US Hispanic Caribbean literature as a "relatively new field in literary history and criticism," Luis argued that "the Civil Rights and Black Power movements and Young Lords Party drew attention to the plight of Blacks and Hispanics in the United States."[129] These social movements encouraged Latino college students to demand culturally relevant curricula and "Latin American or Puerto Rican Studies programs." Student activism was "paralleled by community activists and organizers who sponsored events to promote ethnic awareness and artistic expressions emerging from the *barrios* and ghettos."[130] Luis divides US Hispanic Caribbean literature into two categories. The first is Spanish-language literature written by immigrants from Cuba, Puerto Rico, the Dominican Republic, and other Hispanophone countries in the Caribbean Basin.[131] "The second category," writes Luis, "includes writers who were either born or raised in the United States, and who for the most part write in English."[132] In his second category, Luis includes Piri Thomas, Nicholasa Mohr, Miguel Piñero, Miguel Algarín, Pedro Pietri, Tato Laviera, Martín Espada, Sandra Maria Esteves, Judith Ortiz Cofer, Oscar Hijuelos, and Julia Alvarez, among others.

Luis is right in noting that the Civil Rights/Black Power movements, on a macro-level, shaped and brought renewed attention to US Hispanic Caribbean literature. However, greater attention needs to be brought to the microlevel, to the interpersonal influences African American authors and literature had on US Hispanic Caribbean writers. Nuyorican poet Louis Reyes Rivera reminds us that both Thomas and Mohr were mentored by his father-in-law, John Oliver Killens, the radical African American novelist and cofounder of the Harlem Writers Guild.[133] Julia Alvarez says she was inspired to write poetry by James Weldon Johnson's poem "The Creation" and that she studied under the African American poets Lucille Clifton and June Jordon.[134] These intercultural relationships between African American and US Hispanic Caribbean writers not only raise interesting questions about the nature, utility, and scope of Latinidad, they also challenge conventional conceptions of African American identity. Theorizing the copiousness of what it means to be Latino, Claudia Milian coined the term "Latinities" to describe "how cultural signifiers for the U.S. Latino or Latina have been accessed by an unexpected circle of Latin participants: U.S. African Americans and 'problematic' subgroups like Central Americans."[135] Concerned with the "detours Latinoness and Latinaness take—through blackness, dark brownness, indigence, Indianess, [and] 'second-tier' Latino status," Milian investigates "how a panoply of U.S. African Americans, Latinos, and Latinas walk in and out of their traditional designations."[136] In other words, people of various races or ethnicities strategically pass in and out of Latinidad in the US. If African American and Latino subjectivities can be interchangeable, how does that challenge what we think of when we think of African American literature?

Since the election of Barack Obama, some studies have questioned what African American literature is and how African American literary history should be represented. *In Chaotic Justice: Rethinking African American Literary History* (2009), John Ernest asks, "What is African American about

African American literature, and why should we identify this as a distinct tradition?" and "What is African American about African American literary history?"[137] Using cultural poetics, as informed by the discourse theory of Clifford Geertz,[138] Ernest explores "a consideration of American literary history with Black Studies at its center," a consideration that accounts for "black scholarly and activist history in shaping the tradition of African American expressive culture."[139] *Chaotic Justice* invites us to interrogate the social order that constitutes the notion of race, to question the cultural order beyond the social identity of authors, beyond the subject matter of texts, and beyond the institutional mechanisms that codify African American literature and literary history. In *Representing the Race: A New Political History of African American Literature* (2011), Gene Andrew Jarret argues that African American literature functioned as an instrument for political and social change. Inspired by Eddie S. Glaude's call for a "'post-soul' paradigm," Jarret develops a "political historiography" that tells the story of African American literature's ideological diversity and complexity, a historiography that challenges the four core assumptions of the Black Power, Black Arts, and Black Studies grand narrative of African American literature. According to Jarret, those core assumptions "include the definition of successful African American politics in terms of the racial authenticity of leadership; the utter ideological cohesion of racial constituencies; the primacy of popular over intellectual forms of expressive culture; and the nationalism, rather than internationalism, of African American identity."[140] In *What Was African American Literature?* (2011), Kenneth W. Warren agrees that African American literature was instrumentalized for social change, but posits that African American literature only existed during the Jim Crow era, which he narrowly defines as spanning from 1896 to the 1960s. Unimpressed by critical race theory's observation of the persistence of racism,[141] Warren argues "that with the legal demise of Jim Crow, the coherence of African American literature has been correspondingly, if sometimes imperceptibly eroded as well."[142] Citing the transnational turn in literary and cultural studies, Warren contends that "African American literature might be viewed as a 'historical entity' rather than as the ongoing expression of a distinct people . . . African American literature as a distinct entity would seem to be at an end, that the turn to diasporic, transatlantic, global, and other frames indicates a dim awareness that the boundary creating this distinctiveness has eroded."[143] In *What Is African American Literature?* (2021), Margo N. Crawford, challenges Ernest, Jarret, and Warren's historical determinism, arguing that African American literature is distinct and that its distinctiveness is defined by its moodscape. Informed by

Raymond Williams concept of "structures of feeling" and Althusser's concept of interpellation, Crawford, using reader response theory, contends, "An open system of black nervousness (an open system of black feeling) distinguishes African American literature from other literary traditions."[144] For Crawford, African American literature is a metaphysical Black body: "the is-ness of African American literature is a collective nervous system"; "the is-ness of African American literature is stranded in a space of diasporic shivers."[145] "African American literature is best understood," concludes Crawford, "as writers' and readers' co-creation of a black mood, of a black *feeling world*."[146] Crawford's notion of the ideal Black reader is the site at which her affective theory converges with Ernest, Jarret, and Warren's concerns about the burden of representation. Crawford suggests that the New Negro movement, the Black Arts Movement, and post-soul era literature share the conviction that African American literature should move away from posing to being poised, that is from interpreting Black life for a mainstream audience to expressing Black life for, with, and through Black readers.[147]

One of the virtues of *What Is African American Literature?* is its examination of the role of the African diaspora in African American literature. Using Édouard Glissant's trope of the "shock of elsewhere,"[148] Crawford reminds us of the African American writers who wrote in the African diaspora, and of the Afro-Caribbean, Afro-British, and African writers who either wrote in the US or were influenced by African American literature in their homelands. The list of writers whom she weaves into her close reading includes Zora Neal Hurston, Edwidge Dandicat, Chimamanda Adichie, Ama Ata Aidoo, Zadie Smith, Bessie Head, Aquah Laluah, and Keorapetse Kgositsile. "The impulse not to freeze the diasporic shivers of blackness," argues Crawford, "is the most radical zone of the global black consciousness in African American literature."[149] Yet, Crawford, like Jarret and Warren, freeze writers of Hispanic descent out of her narrative of African American literature's "global black consciousness." Ignoring the Latino contribution to the "diasporic shivers of blackness" of African American literature renders incomplete portraits of African American literary history.

Anthologies of African American literature use the institutional narratives and periodization schemes of conventional literary history, the narratives and schemes that concern Ernest, Jarret, and Warren. In some cases, these anthologies are attuned to the Latino presence in African American literature. Since its initial publication, the *Norton Anthology of African American Literature* (1997) has included a small number of writers of Hispanic descent or affiliation in its canon. For example, the first edition of the anthology includes Arthur A. Schomburg from Puerto Rico and Eric Walrond, a British Guianese writer who spent his teenage years, 1911–18, in Panama.[150] Subsequent editions inexplicably include Nicolás Guillén, a Cuban poet who "made two brief but important trips to the United States, which influenced some of his poetry," notes Luis.[151] Like the *Norton Anthology of African American Literature*, the *Oxford Companion to African American Literature* (1997) includes Nuyoricans Victor Hernández Cruz and Piri Thomas. The *Norton Anthology of Contemporary African American Poetry* (2013) includes Lorenzo Thomas and John Murillo. Thomas was a Panamanian immigrant and Murillo's mother is Mexican and his father African American. The inclusion of Hispanic heritage writers in anthologies of African American literature speaks to Milian's concept of the mutual copiousness of Latinidad and African Americanity. In addition to the ethnoracial categorization and inclusivity conundrum that vexes the editors of African American anthologies and encyclopedias, there is also the problem of naming, defining, and temporally bracketing literary periods and movements. This is particularly true of the Norton anthology's exercise in defining what it means to be African American in the post-Black Arts era.

The three anthologies adopt varied and varying periodization nomenclature for late twentieth-century African American literature. For example, the *Norton Anthology of African American Literature* refers to the post-1975 era as "The Contemporary Period." The first line of the description of "The Contemporary Period" reads: "The fabled awakening in Harlem during the 1920s notwithstanding, one could argue that the true African American renaissance occurred during the last quarter of the twentieth century."[152] The definition identifies six trends that distinguish this period from previous ones. The first of these trends is "(1) the acknowledgement of the multiplicity of African American identities."[153] The subsection titled "Movement Legacies" goes on to refer to the contemporary period as a "literary and cultural renaissance" and stresses that the reflective practice of the period's zeitgeist revealed that "African American communities differed according to geography and region, class, and ethnicity."[154] "Remapping the African American Literary Terrain," another subsection of the introduction to "The Contemporary Period," deals with the diversity of Afroethnicity in the US. It notes that the transnational consciousness of the Contemporary era "reflected both the increasing influence of African and Afro-Caribbean writers on the development of African American literature and the fact that a number of Black writers in the United States were themselves immigrants."[155] The description of "The Contemporary Period" accurately defines major aspects of the period's historical development and cultural temperament, but a competing and contested term for this moment in African American literature and culture is the post-soul era.

Greg Tate's 1986 article "The Cult-Nats Meet Freaky Deke," Trey Ellis's 1989 essay "The New Black Aesthetic," and Nelson George's book *Buppies, B-Boys, Baps, and Bohos: Notes on Post-Soul Black Culture* (1992) are products of the culture wars of the late 1980s and early 1990s, an era rife with debates about the merits and shortcomings of multiculturalism, interculturalism, and multiracialism.[156] The aforementioned works by Tate, Ellis, and George are the founding texts of the post-soul aesthetic. The term "post-black," which was coined in 2001 by Thelma Golden and Glenn Ligon,[157] is synonymous with the term post-soul.[158] In this study, I use the terms post-soul and post-black interchangeably. With its investment in multiculturalism, cosmopolitanism, aesthetic experimentation, social inclusion, liberal individualism, and ideological freedom, the post-soul sensibility has been theorized, celebrated, and bemoaned by a host of scholars and cultural critics over the last thirty-five years.[159] A subset of these cultural critics and theorists champion the post-soul concept because it privileges liberal individualism and deemphasizes political activism. These advocates posit the post-soul aesthetic as a needed corrective to the sexism, heteronormativity, racial essentialism, revolutionary politics, and righteous indignation of the Black Arts Movement.[160] Post-soul advocates view the cosmopolitism of the post-soul aesthetic as more politically, aesthetically, and socially inclusive than the Black Aesthetic.[161] They want contemporary Black subjectivity to be as socially open and intellectually progressive as it possibly can be. They want African Americans to be more accepting of the myriad shades and temperaments of Black individualism, even if that individualism includes disidentifying with political activism and long-standing pieties about slavery and the Civil Rights movement.[162] A minority of post-black pundits go so far as to call for African Americans to be more patriotically appreciative of their US citizenship and the educational, social, and economic opportunities that the postsegregation era has afforded them.[163]

Triumphalist and liberal individualist conceptualizations of post-blackness are not without their detractors. Randall Kennedy views the "libertarian absolutism" of some post-black advocates as wrong-headed.[164] K. Merinda Simmons faults these advocates for defining the ideological heterogeneity of post-blackness against a transhistorical conception of White subjectivity as an ideological monolith.[165] In *Black Post-Blackness: The Black Arts Movement and Twenty-First Century Aesthetics*, Margo N. Crawford takes issue with

post-black advocates who fail to see the social, political, and aesthetic continuities between the Black and post-black aesthetics.[166] Emily J. Lordi also
focuses on the aesthetic and ideological continuities that triumphalist post-
soul theorists tend to ignore. In *The Meaning of Soul: Black Music and the Resilience since the 1960s*, Lordi, like Crawford, takes issue with theorists who
define the post-soul by making soul "stand in for the most restrictive heteropatriarchal impulses of the Black Arts and Black Power movements"; she
takes issue with scholars who theorize "soul as a force of convention and
simplicity that serves as a foil to post-soul eccentricity."[167] In contradistinction to depoliticized, liberal individualist configurations of the post-soul,[168]
Lordi reads the post-soul as a "call to arms" rather than as an academic trope
for and ideological defense of Black elitism, eccentricity, and exceptionalism.[169] Lordi's call for post-soul theorists to be more cognizant of the internal
diversity of African American political thought and cultural expression in the
soul era inspires my own call for scholars in African American cultural studies
to be more attuned to and attentive of the ethnic diversity and interculturalism that characterizes African American literature as well as its intersection
with other ethnic American literatures. Since, but not with, the demise of
Jim Crow something has changed about African American culture and literature. The 1965 Hart-Celler Act, one of the nails in the coffin of Jim Crow, was
the catalyst for the fourth great migration, a wave of immigration that re-
Africanized the US. That process, however, started much earlier when immigrants from Africa and the Caribbean started arriving from their newly
independent countries. The Hart-Celler act accelerated a migration that was
already taking place. The fourth great migration, more so than the demise of
de jure segregation per se, signals a changing same in African American literature and culture, a changing same that I call the Afroethnic Renewal. As the
range of ethnicity in the Black/African American demographic becomes increasingly diverse, Warren's call to ask questions about how ethnic literatures
respond to sociopolitical transformation and Lordi's conception of post-soul
insurgency become progressively relevant as conceptual hinges between Latino and African American studies, fields which should be more engaged with
each other than they currently are because of the historic and increasing
Afro-Latino presence in the US.

The contradiction that I find interesting about the liberal individualist
conception of the post-soul aesthetic is that it uses Ellis's "cultural mulatto"
trope to call for the acceptance of ideological diversity among Black people
in America but has very little to say about the actual ethnic diversity of Black
people in America. At *The End of Blackness*, Debra Dickerson defines Blackness

in strict ethnonationalist terms: "For our purposes, *blacks* are those Americans descended from Africans who were brought here involuntarily as slaves. This definition would include free blacks, even those who owned slaves. Immigrants of African descent, even if descended from South American or Caribbean slaves, are not included in this definition. *The End of Blackness* is specific to the American experience of slavery and its aftermath."[170] While I can appreciate thinkers who narrowly define the scope of their research, the lack of inclusivity in Dickerson's strain of ethnonationalism is counterproductive to the project of Black panethnic solidarity. While post-soul pundits and post-black theorists were fretting over what it means to be African American in postsegregation America, Latinos displaced African Americans as the nation's largest ethnic minority and Afro-Latinidad became increasingly popular in public and scholarly discourse. One would think that post-soul scholars would have ample amounts to say about this historical convergence, but they rarely include Latinos in their discussions of Blackness, and when they do it is either superficially or obliquely. There are, however, a few notable exceptions. In "Television Satire in the Black Americas: Transnational Border Crossings in *Chappelle's Show* and *The Ity and Fancy Cat Show*," Sam Vásquez calls for expanding the canon of post-soul African American satire to include Afro-descendants from and in the Caribbean and Latin America.[171] In her book *Sounding Like a No-No?: Queer Sounds and Eccentric Acts in the Post-Soul Era*, Francesca T. Royster considers Junot Díaz's *The Brief Wondrous Life of Oscar Woa* to be a "post-soul" text.[172] Royster's nod to Junot Díaz is important because it harkens back to Nelson George's understudied pronouncement on Afro-Latino and African American relations in the post-soul era. In his 2005 interview with Ed Gordon on NPR, George said that in the next twenty years it would be "crucial" for African Americans and Latinos to "build bonds" since so many "Hispanic immigrants are brown-skinned, in fact, are black."[173] *Post-Soul Afro-Latinidades*, a special issue of *The Black Scholar*, is one of the few sustained scholarly treatments of the relationship between the post-soul and Latinidad.

Chapter Overview

The Afro-Latino Memoir does not seek to offer a grand theory of Latino or African American literary history. What it does offer is a series of modest close readings designed to start, rather than close, a conversation about the intersection of Latino and African American literary and cultural history. *The Afro-Latino Memoir* is my way of expressing my gratitude to two cultures and literary traditions that continue to enrich my life as well as that of my students. The organizational template for the chapters in this book includes introductory sections that profile the author, the text, the reception history of the text, and the conceptual tools used to examine the text. The introductory sections are followed by interpretive analysis that employs the close reading methods of cultural poetics and cultural materialism. Chapter 1 explores African American literary ancestries and narrative strategies in *Down These Mean Streets* (1967), a memoir by Piri Thomas. In chapter 1, I call attention to Thomas's literary apprenticeship under John Oliver Killens. Killens and Thomas were both members of the Harlem Writers Guild (HWG), of which Killens was one of five cofounders. The HWG had aesthetic roots in the Popular Front and its members played decisive roles in the development of the Black Arts Movement. The analytical sections of the chapter examine the relationship between Latinidad, heteronormative masculinity, and Black consciousness. In these sections, I focus on two instances of Thomas's use of African American racial humor and vernacular culture. I analyze a cowardice joke that contrasts the trope of Indigenous bravery with the stereotype of African American pusillanimity as responses to White racial terror. In addition, I demonstrate that Thomas's use of signifying to resist White infantilization intertextually "tropicalizes" an African American protest joke derived from *Youngblood*, the debut Killens novel that inspired *Down These Mean Streets*. The analysis of the immersion narrative, the cowardice joke, and the signifying protest joke reveals that *Down These Mean Streets* is a transcanonical text, that it is as much a foundational text of the Black Arts Movement as it is of the Nuyorican Movement.

Chapter 2 brings attention to an understudied Afro-Latino memoir, Carlos Moore's *Pichón: Race and Revolution in Castro's Cuba* (2008). Moore was born in Central Lugareño, Cuba in 1942. However, from 1957 to 1961, he lived in New York City. During this adolescent period of his life, Moore came of age ideologically and politically. I explore the uneasy tension between his bohemian liberal humanism and the flowering of his radical Pan-African consciousness, a flowering that was nurtured by his Afro-Panamanian English teacher and through encounters with African American intellectuals and activists like Lewis H. Michaux, Maya Angelou, Harold Cruse, and Malcolm X. This chapter examines this tension by analyzing the role that African American jazz/blues interventions and Black nationalist oratory play in the transformation of Moore's political consciousness.

In chapter 3, I turn my attention to the relationship between the post-soul aesthetic and *When the Spirits Dance Mambo: Growing Up Nuyorican in El*

Barrio (*WSDM*; 2004) by Dr. Marta Moreno Vega.[174] In *WSDM*, Vega chronicles her life growing up as Afro-Puerto Rican in New York City during the twilight of Jim Crow segregation in the 1950s. Although *WSDM* is set in the 1950s, the context of its composition and publication are mediated by the Afrocentric and multiracial discourses of the post-soul era. As an Afrocentric Puerto Rican scholar and memoirist, Vega complicates the debates about Black cynicism and authenticity in Nelson George's *Post-Soul Nation* and Debra Dickerson's *The End of Blackness*, two post-soul treatises that were published in the same year as *WSDM*. Although George and Dickerson are both concerned with the ideological and socioeconomic diversity of Black subjectivity, they give little, if any, attention to Black ethnic diversity. They do not, for example, directly address the Afro-Latino community's relationship to the post-soul and the end of Blackness. In this chapter, I examine the philias and phobias of Afro-Latino and African American interculturalism in *WSDM* to enrich and invite conversations about Afro-Latinidad's relationship to the post-soul condition. Vega represents Afro-Latino and African American interculturalism positively through her association with Katherine Dunham, the famous African American choreographer, with La Dominadora, a spirit guide in Afro-Caribbean religions. Dunham was one of the many African American celebrities whom Vega idolized. La Dominadora was one of the many spirit guides represented on Vega's grandmother's Santerismo altar. Unlike the male writers in this study, Vega calls attention to the relationship between Afro-Latino subjectivity and African-derived religions such as Santería, Espiritismo, and Santerismo. I reveal that the representation of Dunham in *WSDM* is informed by Vega's research on the history of Latin jazz and Santería in post-war New York, a history in which Dunham played a major role. The figurative fusion of Dunham and LA Dominadora reifies Vega's theory of the Black Global Aesthetic (BGA), an aesthetic of which the Black Aesthetic is merely a part.[175]

In the final chapter, I examine post-soul representations of Black nationalism and speculative realism in Veronica Chambers's *Mama's Girl* (1996) and Raquel Cepeda's *Bird of Paradise: How I Became Latina* (2013). Afro-Latina coming-of-age memoirs written after the advent of the Black Arts Movement often include a significant admixture of African American history, culture, and political ideology. This is true of both *Mama's Girl* and *Bird of Paradise: How I Became Latina*. Chambers and Cepeda were raised in New York City in the wake of the Black Power movement. As they came of age, Chambers and Cepeda were attracted to the antipodes of Black nationalism. Chambers repeatedly invokes the civil rights movement's integrationist agenda in

Mama's Girl, and she does so in a way that valorizes Talented Tenth elitism and neoliberal luck egalitarianism. In contrast, Cepeda was aligned in spirit, if not in practice, with the cultural separatist pole of Black nationalism. She was attracted to the hip hop and theosophy of the Five Percent Nation, a splinter sect of the Nation of Islam. In addition to FPN mysticism, Cepeda evinces a generic belief in kismet, *gilgul neshamot,* and the gods and spirit guides of three Afro-Hispanic Caribbean religious practices: Santería, Espiritismo, and Santerismo. Cepeda's conviction in the supernatural is equally matched by her faith in the scientific. Cepeda's promotion of genetic profiling in general and of a specific genetic profiling company, in particular, entices scholars to interrogate the privacy ramifications of a cross-promotional marketing strategy that genetically targets communities of Afroethnic descent. I argue that the ways in which the antipodes of Black nationalism mediate Latinidad in *Mama's Girl* and *Bird of Paradise* reveal the significance of the African American presence in Latina autobiography and highlight the commensurability between Latino and African American studies.

CHAPTER ONE

Laughing the Demons Away
Piri Thomas and the Black Aesthetic

Born in Harlem Hospital in 1928,[1] Piri Thomas was an American writer of Puerto Rican and Cuban descent who grew up in Spanish Harlem.[2] *Down These Mean Streets*, Thomas's best-selling memoir, is a coming-of-age story about the intersection of racial and masculine identity formation, a memoir about the struggle to be ethnically Afro-Puerto Rican and ideologically Black in the 1940s and 1950s New York City. Thomas published *Down These Mean Streets* in the same ten-year Black Arts Movement (BAM) window in which Claude Brown, Malcolm X, Eldridge Cleaver, Anne Moody, H. Rap Brown, Maya Angelou, and Angela Davis published their life stories.[3] Reviewers likened Thomas to James Baldwin, Claude Brown, Stephen Crane, Richard Wright, and Malcolm X.[4] What reviewers and scholars often fail to mention about Thomas is that he was inspired to become a writer by reading African American fiction. More significantly, Thomas deeply embedded himself in the literary organizations, networks, and aesthetics of the BAM.

Thomas embraced, and was embraced by, the African American Old Left literary elites of Harlem. In his published interviews, Thomas reveals the origins of his membership in the Harlem Writers Guild (HWG) and the ethnoracial identity crisis he faced in the wake of his memoir's critical and commercial success. Between 1962 and 1969, Thomas identified so profoundly with the literary nationalism of the BAM and its architects that he began to lose his sense of his Latinidad. Thomas recalls his existential crisis in a 1980 interview with Wolfgang Binder, in Erlangen, West Germany:

> During the sixties I was so strongly into the Black movement, that almost all my friends were *Black*, Black. And I was talking Black, and I was feeling Black. There was a Puerto Rican woman who was married to a Black doctor, Dr. Barrows, and sitting one day in her house she looked at me and said, "Ay bendito, Piri, te vamos a perder." ("Oh, what a pity, Piri, we are losing you.") She meant that culturally, and it

shook me. I was shaking! It must have been around '68, '69. She had said that with such pain; I was ready to become an American Black, and yet I knew that I was not fully accepted by the Blacks! I sensed that also when I was a member of the Harlem Writers' Guild.[5]

With its roots in the African American cultural organizations of the Popular Front, the HWG functioned as the site of Thomas's ethnoracial apprenticeship in the freemasonry of the Black Aesthetic. Thomas's gripping representations of Black subjectivity under Jim Crow and his mastery of the Black Aesthetic contributed to the reception of his memoir as an African American text.

Thirty years after the publication of *Down These Mean Streets*, Thomas's fear of being African Americanized was realized by his inclusion in *The Oxford Companion to African American Literature* (1997). The entry in the *Companion* on Piri Thomas was written by David L. Dudley, who also wrote the *Companion's* entry on Claude Brown. In the entry on Thomas, Dudley highlights Thomas's Afro-Latinidades, noting his Cuban as well as his Puerto Rican heritage. *Down These Mean Streets*, Dudley writes, depicts "a previously 'silenced' group—the negritos, or black Puerto Ricans, of Spanish Harlem. Thomas was compared favorably with James Baldwin and Claude Brown as a writer documenting his successful struggle to achieve personhood despite the dehumanizing conditions of minorities in America."[6] Machismo, street life, drug addiction, gang and prison culture, and fraught scenes of racial and sexual identity formation are central themes in *Down These Mean Streets*, observes Dudley: "The book provides readers with the satisfaction of seeing Thomas escape from the horror of his early life—a story told in African American autobiography and fiction."[7] How and why did Thomas, a Latino author, receive an entry in an African American literary encyclopedia? To answer this question, I queried Dudley. Dudley, suspects that William L. Andrews, the lead editor of the *Companion*, asked him to write the entries on Thomas and Brown because Andrews was familiar with Dudley's research on African American male autobiography, having reviewed his 1991 book, *My Father's Shadow: Intergenerational Conflict in African American Men's Autobiography*.[8]

Like Dudley, Andrews does not recall the discussions that led to Thomas being included in the *Companion*, but he told me, via email, that he first read *Down These Mean Streets* in 1970 in a graduate seminar called Afro-American Autobiography taught by Professor Blyden Jackson at the University of North

Carolina.[9] The inclusion of Thomas in the *Companion* encourages readers to embrace the idea that the Negro/Black/African American racial category has always been Pan-African and inclusive of Afroethnic diversity. One sees this at work with the inclusion of immigrants like Marcus Garvey, Claude McKay, Eric Walrond, and Edwidge Danticat in African American literary handbooks and anthologies. The problem with these handbooks and anthologies, the *Companion* notwithstanding, is that they tend to give minimal attention to US Afro-Latinos writing in English. This oversight is strange given that the rise of Afro-Latino literary criticism in the US was coterminous with the BAM and nurtured in the Spanish Department at Howard University.[10]

The relative silence on *Down These Mean Streets* in African American literary studies is a problem and an opportunity.[11] Bringing attention to *Down These Mean Streets*'s engagement with the Black Aesthetic and its entanglement with the BAM encourages scholars in both African American and Latino studies to fill in the gaps in the history of Thomas's memoir as well as those in the history of the Latino presence in the BAM. Combining social theory, archival analysis, and the close reading techniques of cultural poetics, scholarly studies on *Down These Mean Streets* by researchers in African American and Latino studies tends to examine how ethnoracial identity formation and intersectional subjectivity constitute Thomas's racial awakening as a Puerto Rican who identifies as a person of African descent.[12] Much of the Latino studies scholarship does this by putting *Down These Mean Streets* in conversation with autobiographical narratives by Latino authors such as Bernardo Vega, Jesús Colón, Nicholasa Mohr, Oscar Zeta Acosta, and Richard Rodriguez.[13] Marta E. Sánchez is perhaps the only Latino studies scholar who draws intercultural connections between Thomas and the African American autobiographical tradition. In *"Shakin' Up" Race and Gender: Intercultural Connections in Puerto Rican, African American, and Chicano Narratives and Culture* (2005), Sánchez, like several of Thomas's reviewers, puts *Down These Mean Streets* in conversation with *Manchild in the Promised Land* (1965), Claude Brown's gritty, best-selling autobiography of growing up African American in Harlem during the 1940s and 1950s. Sánchez uses the Chicana trope of La Malinche to conduct an intersectional analysis of ethnic, racial, and gender identity formation in *Down These Mean Streets*, *Manchild in the Promised Land*, and Acosta's *The Autobiography of a Brown Buffalo* (1972). Sánchez uses the shared intercultural histories among the ethnic minorities in these texts to refute the narratives of Puerto Rican, African American, and Chicano cultural pathology proffered by the social researchers Octavio Paz, Daniel Patrick Moynihan, and Oscar Lewis. In their scholarship and editorial work Sánchez, Dudley, and Andrews link Thomas to the African American literary tradition. However, what literary historians and scholars have yet to do is analyze the relationship between Thomas, the BAM, and Black Aesthetic.

In this chapter, I argue that the African American narrative strategies and cultural tropes in *Down These Mean Streets* are due to the influence of John Oliver Killens and the HWG. In the first section of the chapter, I use Thomas's published interviews and biographies of Killens to construct a story of how Thomas joined the HWG and became a fixture in the literary conferences of the BAM. In addition, I use cultural studies of the BAM and the Popular Front to reconstruct the origins of the HWG. In the subsequent three sections, I use conceptual tools from life writing, trauma, humor, and ethnic studies to analyze and interpret how Thomas uses African American narrative strategies and cultural tropes to thematically inform and structure the discourse of masculinity and ethnoracial identity formation in his memoir. I illuminate these Black Aesthetic strategies and tropes by focusing on two understudied instances of Thomas's use of African American racial humor and vernacular culture. These African American narrative strategies and cultural tropes are particularly apparent in Thomas's nuanced negotiation of an ethnic joke about African American cowardice and in his use of signifying to protest a White Merchant Marine officer's infantilizing treatment of him. The first instance of African American humor contrasts the trope of Indigenous bravery with the stereotype of African American pusillanimity. My analysis of this stereotyping ethnic joke refines Marta E. Sánchez's La Malinche thesis, which uses a trope from Chicano studies to evaluate the construction of African American racial consciousness and masculinity in *Down These Mean Streets*. In my second close reading, I use Frances Aparicio and Susana Chávez-Silverman's theory of "tropicalization" to argue that Thomas Latinizes an African American protest joke derived from *Youngblood* (1954), the Killens novel that inspired him to become a writer. Historicizing and analyzing the Black Aesthetic vernacular practices in Thomas's memoir reveals how deeply it is shaped by African American narrative strategies and cultural tropes, supporting my claim that *Down These Mean Streets* is as much a foundational text of the BAM as it is of the Nuyorican Movement.

Literary Ancestors and Relatives: The Genesis and Rebirth of *Down These Mean Streets*

> While one can do nothing about choosing one's relatives,
> one can, as artist, choose one's "ancestors."
>
> —RALPH ELLISON, "The World and the Jug," in *Shadow and Act*

Although *Down These Mean Streets* is unambiguously a Latino memoir, it is deeply mediated by the African American literary tradition. The parturition, aesthetics, and African American readership of *Down These Mean Streets* are indebted, in no small way, to the literary nationalism of John Oliver Killens, the HWG, and African American magazines such as *Negro Digest/Black World*, *The Crisis*, *Ebony*, and *Jet*. Killens, an African American novelist and cultural critic, was one of the founders of the HWG, a proponent of the BAM, and Thomas's mentor, personal friend, and *literary ancestor*. In *Shadow and Act*, Ralph Ellison uses the concepts of relatives and ancestors to describe his theory of literary influence. Relatives are one's literary equals whereas ancestors are one's literary superiors, writers from whom one can learn something new about the world, life, and the craft of writing. The defining distinction between relatives and ancestors, for Ellison, is that one chooses one's ancestors rather than one's relatives.[14] For Thomas, Killens was a literary ancestor.

Scholars in both Latino and in African American studies often overlook the fact that *Youngblood*, Killens's debut novel, inspired Thomas to become a writer. Thomas encountered *Youngblood* when he was incarcerated. He spent nearly six years, 1950 to fall 1955, in prison for armed robbery and attempted murder.[15] Thomas credits *Youngblood* as the book that psychologically saved him from the degradation of prison life by inspiring him to become a writer.[16] After reading it, Thomas says, "I began to write what would one day be known as *Down These Mean Streets*. At that time, it was entitled *Home Sweet Harlem*."[17] Thomas used writing to counter the threats imprisonment posed to his mental health and to process the traumas of his past. When he was released, Thomas had the manuscript smuggled out of the prison by the prison chaplain.[18] He continued to work on the manuscript while he was on parole.[19] The opportunity to publish the memoir arose in 1961 or 1962, when *Petey and Johnny* was being filmed, a documentary about Thomas's job as a social worker in Harlem for Youth Development Inc.[20] After learning that Thomas had written a manuscript about his life, Richard Leacock, one of the producers of *Petey and Johnny*, introduced Thomas to Angus Cameron, a senior editor at

Alfred A. Knopf. Between his discussion with Leacock and his meeting with Cameron, Thomas went home to retrieve his manuscript only to discover that his wife, Daniela, who was unsupportive of his literary ambitions, had burned it, thinking that it was unimportant garbage.[21] Cameron, a member of the advisory board for the Louis M. Rabinowitz Foundation,[22] was instrumental in securing Thomas a $5,000 grant from the foundation to rewrite the manuscript,[23] which it took Thomas five years to do.[24]

When Thomas started rewriting his memoir in 1962, he joined the HWG, connecting to the organization through meetings at the home of Lonne Elder III, an African American actor and HWG member.[25] Killens invited Thomas to become member.[26] Thomas's fellow guild members included Sarah Wright, Paule Marshall, and Alice Childress. Although Thomas was the only Puerto Rican in the HWG, he was thankful for its support because there were no Puerto Rican writing groups of which Thomas knew. There were, however, other Spanish language writing groups, but Thomas considered publishing in English to be more marketable. Thomas and Killens bonded the moment they first met. "John Oliver Killens," says Thomas, "immediately had a rapport with me."[27] Killens read Thomas's manuscript and served as a mentor and advocate for his writing.[28] Although Thomas was in the HWG on and off, he says, "I was always John Killens's friend, his brother."[29] During the 1960s, their brotherly relationship served them well as they traveled to universities in the South championing civil rights, freedom, justice, and peace.[30]

Extant scholarship on Thomas often fails to discuss Thomas's membership in the HWG and his close friendship with Killens, who cofounded the guild in 1950 along with Rosa Guy, Dr. John Henrik Clarke, Willard Moore, and Walter Christmas. The HWG, writes cultural historian James E. Smethurst, was a "Left-influenced" cultural organization.[31] By "Left-influenced," Smethurst means that the founding members of the HWG had ties to the Communist Party USA (CPUSA) and roots in its racially specific Popular Front organizations. According to Smethurst, the long Popular Front in the US lasted from 1935 to the 1950s and called for interracial alliances between "various liberal or social democratic groups and individuals."[32] Within the Popular Front there were several African American led and focused organizations. For example, the National Negro Congress (NNC) and its youth wing, the Southern Negro Youth Congress, were Popular Front organizations dedicated to achieving and advancing social, political, and economic justice for African Americans. Founded in 1935 at Howard University, the NNC was an interracial CPUSA Popular Front organization dedicated to ensuring that African Americans received the benefits of FDR's New Deal reforms. The literary and cultural historian Brian Dolinar claims that after the NNC dissolved in 1947 its "Cultural Division changed its name to the Committee for the Negro in Arts" and continued to do its work.[33]

Three years later, the Committee for the Negro in Arts (CNA) transformed itself into the HWG. According to Katrina Myers Caldwell, Guy, Killens, Clarke, and Christmas "met while working with the Committee for the Negro in Arts, a political and cultural organization created to help enrich opportunities for African Americans in the theater."[34] During the Second Red Scare of the late 1940s to the 1950s, the US attorney general included the CNA on the Justice Department's list of subversive organizations, which, presumably, provided the incentive for the CNA to rebrand itself as the HWG in 1950. The nationalist, Black Aesthetic politics of the HWG arose out of the ethnic pluralism and cultural poetics of the US Popular Front. Aesthetically speaking, three broad thematic and formal concerns defined the cultural poetics of the Popular Front: (1) intercultural fusion; (2) the intersectional relationship between class, racial, ethnic, and national identity; and (3) the significance of place, as realized through the concepts of diction, dialect, neighborhood, region, rural provincialism, and metropolitan urbanity.[35] These Popular Front aesthetics informed the cultural poetics of Old Left-inspired African American literary organizations like the HWG from the 1930s to the 1950s.

The political genealogy of the HWG provides the context for understanding the literary nationalism that informed the thinking and actions of guild members during the 1960s and 1970s, when Thomas was affiliated with the group and its activities. The HWG professional network was crucial to the positive critical reception of *Down These Mean Streets* among African Americans. Through the HWG and Killens, Thomas became deeply involved in the Black Arts Movement. For example, when *Down These Mean Streets* was published in 1967, Killens asked Hoyt Fuller to have it reviewed in *Negro Digest*.[36] Killens himself wrote the glowing review of *Down These Mean Streets* in the January 1968 issue of the magazine.[37] The issue features thirty-eight African American writers who theorize the Black Aesthetic and the "Black Consciousness Movement." In addition to the interviews with the writers, the issue also contains a critique and a defense of Black cultural nationalism by James Cunningham and Ron Karenga, respectively. The issue also includes "Negro Writers' Conferences—The Dialogue Distorted," the scathing twenty-fifth chapter of Harold Cruse's *The Crisis of the Negro Intellectual* (1967). In this chapter, Cruse lambasts John Oliver Killens, the HWG, and their Negro Writers' Conferences as self-promoting tools of the integrationist, Old Left literary elite. In the process, he reveals the HWG's affiliation with the American Society for African Culture,[38] the US branch of the Paris-based Society of African Culture (SAC). Led by Léopold Sédar Senghor, SAC was dedicated to the diasporic promotion of Negritude, a diasporic philosophy of cultural nationalism that affirms African heritage and culture.[39] This connection between the proponents of Negritude in France and the advocates of the Black Aesthetic in the US provides more context to Thomas's claim that almost all of his friends in the 1960s were "*Black*, Black."

In the late 1960s, Thomas and Killens performed and presented together at conferences on African American literature around the country. Many of these conferences were held at historically Black colleges and universities (HBCUs).[40] Starting in 1966, Killens organized three conferences focused on African American literature and the Black Aesthetic at Fisk University, the HBCU where he taught as a writer-in-residence. The theme of the 1966 conference was "The Image of the Negro in American Literature," the 1967 conference theme was "The Black Writer and Human Rights," and the theme of the 1968 conference was "The Black Writer's Vision for America." According to Killens's biographer, Keith Gilyard, Thomas was a panelist at the 1968 conference, which was held in April, just two weeks after Dr. Martin Luther King Jr.'s assassination.[41] In his opening remarks to the conference attendees, Killens promoted the idea that African American literature should highlight "black legends, myths, and heroes . . . celebrate African American people and promote resistance against oppression, and . . . be presented in the African American vernacular."[42] Thomas would have been a celebrity figure at the conference not only because of his best-selling memoir but also because on February 19, 1968 "The World of Piri Thomas" aired on national TV. Thomas wrote, narrated, and acted in the documentary, which was reviewed descriptively in the few reviews it received.[43] Gordon Parks, the famous African American photographer, directed the documentary, further demonstrating Thomas's connection to the Black elite creatives of Harlem.[44]

In May 1968, Thomas and Killens also participated in the "Arts and the Inner City" conference at Columbia College in Chicago.[45] In the spring of 1969, Thomas performed at the book launch party for Nikki Giovanni's poetry collection, *Black Judgement*.[46] Giovanni had been a student in Killens's creative writing workshop at Fisk, and Killens sponsored the party for her at Turntable, a New York City nightclub owned by the Louisiana, R&B singer Lloyd Price.[47] In the 1970s, Killens accepted a writer-in-residence appointment at Howard University, and he hosted conferences there from 1974 to 1978. Gilyard asserts that the first conference at Howard was the most significant. The name of the conference was The National Conference of Afro-American Writers; it was held in 1974 from November 8 to 10.[48] The theme of this conference was the same as the 1966 Fisk conference, but the title of the theme was changed to "The Image of Black Folk in American Literature."[49] Thomas's presence at Fisk and Howard during the 1960s situates him in the long and understudied history of the Cuban and Puerto Rican presence at HBCUs, a history that begins in 1898 in the wake of the Spanish-American War.[50] Thomas's presence at Howard is also significant because Howard is an important site in the development of Afro-Hispanic literary criticism.[51] In a photo of the 1974 conference, Thomas is featured on stage with his fellow HWG members Dr. John Henrik Clarke and Maya Angelou.[52] As a member of the HWG and a regular attendee of Killens's conferences, Thomas would have been steeped in the theory and practice of the Black Aesthetic. From 1968 until the early 1980s, major magazines like *The Crisis*, *Negro Digest*, *Jet*, and *Ebony* reviewed and sold Thomas's books, suggesting that he had a sizeable African American readership.[53] With the exception of *Ebony*, these magazines kept their readers abreast of the censorship cases that plagued *Down These Mean Streets* from 1971 to 1982.[54] Thomas's membership in the HWG, presence in the BAM literary conferences, and representation in African American magazines demonstrate a profound African American influence on the aesthetics of *Down These Mean Streets* and its commercial success.

"When You Can Laugh, the Demons Go Away": The Post-Traumatic Perils of Life Writing

Down These Mean Streets chronicles the physical, emotional, and psychological abuse Thomas suffered as he came of age in New York. What *Down These Mean Streets* does not chronicle is the post-traumatic stress Thomas suffered reliving those events as he composed both the first and second drafts of the manuscript. In his published interviews, Thomas repeatedly uses the tropes of time travel, demons, and Pandora's box to describe how life writing not only saved him from losing his mind in prison but also how it nearly cost him his sanity when as a freed man he had to rewrite the burned manuscript from scratch. When Thomas composed the first draft, he was practicing a form of self-care that is variously called scriptotherapy, writing therapy, and pathography.[55] Suzette A. Henke, a literary studies scholar, defines scriptotherapy as "the process of writing out and writing through traumatic experience in the mode of therapeutic reenactment."[56] Humanities scholar Anne Hunsaker Hawkins argues that the impulse to write about one's trauma is often ritualized: "the motive to testify to one's experience — often taking place as a ritual action — emphasizes the truth value and the factual nature of autobiographies about illness . . . autobiographies about illness or trauma have achieved a validity and an authenticity that is in part a reflection of the way we in our culture privilege personal narrative."[57]

Ritual played a significant factor in Thomas becoming a writer. In a March 1995 interview with Carmen Dolores Hernández, Thomas describes himself as a "very symbolic" person as he recalls the "ceremony" he performed to reify his decision to become a writer after reading *Youngblood*:

> One time they gave me a canary as a present and I had it for two or three days . . . I got up and took the canary out of its cage and the windows across from the bars were open a little bit. . . . And I let the bird fly . . . And I smiled at him, "At least he'll die free, not in a bird cage like me," I said. And I looked inside and thought "you [the prison system] only got my body, you don't have my mind. And I promise you one thing: I won't serve time, I'll make time serve me. I'll educate my mind, not eradicate it. I, Piri, Thomas, will be born anew." So I changed my name from Pete, as they used to call me, and named myself Piri, like my mother called me. I took a piece of paper and said, "Paper, I'm going to tell you a story and whoever reads it is going to walk in it and hear it and feel it. Just like when you've stepped into Alice in Wonderland." And then I began to tell the paper a story and in the writing what you are doing is drawing it out of you. You can feel the conversations going on instead of hearing them. You transpose those feelings into words. I was delighted to know that it was all pouring out.[58]

The ritual of freeing the canary takes on greater significance as an act of heroic self-transformation because it also involves a renaming ceremony, a conventional trope of the fugitive slave narrative. Thomas stopped using the name Pete and adopted the moniker Piri, his mother's pet name for him. This ritual act of self-naming/self-determination affirms not only the memory of his mother but also his Puerto Rican heritage, his Latinidad. Thomas prefaces his recollection of this ritual moment by attesting to writing's power to restore and sustain mental health: "Creativity: it's the strength, the power, it's healing. Creativity was my salvation in prison because it kept me from becoming a vegetable or a psychopath. It opened worlds up to me where

I could time travel with the power of my mind because of the anguish to be free, out of that canary cage."[59] After the recollection of the ritual, Thomas goes on to discuss how he used humor to balance the cathartic benefits with the post-traumatic harms of memoir writing as scriptotherapy:

> Humor's always been important for me. If I could laugh, the demons would go away. So, I had to add a little humor and then things became a little better. But getting that out of me was a catharsis. I had taken the demons and put them into it. I was writing prose, I was writing my feelings and my feelings danced like musical notes. What a lot of people don't understand is that in writing *Down These Mean Streets* I could not realize the psychological damage it would do to me by opening up Pandora's Box again and bringing back to mind all those things I had gone through.[60]

Thomas returns to the time travel, demon, and Pandora's box metaphors in a fall 1996 interview with Ilan Stavans, revealing that the initial manuscript of *Down These Mean Streets* was never intended to be published. Writing that manuscript was a therapeutic coping mechanism and the final product was intended strictly for private consumption:

> Many people do not understand that to write that book I almost blew my mind. Because I had to force myself back in time and feel all the feelings again which included all the agony and the pain. That book was supposed to be something swept under the rug and forgotten but I went and opened Pandora's Box, and out came not only the demons, but also the truths. That's why I could not a leave a chapter unfinished; I would work on it three or four days straight, reliving all the emotions from that time. But once I discovered that the truth brought relief from the pain, it was wonderful. I then added humor and when you have humor you can laugh, and when you can laugh, the demons go away.[61]

Thomas added the humor for the benefit of his readers as much as for himself. He uses humor, I contend, to cultivate a sympathetic audience. Psychiatrist Judith Lewis Herman notes that a sympathetic audience is an important component of a trauma victim's survivorship.[62] Hunsaker Hawkins, in her research, finds that writing with the expectation of publication, writing for an audience of sympathetic readers, is just as therapeutic as the act of writing strictly for one's self.[63] However, striking a note of caution, she says that trauma theorists have taught her a "great deal . . . about the motives and function of pathography. They've taught me that the medical and legal models for trauma and recovery that I call 'therapy' and 'testimony' are not without their psychological risk. Either can so fixate and imprison the survivor in the trauma that it is so much survived as it is perpetuated."[64] Published life writing is rife with psychological risks because it exposes writers to the additional traumas of ridicule and censure as well as to charges of libel and fraud, especially when expectations of veracity are unmet, note life writing scholars Leigh Gilmore and G. Thomas Couser.[65]

Exposing one's private life to public scrutiny through memoir is not without its perils, be they ethical, legal, or psychological. Thomas experienced intense psychological harm as he rewrote his lost manuscript. In a fall 2001 interview with Dorothee von Huene Greenberg, Thomas focuses on the post-traumatic stress of life writing for publication and on the relationship between catharsis, humor, narrative selectivity, and autobiographical fidelity:

There were little energies there that may have happened that I made a little less of, and there were ragings that I didn't want to put in as they happened. You must understand that when I was writing the book I did not realize that I was going back in time to see the sees and do the dos and hear the hears and feel the feelings over and over again seven times stronger, and I broke walls in my kitchen writing the book, and that is why I had to temper some of it down, or the rage would destroy me. That is why when I finished a book my agent, a woman, said, "This book certainly has had to have been a catharsis for you." And I didn't know what the word "catharsis" was, but I was too proud to admit it, so I said, "mhm," and when I got to where I could look up 'catharsis' and it meant getting it off my shoulders, I said to her via spirit, "yea."

So there is nothing in *Down These Mean Streets* that didn't happen to me. . . .

The writing of *Down These Mean Streets* put a *tremendous pressure* on me emotionally. I could feel my life going out of me. . . . I knew in *Down These Mean Streets* that the reader would not be able to put the book down, would have to keep on reading, and I learned that I was being so intense that I would affect my readers also, so I learned that I had to put humor in it too, so that people laugh from time to time. And what humorous thing could I write about in *Down These Mean Streets* that would relate to everyone? O, maybe a little thing like taking a bath and laying a little fart, you know, passing wind, and hearing the bubbles come up in the bath water, and the "phewy" of my brother. Everybody has done that at one time or another.[66]

Thomas's conviction in humor's therapeutic benefits for himself and his implied reader is supported by cultural and clinical studies that confirm humor's ability to improve mental and physical health, its ability to ameliorate psychological symptoms of trauma such as anxiety, depression, and rage.[67]

Thomas's scatological humor reflects his empathy for a universal reader, but his familiarity and facility with African American vernacular practices such as the dozens and signifying suggest that he was also writing with an ethnically specific, ideal reader in mind. In the memoir, Thomas is self-aware of the dozens and signifying as ethnically specific vernacular practices, identifying them by name in his interactions with his African American best friends Crutch and Brew.[68] According to Amuzie Chimezie, the dozens is a West African-derived verbal game of insults "in which two contestants, in the presence of a spurring audience of peers, try to best each other in casting aspersions on each other or each other's relatives, particularly the mother."[69] The ritualized verbal dueling that constitutes the dozens serves important expressive, psychological, social, and educational functions in African American culture, especially among adolescent and adult males.[70] Signifying, in the African American vernacular tradition, refers to two types of artistic African American speech practices. According to Claudia Mitchell-Kernan, the first is humorous "verbal dueling" and the second is "a way of encoding messages or meanings in natural conversations which involves, in most cases, an element of indirection. This kind of signifying might be best viewed as an alternative message form, selected for its artistic merit, and may occur embedded in a variety of discourses."[71] Thomas's explicit use of and references to the dozens and signifying reveal the depth of his familiarly with the Black Aesthetic and the rich tradition of African American ethnic humor in conversational joking.

"What the Hell Indians Had to Do with All This": Indigeneity, Anti-Blackness, and the Black Mask of Ethnic Humor

> Americans began their revolt from the English fatherland when they dumped the tea in to the Boston Harbor, masked as Indians, and the mobility of the society created in this limitless space has encouraged the use of the mask for good and evil ever since.
>
> —RALPH ELLISON, "Change the Joke and Slip the Yoke" in *Shadow and Act*

Although *Down These Mean Streets* is primarily set in 1940s and 1950s New York, a thematically significant portion of it is set in the Deep South, where

Killens was born and raised. Thomas's friendship with Killens and their membership in the HWG provides the context needed to understand Thomas's familiarity with the African American autobiographical tradition and his mostly sympathetic but sometimes problematic treatment of African American literary and cultural tropes in *Down These Mean Streets*. Concepts like colorism, minstrel dialect, folk humor, signifying, playing the dozens, passing, racial emasculation, and lynching are highly concentrated in *Down These Mean Streets*. They are particularly dense in chapters thirteen to nineteen. Over the course of these six chapters, seventeen-year-old Thomas joins the Merchant Marine as a way to make it down South in order to discover what it means to be a "black man."[72] Thomas travels with Brewster "Brew" Johnson, his nineteen-one-year-old, African American best friend. In their relationship, Brew is cast as an adept and Thomas as a neophyte. Brew initiates Thomas into the fraternity of African American male identity politics and consciousness. On this seven-month, ritualized journey of racial initiation, Thomas and Brew make stops in Washington, DC; Norfolk, Virginia; Mobile, Alabama; New Orleans, Louisiana; and Galveston, Texas.

Scholars in Latino Studies have brought critical attention to Thomas's Southern journey of racial identity formation, but few have used conceptual tools from African American studies in their examinations.[73] Scholars in African American studies will immediately recognize that Thomas's Southern journey of racial identity formation is analogous to the African American immersion narrative. Thomas's journey, for example, has much in common with the immersion narratives one finds in classic African American texts like *Twelve Years a Slave*, *Up from Slavery*, *The Souls of Black Folk*, *The Autobiography of an Ex-Colored Man*, and *Cane*.[74] The impetus for the immersion narrative in *Down These Mean Streets* is Thomas's confusion about where he, as an Afro-Latino, ranks in the racial social order of America. I categorize Thomas as an Afro-Latino because that is how he increasingly characterizes himself over the course of the memoir. Thomas and his father are the darkest members in their family of six, which includes Thomas's mother, sister, and two brothers, who are all considered White. Thomas and his father are routinely racialized (i.e., unintentionally passed) by the public at large as Black, where Black is implicitly defined as being a descendant of Africans enslaved in the US.

A bitter argument between Thomas and his brother José dramatizes Thomas's increasing identification with his African heritage and Pan-African identity. Thomas and José argue about whether dark-skinned Puerto Ricans are dark because of "Indian" or "moyeto" blood, moyeto being a Puerto

Rican slang term for a very dark-skinned person of African descent.[75] The idea that dark-skinned people of Hispanic Caribbean descent may be dark because of Indigenous Caribbean ancestry is often associated with the popular and official racial discourse of the Dominican Republic.[76] This racial discourse, however, is not unique to the Dominican Republic, given that it appears in the memoirs of Afro-Puerto Rican and Afro-Cuban writers like Piri Thomas and Carlos Moore. During the argument with Thomas, José says, "Maybe Poppa's a little dark, but that's the Indian blood in him."[77] As the argument progresses, José asserts that Thomas is "Indian" just like their father.[78] Furthermore, José insists that "Indian blood" not only makes dark-skinned Puerto Ricans dark but that it also makes them socially distinct from, if not superior to, people of African descent. Thomas counters José's Indian blood thesis by recounting the history of African slavery in Puerto Rico: "What kinda Indian? I said bitterly. Caribe? Or maybe Borinquén.[79] Say José, didn't you know the Negro made the scene in Puerto Rico way back? And when the Spanish spics ran outta Indian coolies, they brought them big blacks from you know where. Poppa's got *moyeto* blood. I got it. Sis got it. James got it. And mah deah brudder, you-all got it."[80] Marta Caminero-Santangelo argues that José uses "Indian blood" as a whitening strategy:

> In the polarized racial dichotomy of white/black, "Indian blood" gets "read," at least by Piri's brother, as a defense against blackness. . . . As a first step towards repudiating white privilege and constructing a sense of solidarity with African Americans, Piri rejects the comforting excuse of "Indian blood" for the insistence on "moyeto" or black blood; but in so doing, he relies on the very notions of race as biology and the one-drop rule that are the foundations of the racial structure of American society. In other words, he bases his argument on the grounds of biological essentialism, which will connect him to African Americans.[81]

The argument between Thomas and José escalates into a brutal physical altercation which hastens Thomas's resolve to travel down South to discover what it means to be a "black man." Clearly, Thomas does not deny or disparage the African contribution to the cultural and phenotypical make up of modern-day Puerto Ricans. Thomas seemingly ascribes to a tripartite conception of *mestizaje*, the idea that Puerto Ricans are a mix of Spanish, Indigenous, and African peoples. This is closely related to Juan Flores's concept of "triple consciousness," a concept that defines US Afro-Latinos as nationally American, ethnically Latino, and racially of African descent.[82]

However, like his father and his brother, Thomas also rejects being categorized as Black, but he rejects it for two different reasons. First, Thomas objects to being racially categorized as Black because it obscures his ethnic identity as a Puerto Rican, and, in the context of the 1940s, suggests that he is ethnically African American. The fact that Thomas suppressed his Afro-Cuban heritage in constructing Thomas, his narrative self, adds another layer of nuance, if not complexity, not only to Thomas's objection to being categorized as African American but also to the limits of his commitment to the autobiographical pact and its ethos of complete disclosure. Thomas never mentions his Afro-Cuban heritage in *Down These Mean Streets*. Antonio López reveals that Thomas's father migrated from Cuba to Puerto Rico in 1923, spent a year working on his Puerto Rican accent, and then, pretending to be Puerto Rican, migrated to Harlem, as a US citizen.[83] Thomas, who is so brutally candid about other matters in his life, probably chose not to disclose his Cubanidad because of a combination of factors: market aesthetics, US anti-Cuban sentiment, and the fear of deportation. In any case, Thomas resists the strict US binary racial logic of hypodescent: "A black man is so important that a drop of Negro blood can make a black man out of a pink-assholed, blue-eyed white man."[84] Even as a Harlem-born Puerto Rican, Thomas still feels that he is ethnically distinct from, if not socially superior to African Americans like his "tight *amigos*" Crutch and Brew.[85] For example, when Brew attempts to use the one-drop rule to build a Pan-African solidarity with Thomas, Thomas rejects it because it threatens his conception of himself as a Puerto Rican:

> "Yeah, Brew," I said, "it must be tough on you Negroes."
> "Wha' yuh mean, us Negroes? Ain't yuh includin' yourself? Hell, you ain't but a coupla shades lighter'n me, and even if yuh was even lighter'n that, you'd still be a Negro."
> I felt my chest get tighter and tighter. I said, "I ain't no damn Negro and I ain't no paddy [White]. I'm Puerto Rican."[86]

Thomas rejects homogenizing panethnic categories like White, Black, and Indian in favor of territorially specific and ethnoracially mixed categories of identity like Puerto Rican.

Second, Thomas rejects identifying as African American because it threatens his masculinity. As I explore in greater detail further on, Thomas's belief in the Hegelian notion of "national character" leads him to believe that African Americans, relative to Indigenous Americans, are an emasculated and feminized people.[87] Critical humor specialist Michael Pickering argues that the stereotyping function of the national character concept derives its power, over time, from the force of repetition in mass media and popular culture:

> The idea of national character emerged in the eighteenth century, and, for philosophers such as Hume, Rousseau and Herder, ideas of national genius and character were considered as expressive of a collective unity and uniqueness. . . . The idea of "national character" was typical of the kind of essentialist thinking applied to categories of association and identity in the nineteenth century. Being English or French distilled a defining racial essence, given by nature and taken as hereditary. . . . Continuing reference to an essentialized national character shows how difficult it is to defuse and nullify certain stereotypes, especially when the historical accretions built up around them seem to provide evidence of long-term continuities and deeply innate characteristics.[88]

For Thomas and Brew, the histories and popular culture images of Indigenous nations fighting wars against the US are models of heroic masculinity. Thomas and Brew empathize with the Indigenous armed struggle against White racism. Engagement with the trope of Native American bravery seems to have been a staple feature of African American boyhood from slavery until the 1950s. For example, the historian Leon F. Litwack reminds us of the longevity of this trope in his discussion of how racial subordination and difference structured "interracial companionship and play." Litwack writes, "That difference was made perfectly clear in the games a Virginia black remembered of a childhood spent both in slavery and freedom. When they played 'Injuns an' soldiers,' the white boys had been the soldiers and the black boys the Indians. When they later played 'Yankee an' 'Federates,' the actual outcome of the Civil War was irrelevant."[89] Litwack uses this example to support his concept of "racial initiation," which he defines as a child's initial encounter with "racial insult."[90] In the opening of his 1965 debate with William F. Buckley Jr. at Cambridge University, James Baldwin provides a second example of how the trope of Indigenous bravery can catalyze African American sociopolitical awakening in boyhood: "It comes as a great shock around the age of five or six or seven to discover the flag to which you have pledged allegiance, along with everybody else, has not pledged allegiance to you. It comes as a great shock to discover that when you were rooting for Gary Cooper killing off the Indians, that the Indians were you."[91] Admittedly, it is not safe to generalize about the role of the Indian bravery trope in African American literature and culture based solely on the examples from Litwack and Baldwin, but

I call attention to them because they are thematically linked to how Marta E. Sánchez similarly uses an Indigenous trope to analyze and interpret how men of African descent construct and perform heteronormative masculinity.

In her book *"Shakin' Up" Race and Gender*, Sánchez uses La Malinche, an Indigenous figure from Chicano history and culture, to evaluate Thomas's masculine identity formation and performance. La Malinche was the Indigenous concubine of the Spanish Conquistador Hernán Cortés. "La Malinche," writes Sánchez, "is coded as a mother-traitor to the nation because she collaborated, sexually and politically, with the Spanish colonizers of Indian civilizations." Using the lens of the La Malinche trope, Sánchez argues that Thomas "compensates for the racialized and feminized abjection of black men in the United States by making the abjection of women the guarantor of his ethnic and masculine privilege." Sánchez's point about the "feminized abjection of black men" primarily focuses on how Thomas reads and treats Gerald Andrew West, an effete African American trickster figure.[92]

On the second stop of their journey to the South, Thomas and Brew meet Gerald Andrew West in Norfolk, Virginia. According to Thomas, West is "tan-colored and not really very negroid-looking."[93] West is a Du Boisian figure who lives and works among the African American masses in Norfolk, where he gathers material for a book on the "Negro situation,"[94] a book that calls to mind Du Bois's *The Philadelphia Negro*. Sánchez suggests that West's book project, polite manners, speech affectation, light complexion, and disavowal of "blackness" become markers of femininity, in the minds of Thomas and Brew. West's opportunistic use of his racial ambiguity is particularly troubling for the two young men. Over the course of his conversation with Thomas and Brew, West declares that he is "one-eighth colored," part English, part Malaysian, part Spanish, and part Indian, having "Indian blood from, uh, India."[95] By the end of the conversation, West admits that he is trying to pass for Puerto Rican so he can "make the next step to white," declaring that he looks and feels White and that he intends to go "back to Pennsylvania and *be* white."[96] Caminero-Santangelo claims that West's self-representation as thoroughly "blended" fits Gloria Anzaldúa's conception of the "new mestiza [who] learns to be an Indian in Mexican culture, to be Mexican from the Anglo point of view."[97] However, West's pride in being East Indian rather than Native American highlights the understudied role that the rejection and acceptance of Indigenous identity can play in racial identity formation in the African American cultural imaginary.

In contradistinction to Sánchez, I argue, that Thomas's view of African Americans as a feminized people is primarily manifest in his perception that

African Americans did not use mass armed resistance to defend themselves against lynching. Caminero-Santangelo comes close to making this point when she says, Thomas's insistence on Puerto-Ricaness is "clearly a self-protective denial of shared experience with African Americans in a US context; if he is not black, he assumes, he need not fear being lynched."[98] Because of the premium he places on machismo, Thomas does not want to be associated with a people whom he perceives to be a nation of craven victims, inviting, through their weakness, the violence visited upon them by White terrorists.

Thomas's understanding of cowardice as a defining component of African Americans' national character is linked to paternalist conceptions of African Americans as infantile. Depending on the critic, African Americans are either inherently infantile or infantile as the result of the brutalization of slavery. For example, Stanley Elkins's discredited "Sambo thesis" gave some credence to the brutalization theory in the early 1960s, during the time in which Thomas was writing his memoir.[99] In *Fatal Self-Deception: Slaveholding Paternalism in the Old South*, Eugene D. Genovese and Elizabeth Fox-Genovese write that the notion of inherent "black cowardice" was commonplace in the US cultural imaginary during the Colonial era and well into the age of abolition. "The black abolitionists John Rock and Frederick Douglass," they confirm, "had to reply to charges by Theodore Parker, among others, that blacks showed inherent cowardice by refusing to fight for their own freedom and that John Brown's raid had failed to spark a slave revolt."[100] In Thomas's mind, African Americans deserve their inferior social status because they did not resist slavery, segregation, and racial terror militantly enough. They are a weak people who lack valor, bravery, and, as Brew implies, "heart."[101]

Both Thomas and Brew make clear the connections between "heart," "black cowardice," Indians, machismo, and the lynching of African Americans in *Chapter 13: Hung Up between Two Sticks*. The two sticks in the chapter's title are allusions to the crucifixion of Jesus. However, I argue that Thomas intentionally uses the verb "hung" to call to mind the practice of racial lynching, an equally ritualized form of murder and social terror. By conflating crucifixion and lynching, the title of the chapter suggests that African Americans are sacrificial Christ figures. Chapter 13 contains a crucial scene in which Brew confronts Thomas about Thomas's repeated refusal to identify as a Black man. When playing the dozens with each other, Thomas realizes that his belief in Puerto Rican exceptionalism offends Brew. Using lynching imagery, Thomas interrogates his own idea that Puerto Ricans are socially superior to African Americans, that Puerto Rican lives matter more than Black lives in the racial social order of the US: "I tried to dig myself.

I figured I should get it back on a joke level. What the hell was I trying to put down? Was I trying to tell Brew that I'm better than he is 'cause he's only black and I'm Puerto Rican dark-skin? Like his people copped trees on a white man's whim, and who ever heard of Puerto Ricans getting hung like that?"[102] In Thomas's myopic view of history, the fact that African Americans were routinely lynched suggests that they were socially inferior, if not inherently craven, because they did not oppose lynching in a show of mass armed resistance.

Thomas's position fails to take into account that there was a "continuum of lynching resistance," as Sundiata Cha-Jua notes in the abstract of his conference paper "Beyond the Rape Myth: Black Resistance to Lynching, 1867–1930." The five responses on the continuum include flight, self-defense, protest, collective armed defense, and mass exodus.[103] Scholars of African American history and culture can credibly conjecture that collective armed defense was the least favored option because it could trigger massacres, like those that occurred in Chicago in 1919 and Tulsa in 1921. Clearly, there were practical and pragmatic reasons that account for African Americans' putative lack of "heart," to use Thomas's concept for masculine bravery. However, hegemonic masculinity often interprets African American pragmatism as cowardice, in relation to armed mass resistance. Thomas and Brew's hegemonic masculinity compromises their ability to perceive African American pragmatism in the face of White racial terror as a type of courage.

The "copped trees on a white man's whim" phrase is the first in a series of references to lynching as crucifixion, which is the central motif in the chapter. Three other references follow it. Thomas says to Brew "if you could dig the way I feel, you'd see I was hung up between two sticks."[104] Further along in the conversation, Thomas says, "True, I ain't never been down South, but the same crap's happening up here. So they don't hang you by your neck. But they slip an invisible rope around your balls and hang you with nice smiles."[105] And finally, Thomas asks Brew, "A cat's gotta be hung before he knows what's happenin'?,"[106] by which Thomas means that one can conceptually acknowledge the reality of anti-Black racism and violence in the US without having to experience it personally.

Interestingly, Brew is the one who verbalizes the notion that African Americans are craven, a notion that Thomas restricts to his own internal monologue. Brew compares the history of oppression and racial terror suffered by African Americans to the genocide suffered by Native Americans: "Now those Indians sure had some kinda hard way to go, but they had heart." The comment puzzles Thomas who asks "what the hell Indians had to do with all this."[107] Brew replies with a humorous folk expression that his father used to say: "The Indian fought the white man and died / An' us black folk jus' wagged ouah tails, / 'Yas suhses,' smiled and multiplied."[108] This facetious folk poem falls into a US genre of humor known as dialect humor. Thomas uses phonetic spelling and nonstandard English to distinguish African Americans from the host of other ethnic groups in the memoir. This not only celebrates the distinctiveness and variety of African American vernacular culture, but it also serves as a questionable source of dialect humor. Dialect humor is a form of linguistic stereotyping that often indexes racial, ethnic, and socioeconomic differences. When someone uses dialect humor to disparage members of an ethnic group to which they do not belong that humor falls into a category that humor researchers call ethnic joking. Humor scholar Catherine Evan Davies notes that ethnic jokes in western societies focus on the stupidity or canniness of minorities and police social, geographic, and moral boundaries. "They mock groups," argues Davies, "who are peripheral to the central or dominant group or who are seen by them as ambiguous. They ascribe to these groups traits which the group telling the jokes does not wish to recognize among its own members."[109] A typical example of Thomas's use of dialect humor to differentiate Puerto Ricans from African Americans involves Brew describing, in heavy Black Southern dialect, how his English used to be worse: "Ah hates cornbread and sugar watah. Ah hates cardboard in mah shoes. Ah hates wakin' scared. Man, Ah nevah had much o' schoolin', Piri; the only lessons Ah evah got was from my mom. You know, Ah used to speak some terrible English. It's only now that I'm talking better."[110] This specific instance of dialect humor functions as a type of minstrel humor because Brew is a composite character based on up to four of Thomas's actual friends, one being the actual Brew and another being Isaac Nasario.[111] Thomas's choice to mask a Puerto Rican as an African American male from the South amounts to literary minstrelsy, especially when one takes into account the pejorative way in which Brew's Black Southern dialect is used not only as a mark of ethnoregional authenticity but also as an index of Puerto Rican and African American difference. Although Thomas is Afro-Puerto Rican, his intraracial ethnic joking does not function as self-deprecating in-group humor because he is ethnically and culturally distinct from Brew. Thomas's dialect humor functions as what Simon Weaver calls "cultural racism": "Because of its emphasis on culture, it is often seen as a racism that moves away from, or disguises a belief in, a biological basis to racism."[112] Taking issue with the claim that "jokes are just jokes," Weaver argues "that humour is not always benign, nor does it always work for the social good, and, although claims of offensiveness differ, humor can, in particular readings serve ideological functions for serious discourse."[113] Because of their polysemic nature, even intraracial ethnic jokes, especially those between differential ethnic groups, can harmfully reproduce and perpetuate stereotypes based on the notions of biological racism that subtend the concept of national character.

Brew's joke about the distinction between the national characters of Indigenous Americans and African Americans falls into a category of ethnic humor called "black cowardice" jokes. Citing Christie Davies, the late Charles R. Gruner, a professor of communication studies, writes there were "two major stereotypes and/or comic scripts used in anti-black humor, most of which is generated by southern U.S. whites: blacks' supposed tendency to steal chickens and their supposed cowardice when danger looms."[114] Brew's ethnic joke reinforces stereotypes of the Indigenous noble savage and the docile and cowardly African American slave. The joke is morally complex because it simultaneously celebrates and disparages Indigenous Americans for their uncompromising bravery and African Americans for their nonmilitant pragmatism. Using relief theory to defend the case for ethnic stereotype humor, Leon Rappaport contends that its social utility exists in its capacity to grant its audience permission to revel in the joy of transgression, in the pleasures of temporarily skewering liberal ideals and "violat[ing] the rules of conventional morality."[115] Brew's joke does this for members of his ethnic group by employing what humor scholars call a "self-esteem enhancing function." Jacquelyn Rahman writes that African American comedy bolsters African American self-esteem by portraying the group "as strong survivors and repositories of soul."[116] In Brew's joke, this self-esteem enhancing function is realized through what Rappaport calls "protective self-critical humor."[117] Ethnic humor, argues Rappaport, "helps us to cope with the risky or fearful nature of interpersonal relationships."[118] In this sense, Brew's joke functions as an index of the "customary joking relationship" that exists between him and Thomas. As Neal R. Norrick writes, the rapport function of conversational joking relationships between kin, friends, and colleagues allows for both the maintenance of social cohesion and the socially acceptable public expression of aggression.[119] Brew and Thomas's joking relationship reinforces their intraracial kinship, allowing them to bridge the gulf of their ethnic differences and worldviews about the limits of Black identity. After Brew tells the joke, he smiles knowingly at Thomas, suggesting that he knew Thomas had also been thinking that Blacks were cowards. Thomas, acknowledging Brew's knowing smile with a knowing smile of his own, attempts to defend African

Americans from Brew's charge of cowardice. "Maybe," says Thomas, "it wasn't a bad idea to take it low when the weight was all on the other side. Dig it, man, the Indian fought the paddy and lost. And the Indian was on his own turf."[120] Thomas's comment acknowledges the wisdom of African American pragmatism relative to collective armed resistance. The problem is that Brew's *black humor* uses the dispossession of Native Americans as the historical medium in which to dissolve Black and Latino ethnic tension.[121] Brew restores his relationship with Thomas by making the intergenerational trauma of Native American genocide and African American slavery the butt of his tension relieving joke. On the heels of this discourse about comparative ethnic bravery, Thomas decides to go down South to test his manhood and his racial identity by testing his theory of Puerto Rican exceptionalism.

After leaving Gerald Andrew West in Norfolk, Thomas and Brew travel to Mobile, Alabama and New Orleans. Brew disappears in New Orleans, but Thomas continues his quest through the Deep South via the Merchant Marine. After New Orleans, the *James Clifford* stops in Galveston, Texas. In Galveston, Thomas befriends an unnamed, "olive-skinned," silk-haired, straight-nosed Mexican man at a carnival. He asks the man to take him to a "white cathouse" so that he can have racial revenge sex in Texas with a White prostitute.[122] The only way Thomas can enter the brothel is for him to pretend to be a monolingual, Puerto Rican migrant. "If you do not speak a word of English," says his Mexican friend, "you may pass for Puerto Rican."[123] Despite Thomas's fluency in Spanish, Thomas suspects that his newfound Mexican friend thinks that Thomas is actually a "home boy," an African American, who is passing for Puerto Rican.[124] The notion that some African Americans are sometimes mistaken for Latinos speaks to Milan's concept of "passing Latinities" and reminds one of James Weldon Johnson's unnamed narrator in *The Autobiography of an Ex-Colored Man*. When they arrive at the brothel, the White proprietor is suspicious of Thomas. In Spanish, he asks Thomas where he is from. Thomas says Puerto Rico. Still suspicious, the proprietor asks the Mexican man if Thomas is a "nigger." The Mexican man assures him that Thomas is not.[125] And then the proprietor says something that confirms Thomas's theory of Latino exceptionalism. The proprietor says that he allows "all kinds of foreigners, and Spanish people who come from Argentina and Colombia and Peru and Cuba, and that's all right, but we go to keep these damn niggers down."[126] Satisfied, the proprietor lets Thomas and the Mexican pass into the brothel. Although Thomas is silently outraged at the proprietor's racism, he pays ten dollars for a prostitute, while his Mexican friend pays only five. Everything being equal, it appears that the surcharge is connected to Thomas being dark-skinned. After having sex, Thomas triumphantly proclaims to the prostitute, in English, "I just want you to know that you got fucked by a nigger, *by a black man!*"[127] This false unmasking constitutes a second act of trickster passing, as Thomas is neither a "nigger" nor a "black man" in the sense that the proprietor and prostitute understand the terms.

The ritual act that secures Thomas's rite of passage into Black identity happens in a racially segregated brothel with a White prostitute. This scene is emblematic of what Sánchez means when she says Thomas makes "the abjection of women the guarantor of his ethnic and masculine privilege."[128] Thomas realizes a sad irony—the luxury of his revenge on White America costs him ten dollars and enriches the racial social order he despises. The money, he says, meant nothing to him. He just "wanted to prove something."[129] The something he proved is that race is a social construct, a confabulation of the mind, and not a biological truth. What he also proves is that there is some merit to the reality of Latino exceptionalism, in the sense that the White brothel owner makes an exception for Thomas because he perceives him to be something more than a "nigger."

Change the Joke: Signifying and Tropicalizing Dignity

> The white man's half-conscious awareness that his image of the Negro is false makes him suspect the Negro is always seeking to take him in, and assume his motives are anger and fear—which very often they are. . . . Very often, however, the Negro's masking is motivated not so much by fear as by a profound rejection of the image created to usurp his identity.
>
> —RALPH ELLISON, "Change the Joke and Slip the Yoke" in *Shadow and Act*

In his 1980 interview with Wolfgang Binder, Thomas reflects on the psychological harm White infantilization inflicts on Black males:

> I wanted to be a human being that didn't have to walk down the streets without people constantly either calling me a "boy" in a nasty tone (and they would call you a boy even when you were thirty years old), and then there was the constant "nigger" and "black bastard" and "dirty spic," all that nastiness. It got to enrage me. It got me to the point where I was ashamed of my skin. In fact I would sometimes secretly pray that I could somehow turn white. And later I found out that beyond your color or language there was something more important, called your sense of dignity.[130]

Thomas illustrates this same concern for dignity in the signifying scene between him and the chief mate of the *James Clifford*, the Merchant Marine ship on which Thomas served as a messman. The scene occurs in Norfolk, Virginia. It occurs after the incident with Gerald Andrew West but before the brothel scene in Galveston.

In the *James Clifford* scene, Thomas uses signification to resist the chief mate's attempt to emasculate and infantilize him by calling him "boy." The signifying script Thomas uses to educate the chief mate revises a similar signifying scene in *Youngblood*. The late William H. Wiggins Jr. writes about this scene in his 1971 essay "Black Folktales in the Novels of John O. Killens." In his article, Wiggins analyzes the relationship between race, masculinity, emasculation, and folk humor in three of Killens's novels: *Youngblood, And Then We Heard the Thunder,* and *'Sippi.* Wiggins examines several signifying jokes that protest the infantilization of African American men by Whites. Citing Richard M. Dorson, Wiggins classifies this genre of jokes as "'protest humor'; i.e. they carry the themes of black resentment and resistance to racial prejudice in America."[131] The infantilization folktale to which Wiggins refers, and which I contend that Thomas revises, occurs in the first chapter of the third book of *Youngblood*. The principal characters in the scene are Jim and Oscar, two male teenagers who, like Thomas and Brew, are best friends. Oscar is White and Jim is Black. One night, as Jim and Oscar are hanging out and enjoying each other's company, Oscar, naively, but without malice, says to Jim, "You know some folks say your old man is the strongest colored boy on the plantation, and I b'lieve it's the truth."[132] Perturbed, Jim uses a humorous folktale to indirectly express his displeasure with Oscar having infantilized his father as a "boy": "You know, what you just said remind me of a story I heard the other day, about a colored man in Waycross. This colored man—he was a great big colored man. He was walking down the street in Waycross minding his own business, when this cracker came up to him and said, 'Hey, boy, where you going?' And the colored man looked at the cracker and said, 'Mr. White folks will you tell me something please, sir? How big do mens grow where you come from?'"[133] The punch line of the story turns on the conceptual meanings of the words "big," "mens," and "boy." The "colored" character in the story indirectly asks how big and how old does an African American male have to be before he is acknowledged as a man by Whites?

The confrontation between Thomas and the chief mate of the *James Clifford* intertextually revises and tropicalizes the infantilization scene between Jim and Oscar in *Youngblood*. Recall that Thomas joined the Merchant Marine to make his way down South with his friend Brew. Thomas was a messman on the *James Clifford*. One morning, while serving coffee to the captain and the chief mate, the captain says to Thomas, "Son, please bring me a cup of coffee and make it—" "Yes, sir," I cut in, "black, hot, and no sugar."[134] Ostensibly, being called "son" does not immediately bother Thomas; he does not even seem to notice it. Perhaps, it is not immediately perturbing because it implies a sense of kinship. However, things change when the chief mate says, "Hey, boy, let me have another cup of coffee."[135] Thomas does not confront the chief mate directly about this slight. Instead, he expresses his displeasure by repeatedly bringing the chief mate cold cups of coffee. The chief mate is befuddled; he has no idea what he did to offend Thomas. After breakfast, the chief mate confronts Thomas alone, and asks why he brought him cold coffee on purpose. Thomas, like Jim in *Youngblood*, responds by signifying his displeasure with Whites referring to non-White men as boys: "Well, it's this way. When I was a little kid, my momma told me that someday I'd grow up to be a man, and if I was a good boy and ate a lot, I'd grow into a real *chevere* [sic] man. Well, I've done what Momma asked me and I've grown into a man. If Momma is right, and I believe she is, I ain't no longer a boy. You understand, *sir*?"[136] Thomas's uses signifying to confront White authority in a way that allows him to express his anger and assert his dignity without inviting violence or reprisal. Thomas has mastered the psychological and social functions of signifying. Given Thomas's literary mentorship under Killens and his membership in the HWG, it is not unreasonable to suggest that the chief mate scene in *Down These Mean Streets* is intertextually informed by, if not directly inspired by, the "How big do mens grow" scene in *Youngblood*. As such, the interracial friendship between Jim and Oscar can be read as a literary analog of the interethnic friendship between Thomas and Brew. The difference is that Thomas "tropicalizes" his version of Killens's folktale by using Latino idioms and his own personal experience of growing up Nuyorican. "To *tropicalize*," argue Frances Aparicio and Susana Chávez-Silverman, "means to trope, to imbue a particular space, geography, group, or nation with a set of [Latino] traits, images, and values." When performed by Latinos, tropicalization can be either hegemonic or radical, they contend. When performed by the dominant society, tropicalization tends to be hegemonic. Hegemonic tropicalization sustains negative and/or sexually exotic stereotypes about Latinos and Latinidad. Radical tropicalization, on the other hand, combats negative stereotypes and constructs positive representations of being of Latino identity and culture.[137] The chief mate incident, I argue, gives Thomas the confidence he needs to trick the brothel owner in the subsequent ethnic passing scene, discussed in the previous section. The fact that these two scenes take place in the final part of the last chapter of the immersion narrative in *Down These Mean Streets* signals that Thomas is no longer a neophyte. His courage to use the rhetorical strategy of signifying to confront White power in the chief mate scene and to use trickster passing in the subsequent brothel scene indicates that he is now an adept, that his ethnoracial apprenticeship in the social protest tradition of African American masculinity is complete. Thomas challenges racist White masculinity in the Deep South by confronting one White man, tricking another, and risking his life by sleeping with a White woman. By confronting the Southern racial social order in indirect and direct ways, Thomas learns what it means to be a Black man who not only stands his ground but who also lives to write about it.

Conclusion

Youngblood and *Down These Mean Streets* focus on the intersection of masculinity and racial identity formation, on what it means to come of age culturally and politically as a heteronormative man of African descent in the United States between the 1930s and the 1950s. *Down These Mean Streets* is influenced by several classic African American narrative strategies and cultural tropes. These strategies and tropes include signifying, playing the dozens, valorizing dialect and slang, engaging in hypodescent racial politics, completing an immersion journey into the Deep South, and passing and being passed as an ethnoracial other. Uncovering the African American narrative strategies and cultural tropes in *Down These Mean Streets* enhances our understanding of the transcultural aspect of what Tommie Shelby calls "pragmatic black nationalism."[138] The literary ancestry between John Oliver Killens and Piri Thomas and the high degree of intertextuality between their debut books reveal the ideological continuities between the aesthetics of the Popular Front, the Black Arts Movement, and the Nuyorican Movement. *Down These Mean Streets* proves itself to be transcanonical, to be a foundational text in both the Nuyorican and Black Arts Movement.

Piri Thomas's racial identity crisis in *Down These Mean Streets* sets the stage for Carlos Moore's *Pichón* (2008), a memoir that portrays what happens when a young Afro-Cuban immigrant with a traumatic childhood and affinity for African American culture becomes politically radicalized in postwar New York.

CHAPTER TWO

From Bohemian *Piolo* to Leftist *Jorocón*
The Pan-African Radicalization of Carlos Moore

Carlos Moore, an Afro-Cuban activist, scholar, and author, was born in Central Lugareño, Cuba, in 1942. His family immigrated to the US in 1957 to escape the conflict between the Batista regime and Castro's Revolutionary forces.[1] In the spring of 1961, Moore returned to Cuba to escape the FBI investigation of his activism in New York and to support the revolution.[2] Moore recounts these events in his memoir *Pichón: Race and Revolution in Castro's Cuba* (2008). The reviews of *Pichón* highlight Moore's activism and political ideology and condemn, in their estimation, his stale and "wooden" prose style.[3] As a contemporary Afro-Latino memoir, *Pichón* is important because its bildung narrative fills a gap in the history of Latino and African American interculturalism in the postwar era. Moore devotes a third of *Pichón*, ten chapters, to his teenage years in the US, signaling how significant they were to the development of his radical Pan-Africanist consciousness. Although Moore's experiences in Europe, Africa, Latin America, and the Anglophone and Hispanophone Caribbean also exemplify his Pan-African activism, I exclusively focus on his experience in the US because that is where his radicalism was forged. When Moore arrived in New York in 1957, the second decade of the Cold War was getting underway,[4] the Civil Rights movement was making steady advances,[5] and African and Caribbean countries were rapidly decolonizing.[6] The coming-of-age section of Moore's memoir reveals how he was radicalized in Harlem's hotbed of Black nationalists, Pan-Africanists, and Old and New Left radicals.

As a teenager in New York, Moore declared himself a Marxist and belonged to or was affiliated with a variety of Old Left and New Left groups and ideologies. Between June 1960 and June 1961, he joined the Socialist Workers Party (SWP), the Fair Play for Cuba Committee (FPCC), and On Guard for Freedom.[7] His work for the US branch of the July 26 Movement won him an introduction to Fidel Castro when Castro stayed at Harlem's Hotel Theresa in September 1960,[8] but Patrice Lumumba was Moore's "first political hero."[9] He admired Lumumba for his "Pan-African nationalism" and his efforts to free the Congo from the neocolonial influence of the West.[10] Moore's admiration led him to volunteer in the Congo Mission to the United Nations (UN).

During his brief time in New York, Moore was deeply influenced by the Black nationalist and Pan-Africanist ideology of Lewis Michaux, the proprietor of the National Memorial African Bookstore (NMAB).[11] It was at the NMAB that Moore met Maya Angelou, the person whom he identifies as being the catalyst for his conversion from bohemian *piolo* to Leftist *jorocón*.[12]

In the Foreword to *Pichón*, Maya Angelou praises Moore for his revolutionary resistance, passion, and compassion.[13] Angelou and Moore's friendship was shaped by their mutual love of African American music and their radical Pan-Africanist activism. On February 15, 1961, Blacks who were outraged at the CIA-sponsored assassination of Patrice Lumumba, disrupted Ambassador Adlai E. Stevenson's Security Council meeting at the UN.[14] The Harlem Writers Guild (HWG) and the Cultural Association for Women of African Heritage (CAWAH), one of the HWG's offshoots, organized the protest.[15] The female membership of the HWG, which included Maya Angelou, Rosa Guy, Sarah Wright, and Abbey Lincoln, founded CAWAH in 1960.[16] CAWAH's mission was "to support all black civil rights groups," writes Angelou, in her memoir *Heart of a Woman* (1981).[17] CAWAH and the HWG were inextricably linked through their shared female members and their common admiration for the Congolese liberation struggle.[18] CAWAH, not the HWG, was the ideological source, organizational unit, and public face of the UN protest, says Angelou. CAWAH wanted the UN protest to be nonviolent and peaceful. The plan was to stage a protest that involved standing silently in the chamber of the UN until led out. Women protesters would don black veils, and men would sport black armbands. Only six of the ten women in CAWAH chose to participate in the protest. These six women asked Lewis Michaux to gather the Harlem community in front of the NMAB for their call to arms. Angelou claims that a crowd of thousands congregated to hear Rosa Guy, Abbey Lincoln, and her announce the purpose and plan of their protest.[19]

On the day of the protest, CAWAH smuggled about sixty protesters into the UN, six to seven people at a time. They gained access through Moore,[20] who worked in the UN and whom Angelou had befriended, the previous year, at the NMAB. In recounting the protest, Angelou recalls Moore's good looks and his hot temperament. "Carlos," says Angelou, "was little and pretty and reminded me of my brother"; but she also remembers him as "an angry young man who moved through Harlem's political sky like a luminous meteor."[21] Angelou was unaware of the depth of Moore's anger, unaware that he was using CAWAH's protest and march to mask his plot to "neutralize the Belgians" in the Belgian Consulate.[22]

In this chapter, I argue that African American cultural paradigms, social institutions, activist networks, and political discourse served as models for Carlos Moore's radical Pan-African Latinidad. Moore's *Pichón* occupies a unique space among the five memoirs in this study because it is the only one in the group that is written by an immigrant. As a transnational narrative, it reveals the dialectic between what Neelam Srivastava calls "imperial cosmopolitanism"[23] and what Emily Johansen calls "territorialized cosmopolitanism."[24] Instead of trafficking in the anxieties of ambivalence, deracination, exile, fragmentation, and nostalgia associated with the discourse of cosmopolitanism, the US immigrant section of *Pichón*, I contend, celebrates what Moore calls his "informal schooling" in leftist political ideology, African American culture, and Black nationalism.[25] It depicts the initial stages of Moore's hero's journey as an organic intellectual, portraying his heroic self-transformation as an exemplar of the type of cultural synthesis that Fernando Ortiz, a Cuban anthropologist, famously called transculturation.[26] Moore's transcultural embrace of Black nationalism does not require him to sacrifice his Afro-Latinidad on the altar of what Lorgia García Peña calls "hegemonic blackness—blackness defined through US culture, politics, histories, and the Anglophone experience."[27] Despite its global scope, "hegemonic blackness," notes García Peña, provides the global Afro-Latino diaspora with useful models for shaping the political and cultural language of their social activism.[28] As an Afro-Cuban scholar-activist who has lived in the US, France, Nigeria, Senegal, Trinidad and Tobago, and Brazil,[29] Carlos Moore exemplifies what García Peña calls "global blackness," a Pan-African political and cultural solidarity that is inherently inclusive of "Black Latinidad."[30] Rejecting the discourse of embodied identity, social constructivism, and nationalism, García Peña defines Black Latinidad "as an epistemology . . . a point of entry and a set of methods that move us beyond homogeneous concepts of racial and citizenship exclusion."[31] While I am not prepared to entirely dismiss nationalism, social constructivism, and embodied identity, their shortcomings notwithstanding, I am prepared to read *Pichón* as an exemplary representation of "Black Latinidad" and "global blackness."

Like García Peña, Yomaira C. Figueroa-Vásquez and Margo N. Crawford call for a global turn in Afro-Latino and African American studies, respectively. These three scholars engage in comparative research that explores intercultural relations between Afro-Latinos, Africans, and African Americans. Examining Afro-Latinidades beyond Latin America and the US, García Peña and Figueroa-Vásquez focus on Italy and Equatorial Guinea, respectively. Hailing Paul Gilroy's concept of the Black Atlantic, Figueroa-Vásquez offers the term "Afro-Atlantic Hispanophone diaspora" as an interpretive tool "to engage the complexities within the field of global Hispanophone studies."[32] By substantively focusing on the Hispanic Caribbean and Hispanic Africa, Figueroa-Vásquez's Afro-Atlantic concept amends and exceeds Gilroy's version of the Black Atlantic paradigm. Similarly, Crawford explores the intertextual role of Caribbean, African, and Afro-British writers in African American literature. Using Édouard Glissant's theories of relationality, "shock of elsewhere," and "poetic force,"[33] Crawford examines the Afro-diasporic aesthetic impulses that "move through the national boundaries of African American literature."[34] Through the poetics of relation,[35] these intercultural aesthetic impulses structure a "global black consciousness," contends Crawford: "The impulse not to freeze the diasporic shivers of blackness is the radical zone of global black consciousness in African American literature."[36] Like Gilroy's Black Atlantic paradigm,[37] Crawford's concept of "global black consciousness" challenges the exceptionalism and nationalism of American and African American cultural studies.[38] In using global and Afro-Atlantic constructs to disrupt "hegemonic blackness," Hispanidad, and Latinidad, Crawford, Figueroa-Vásquez, and García Peña, underscore the value of "intercultural and transnational" units of analysis like the Black Atlantic.[39] Building on the work of Crawford, Figueroa-Vásquez, and García Peña, I reveal, through the lens of literary interculturalism, how and why Black nationalism amplified rather than diminished Carlos Moore's Afro-Atlantic Hispanidad.

The immigrant bildung narrative in Pichón, I argue, speaks to and through the "shock of elsewhere" in the language of Black nationalism and Pan-Africanism. The feature that most distinguished Black nationalism in the 1960s, writes William L. Van Deburg, was a preoccupation with the "psychological process of becoming black," a belief that the "revolution of the mind . . . was a prerequisite for . . . revolutionizing society."[40] Pan-Africanism is Black nationalism brought up to global scale. Pan-Africanism is both a cultural philosophy and an institutionalized political movement, George Shepperson reminds us, locating examples of institutional Pan-Africanism in the five Pan-African Congresses, the 1956 publication of George Padmore's Pan-Africanism or Communism, and the 1958 All-Africa Peoples Conference.[41] As a cultural philosophy, Pan-Africanism, writes Wilson Jeremiah Moses, is a type of macro-nationalist ideology that posits "all black people have interests in common. Its adherents accept as axioms the ideas that no black person is free until all are free, and that the liberation and unification of Africa is essential to the dignity of African people everywhere."[42] The Black nationalist focus on the psychology of racial self-fashioning, I contend, is a central motif in the bildung narrative of *Pichón*. To understand how Moore's "informal schooling in Harlem" shaped his radical Pan-African Latinidad,[43] it is necessary to investigate four specific vectors of transculturation: the memory of slavery, the blues impulse, Black nationalist oratory, and African American intellectual mentorship.

Diasporic Shivers of Blackness: The Erotics of Terror and the Timbre of Sincerity

In *Scenes of Subjection: Terror, Slavery, and Self-Making in Nineteenth-Century America*, Saidiya V. Hartman defines representations of sexual exploitation in the collective memory of slavery as the "erotics of terror" and reminds us that the "precariousness of empathy" is what is at stake when we hail the memory of slavery.[44] Hartman excavates the archive of the memory of slavery "to illuminate the practice of everyday life—specifically, tactics of resistance, modes of self-fashioning, and figurations of freedom— and to investigate the construction of the subject and social relations contained within [its] documents."[45] Gilroy argues that Afro-descendants in the Black Atlantic "make creative, communicative use of the memory of slavery."[46] "Artistic expression," he contends, "becomes the means towards both individual self-fashioning and communal liberation. Poiesis and poetics begin to coexist in novel forms—autobiographical writing, special and uniquely creative ways of manipulating spoken language, and above all music."[47] I am interested in the ways Moore uses representations of Black female blues/jazz singers and the sermonic power of Black nationalist oratory to signify the episodic transformation of his social consciousness, of his Afro-Latinidad. To signal these moments of episodic transformation, Moore employs aesthetic strategies that are atypical in conventional life writing. He uses the lyricism of poetry and the dialogic techniques of narrative fiction to mark the "psychological process of *becoming* black."[48]

What interpretive tools can we use to understand the relationship between the Black autobiographical tradition, the memory of slavery, and the icon of the Black female blues/jazz singer? In *Hot Music, Ragmentation, and the Bluing of American Literature*, Stephen C. Tracy interprets the trope of the Black female blues singer as a reification of the foundational I-as-We motif in African American literature and culture. In his analysis of Countee Cullen's poem "Colored Blues Singer," Tracy describes the African American female blues singer as an icon of personal suffering, creative self-expression, and transformative endurance in the face of a tragic past and present. Tracy writes that "the blues singer's song is a lament with agency—'You make your grief a melody' (line 7)."[49] Tracy argues that a Black blues singer's subject matter is inherently personal and restorative: "This is the great comfort of the blues, that it fosters creativity and provides solace, ameliorates rather than merely dramatizes a situation. Further, the songs of the blues singer connect to hidden personal origins, not merely mythological stories from foreign cultures but real songs and occasions of loss."[50] As Tracy points out, the trope of the Black female blues singer recognizes Africa, Africans, and the histories of slavery and racialization in the Americas as "the source tragedies of the triumphant blues."[51] Understanding the trope of the Black female blues singer and the work that it performs in the Afro-Atlantic provides a cultural heuristic for articulating its transcultural significance in *Pichón*.

In *Black Resonance: Iconic Women Singers and African American Literature*, Emily J. Lodi offers the concept of "spaces of sincerity" as a cultural heuristic for the I-as-We motif of the Afro-Atlantic experience. Spaces of sincerity are spaces and times in which African Americans feel free to drop the pragmatic mask of double consciousness. Lordi's spaces of sincerity concept is part of a quartet that includes the concepts "timbre of sincerity," "sincere ambivalence," and "integrative practice." Lordi adopts the concepts from "As the Spirit Moves Mahalia," Ralph Ellison's review of Mahalia Jackson's performance at the 1958 Newport Jazz Festival. The draft title of Ellison's article was "Mahalia, The Timbre of Sincerity." This was Ellison's "only article on a female (sacred) singer."[52] Lordi's four concepts articulate the love-hate relationship—the sincere ambivalence—African Americans often have with the dominant culture in the US. The freedom from masking one's sincere ambivalence can be particularly pronounced in certain ritualized spaces and at certain ritualized times. For Lordi, these ambivalently charged "spaces of sincerity" are "those *moments* when the obligation to wear the mask diminishes—as it might in safe spaces that are located, in Sondra O'Neale's words, 'beyond the mask.'"[53] Lordi defines "spaces of sincerity" in terms of time and space. Lordi's emblem of the space/time of sincerity is a Sunday morning in a Black church. Free from the "white gaze," an African American congregation can experience a catharsis as a result of a gospel singer's "timbre of sincerity." The Black church is a space for authenticity, for the timbre of sincerity. According to Lordi, the timbre of sincerity is a moral trait, an "ethical function," characterized by "integrative practice." Integrative practice is "the performance of stylistic variation and citational range."[54] In other words, integrative practice is the act of harmoniously fusing heterogeneous aesthetics, themes, styles, modalities, subjects, and affects; it is a valorization of multiplicity over singularity, simultaneity over antiphony, and hybridity over purity. Put simply, reading for the timbre of sincerity means analyzing how artists "engage at once subversively and affirmatively with the prior texts they cite and refashion."[55] Reading for the timbre of sincerity in *Pichón* means reading for the intertextual narrative strategies and cultural tropes that constitute the I-as-We in the spaces of sincerity in which Moore employs the trope of the Black female blues singer.

"My Informal Schooling in Harlem": A Portrait of an Activist as a Young Man

Like *Down These Mean Streets*, *Pichón* documents a challenging interpersonal struggle for self-love, for Black pride. Moore, however, was not involved in street life and gang violence. *Pichón* is a portrait of an activist as a young man. Moore's coming of age story documents a life of the mind, a life of radical politics and militant direct action. His awakening as a revolutionary Pan-Africanist hinged on his chance encounter with Maya Angelou at the NMAB. Angelou shaped his ideas about the supposed ills of interracial dating, the benefits of cultural nationalism, and the urgency of the Third World struggle for decolonization. Prior to meeting Angelou, Moore spent his leisure time in Greenwich Village receiving an informal education in Leftist radicalism and Black nationalism. In the Village, Moore meets Arnold (Arnie) and Nina, a Jewish couple that guides his political education. They introduce him to radical theories of government and political economy. With Arnie and Nina, Moore discusses anarchism, anti-Semitism, Bolshevism, capitalism, fascism, imperialism, Marxism, socialism, Stalinism, and Trotskyism; they also discuss jazz, racism, and *Homage to Catalonia*, George Orwell's memoir about fighting fascism in the Spanish Civil War.[56] Influenced by Arnie, Moore joins the FPCC, and they routinely attend meetings together. Through the FPCC, Moore becomes connected to the SWP and begins reading its weekly magazine, *The Militant*. By October 1960, Moore considers himself to be a Marxist, but a Marxist who has a growing affinity for Garveyite Pan-Africanism and NOI Black nationalism.

Moore meets several mentors of African descent who introduce him to people, books, organizations, and ideas that challenge his belief in the value of Marxist socialism, internationalism, and liberal humanism, beliefs he had learned from White radicals in Greenwich Village. These Black mentors and associates include Mr. Callender, J. A. Rogers,[57] Lewis H. Michaux,[58] Richard T. Gibson, Dan Watts, Robert Maynard, Calvin Hicks,[59] LeRoi Jones,[60] Harold Cruse,[61] Maya Angelou,[62] Abbey Lincoln,[63] Max Roach,[64] Laura (an African American lover), and Mburumba Kerina. Callender, Michaux, Cruse, Angelou, Laura, and Kerina have significant impacts on the clash between Moore's internationalism, liberal humanism, and Black consciousness.[65] Of the several "black leftists" Moore meets, Cruse is the one who convinces him that Marxist socialism is ill-equipped, if not unprepared, to solve the problem of White supremacy and anti-Black racism.[66] Moore meets Cruse after Cruse returns from his first trip to Cuba. Both Moore and Cruse were Trotskyite Marxists and members of the SWP and FPCC. However, before Moore meets Cruse, Mr. Callender is the mentor who first introduces Moore to the politics of Black cultural nationalism.

Callender, a Christian Scientist, was Moore's high school English teacher. An Afro-Panamanian of Jamaican descent, Callender introduces Moore to African American music, history, literature, and print culture like *Amsterdam News*, *Ebony*, and *Jet*. Callender inculcates Moore's love of reading and public libraries. Due to Callender, Moore reads Bertrand Russell's *Why I'm Not a Christian* (1927) and meets J. A. Rogers at a Christian Scientist political lecture.[67] Rogers was a biracial Jamaican American journalist, novelist, and autodidact historian who wrote works that vindicated the achievement of people of African descent and debunked the discourse of scientific racism.[68] Rogers encouraged Moore to purchase his books "at the National Memorial African Bookstore in Harlem, which Callender had already mentioned."[69]

Known by its tagline, the "House of Common Sense and Proper Propaganda," Moore describes the NMAB as a depot for Harlem's activists. David Emblidge, a historian of American booksellers, concurs. Emblidge says NMAB "attracted a loyal clientele, championed famous writers and artists, and hosted international leaders (especially Africans). A rallying point for political speeches, often delivered in front of the store, in its period, there was no other black bookstore in America with Michaux's influence."[70] In 1960, Moore goes to NMAB for the first time, staying there past midnight.[71] Lewis H. Michaux, the proprietor of NMAB, is a "fire-and-brimstone black nationalist" whose singular passion is "to talk to people about Marcus Garvey, Africa, and the history of black people."[72] At the time Moore discovers the NMAB, international media is focused on the revolution in Cuba and Congo's independence movement. During this period, Moore becomes infatuated with Patrice Lumumba and the history of the Congo. To satiate Moore's preoccupation with the Congo, Michaux gives him *King Leopold's Soliloquy* by

Mark Twain. The book initiates Moore's interest in Africa and the development of his Pan-Africanist worldview and decolonial consciousness.

Using teaching and learning metaphors, Moore describes the NMAB "as the academy that set my mind ablaze and groomed my soul. It was there that the most compelling encounter of my youth took place; thereafter nothing in my life would be the same."[73] That encounter is with Maya Angelou, the African American mentor who convinces him to stop dating interracially, and who convinces him that humanism and internationalism are not "worthwhile" for Black people if Black people do not have Black pride.[74] Angelou's intervention in the development of Moore's political consciousness is the first in a series of four episodic encounters that result in Moore embracing radical Pan-Africanism. The four pivotal episodes in the development of Moore's Pan-Africanism consist of two encounters with the Black female blues impulse and two encounters with Black nationalist oratory and sermonic rhetoric. According to Craig Werner, the blues impulse is the need to use the cathartic and communal function of the blues as a source of personal affirmation, historical continuity, and ameliorating resilience in times of joy and pain.[75] Though eschatological and teleological, the function and expression of African American sermonic rhetoric, according to Dolan Hubbard, is categorically and historically related to the blues impulse. Hubbard makes several significant points about the relationship between African American sermonic rhetoric and the blues. First, like the blues, "survival and resistance" is the "central impulse" of the African American sermon.[76] Second, the African American sermonizer is a "transformational agent," much like the blues, jazz, or gospel soloist.[77] Third, the sermon's "mode of expression is colored by a blues sensibility, if by blues one means the working out of the tension between what Richard Wright in 'The Literature of the Negro in the United States' refers to as the sensualization of pain and pleasure as opposed to the transcending of pain and pleasure."[78] The four transformational episodes in Moore's conversion narrative display the characteristic features of the blues impulse and African American sermonic rhetoric, but two of them deploy these features in stylistic patterns that are more common in lyric poetry and narrative fiction than in life writing.

The first and third episodes in Moore's Pan-African conversion narrative involve female blues interventions. The first intervention is with Maya Angelou, the most significant of Moore's New York mentors. The third intervention involves Laura, one of Angelou's acquaintances. These female blues encounters with Angelou and Laura occur in what Lordi calls "spaces of sincerity."[79] The second and fourth episodes in Moore's Pan-African conversion involve Black male oratorical interventions. The first male encounter is with the Garveyite soapbox orator. Repeated and prolonged exposure to the orator's moral suasion convinces Moore to value the Africanity of his own body by relinquishing the practices of hair-straightening and skin-bleaching. The second Black male encounter is with the political speeches and sermons of Malcolm X. Malcolm's orations seduce Moore into moving from rhetorical resistance to the resistance of direct action. I read Moore's encounters with Malcolm X through Hubbard's analysis of the political and psycho-affective value of sermonic rhetoric in the African American literary imagination. I use a close reading of the four pivotal episodes in Moore's bildung conversion narrative to explore the gendered relationship between the jazz-rendered blues "spaces of sincerity" and the transformative power of Black nationalist oratory and sermonic rhetoric.[80]

Maya Angelou and the Politics of Interracial Dating

The most significant mentor in the development of Moore's Pan-Africanism is Maya Angelou, whom he met at the NMAB by chance. At the time, the revolution in Cuba was in the national news. Like many of the people Moore meets in this period, Angelou takes an interest in him primarily because he is Cuban. However, part of her interest in Moore is no doubt racial, maternal, and sororal. Fifteen years older than Moore, Angelou calls him "little brother." Moore becomes the object of her "pragmatic black nationalism," a term coined by Tommie Shelby.[81] Moore becomes Angelou's personal racial uplift project. Angelou introduces Moore to her friends Abbey Lincoln and Max Roach, and she invites him to listen to the couple perform songs that would later become part of their album *We Insist! Max Roach's Freedom Now Suite* (1960). Moore brings Helen, his White lover, with him to hear Lincoln and Roach perform in the Village.[82] Another of Moore's lovers is Karina, an Irish woman who attends the Martha Graham School of Dance and introduces Moore to poetry readings, "modern dance, theater, and ballet."[83] During his time with Karina, Moore slowly comes to realize the fact that the disapproving looks that he and Karina receive in public have nothing to do with his being Cuban, with his "foreign ways, halting accent, and non-American body language"; it had everything to do with his being Black.[84]

No longer able to maintain his self-delusion, Moore begins to wonder if he is a *piolo*, a Cuban term for a Black person who exclusively associates with Whites.[85] The prospect of being a *piolo* confuses Moore because he appreciates the intellectual and cultural progress he has made by fostering interracial friendships and romances. He says, "I liked *whites*—period! I felt good being around them; they accepted me. Thanks to consorting with liberal whites in the Village, I had graduated from black to Human Being."[86] Before he started moving in interracial circles, Moore, was politically naive, having little to no knowledge about the revolution in Cuba, the US Civil Rights movement, or the decolonial movements in Africa, Asia, and the Caribbean. Of this period Moore writes, "I was interested in nothing that might disrupt my maiden voyage to the utopia of interracial delights. I was living in a wonderful cocoon, self-immured within walls that made me impervious to any telling realities."[87] Notice that Moore uses figurative language that invokes conventional bildung narrative tropes: intellectual maturation, conviction in the idea of perfection, the transformative power of first experiences, and the blissful ignorance of an immature sociohistorical consciousness. While it is tempting to suggest that Moore's preoccupation with interracial dating and color-blind liberal humanism is an example of existentialist bad faith, it is important to keep in mind that Moore was just a teenager, a teenager who had been conditioned as a child to valorize Whiteness and disparage Blackness. If we are prepared to take Moore at his word, then he was more immature than he was self-deluded.

After his date with Helen at the jazz club, Moore learns that Angelou, Lincoln, and Roach "were displeased at the way I had come into the club exhibiting a white woman as if she were the sole symbol of my worth. . . . They had hoped I would connect with the message of black pride their music sought to convey."[88] Angelou becomes so concerned with what she considers to be Moore's internalized racism that she stages a one-on-one intervention. She invites him over to her house on what Moore thinks may turn out to be a sexual escapade. However, Angelou, wearing an Afro, spreads out the albums of Nina Simone, Odetta Holmes, and Miriam Makeba on a table. Moore is unfamiliar with the singers, but he notices that they "all wore their hair natural like Maya's. That made a powerful impression on me, since my own hair was straightened and fell slickly over my head."[89] It has a powerful impression on him because, as a child, Moore's mother applied clothespins to his nose to make it narrower, advised him to suck in his protruding lips when speaking, routinely straightened his hair with commercial and amateur chemical treatments.[90] It was not until Moore was forty years old that he learned why he was the target of his mother's racial animus. His hair was curlier and his skin darker than the rest of his siblings because he was the result of an extramarital affair.[91] As a child, Moore was the incarnation, the constant reminder, of his mother's infidelity. Her guilt and shame, reasons

Moore, caused her to emotionally and physically abuse him for the first ten years of his life.[92] The subtitle of chapter 4, "My Mother's Blot," suggests that Moore's unambiguous Blackness—his hair quality, facial features, and dark skin—is a stain on his mother's conscious, a stain that she tries to erase with repeated physical abuse, the worst of which being her attempt to drown Moore in a barrel of rainwater when he was seven years old.[93]

Moore listens to the music and Angelou signs and gives him a copy of her 1957 album *Miss Calypso*. The biographical profile on the album cover claims that Angelou is the Cuban-born child of a Watusi immigrant. The fake profile was a "marketing gimmick," says Angelou.[94] To get work as a Black singer in the US, she had to deny her African American identity and pass as an Afro-Cuban immigrant. Angelou and Moore poignantly laugh at the subterfuge necessary to counter the absurdity of US racial logic and subordination. Their sense of a common African heritage and a common racial oppression brings them together ideologically. In their space of sincerity, Angelou feels comfortable enough to have a long conversation with Moore about self-esteem, racism in the US, the Civil Rights movement, and what she sees as his racial obligation to date women of African descent. "Listen, little brother," she tells him, "next time I invite you some place, don't march in with one of those white women as if you were a gladiator! If you can't come with a *sister*, come by yourself."[95]

Angelou's appeal for racial endogamy reflects the social space and circles she moved in during that window of her life. It is important to remember that before she moved to New York she was married to Tosh Angelos, who was Greek, and that in the early 1970s she married Paul du Feu, who was Welsh. Angelou's female blues intervention set Moore's ideological transformation in motion. Looking at his transformation through the lens of the spiritual conversion narrative raises an interesting question. Would Moore have become the Pan-Africanist that he became if he had not first been a *piolo*? Without his interracial social experiences, Moore's conversion narrative would be less compelling than it is for his ideal reader because the magnitude of change would be less profound. As we shall see in the fourth stage of his episodic transformation, Moore, like the apostle Saul, has to move from one extreme to the other to make his conversion narrative memorable and exemplary for the ideal reader of *Pichón*. In *Spiritual Autobiography in Early America*, Daniel B. Shea Jr. notes that conversion narratives are proselytizing texts. They are designed to bring potentials into the fold through grace: "The spiritual autobiographer is primarily concerned with the question of grace: whether or not the individual has been accepted into divine life, an acceptance signified by psychological and moral changes the autobiographer comes to discern in his past experience."[96] Moore's female blues intervention with Maya Angelou is about him receiving the secular grace of her communal approval in an Afro-diasporic space of sincerity, a space that invites him to unmask himself.

The Garveyite Orators

Moore leaves Maya's apartment on good terms, realizing that the point of the intervention was his general flight from his "black self."[97] However, Moore is not immediately converted. Angelou's "foolishness about 'black pride'" does not sink in until a Garveyite soapbox orator at Nostrand Ave. and Fulton St. mocks Moore's processed hair in front of a crowd of "fifteen or so other people."[98] Moore styled his hair like that of his African American idols: Nat King Cole, James Brown, the Platters, Brooke Benton, and Jackie Wilson. "The men," says Moore, "fashioned their artificially straightened hair into marcel waves. To have a marcel became my goal."[99] The orator calls out, "Hey, hey, hey, Mr. Negro!"; "Look at your hair, Mr. Negro! You're ashamed of your hair!"; and "Look at Mr. Negro! He doesn't know he's a lost African."[100] The taunts trigger a flashback, a reverie in which Moore recollects the days when his mother used to chemically process his hair. He recalls how "the white boys laughed at our features, likening our nostrils to saxophones, our lips to bloated beef, and our hair to the *marabu* bush that was full of prickly thorns."[101] Worming their way into his psyche, the orator's taunts haunt Moore long after the public shaming is over. "I could not," says Moore, "get that man's litany out of my mind":

Hey, Mr. Negro, you're ashamed of your lips.
Of course I was not ashamed of my lips!
Hey, Mr. Negro, you're ashamed of your nose.
Nonsense, I was not ashamed of my nose.
Hey, Mr. Negro, you're ashamed of your African hair.
Ridiculous, I was not ashamed of my hair; it was just easier to handle
   when straight.[102]

Taking the advice of his mentor Lewis Michaux, Moore returns to listen to a variety of street corner orators lecture about Garvey, the UNIA, the glory of Africa, and being of African descent. The lectures have the desired effect. Moore disposes all of his skin bleaching and hair straightening products. What is aesthetically interesting is how Moore stylizes the experience of his first encounter. The antiphonal italicized accusations and nonitalicized remonstrations are set in the memoir as if they were a stanza in a poem. This aesthetic choice visually calls attention to the significance of the passage's content. It exemplifies Gilroy's contention that Black Atlantic expressive culture merges poises and poetics by innovatively manipulating spoken language and music.[103] In this case, Moore stylizes the lecture as music, as poetry, to highlight the psychological process of developing a decolonial consciousness, underscoring the emphasis that the discourse of Black nationalism places on the prerequisite of revolutionizing the mind.[104]

The Erotics of Terror and the Terror of the Erotic

When Moore receives a second invitation from Maya Angelou to listen to Abbey Lincoln and Max Roach, he comes alone to the club. He recounts this story in chapter 14, "Encounter with Myself." At the club, Angelou introduces Moore to Laura, a twenty-four-year-old African American woman. Moore goes home with Laura after leaving the club in the early morning hours. Laura draws Moore into a conversation about his life in Cuba, the circumstances of his immigration, and his relationship with his mother. The interrogation frustrates Moore because it exposes his ignorance about his parents' origins and lives in Jamaica. On the record player, Sarah Vaughan sings "If You Could See Me Now," as Moore and Laura lay naked in bed. When Laura finally concedes to sex, she mounts Moore, which intimidates him so much that he is unable to perform. "With Laura," says Moore, "I felt inadequate, overpowered by her assertiveness."[105] Ella Fitzgerald scats in the background on the record player as Moore spirals into panic and shame. Instead of acting on his impulse to leave, Laura has Moore stay and continue a conversation in which she explicitly links his lack of "virility" to her being a woman of African descent. During the conversation Moore asks Laura why African American women are racist, why they disparage "black men who date white women."[106] Laura explains, that it is not racism per se, but offense at the fact that Black men perfunctorily afford White women a level of prestige and esteem that they do not afford Black women. Black men, says Laura, treat Black women like "dirt" and White women like "war trophies" and "goddesses."[107] Invoking the memory of slavery, Laura puts her sense of insult into historical context, starting with the brutalization and violation of enslaved Black women by White men. Moore counters her narrative by arguing that Black men suffered during slavery, too, and that dwelling on the past will not change the present. Moore's riposte about the suffering of Black men calls to mind Hartman's contention that the range of sexual violence in the memory of slavery includes "the sexual exploitation of slave women . . . and the castration and assault of slave men." It is important to remember this range of sexual violation, says Hartman, "because of the elusiveness or instability of gender in. . . . the erotics of terror in the racist imaginary."[108]

What is aesthetically interesting about Moore's representation of his conversation with Laura is his poetic stylizing of the erotics of terror and the terror of the erotic. As with the Garveyite orator, Moore's encounter with Laura triggers a crisis of identity. The conversation reads like the stylized litany of the orator, like a sort of blues poem:

> "For four hundred years we black women had to fend
>   for ourselves . . ."
> Was that the black man's fault? Of course not!
> ". . . raise children we had not desired, or have those we
>   desired seized from us . . ."
> But black men were in chains, too.
> ". . . our bodies defiled, our lives trampled, our humanity torn to
>   shreds . . ."
> My chest was heavy. The weight of hundreds of years had settled
>   upon it. . . .
> ". . . black women endured those centuries completely on their
>   own . . ."[109]

Before Laura can become intimate with Moore, she has to have him confront the "terrors of the past," "the epoch of blood," and the "perilous abyss" of the memory of slavery.[110] Moore's aestheticization of their dialogue holds the trauma in abeyance, lyrically suspends it in belatedness, as it simultaneously presages the revolution of his racial consciousness. As the memoir writer, Moore is both a spectator and narrator of his past. By sharing his space of sincerity with his ideal reader, Moore fulfills one of the expectations associated with contemporary memoir—the aestheticized performance of vulnerability and trauma.

Laura's recitation transports Moore from their space of sincerity into the space/time of the enslaved: "I wanted to stay in that world a little longer, long enough to change the course of the history that produced people like Laura and me. I wanted to obliterate that past, bring down the wall between us."[111] At stake in confronting these scenes of subjection, Hartman writes, is "the precariousness of empathy."[112] After coming through the memory of slavery and arriving at a mutual point of empathy, Billie Holiday's "Don't Explain" plays on the record player as Laura reads poetry to Moore. When Dinah Washington's "Bitter Earth" plays, Moore and Laura begin to make love in the sunlight of the new day. The Black female blues/jazz singers featured in Angelou and Laura's interventions, in their spaces of sincerity, impress upon Moore the particularized suffering of Black women and womanhood. Although Moore kisses Laura all over her body, ultimately performing oral sex on her until she climaxes, kissing the hair on her head was a transformative experience for him. As he kissed her hair, he noted that it was the first time that he kissed hair that was not straight.[113] The act of kissing Laura's natural hair reflects the new day dawning in the development of Moore's racial consciousness; it is an act of self-love, an act that starts to free Moore from "the weight of centuries," from the memory of slavery.

The Ecstasy of Malcolm X

Maya Angelou, the Black nationalist street corner orators, and Laura collectively prepare Moore for the encounter that radicalizes him. In the summer of 1960, Moore attends two lectures by Malcolm X. The first takes place at a Nation of Islam mass rally inside the 369th Field Artillery Armory in Harlem at 142nd St. and Fifth Ave.[114] Like the NMAB, the Armory is an Afro-diasporic space of agency and activism. At the mass rally, Malcolm X discusses how the US, as an empire, oppresses people of color globally and how internalized racism undermines the African American capacity for self-government, erodes African American self-confidence, and leads to a culture of self-debasement.[115] After the speech, Moore becomes an avid reader of *Muhammad Speaks*, a weekly magazine that the Nation of Islam began publishing in May 1960. The second lecture is held at "the Muslim mosque in Harlem that was under Malcolm's leadership."[116] Like the Black church, the Armory and the mosque, are spaces of sincerity, spaces where Moore can, in congregation, drop the mask that the White gaze requires. Moore attends the lecture in Harlem with "Mburumba Kerina, an Ovaherero nationalist" who was introduced to him by Maya Angelou.[117] Kerina and Moore "disagreed sharply" on the efficacy and relevance of Malcolm X's speech at Temple Seven. Without providing specifics, Moore describes the lecture as an "electrifying speech" about Black people. Kerina, however, was disgruntled because the speech was less about Islam than it was about the politics of racial oppression.

It is the transformative impact of the first speech that warrants attention. After the first speech, Moore says, "I felt that something beyond the merely unusual had happened to me," but after the second lecture Moore says, "I had been seeking precisely the political explanations Malcolm offered."[118] Moore describes the effect of Malcolm X's sermonic rhetoric in military and biblical terms: (1) "Malcolm X took my mind and soul by storm" and (2) "But the scales had fallen from my eyes."[119] The second metaphor, the revelatory one, is an allusion to the faith healing of Saul of Tarsus by the prophet Ananias. When Saul arrives in Damascus, Ananias, a disciple of Christ, receives him, and, as previously instructed by the voice of Jesus, Ananias lays hands on Saul, miraculously restoring his sight.[120] Like the soapbox orator, Malcolm X takes on the role of what Hubbard calls the transformational agent, the same role Hubbard ascribes to the African American preacher. This is the same ameliorating and transformative function that Tracy and Lordi ascribe to African American blues and gospel singers. In comparing his political awakening to St. Paul's conversion to Christianity, Moore taps into the religious roots of life writing. Spiritual conversion narratives, autobiographies, and bildungsromans have thematic roots in the Christian pietism of the seventeenth and eighteenth centuries.[121] Rodger M. Payne notes that the development of what we might call the autobiographical self was coterminous with "the rise of various pietistic traditions that emphasized personal and affective experience."[122] Payne goes on to say, "Only the transforming self constitutes both the subject and the object of proper autobiographical activity" and that "true salvation implied the negation or extinction of the self."[123] Patricia Caldwell argues that the Puritan conversion narrative is uniquely characterized by transnational disenchantment: "It is as if, for most of the people, there is an unexpected deadlock between their experiences of the migration and the fulfillment of their religious hopes."[124] The Puritans' disappointment in America anticipates Moore's immigrant disillusionment when he realizes that America is not the unadulterated Black promised land he imagined it to be when he lived in Cuba.[125] Although the US was no Black utopia, it did turn out to be the site of Moore's ethnoracial apprenticeship in Black nationalism and Pan-Africanism.

Conclusion

Moore's brief time in New York is a classic ascent narrative, one of the defining features of the African American autobiographical tradition.[126] In immigrating to New York from Cuba, Moore moves from a state of political innocence to a state of political engagement. But his ascent narrative is also a spiritual conversion narrative, a spiritual conversion in which political ideology stands in for religious conviction. The two one-on-one blues interventions with Maya Angelou and Laura employ the experience of Black women and the memory of slavery to represent the affective shock of elsewhere, the "black diasporic shivers" that bind African Americans to the rest of the Afro-Atlantic world.[127] The two one-to-many oratorical encounters answer those blue interventions with appeals for revolutionary self-love, self-reliance, and self-transformation. Moore's ideological exposure to anti-colonialists, Black nationalists, and Pan-Africanists reveal how African American influences shaped his Afro-Latinidad and provided him with a translatable "political and cultural language" for his activism.[128] The photos in Moore's memoir provide visual evidence of how connected Moore was to Black nationalists and to the Black Left. The photos document that he spoke with Castro when Castro visited the Hotel Theresa in Harlem; that he served as a translator for Robert F. Williams in Havana in 1961; and that he had a conversation with Malcolm X in 1964. Moore's ethnoracial apprenticeship in Harlem under the influence of Black nationalist, Pan-African, and Old and New Left mentors speaks to how diasporic understandings of Black identity can lead to productive intercultural solidarities among Latinos and African Americans. We see those connections, and disconnections, vividly realized in Marta Moreno Vega's memoir *When the Spirits Dance Mambo: Growing Up Nuyorican in El Barrio*, the subject of the next chapter.

CHAPTER THREE

Morenophilia/Morenophobia

Marta Moreno Vega, Afro-Caribbean Religion,
and Ethnic Intermarriage

In January 2004, Nelson George and Debra J. Dickerson published *Post-Soul Nation* and *The End of Blackness*, respectively, setting the stage for popular and scholarly discussions about Black authenticity and racial progress in contemporary America. Five months later, those discussions kicked into high gear after President Barack Obama delivered his "The Audacity of Hope" keynote address at the 2004 Democratic National Convention. Obama's stunning speech fueled his rise to national prominence and put him on the path to becoming the nation's first African American president. As a biracial, US-born child of a Kenyan immigrant, Obama, with his Harvard education and professional success as a lawyer, scholar, memoirist, and US Senator, challenged conventional notions of African American identity and authenticity in the US.[1] Obama embodied the central concerns of *Post-Soul Nation* and *The End of Blackness*. In *Post-Soul Nation*, George examines how the neoliberal policies of the 1980s kept the Black masses socially, economically, and politically disenfranchised even as the national appetite for African American popular culture and celebrity figures came to embody "the unprecedented acceptance of black people in the public life of America."[2] Noting the social and financial success of the Black elites, Dickerson, in *The End of Blackness*, counsels African Americans to divest in constrictive notions of Black identity and stop using institutional racism as an excuse for a failure to thrive.[3] It was in this climate of African American debates about postracialism and the post-soul condition that Dr. Marta Moreno Vega published *When the Spirits Dance Mambo: Growing Up Nuyorican in El Barrio*.

Who is Vega and why does she matter? Does her memoir advance what is known about the relationship between Latinidad, post-soul subjectivity, and the end of Blackness? Vega is a Harlem-born Puerto Rican memoirist, filmmaker, Afrocentrist scholar, and Santería priestess, but long before she earned those four distinctions, she had an established reputation as a community organizer and institution builder. In 1976, Vega founded the Visual Arts Research and Resource Center Relating to the Caribbean, known today as the Caribbean Cultural Center African Diaspora Institute. Between

1976 and 2006, Vega played a role in founding and/or directing Amigos del Museo del Barrio, the Association of Hispanic Arts, and the Global Afro-Latino and Caribbean Initiative. Vega's first book, *The Altar of My Soul: The Living Traditions of Santería*,[4] is equal parts cultural history and authoethnography. In *Altar*, Vega tells the story of her religious conversion. On August 11, 1981, during her second trip to Cuba, Vega was initiated into Santería as a follower of "the *orisha* Obatalá Ayáguna."[5] Vega's expertise in Santería history and culture is grounded not only in her personal experience but also in her scholarly training as an Afrocentrist. In the spring of 1995, Vega successfully defended her dissertation, *Yoruba Philosophy: Multiple Levels of Transformation and Understanding*, earning her PhD in African American Studies from Temple University.[6] Dr. Molefe K. Asante, her dissertation adviser, is the premier proponent of Afrocentricism, a critical method of cultural studies that underscores the agency of peoples African descent and critically examines the value of their cultures, epistemologies, and contributions to world history.[7] During the cultural wars of the 1980s and 1990s, Afrocentrism's detractors charged it with being racially chauvinist and lacking analytical rigor. Afrocentrism, however, has passed the test of time and dispelled the caricatures of its detractors.

As a Puerto Rican scholar and memoirist, Vega's Afrocentricity and Afro-Latinidad complicate the discourse of Black cynicism and authenticity in *Post-Soul Nation* and *The End of Blackness*. Although George and Dickerson are both concerned with the ideological and socioeconomic diversity of Black subjectivity, they give little, if any, attention to Black ethnic diversity.[8] They do not, for example, directly address the relationship between the post-soul, the end of Blackness, and Afro-Latinidad. In this chapter, I tackle George and Dickerson's marginalization of Afro-Latinos by examining philias and phobias of Black interculturalism in Vega's *When the Spirits Dance Mambo* (*WSDM*; 2004). I focus my analysis on Vega's preoccupation with Yoruba religion, the mambo and Latin jazz craze, African American feminist role models, and intermarriage between Latinos and African Americans. In *WSDM*, Vega chronicles her life growing up as Afro-Puerto Rican in New York City during the twilight of Jim Crow segregation. Although *WSDM* is set in the 1950s, the context of its composition and publication are mediated by the post-soul discourse of the 2000s.

Is *WSDM* a post-soul text? Is the post-soul an appropriate interpretive tool for analyzing Afro-Latino literature and culture? The short answer to these questions is yes. Since the late 1990s, there have been several influential studies that put Latino, Afro-Latino, and African American literary and cultural histories in conversation with and among each other.[9] These studies reveal that social relations between Latinos, Afro-Latinos, and African Americans have always been transcultural. Comparative scholarship in Afro-Latino and African American studies should reflect that transcultural engagement in its theories and methods. This type of research can be especially fruitful when it is interdisciplinary, when it uses conceptual tools from two or more disciplines and their associated fields and areas of study. The post-soul is an appropriate interpretive tool for analyzing WSDM not only because the memoir was produced in the post-soul era, but also because US Afro-Latino and African American literary and cultural production are bound in a Pan-African poetics of relation.

Exploring the complex ways in which WSDM's Afrocentricity and its ethnic intermarriage trope speak to the anxieties that animate Dickerson's end of Blackness thesis and George's fear of African Americans losing their changing role in the American cultural imaginary is one way of trying to answer this question. Recall that George's anxiety about African Americans becoming obsolete due to multiracialism and demographic diminution concludes Post-Soul Nation: "It's time for a new look at our role, as an ethnic community and as part of the United States. We are still instigators, creators, and animators of much of what defines this nation. We are no longer post-soul. We are something else. For now, I leave that new definition to you."[10] That new definition, that new something else, is apparently "post-black." Increasingly, scholars and cultural critics are using the term post-black rather than post-soul to describe the contemporary African American condition. Recall that Thelma Golden and Glenn Ligon coined the term post-black in 2001. Between 2007 and 2020, pundits and scholars such as Paul Taylor, Ytasha L. Womack, Touré, Derek Conrad Murray, Margo N. Crawford, and Ilka Saal and Bertram D. Ashe began to critically deploy post-blackness.[11] Saal and Ashe "consider the terms post-soul and post-black as largely synonymous with regard to [the terms'] poetics and politics."[12] Hailing Raymond Williams, they define post-blackness as a structure of feeling,[13] as both an aesthetic and a theory of representation that marks "a decisive artistic and ideological break in the works of artists who were either born or came of age after the civil rights movement."[14] Relying on Ashe's 2007 theory of the post-soul aesthetic,[15] they go on to describe the three essential features of post-blackness: "This break displays three distinctive characteristics: (a) 'a hybrid, fluid, elastic, cultural mulattoesque sense of blackness,' which works alongside (b) the playful, often humorous, and frequently iconoclastic Signifyin(g) on established narratives, tropes, images of blackness in order to (c) trouble habitual notions of blackness, or, as Ashe suggests, to execute a sense of 'blaxploration.'"[16] As their nod to the New Black Aesthetic suggests, Saal and Ashe's vision of post-blackness is theoretically grounded in Ellis's liberal individualist cultural mulatto trope, a trope that intertextually links African American, Afro-Latino, and Latino studies through the shared discourse of *mulatez*.[17] Saal and Ashe view post-blackness as a "spectrum" bounded by "radical individualism," on the one end, and the need for socially inclusive "new forms of collectivity," on the other.[18] By collectivity, I understand Saal and Ashe to mean a pluralistic Black consciousness, a big-tent philosophy of racial identity that Tommie Shelby calls "pragmatic black nationalism."[19] Womack argues that post-blackness rejects narratives of Black despair, pathology, and ideological homogeneity. She contends that African and Caribbean immigrants, Black alternative Christians and non-Christians, biracial and multiracial Blacks, and Black sexual minorities are redefining conventional notions of what it means to be Black/African American.[20] Touré's brand of post-blackness refutes post-racial ideology and essentialist notions of Black authenticity, trumpeting a call for the total acceptance of a "modern individualist Blackness."[21] Aligned with Touré's vision of an ideologically pluralistic Black subjectivity, Murray focuses on how post-black art and artists challenge heteropatriarchal scripts of Black identity and solidarity.[22] Touré's triumphalist post-black discourse has its detractors. Randall Kennedy, Houston A. Baker, K. Merinda Simmons, and Margo N. Crawford fault Touré's post-blackness for its elitism and "libertarian absolutism,"[23] its failure to understand Whiteness as a historically contingent social construct,[24] and its celebratory tone.[25] Crawford takes post-black advocates to task for overlooking the BAM's celebration of weirdness, abstraction, eccentricity, improvisation, and transnationalism: "Many post-black advocates fail to understand black abstraction, black improvisation, and even *black* post-blackness. The irony of the post-black critiques of essentialized blackness is that the emerging post-black 'marketing' obscures the transnational motion that was created when 'black' was mobilized as a unifying concept full of layers and different temporalities. Post-blackness is often stuck in a misunderstanding of the black aesthetic movement."[26]

What does Crawford mean by "*black* post-blackness"? She defines her enigmatic concept in several ways: (1) a "wide horizon of shaping and unshaping blackness," (2) an analog to Amiri Baraka's concept of "the changing same," (3) "the circular inseparability of the lived experience of blackness and the translation of that lived experience into the world-opening possibilities of art," and (4) a "state of suspension" in which "black consciousness-raising and black experimentation are inseparable; being and becoming cannot be separated."²⁷ She goes on to say, "Black post-blackness is a way to understand the continuity between the BAM and the twenty-first-century African American literature and culture that seems to be 'post-black' . . . Black post-blackness was the cultural mood of the BAM's simultaneous investment in blackness *and* a type of freedom that broke the boundaries of blackness."²⁸ Black post-blackness, writes Crawford, is the ability to take Blackness "for granted and therefore not needing to remain defined by that term."²⁹ Blackness, as a form of ethnoracial nationalism, then is both a prerequisite and a condition of post-blackness. Its haecceity makes it distinct from other ethnoracial constructs, but like Heraclitus's river, Blackness is a changing same. In short, Blackness always was, always is, and always will be socially constructed and historically fluid. The fluid quiddity of Blackness defines what it means to be post-soul, to be post-black.

What, if anything, is post-soul about the representations of Latino and African American interculturalism in *WSDM*? *WSDM* is a post-soul text because of its historical positionality, but is it a black post-black text, I contend, because of its author's ideological commitment to the transnationality of Blackness and the poetics and politics of the Black Arts Movement. In this chapter, I argue that *WSDM* is informed by a black post-blackness that engages the contending forces of racial neoliberalism and decolonial Afrocentricity that mediate it. I use the terms *morenophilia* and *morenophobia* to define the affinities and tensions that inform Latino and African American intercultural engagement. Examining Vega's preoccupations with intercultural relations between Latinos and African Americans, particularly in the realms of religion, music, dance, and marriage, reveals the intertextual mechanics that structure the black post-blackness of *WSDM*.

African Diasporic Interculturalism: Afro-Caribbean Religion, Mambo, and the Black Global Aesthetic

Contemporary spiritual life for many Latinos of Hispanic Caribbean heritage is informed by Santería, Espiritismo, or Santerismo. Santería, a polytheistic Lucumi religion, arrived in Cuba, Puerto Rico, and the Dominican Republic with enslaved West African people during the colonization of the New World. Santería adherents worship a pantheon of Yoruba gods called *orisha*; in addition, adherents also practice divination and animal sacrifice.³⁰ Conventional scholarship holds that the postwar boom of Santería worship in the US began in 1946 with the arrival of Francisco Pancho Mora, a *babalawo*,³¹ from Havana.[32] Within thirteen years, orisha worship became increasingly popular among African Americans. Walter Eugene King is thought to be the first African American initiated into Santería; he entered the faith in 1959, in Matanzas, Cuba.[33] Two years later, Margie Baynes Quinones was initiated in New York City as the first Santería *iyalawo* (i.e., priestess) of African American descent.[34]

In addition to Santería, many people of Hispanic Caribbean heritage also practice Espiritismo. Known as Spiritism in English, Espiritismo originated as a progressive quasi-religious philosophy clothed in the rituals of positivist science and veiled in "Christian morality, and mysticism."[35] Hippolyte Léon Denizard Rivail, an educator in France, started the movement in the 1840s when he became preoccupied with the supernatural and paranormal. Under the pen name Allan Kardec, Rivail published several books that popularized his prayers and liturgy, his theories about reincarnation, and his methods of communicating with the dead through mediums in séances.[36]

In the Hispanic Caribbean, Santería absorbed some of the core principles and practices of Espiritismo, resulting in Santerismo. Like Santería, Santerismo includes beliefs in magic, herbal rituals, *orishas*, and spirit guides.[37] Santerismo in Puerto Rico, notes George Brandon, was tightly associated with lower-class Afro-Puerto Ricans. However, in the US, Puerto Ricans of various ethnoracial backgrounds embraced Santerismo, using it as a decolonial form of cultural resistance and self-determination.[38] Among Nuyoricans, for example, Santerismo became a nationalized symbol of Puerto Rican identity, contends Brandon: "Practice of Espiritismo becomes a symbol of the homeland, almost a national or ethnic symbol representing an identity that contrasts with general American norms and values. The eruption of blackness, in the form of the Seven African Powers present in Santerismo, therefore represents an affirmation of Africa as an aspect of Puerto Rican ethnic identity."[39] Puerto Ricans in the US grew more accepting of Santerismo's Afrocentricity during the 1950s and 1960s because Puerto Rican and Cuban popular music was infused with "Santeria chants and instruments" and because mainland Puerto Ricans highly identified with the African American "social consciousness movements" and political "struggles" of the Civil Rights era.[40]

Steeped in the anthropological literature on African cultural retentions in the Americas,[41] Vega has published several articles on Santería, Espiritismo, and interlocking African diaspora cultures.[42] In these articles, Vega often explores how Pan-African solidarities between Latino and African American professional dancers and musicians facilitated the postwar boom of Santería in New York City. Vega makes a provocative, if not essentialist, theoretical intervention in the literature on the Black Arts Movement when she posits that the West African concept of àse, "sacred ancestral energies," constitutes what she calls a Black Global Aesthetic (BGA).[43] Rowland Abiodun, one of Vega's scholarly sources, defines àse as "an enigmatic and affective phenomenon in Yoruba art and culture, the creative power in the verbal and visual arts." He goes on to say that àse is "the most important religio-aesthetic phenomenon to survive transatlantic slavery almost intact."[44] Àse, asserts Vega, "unifie[s] the aesthetic vision" and "permeates the consciousness" of the Yoruba, West Africans, and their descendants in the Americas.[45] As an aesthetic that originates out of religious philosophy, traditions, and sensibilities, àse is anathema to the secularity of "the Western European concept of 'art for art's sake.'"[46] "Àse," Vega explains, "is found in a number of African Diasporan religions—Espiritismo, Santería, vodoun, vandomblé, Shangó, Palo Monte, among others share a common aesthetic vision and inconographic narrative that is traceable to origins in traditional West African cultures."[47] Africans and their descendants in the diaspora, argues Vega, "blend the boundaries between the sacred and the secular, connecting divine and aesthetic knowledge to worldly artistic endeavors."[48]

In the global Black diaspora, contends Vega, the world of intellectuals, artists, singers, musicians, and dancers is suffused with àse. Vega supports her claim by demonstrating how figures like Katherine Dunham, the African American anthropologist, choreographer, and Haitian Vodun initiate, held workshops and salons that were attended by Afro-Caribbean intellectuals and creatives like Aimé Césaire and Sèdar Senghor in Paris and by "Perez Prado, Celia Cruz, Wilredo Lam, and Tito Puentes" in New York at Dunham's monthly Boule Blanche events.[49] Vega credits Dunham as being inadvertently responsible for the postwar boom of Santería in New York City.[50] Julito Collazo, a drummer Dunham recruited from Cuba, "would become one of the pioneer members of a small group of Yoruba traditional practitioners who were instrumental in establishing Orisha worship in New York City," writes Vega.[51] Dunham and her dancers honed their skills in Afro-Cuban music and dance by practicing mambo and cha-cha-cha at the Palladium with the *Afro-Cubans*, Frank "Machito" Grillo's Latin jazz band, I discuss this in more detail further below.[52] Like Dunham, Dizzy Gillespie was an African American artist whose work was informed by the BGA. Chano Pozo, Gillespie's Afro-Cuban collaborator introduced him to sacred Yoruba chants and rhythms, resulting in new genres of music like Cubop and Latin jazz.[53] In Santería, sacred rhythms are bijectively bound to sacred dance choreographies. It is not surprising then that Dunham, a professional dancer, eventually produced music. Dunham's 1955 album, *Singing Gods*, "focused on the ritual music and chants of vodun, Santería, and Candomblé."[54] *Singing Gods*, like Cubop and Latin jazz before it, demonstrates how the sacred and secular mutually inform one another in the BGA.

No less than mambo, Cubop, and Latin jazz, the Black Arts Movement, claims Vega, is a manifestation of the BGA and its religio-philosophical grounding in àse. Vega contends that Amiri Baraka and Larry Neal, architects of the BAM, understood the value and power of religion in the fight for Black self-determination. Baraka, writes Vega, viewed religion as a decolonial weapon: "anytime there is a political energization, Africa is central, therefore religion is part of it. The stepped-up consciousness in fighting imperialism, colonization has motivated the creation of Black Movements to counter oppression. . . . religion is a weapon against injustice, for us it is a return to authenticity, it is the spread of African consciousness, Afrocentricity, people will pick up religion faster than a gun."[55] Yoruba religious philosophy shaped the curriculum of Baraka's Black Arts Repertory Theater/School (BARTS). Chris Oliana and Oba Oseijeman (Walter Eugene King), the first two African Americans initiated into Santería in Cuba, taught at BARTS, where they "formalized aesthetic criteria culturally grounded in the black global sacred experience," contends Vega.[56] In "Some Reflections on the Black Aesthetic," Larry Neal assigns positive value to orishas, ancestor worship, voodoo, macumba, and African gods.[57] Neal's engagement with West African religious practices and philosophies are more personal than commonly thought. Neal and Ted Wilson, another BAM activist, were initiated into the Yoruba religion, Vega asserts.[58] For Vega, Neal's outline of the Black Aesthetic "provides the essential elements that form the foundation of African Diaspora aesthetics and creative expressions."[59] Vega's intervention disrupts conventional nationalist narratives of the Black Aesthetic by underscoring its transnationality. For Vega, Neal's Black Aesthetic was always already a "global black aesthetic."[60]

Morenophilia: Àse Feminism, Spiritual Mestizaje, and Santa Marta La Dominadora

I contend that àse feminism informs how Vega critically constructs her Latinidad in *WSDM*. I define and theorize àse feminism as a practice of gender equality that is informed by reverence for the decolonial feminine divine in African diaspora religions like Santería, Espiritismo, and Santerismo. In

WSDM, àse feminism is embodied by Vega's grandmother, a practitioner of Santerismo, and the female spirit guides she worships: Dominadora, Gitana, and La Madama. Although Vega's memoir will be twenty years old in 2024, it has yet to receive the scholarly attention it deserves. The two exceptions to this oversight are book chapters by Juanita Heredia and Theresa Delgadillo. A decade stands between the publication of Heredia's chapter in 2009 and the publication of Delgadillo's in 2019. Heredia examines the formation of Vega's diasporic Afro-Latina identity, whereas Delgadillo explores the decoloniality of Vega's feminism. Both chapters provide substantive summaries of Vega's memoir and offer close readings of key scenes and thematic elements. I build on the work of Heredia and Delgadillo by bringing specific attention to how Vega's Afrocentric scholarship and her provocative theory of a BGA mediate her representations of Latino and African American interculturalism in *WSDM*.

Vega's scholarly training as an Afrocentrist informs the thematic emphasis she places on the BGA in *WSDM*. In her memoir, Vega explores the roles that colorism, music, dance, and Santerismo played in shaping her racial consciousness as she came of age in 1950s New York City. Born in East Harlem in 1942, Vega was the youngest of three children: "Alberto, called Chachito; Socorro, nicknamed Chachita; and me, Cotito."[61] Puerto Rican colorism mediated Vega's racial consciousness. Vega's sister was "light skin," like their mother, whereas Vega and her brother shared their father's "dark complexion."[62] Although Vega describes herself as "a skinny girl with caramel skin,"[63] relatives nicked named her Negrita. Negrita, which means little black girl, is a common diminutive in Hispanic Caribbean cultures. Puerto Rican colorism heightened Vega's racial consciousness and made her feel like she did not "fit into anything."[64] However, her grandmother's Santerismo and the sacred rhythms of Tito Puente, Celia Cruz, Francisco Raúl Gutiérrez "Machito" Grillo, and Felipa "Graciela" Pérez y Gutiérrez's mambo music "brought Africa to [her] home," shaping Vega's sense of racial pride.[65]

Santerismo also shaped Vega's sense of what it meant to be an Afro-Latina. Doña Luisa, Vega's paternal grandmother, was a respected medium and spiritual guide for the Puerto Rican community in Vega's apartment building. On the same floor as Vega's, Luisa's apartment contained a sacred altar room: "Abuela's sacred room was covered by large murals of Catholic saints. Shelves were filled with statues of Africans and Native Americans that came alive when she played the special music that called the power of the divinities."[66] Proud of her African matrilineage, Luisa told Vega stories of Tomasa and María de la O. Tomasa, Luisa's mother, was "a tall mulatta the color of sweet golden-brown tamarind" who had abandoned Luisa at birth because she was "the color of strong dark wood."[67] María de la O, Tomasa's mother, raised Luisa. María de la O was "born into slavery" and "called herself *una africana de verdad*—a true African—and spoke a mixture of Spanish and African words."[68] The narrative of María de la O functions as an ethnoracial authenticating device, establishing Vega's matrilineal pride in African heritage. Colorism, mambo music, and family lore each informed the Afrocentric scholar Vega came to be, but Santerismo uniquely informed Vega's feminism.

In *WSDM*, Vega references four Santerismo female spirit guides as archetypal feminist role models: La Madama, La Gitana, La Conga, and Santa Marta la Dominadora. In Santerismo, La Madama is "a Black 'mammy' type, turbaned and rotund in a gingham dress, representing the *curandera* or faith healer"; La Gitana is a gypsy "who is in touch with the future;" and La Conga is "a wise old African man or woman, familiar with nature, magic, and time-honored healing remedies."[69] For Vega, Madama represents the importance of family.[70] The spirit guides Gitana and Conga are also two of Vega's three personal spirit guides.[71] Vega's Conga is a fugitive slave woman who adopts the name of Vega's great-great-grandmother, María de la O: "There is a *conga* that stands on your right. She is a warrior, a *cimarrona*, a runaway slave."[72] Vega's Gitana is a "gypsy of two waters . . . a daughter of *las dos aguas*—of sweet and salt water." Vega's Gitana represents the importance of music, dance, mobility, and the cleansing capacity of life's joys.[73]

Of the four spirit guides she references, Vega reifies àse feminism most ardently in her representations of Dominadora. Whereas Madama, Conga, and Gitana are archetypal spirit guides in Puerto Rican and Cuban Santerismo, Dominadora, according to Martha Ellen Davis and Milagros Ricourt, is an archetypal deity in Dominican vodú and spiritualism.[74] Possessing the power to dominate and control males, Dominadora is most often depicted as an Afro-descendant woman in a green dress holding a snake above her head in her right hand as a second snake ascends her body, nestling its head between her breasts.[75] Davis claims that Dominadora has no counterparts among the Catholic saints, but Vega and other popular sources syncretize Dominadora with Saint Martha,[76] who, according to French medieval legend, tamed a dragon called the Tarasque.[77]

Dominadora, Saint Martha's African diasporic counterpart, is a BGA archetype of Black female beauty, seduction, sensuality, and strength.[78] One of Vega's key models of beauty and womanhood was her grandmother's statue of Dominadora. Vega's initial description of the statue is worth quoting in full:

Taking as my model the Catholic Santa Marta la Dominadora on Abuela's altar, who sat cross-legged on the ground and held in her hands a large serpent that she had subdued with her charm, I dreamed of placing the handsomest guys at the club in a trance. The seductive image of La Dominadora, with her hypnotic eyes and defiant posture, danced in my head. Her youthful, sensual body was always adorned in bright green, her breasts and hips full, healthy. I imagined her voice as mysterious and enthralling, one that drew her prey nearer with each word. I posed for the mirror in my bedroom with my hands on my slim hips.

My vision of La Dominadora was a composite of the statue and of actresses and women in the neighborhood that I thought beautiful. My imagination created a perfect image eliminating Rita Moreno's irritating accent in *West Side Story*, which did not sound like anyone I knew, adding the powerful legs of Katherine Dunham dancing in the movie *Mambo*, including the swaying hips and enticing smile of Dorothy Dandridge, and encompassing even the piercing eyes of Abuela as they had appeared in that sepia photograph of her as a proud young woman and the elegant strut of my mother.

Like La Dominadora, my skin was infused with warm caramel. Her lips were a rich bright red, and I wished I were allowed to wear lipstick. I reasoned that if La Dominadora was on Abuela's altar, there was nothing wrong with me wanting to look like her. I admired and wanted to emulate the saint's unapologetic strength.[79]

Vega's Dominadora fuses spiritual, familial, and African American women celebrity figures to create a role model for, as Heredia notes, "a coalition of young women of color such as African Americans, Puerto Ricans, and Afro-Latinas."[80] Vega's amalgamated Dominadora not only replicates the syncretism inherent in Santería and Santerismo, but it also embodies Gloria Anzaldúa's concept of spiritual *mestizaje*. Delgadillo defines Anzaldúa's spiritual *mestizaje* as an interpretivist process, theory, and practice of critiquing oppression, honoring the sacred, reconfiguring the self and social relations, and developing a decolonial political consciousness.[81] Vega uses the spiritual *mestizaje* of the Dominadora conglomerate to concretize BGA interculturalism and its function in Afro-Latina agency and subject formation. Vega's composite Dominadora performs an Afro-Latina subjectivity that is grounded in the interpretivist epistemology of Santerismo, a BGA epistemology that I call àse feminism.

As an archetype of àse feminism, Vega's amalgamated Dominadora makes space not only for the African American beauty of the dancer Katherine Dunham but also for the Afro-Latina voices of the singers Celia Cruz, Xiomara Alfaro, Felipa "Graciela" Pérez Gutiérrez, and Celina Gonzalez Zamora. As a teenager, Vega incorporates Dunham into her vision of Dominadora because of Dunham's beauty, dancing prowess, and celebrity status. However, Dunham's inclusion in Vega's composite Dominadora takes on additional layers of intercultural meaning and depth when one recalls that Dunham was one of the many women Vega studied in her research on Yoruba thought in the African diaspora. As a scholar of Africana studies, Vega moves beyond her teenage interest in Dunham's looks and fame. Vega becomes fascinated with Dunham as a subject of study because of Dunham's personal and professional engagement with African religions and their àse aesthetic.[82] Dunham, an initiate of Haitian Vodun, became a follower of Santería through her professional associations with Latino musicians and singers who practiced Santería. In her own words, Dunham describes how she entered the faith: "Santería, or Cuban Vodun, was just entering my life by way of two Cuban drummers, La Rosa Estrada and Julio Mendez, as well as Dutch Antilles drummer, Gaucho Vanderhans . . . Little by little I was being introduced into the Cuban-Yoruba-West-Coast African belief, close to, but different from the Haitian Rada-Dahomey-Congo-Pétro experiences of mine in Haiti."[83] Dunham embraced Santería and Afro-Cuban music and dance. Vega notes that a knowledge and appreciation of Santería informs Shango,[84] a suite in Dunham's 1946 dance revue Bal Negre. The Shango suite, writes Vega, is Dunham's translation of a bembé, a Santería ritual that features the sacred rhythms and choreographies of the orishas.[85] Vega reveals that Gilberto Valdez, Dunham's musical director, was familiar with the sacred instruments and rhythms of Santería. In the 1930s, Valdez was the first director "to include the ritual batá drums of Santería in a symphonic orchestra in Cuba," writes Vega.[86] Vega's interviews with Ramón "Mongo" Santamaría, a famous Afro-Cuban drummer and bandleader, and Felipa "Graciela" Pérez Gutiérrez are instructive: "Santamaria recalled that, when musicians completed their gigs at the Palladium, they would go to the Dunham school to jam with the Dunham musicians and watch the dancers. Graciela [Perez], the vocalist from Machito and his Afro-Cubans, recalled in an interview on January 10, 1997, that Dunham and her dancers were frequent visitors to the Palladium, where they would dance the night away practicing the steps of mambo and cha-cha-cha, which were later integrated into their staged performances."[87]

Vega's research reveals Dunham's personal and professional engagement with the Cuban music and dance communities in New York City.

For Vega, Dunham embodies the spiritual *mestizaje* of Latino/African American interculturalism. Delgadillo notes the intercultural significance of Vega's recollection of attending a Celia Cruz concert at the Apollo Theater: "One of a few key moments in the narrative when Cotito recognizes the groundbreaking fusion of sacred Orisha sonic traditions with secular musical forms occurs at a Celia Cruz concert she attends with her brother Chachito at the Apollo Theater (Vega 2004, 242–43). Orisha and African diaspora practices here represent not a static past but a dynamic, ongoing, transformative cultural experience that comes to inhabit new sonic spaces in New York of the 1950s."[88] Degadillo goes on to note the importance of African American/Latino "sonic fusions" and "musical networks" in Vega's recollection of dancing mambo to Machito's song "Changó Ta Veni":

> Moreno Vega recognizes the song's Orisha references and rhythms, underscoring how sacred forms of dance and music influenced the new 'mambo' sound and movement by connecting it to the sight of her abuela engaged in sacred dance. While a number of cultural and music critics have also written about the important sonic fusions of this period, providing in valuable insight into African American and Latina/o musical networks, innovations in form, transnational musical movements, and the emergence of Latina/o musical genres, Morena Vega's memoir provides an insider narrative of what it felt to be among those hearing and experiencing this new music for the first time, and her narrative innovatively emphasizes the fusion of sacred and secular in the sonic realm by highlighting the inter relationship between worldview, body in motion, and sound—or Orisha worship, dance, and music, as it also examines how these figure in the generational and gendered differences within her own family.[89]

Delgadillo provides substantive textual evidence and critical analysis of the spiritual *mestizaje* of Vega's BGA interculturalism, but to advance our understanding of Vega's áse feminism we must also consider the profuse peritextual elements in *WSDM*.[90]

Vega explicitly incorporates Dunham into her vision of Dominadora, but she implicitly incorporates the voices of Afro-Latina singers like Xiomara Alfaro into Dominadora through her peritextual use of their song lyrics.[91] Each of the sixteen chapters in *WSDM* uses the lyrics of popular mambo and Latin jazz songs as epigraphs. Three of the sixteen epigraphs reference the orishas and five of the sixteen are drawn from songs by Afro-Latina singers. The epigraphs from the first, third, fourth, fifth, and fifteenth chapters derive from songs by Celina González Zamora,[92] Celia Cruz,[93] Xiomara Alfaro, Felipa "Graciela" Pérez y Gutiérrez (aka Graciela Grillo),[94] and Celia Cruz, respectively. The connection between Dunham, Xiomara Alfaro, and Dominadora resides in "Negrita Linda," the fourth chapter of the memoir. Vega uses lyrics from Alfaro's song "Angelitos Negros" as the epigraph for "Negrita Linda." The epigraph, in translation, reads: "Even if the Virgin is white, paint black angels. All the little black angels also go to heaven." According to Heredia, Alfaro was a member of Dunham's dance troupe. What Heredia does not mention is that Alfaro also acted and sang with Dunham in *Mambo*, the 1954 film that captured Vega's attention as a teenager. Alfaro, then, can be credibly read as a Dominadora role model because of her connection with Dunham and because of the thematic resonance between her epigraph and the subject of the chapter it introduces.

"Negrita Linda" recounts the struggles Vega faced in developing a positive image of Black beauty and womanhood. In "Negrita Linda," Vega explores the mixed messages she receives from her family and community about Black women as objects of beauty and desire. Vega tells the story of how her brother wounded her by mockingly calling her an African because of her complexion and hair texture. As her brother teases her, the song "Babalú, Babalú Ayé," by Miguelito Valdés, plays on the radio. Valdés, writes Vega, "sang addressing the Yoruban god of healing, the rhythmic beats of Afro-Cuban drums in the background. *'Yo le quiero pedir que mi negra me quiera.'* I want to ask that my black woman love me."[95] Hurt and insulted, eleven-year-old Vega throws a glass at Chacito. Her father rewards her with five lashes for her violent outburst. Vega uses Alfaro's song as an epigraph not only to foreshadow but also to counter the anti-Black discourse of her brother's insults.

Vega's intertextual referencing of Alfaro takes on even more significance because of Alfaro's membership in the Santería community. Heredia writes that Alfaro's sister "Olympia Alfaro or Omí Sanyá, was a priestess or 'apuón' in the Lukumí Orisha religious community, performing a type of gospel music particular to this following." Heredia goes on to say, "In the 1970s, [Xiomara] Alfaro became ordained by her sister in the Oshún faith, which is related to Santería."[96] As Heredia notes, by intertextually citing well-known Afro-Latina singers like Celia Cruz and lesser-known ones like Xiomara Alfaro, Felipa "Gracielas" Pérez Gutiérrez, and Celina Gonzalez Zamora, Vega intervenes in the male-centered historiography of Latino popular music.[97] WSDM does the cultural work of recuperating and reclaiming the Afro-Latina presence in the history of mambo, Cubop, and Latin jazz. Arguably, when Vega eliminates Rita Moreno's performance of Latina sonority from her vision of Dominadora, she, through the discursive force of intertextuality, replaces it with the voices of Cruz, Alfaro, Pérez Gutiérrez, and Gonzalez Zamora, women who, because of their exceptional talent, were Dominadoras in the world of Latin jazz.

Examining how Santerismo informs the intercultural relationship between Katherine Dunham and Xiomara Alfaro in WSDM underscores the utility of àse feminism as a tool for analyzing spiritual *mestizaje* and ethnoracial identity formation in Afro-Latina memoirs. Vega concretizes Latino and African American relations in Dominadora, situating Dominadora as a BGA figure of the decolonial feminine divine, as a trope of àse feminist mutual aid and collaboration. As an "objective correlative" of intercultural solidarity,[98] Vega's Dominadora conglomerate refutes popular narratives of Latino and African American enmity. Although Vega offers Dominadora as a symbol of Afro-Latina agency and Latino and African American cultural solidarity, she balances this portrait when she addresses the topic of Latino and African American intermarriage.

Morenophobia: Ethnic Intermarriage and Puerto Rican Exceptionalism

In chapters 8 to 13 of WSDM, Vega complicates the feminist agency aspect of her Dominadora archetype when she recounts her sister Chachita's illicit courtship with and forced marriage to Joseph "Joe" Singleton, an African American. How does the intermarriage narrative in WSDM reflect Vega's commitment to Afrocentrism and speak to the post-soul moment into which it emerged? What, if anything, can we learn by putting Vega's representation of Latino and African American intermarriage in conversation with Latinos demographically displacing African Americans as the nation's largest ethnic minority? What challenges does intermarriage pose to social categories like Black, African American, Afro-Latino, and Non-Hispanic Black? Does Chachita and Joe's intermarriage reveal insights about the relationship between patriarchy, *mulatez/mestizaje*, and the post-racial/multicultural/intercultural debates of the early 2000s? These are the questions I seek to answer about the intermarriage narrative in WSDM. In the context of Vega's memoir, Chachita and Joe's marriage seems exotic and anomalous, but the history of Afro-Latino American and African American intermarriage in New

York City goes back as far as the late nineteenth century. Arturo A. Schomburg, the Afro-Puerto Rican namesake of the Schomburg Center for Research in Black Culture, epitomizes how common it was. Jesse Hoffnung-Garskof reveals that each of Schomburg's three marriages were to African American women.[99] Schomburg was not an outlier. The common oppression of Jim Crow segregation inspired Afro-Cuban, Afro-Puerto Rican, and African American social organizations and political solidarities. Through their intercultural contact in social and political organizations, the three communities grew closer, intermarrying more often than realized.[100]

Before examining intermarriage in *WSDM* as a site of anxieties about interculturalism, multiculturalism, and post-racialism, it is necessary to define the terms of critical analysis. Post-racial is a multivalent descriptor. On the one hand, post-racial denotes a period or society in which state-sanctioned racism is constitutionally illegal.[101] On the other hand, post-racial describes an idealized society in which systemic racism is extinct and racial identity is socially irrelevant.[102] For example, in the US post-racialism, as an ideological stance, triumphantly asserts that the victories of the Civil Rights movement in the 1960s and the election of Barack Obama in 2004 indicate that de facto structural racism no longer exists in America.[103] "Post-racial ideology," writes Alexandre Emboaba Da Costa, "circulates in situations where various degrees of race and/or color-blindness, denial of racism and colonialism, and racist sentiment endure alongside persistent, implicit race-consciousness in peoples' minds and in state policy . . . post-racial ideology seeks to depoliticize race, racism, and difference in ways that demobilize anti-racist politics, substantive cultural recognition, and material redistribution."[104] Through willful ignorance, post-racialism denies the reality of structural racism by asserting that it does not exist or by focusing on a normative future in which race will no longer matter. Post-racialism informs the multiculturalism/interculturalism debates of the 1980s and 1990s. Multiculturalism and interculturalism are competing models of managing a society based on the recognition and accommodation of ethnocultural diversity. As philosophies of citizenship and belonging, interculturalism and multiculturalism take the form of political theories, state policies, and moral stances about how to best live in a culturally pluralistic society.[105] Da Costa contends that there are various persuasions of multiculturalism and interculturalism: "conservative, liberal, corporate, and critical." Liberal multiculturalism argues Da Costa, "tends to emphasize cultural 'diversity' and 'tolerance' of difference over a more direct, critical engagement with race, racism, and histories of inequality. In contrast, more critical anti-racist and anti-colonial versions of multiculturalism (and interculturality) challenge some of the depoliticizing, paternalistic, and culturalist tendencies of liberal versions by foregrounding power structures and intergroup relations as well as anti-racist and critical pedagogies."[106] In other words, multiculturalism advocates for the recognition, cultural autonomy, and legal accommodation and protection of ethnic and national minorities, whereas interculturalism is variously cast as either an amendment of multiculturalism or multiculturalism's arch competitor.[107] Interculturalism, its exponents claim, differs from multiculturalism in that it takes into account the needs, fears, and aspirations of the majority culture as well those of minority communities.[108] Unlike multiculturalism, they argue, interculturalism emphasizes cross-cultural dialogue, interethnic contact, social integration, and national unity.[109] Based on this definition, Chachita and Joe's intermarriage represents the epitome of Latino and African American interculturalism.

Intermarriage, as it is conventionally defined, refers to the legal union of two spouses of differing faiths, ethnicities, races, or nationalities. Although intermarriage threatens an ethnic group's sense of cohesion and particularity, it is a marker of a nation's comfort with interculturalism, given that the rate and number of intermarriages quantifies the decline of traditional social divisions.[110] The critical distinction between ethnic intermarriage and racial intermarriage is that the latter is a subcategory of the former.[111] This distinction is particularly relevant in the case of Chachita and Joe, whose marriage takes place in 1956, eleven years before the US Supreme Court rules that anti-miscegenation laws are unconstitutional in *Loving v. Virginia*.[112]

Although Chachita and Joe's exogenous romance is not interracial, it is fraught with interethnic tensions about skin color and miscegenation. The anti-Black discourse of pigmentocracy, colorism, and *mulatez/mestizaje* informs the context of their courtship and marriage. Pigmentocracy, a hierarchal system of privilege and power based on the skin color of a society's dominant group, favors White and lighter skinned people in the US, the Caribbean, and Latin America.[113] Colorism is the application of light skinned privilege in minority communities of the same nondominant ethnoracial group. In the US, colorism has deleterious social, mental, and physical health effects for people raced as Black/African American.[114] *Mestizaje* is one of the popular modalities of post-racial ideology in the Americas, contends Da Costa, the others being "racial democracy . . . colorblindness, and liberal, neoliberal, and post-neoliberal multiculturalisms."[115] *Mulatez/mestizaje* informs the phrases "*adelantar la raza*" and "*mejorar la raza*."[116] These eugenic phrases describe the impulse of non-White people to "advance" or "improve"

the social opportunities and outcomes of their ethnoracial group by repro-
ducing with White or lighter skinned people.[117] Jared Sexton, one of the leading detractors of multiracialism, argues that its fixation with racial hybridity
not only subtends White supremacy, but that it also projects heteronormative reproduction and family structures as social norms.[118] In sum, *mulatez/
mestizaje* stages multiracial mixture as a paradigm for post-racial social har-
mony in a way that promotes Whiteness as a societal ideal and standard of
human worth.

Puerto Rican nationalism and *mulatez/mestizaje* shape the fraught interethnic courtship and marriage of Chachita and Joe. In chapter 8, "Mi Amiga,"
Vega first learns that her sister, Chachita, has a secret boyfriend. Having a
boyfriend was "unacceptable" for the girls in Vega's family,[119] having an African American boyfriend was even more so because of Puerto Rican's "in-
grained prejudice toward dark skin" and Vega's parents' belief in "'*adelantar
la raza.*' 'Advancing the race' by marrying someone with a lighter complexion."[120] In her assessment of Chachita's exogenous relationship, Heredia writes, "she has to sneak behind the parents' back to date her African
American boyfriend, Joe, to hide his gender and race. This implies that one's
skin color is a critical issue for the Moreno parents as they try to assimilate
to the U.S. mainstream."[121] Heredia implies that Joe's skin color is more of
an issue for the parents than his ethnicity and nationality, but a close textual analysis yields a more ambiguous answer. Chachita takes pains to underscore Joe's light complexion: "He's *un negro*, but light . . . He's the same
color as I am . . . Whether Chachita's boyfriend was lighter than us or not
would not matter as much to our parents as '*que era un negro.*'"[122] Chachita
and Vega use the word *negro* to differentiate Non-Hispanic Blacks from other
American citizens and immigrants of African descent. In the context of the
passage, "*negro*" refers not to Joe's skin color but to his nationality, to his ethnic heritage as a descendant of Africans enslaved in the US. Contradicting
Heredia, Vega claims that an African American suitor's ethnicity/national-
ity would be more of an issue of contention for her parents than his actual
color. Heredia, however, is not wrong about the importance of skin color to
Vega's parents. Vega's parents share a socially conservative, anti-Black, Puerto
Rican nationalist vision of courtship and marriage for their daughters, whose
virginity they police and prize as a badge of family honor. They prefer
that their daughters only date men whom the daughters intend to marry,
and that those men be "light skinned, have good hair, come from a good
family, and be Puerto Rican."[123] As Heredia suggests, colorism and gender
shape Vega's parents' and grandmother's patriarchal ideas about courtship

and marriage, but ethnicity and nationality are equally constitutive of their stance. From an interculturalist point of view, Vega's parents' cultural insularity is indicative of multiculturalism's encouragement of ethnic separatism. Vega portrays the depth and scope of her parents' cultural conservatism and ethnic insularity in chapter 9, "Voy a Apagar la Luz."

Chapter 9, "Voy a Apagar la Luz," violently reveals the patriarchal double standard Vega's parents hold regarding dating and sex outside of marriage. Chachito, their son, was not subject to their sexual policing. They allowed him to date "tons of women," whereas Chachita felt like "a prisoner in [her] own house."[124] Under the ruse of spending seven weeks away from home as a summer camp counselor, Chachita pursues her sexual freedom with Joe. The ruse unravels when the camp, at the end of the seven weeks, calls Vega's residence to say that Chachita never arrived. Vega was just as shocked as her mother to learn that Chachita had never attended the camp. When Vega's mother and grandmother ask Vega if she knows anything about Chachita's whereabouts, Vega tells them that Chachita has a boyfriend who lavishes gifts on her. Realizing that Chachita probably spent seven weeks with a secret boyfriend, Flora calls her a "disgrace," a "lowlife," and "una puta."[125] Luisa agrees with Flora on the latter two aspersions but not the first. Flora enacts the discourse of "marianismo" by disparaging Chachita's sexual agency. Marianismo is a Latin American/Hispanic Caribbean ideology that assigns chastity, docility, domesticity, femininity, maternalism, obedience, moral rectitude, and self-sacrifice to the female gender role.[126] When Chachita arrives home, Flora is less concerned with her daughter's immediate well-being than she is with the perception that Chachita's sexual escapade has dragged the family name "through the mud."[127] Equally outraged, Chachita's father beats her until she slumps to the floor and blood runs from her nose. To preserve the family's honor, he calls for Flora to find out who Joe is and "arrange the wedding immediately."[128] In chapter 10, "Toda Una Vida," Vega recounts how Chachita's destiny was "sealed with a handshake between our father and a man with whom she had just hoped to find a little bit of freedom."[129] Chachita's "stupidity," Flora tells Vega, "is leading her to an even worse future than mine, with a man she barely knows."[130] Joe being unemployed only adds insult to that injury.

Six to seven months after Chachita's secret is revealed, a date is set for her marriage to Joe. In chapter 13, "Que Pena, Here Comes the Bride," Vega introduces readers to Joe's family. For the first and only time, readers see the interethnic marriage from Joe's family's point of view. By bringing the two families together, Vega provides a significant commentary on Puerto Rican and African American relations in postwar New York City, a commentary that sheds more light on Vega's theory of the BGA in regard to the politics of colorism, ethnonational insularity, and interculturalism. Joe's family, writes Vega, "did not approve of his marrying a Puerto Rican girl, just as our family disapproved of Chachi marrying outside of her ethnic group."[131] Joe's mother, whom Vega characterizes as overweight, uncouth, loud, disheveled, and possibly inebriated, says to Joe, in front of his new family, "Son, you happy with your Puerto Rican gal? She looks like one of us, doesn't she? So what's the big deal?"[132] Joe's mother's radical candor counters the notion that *mulatez/mestizaje* makes Puerto Ricans racially distinct from African Americans. Sonia Song-Ha Lee cogently explains how Puerto Rican migrants' sense of racial exceptionalism was rooted in the politics of *mulatez/mestizaje*:

> Puerto Ricans claims to "racial exceptionalism" was based on two notions: that racial mixture in Puerto Rico naturally produced racial equality and that notions of racial hierarchy were fluid because they were inflected with class qualifications rather than biological markers. Both notions, however, hid the deeper foundations of racism that grounded Puerto Rican society. Racial mixing was celebrated in Puerto Rico not so much because it reflected the Spanish, African, and Native ancestries of the people equally, but because it was assumed to be a stepping-stone toward the "whitening of the race," or in other words, the disappearance of blacks.[133]

The subtext of Joe's mother's comment is that as a consequence of colonial history racial hybridity is as characteristic of what it means to be African American as is characteristic of what it means to be Puerto Rican. Like Chachita, Joe's mother sees Puerto Ricans and African Americans as belonging to the same African diaspora family, implying that because they share a common Jim Crow condition and settler colonial history that they share a common fate and political agenda in the US. As Paul Ortiz notes, it is vital for Latino and African Americans to recognize their linked fate: "Today, the descendants of former slaves and the descendants of people in Latin America and the Caribbean are heirs to oft-forgotten lineages of democratic struggle that provide vital reminders of how linked our histories are in the Americas."[134] Chachita and Joe's marriage epitomizes this linked fate not only because it dramatizes Puerto Rican migrants' "dislocation within the North American racial system," but also because it anticipates their "relative ease in coexisting with African Americans as well."[135] That relative ease, in regard to intermarriage, is reflected not only by the history of Black and Latino intermarriage in the late nineteenth century but also by the post-soul moment from and into which *WSDM* emerged. Contextualizing the narrative of Chachita and Joe's marriage in the longer trajectory of Latino and African American interculturalism demonstrates how Vega's memoir speaks not only to the distant past but also to the post-soul anxieties of its historical moment.

In the early 2000s, the period in which George, Dickerson, and Vega published their books, debates about the social and political fate of African Americans loomed large in the public imagination. A key aspect of the debates involved the clash between traditional civil rights interest groups and the multiracial identity movement. The Center for the Study of White American Culture defines the multiracial identity movement as "30 grassroots support groups composed of interracial couples, transracially adoptive families, and individuals of multiracial heritage" united by a four-point agenda focused on ending White supremacy, the one drop rule, monoracism, and the racial categorization of people by the state.[136] Since the 1980s, the movement has been advocating for a multiracial identity category to be added to the US Census. In 2000, it was partially successful in achieving that goal. Although the 2000 Census did not include "Multiracial" as a distinct racial identity, it did allow respondents to check one or more categories of ethnoracial heritage.[137] According to demographer William H. Frey, respondents could identify themselves using "combinations of up to six specific racial categories, including 'some other race.'"[138] Hispanic, Asian, Native, and African American interest groups feared the unintended consequences of allowing respondents to identify as multiracial. These "civil rights advocates," as sociologist and historian Joel Perlmann calls them, were opposed to the multiracial movement's push for a separate identity category because the state uses traditional ethnoracial categories and statistics to assess racial discrimination in housing, education, employment, and voting.[139] Concurring with Perlmann, political scientist Kim M. Williams writes that the civil rights advocates felt that "a multiracial category would imperil the statistics needed to enforce civil rights laws."[140] From the civil rights advocates' point of view, multiracialism serves the neoliberal agenda to dismantle the victories of the civil rights movement. For example, civil rights scholar Tanya Katerí Hernández explores how the multiracial identity movement's quest for recognition disrupts "the antidiscrimination law legal context": "Even United States Supreme Court litigation has begun to associate the growth of multiracial identity with the obsolescence of civil rights policies. Particularly worrisome has been the judicial suggestion that the growth of multiracial identity undercuts the legitimacy of affirmative action policies that have long sought to pursue racial equality."[141] Hernández, Williams, Perlmann, and Frey provide the historical and cultural context for understanding how and why *WSDM* embodies and speaks to Black nationalist fears of multiracialism, demographic contraction, and gentrification.

The intermarriage narrative in *WSDM* speaks to the cultural moment in which it was published because it reifies post-soul anxieties about the relationship between the Latino population boom, multiracialism, interculturalism, and the demise of Blackness. Recall that the first of George's four points about the contemporary African American condition focuses on African Americans' fallen status as the nation's largest ethnic group and underscores the need for African Americans to rethink how their shrinking numbers will impact their cultural and political clout as a national minority. In 2003, the US Census Bureau declared Latinos to be the largest ethnic minority group in the US.[142] Curiously, George chooses not to mention this fact, chooses not to identify Latinos as the group who displaced African Americans. George's reticence about naming Latinos betrays a reluctance to address the history of African American/Latino relations as well as a reluctance to consider Latinos as inclusive of Blackness. Dickerson goes even further in her evasion of the ethnic diversity of Black America. She limits her definition of Black to "those Americans descended from Africans who were brought here involuntarily as slaves. . . . Immigrants of African descent, even if descended from South American or Caribbean slaves, are not included in this definition. *The End of Blackness* is specific to the American experience of slavery and its aftermath."[143] George and Dickerson are not only both evasive on the Latino question but they also share similar views on multiracialism.

George includes multiracialism as one of the four comorbidities of the post-soul era, posing it as an existential threat to African American identity and demographics. In a similar vein, Dickerson, who is interracially married,[144] sees the push for multiracial identity as validation of White America's conviction in Black inferiority: "Instead blacks have meekly accepted whites' cramped vision of themselves as always and only black, and of blackness as always on and only something less than. This explains the current white push for the understanding of their children with blacks as bi- or multiracial, not as black. Now that they are ready to legitimize such unions and their offspring, they are tacitly acknowledging that 'black' is bad, less than, or at least an amputation of healthy limbs. At a minimum they are acknowledging that 'blackness' is meaningless."[145] In some ways, it is not surprising that George and Dickerson converge on multiracialism. Hybridity, as expressed in the form of Ellis's "cultural mulatto" metaphor, is an essential element of the New Black Aesthetic, which conceptually travels with the concepts of post-soul and post-blackness. George and Dickerson's fears about multiracialism's capacity to thin the demographic numbers of people who identify as Black is related to "black denial." In the popular imagination, Black denial describes the impulse of some Afro-Latinos to account for their dark complexions through the claim of Indigenous heritage.[146] Although Kimberly Eison Simmons and Raj Chetty challenge the popular understanding of Black denial,[147] it is not hard to imagine how anxieties about Black denial and Latino exceptionalism might implicitly inform post-soul anxieties about Latinos demographically displacing African Americans.

The intermarriage narrative in WSDM is the epitome of African American and Latino American interculturalism, but what makes the narrative even more significant is that it challenges George and Dickerson's conceptions of and concerns about the nature and scope of Black identity. The African American diminution and end of Blackness themes in George and Dickerson's jeremiads fail to take into account that Afro-Latinos and other immigrants of African descent have been renewing the Black/African American demographic since 1965. The intermarriage narrative anticipates George's call for African Americans to reassess their role as a relevant ethnic minority in the US, his call for African Americans to seek a "new definition" to define their fallen station. George leaves it up to the reader to coin the new term and definition. However, reading the intermarriage narrative through the lens of Dickerson's end of Blackness thesis yields an alternative interpretation. Joe and Chachita's interethnic marriage buttresses Dickerson's call for African Americans to be more intercultural. She is frustrated by insular expressions of African American identity, expressions that tend to limit the history of African American culture to the history of slavery and Jim Crow segregation. She calls for African Americans to reject forms of Afrocentrism and multiculturalism that view Western culture as "innately oppressive."[148] For Dickerson, true multiculturalism and true Afrocentrism call for African Americans to stop "tout[ing] only black history and culture" and to embrace their "historic interconnectedness" with Africa and Asia. Wearing African clothing and decorating one's living space with African art is performative Afrocentrism, claims Dickerson. Expressions of true Afrocentrism, for Dickerson, include "traveling to Africa," "learning the classical Arabic in which Sudanic Africa's precolonial history is recorded," and "taking an interest in the continent, or at least in West Africa, the way American Jews do in Israel."[149] In uniting two parts of the African Diaspora, Joe and

Chachita's marriage would seemingly satisfy Dickerson's call for African Americans to break out of their ethnonational parochialism.

Recalling that each of Arthur A. Schomburg's three wives was African American reminds us that Afro-Latinos have been shaping Black subjectivity through intermarriage since at least the 1870s. Post-black critics tend to overlook this history of mutual affiliation, affinity, and identity formation. Like multiracialism, Afro-Latino/African American intermarriage contests narrow conceptions of Black identity. If post-soul theorists are truly committed to opening up and expanding the definition of what and who counts as Black in America, then they will have to embrace the ethnic diversity of contemporary Black America, the prospect of increased ethnic intermarriage, and the ascendency of Latinos as the nation's largest ethnic minority group.

Conclusion

African American and Puerto Rican intercultural relations in postwar New York laid the groundwork for the cultural and political solidarities between African Americans and Puerto Ricans in the Black Arts, Nuyorican, and post-soul aesthetics. WSDM advances what is known about the development of Afro-Latinidad by putting postwar African American and Puerto Rican intercultural relations in conversation with the twenty-first-century politics of post-blackness. Grounded in her faith in Santería, Afrocentrism, the BGA, and community organizing, Vega wrote a memoir that traffics neither in post-soul cynicism nor post-black preoccupations with Black identity and authenticity. Putting WSDM in conversation with Post-Soul Nation and The End of Blackness is significant because it complicates the interculturalist versus multiculturalist, integrationist versus nationalist, and individualism versus communitarianism narratives about post-soul America. During the post-soul era, African American intellectuals variously critiqued the Black Arts Movement as passé, essentialist, retrograde, and/or chauvinistic,[150] theorizing new norms for Black identity, authenticity, and futurity in post-racial America.[151] As African American cultural critics were fretting over demographic diminution and championing the demise of Blackness, their Latino counterparts were increasingly affirming their investment in Afro-Latinidad, if not Afrocentricity.[152] As African American intellectuals were questioning the nature, utility, and cohesiveness of Blackness, Afro-Latino intellectuals were productively expanding and consolidating it.

The major exponents of the post-soul aesthetic are invested in the diversity of Black subjectivity, but their conceptions of that diversity rarely extend beyond examinations of African American literary and cultural production. They tend to marginalize Afro-Latino literature in general and the Afro-Latino memoir in particular, leaving the conceptual links between Afro-Latinidad, the post-soul, and the end of Blackness unexplored. Vega illustrates those links in her memoir. In *WSDM*, Vega fuses Katherine Dunham and La Dominadora to illustrate her theory of the BGA.[153] The BGA that informs *WSDM* is what qualifies the memoir as a black post-black text. Whereas the fusion of Dunham and Dominadora represents a *morenophilia* (a love of African Americans), the fraught courtship and marriage of Chachita and Joe represent a *morenophobia* (a fear of African Americans). Vega's decision to focus so much of her personal narrative on the union of Chachita and Joe not only decries Latino exceptionalism and Latino anti-Black racism but also valorizes Latino and African American interculturalism.[154] By examining the African American presence in *WSDM*, I reveal how Afro-Latinidad, in the post-soul era, chooses to celebrate the vitality of Blackness rather than theorize its putative irrelevance and morbidity. By rejecting post-racial philosophies of Black subjectivity that are invested in universalist, assimilationist, and liberal individualist forms of social integration, Vega situates *WSDM* as a black post-black text that advances decolonial Afrocentricity to contend with the forces of neoliberalism, forces that shaped the liberal individualist zeitgeist of the post-soul era, the era that produced Afro-Latina memoirs like *Mama's Girl* by Veronica Chambers and *Bird of Paradise: How I Became Latina* by Raquel Cepeda. Unlike Vega, Chambers and Cepeda came of age in post-soul New York. In *Mama's Girl*, Chambers recounts how her Talented Tenth elitism and neoliberal luck egalitarianism are a consequence of the integrationist victories of the Civil Rights movement. Cepeda, on the other hand, recounts how the separatist theosophy of the Five Percent Nation, a splinter sect of the Nation of Islam, informed her Afrocentric Latinidad. Because Chambers and Cepeda provide compelling post-soul contrasts and complements to Vega's insurgent communitarianism, it is to *Mama's Girl* and *Bird of Paradise* that I now turn my attention.

CHAPTER FOUR

Post-Soul Latinidad

Black Nationalism in the Memoirs of Veronica Chambers and Raquel Cepeda

Since the early 2000s, scholars have been paying increasing attention to Latino memoirists like Piri Thomas, Evelio Grillo, Marta Moreno Vega, Veronica Chambers, and Raquel Cepeda.[1] Published after the advent of the Black Arts Movement, the memoirs by these canonical, understudied, and emerging Latino authors are deeply mediated by African American literary, cultural, and political influences. This is particularly true of *Mama's Girl* (1996) by Chambers and *Bird of Paradise: How I Became Latina* (2013) by Cepeda.[2] Chambers and Cepeda are the only writers in this study who are quintessential post-soul writers, by which I mean Generation X writers who deal with the various and varying themes of the post-soul aesthetic.[3] Both of these Latina memoirists were born in the early 1970s, during the heyday of the Black Power Movement. Chambers was born in Panama and moved to Brooklyn when she was five.[4] Born in Harlem, Cepeda was primarily raised in the Inwood neighborhood of Manhattan.[5] As they came of age, Chambers and Cepeda were attracted to different modalities of Black nationalism: cultural pluralism and cultural separatism. In *Mama's Girl*, Chambers invokes the integrationist agenda of the Civil Rights movement to subtend her investment in neoliberal luck egalitarianism. Cepeda, in contrast, is sympathetic to the decolonial theosophy of the Five Percent Nation (FPN), a splinter sect of the Nation of Islam (NOI).[6] Cultural nationalist groups like the FPN tend to be skeptical of the race neutrality methods and goals of liberal integrationism. In addition to her stock in religious Black nationalism, Cepeda is equally invested in the mystic and supernatural aspects of Afro-Caribbean religions. In this chapter, I argue that the antipodes of Black nationalism and the speculative realism in *Mama's Girl* and *Bird of Paradise* reveal them to be post-soul memoirs.

Scholarship in Latino studies is increasingly focusing on how Latino and African American identity, history, and culture mutually inform one another. Theorizing the copiousness of what it means to be Latino, Claudia Milian coined the term "Latinities" to describe "how cultural signifiers for the US Latino or Latina have been accessed by an unexpected circle of Latin participants: U.S. African Americans and 'problematic' subgroups like Central Americans."[7] Concerned with the "detours Latinoness and Latinaness take—through blackness, dark brownness, indigence, Indianess, [and] 'second-tier' Latino status," Milian investigates "how a panoply of U.S. African Americans, Latinos, and Latinas walk in and out of their traditional designations."[8] In other words, people of various races or ethnicities can strategically pass in and out of Latinidad in the US. Since 2010, scholars like Milian have published trendsetting monographs that examine how Afro-Latino detours complicate and expand conventional notions of Latino American and African American subjectivity.[9] These scholars contribute to the body of research that scrutinizes the utility and efficacy of Latino as a pan-ethnic category of cultural and political analysis.[10] Passing, invisibility, triple consciousness, and transcultural detours formally and thematically structure *Mama's Girl* and *Bird of Paradise*,[11] revealing how they expand conventional conceptions of Latino life writing.

Mama's Girl and *Bird of Paradise* are significant forms of Latino life writing because they archive the African American detours that inform Latina identity formation in the postsegregation era. Collectively, Chambers and Cepeda's memoirs exemplify the five defining features of Latino autobiography: (1) communal portraits of the author's ethnic group, (2) bildungsroman narrative arcs, (3) aesthetic experimentation, (4) sociopolitical critiques, and (5) the author's achievement of the American Dream.[12] As memoir writers, Chambers and Cepeda make themselves subject to public scrutiny and historical analysis in ways that fiction writers do not.[13] Because of Chambers and Cepeda's commitment to the "autobiographical pact" of memoir writing, we can better understand how Black nationalism shapes Latinidad by examining the real-life African American encounters, presences, and influences in their memoirs.[14]

The Black nationalist detours in Chambers and Cepeda's memoirs inspire me to offer the term "post-soul Latinidad" to describe the entanglement of Latino American and African American culture and identity in the postsegregation era. Chambers and Cepeda started their literary careers during the last decade of the post-soul era, a decade that witnessed a boom in postcolonial and multiethnic literature. The Black Arts, Black Power, and Black feminist movements of the 1960s and 1970s, argues Jodi Melamed, set the stage for the market's interest in multiethnic literature by promoting culture as a vehicle for structural change. The multiethnic literary boom was coterminous with the ascendancy of a hegemonic ideology of containment called liberal multiculturalism. Liberal multiculturalism, argues Melamed, encouraged White

Americans to embrace representational ethnoracial diversity, but it stopped short of encouraging them to share institutional power.[15] Spanning from 1980 to 2000, liberal multiculturalism co-opted the "deployment of culture by turning it into aesthetics, identity, recognition, and representation."[16] Caribbean American writers like Chambers and Cepeda can profit from a feature of multiculturalism that Graham Huggan calls the "postcolonial exotic." Two competing principles of value define the postcolonial exotic: anticolonialism as a political stance and foreignness as a cultural commodity.[17] Dominic Head, notes that the "exotic appeal" of postcolonial literature is a result of the "perceived importance of multiculturalism" in the contemporary moment and the genre's concern with cosmopolitanism and "ethnic difference."[18]

Simultaneously interpreted under both postcolonial and multicultural rubrics, Caribbean diasporic writers, argues Elena Machado Sáez, "strive to educate the mainstream readership about marginalized histories and avoid reifying any stereotypes their readers might bring to the text, chiefly the perception that ethnic writers should translate their cultures for effortless and uncomplicated market consumption."[19] Sáez uses the term "market aesthetics" to define how the style and content of these writers reveals "a conflict between [their] pedagogical ethical imperative and the market lens of the reader."[20] The conflict, in other words, arises from the tension between Caribbean diasporic writers' political desire to revise colonial narratives of history and their occupational desire to satiate the publishing industry's appetite for exotic difference. When analyzing nationalism in coming-of-age memoirs written by ethnic minorities, it is important to keep in mind the structural and thematic parallels those memoirs share with coming-of-age novels written by ethnic minorities. Martin Japtok observes two important dynamics at work in ethnic coming of age novels: the idealism/materialism and the individualism/communalism dialectics.[21] The former binary pits conceptions of ethnicity as a metaphysical essence against conceptions of ethnicity as a social construct. The latter pits the politics of personal freedom against the politics of ethnic solidarity. These same binaries appear and recombine in the post-soul detours that *Mama's Girl* and *Bird of Paradise* take through Black nationalism.

Onward and Upward: Talented Tenth Elitism
and Luck Egalitarianism in *Mama's Girl*

The US experienced a boom in the publication of multicultural literature and memoirs in the 1990s. Richard Rodriguez, Judith Ortiz Cofer, Pablo Medina, Julia Alvarez, Victor Villaseñor, Cristina García, Mary Helen Ponce, Abraham Rodriguez Jr., Esmeralda Santiago, Norma E. Cantú are some of the notable Latino American authors who primed the multicultural literary market place for writers like Edwidge Danticat, Junot Díaz, and Veronica Chambers. Like Danticat and Díaz do in their first books, Chambers focuses on the Caribbean immigrant experience in her debut book *Mama's Girl*.[22] Danticat and Díaz's debut books are fiction. *Mama's Girl*, however, is a memoir.[23] While the traditional bias against the memoir in literary studies may partly account for why Chambers received less attention than Danticat and Díaz did from the literary establishment, I argue that Chambers's African American narrative strategies explain why *Mama's Girl* received so little attention as a Latina text. While the quality of Chamber's writing may be another reason why *Mama's Girl* was lauded in neither Latino nor African American studies, what her memoir reveals about the complexities of mother-daughter relationships, the Afro-Caribbean model minority myth, and post-soul Black girlhood more than compensate for perceived shortcomings in lyricism, sublimity, or formal experimentation.[24]

Ifeoma C. K. Nwankwo describes the features that constitute *Mama's Girl* multicultural distinction and sociological merit: "Chambers' text speaks from and of three primary histories, the Panamanian-West Indian, the African American, and the US Latino/a. In terms of Panamanian-West Indian history, *Mama's Girl* speaks implicitly to the origin of Panamanian-West Indian communities and more explicitly to the Panamanian-West Indian experience in the United States today."[25] *Mama's Girl* opens with Chambers playing Double Dutch in Brooklyn in the mid-1970s. It concludes in 1992 when Chambers becomes fully independent as a magazine writer/editor and starts supplying her mother with lavish gifts, upscale experiences, and financial advice. Chambers tells the story of her dogged, if not quixotic, pursuit of academic perfection from grade school through college. Intellectual ambition, divorce, domestic abuse, and sibling rivalry are key themes in *Mama's Girl*, but the emotional core of the memoir is its fraught mother-daughter relationship, as indicated by its epigraph, which is the second stanza of the poem "Black Mother Woman" by Audre Lorde. Like the persona in Lorde's poem, Chambers learns to use her mother's emotional callousness and rejection to define herself as a durable and sacred being, tapping into what Michele Wallace calls the "black Superwoman" trope.[26] The epigraph foreshadows the memoir's mother-daughter conflict and speaks to Chambers' capacity for resilience and forgiveness. In the end, Chambers establishes an imperfect yet healing relationship with her mother.

What can a combination of cultural poetics, paratextual analysis, and close textual analysis of Chambers's memoir reveal about the role of Black nationalism in the Afro-Latina imagination? The answer to the question is partly revealed in "Three Young Voices," an *Essence* magazine article cowritten by Chambers, Danticat, and Sheneska Jackson. In her section of the article, Chambers writes: "My book, *Mama's Girl*, is a memoir about growing up in the post-civil-rights generation and how it has shaped the arc of my relationship with my mother. . . . Once I had the great fortune to meet one of our most prominent writers, Ann Petry, author of one of my favorite novels, *The Street*. . . . Long before I thought about writing a memoir, I was familiar with a great African-American tradition: We've always told our own true tales."[27] Chambers invokes the civil rights movement, claims an African American author as a literary influence, and uses the plural pronouns "our" and "We" to write herself into the African American literary tradition. More important, Chambers never mentions her Afro-Latina heritage, and neither does the accompanying excerpt of the book.

Additional evidence of Chambers's privileging her race over her ethnicity appears in her personal essays. In "Secret Latina at Large" and "The Secret Latina," Chambers writes about how Blackness in the US cloaked her Latinidad and how anti-Black racism in the Latino community caused her to privilege her Blackness over her Latinidad.[28] In "Veronica Chambers '87: Writer and Editor," Chambers writes, "My family was from Panama, but I had been obsessed with African American history for as long as I can remember."[29] Chambers goes on to recall how as an undergraduate at Bard College at Simon's Rock she ideologically aligned herself with Du Bois's nationalist concept of the Talented Tenth: "It meant a lot to me, as a black Latina, that the school was situated in the birthplace of W. E. B. Du Bois. I had not yet read *The Souls of Black Folk*, but I knew about Du Bois and his notion of the Talented Tenth. My heart quickened at the thought of somehow being able to tap into his tenacity, ambition, intellectual curiosity, and cosmopolitan elegance. His connection to the home of Simon's Rock seemed like another sign that this would be the right place for me. *Look for the drinking gourd*."[30] Notice that Chambers is more enamored with the traits of Du Bois's elite class status rather than with his Talented Tenth agenda of service, sacrifice, and racial uplift. Even more curiously, she is silent on the overt machismo in Du Bois's political project.[31] Chambers's preoccupation with African American cultural heroes like Du Bois is evidence of her triple consciousness, her conception of herself as racially Black, ethnically Hispanic, and nationally American.[32] Her admiration of Du Bois speaks to the Pan-African subtext of *Mama's Girl*, to the idea that Afro-Latinos and African Americans share a linked history and sociocultural fate in the Western hemisphere.

Moving from paratextual to close textual analysis illuminates even more about the role of Black nationalism in Chambers's memoir. Although Latinidad is foregrounded in the first three chapters of *Mama's Girl*, it rapidly gives way to a profusion of African American cultural references in the remainder of the text. Representative examples of this market aesthetic include Chambers's references to Zora Neale Hurston, Toni Morrison, Audre Lorde, and W. E. B. Du Bois as Ellisonian literary "ancestors."[33] Chambers even finds role models in sitcoms that feature African American characters and families. The paucity of Latino and the cornucopia of African American cultural signifiers in *Mama's Girl* may explain why many of the reviewers of the memoir exclusively categorized it and Chambers as African American.[34] Chambers's market aesthetics, that is, her decision to frame herself, or allow herself to be framed, as African American, reveal the complexities of Latina identity formation and Black nationalist affinity under the hegemony of America's Black/White racial paradigm. During Chambers's first ten years, her parents socialized her and her younger brother as African Americans rather than as Latinos. They spoke English in their household and Black nationalist politics shaped their civic engagement and personal lives. Chambers's father, for example, "joined the civil rights movement and later the Black Power movement."[35] He was so moved by the sacrifices of radical Black activists that he wanted Chambers's first name to be Angela Davis. The fact that he named his son Malcolm X Chambers is a testament to the father's commitment to Black nationalist identity politics.[36] Every year, during Black History Month, Chambers's parents required Chambers and her brother to write reports about significant African American cultural heroes. Chambers's parents also watched and discussed documentaries about the Civil Rights movement with her and her brother, and they enrolled her in a primary school that taught its students "We Shall Overcome" and "Lift Every Voice and Sing," the African American national anthem.[37]

The specificity and plurality of African American vernacular tropes and cultural references in *Mama's Girl* illuminate how the concepts of racial uplift, upward class mobility, respectability politics, and cosmopolitan exceptionalism inform Chambers's relationship with Black nationalism. Ascension is the extended conceit that thematically unifies *Mama's Girl*. The conceit appears throughout the memoir. References to Michael Jordan and Zora Neal Hurston, for example, reify the personal virtues Chambers promotes: expertise, elitism, virtuosity, racial integration, ideological freedom, and the consumerist pursuit of the American Dream. Chambers's linking of the American Dream, upward social mobility, and the civil rights movement is explicitly expressed in the scene dealing with Chambers's desire to apply to Choate Rosemary Hall, an elite boarding school in Connecticut. Cecilia, Chambers's mother, is not excited about her daughter's interest in Choate. The scene is one of a pair linking individual exceptionalism to the integrationist agenda of the civil rights movement, an agenda that held the promise of dismantling social barriers to the American Dream. In these scenes, Chambers uses jumping and flight as metaphors for personal achievement and social progress, respectively. For example, Chambers uses Zora Neale Hurston's "Jump at de sun" quote as a personal motto,[38] demonstrating that she, like Hurston, values the principle of striving for achievement in every field of human endeavor.

Following the Hurston quote, Chambers mentions how she always imagined herself as Tootie, the African American girl who attends an elite boarding school in *The Facts of Life*.[39] After boarding school, Chambers imagined that she would go to college and become a "credit to her race," as the older women in her neighborhood encouraged her to do when she was young.[40] Chambers's perfectionist desire to become an exemplar of her race is reinforced by the respectability politics of her other favorite sitcoms: *The Cosby Show* (1984–92) and *A Different World* (1987–93). Portraying African American lawyers, doctors, and college students, these shows provided Chambers with "buppie" role models. Buppie, slang for 'black urban professional,' is a post-soul trope that describes people who are "ambitious and acquisitive, determined to savor the fruits of integration by any means necessary."[41] The shows stressed the significance of undergraduate and postgraduate credentials, employment in the professional class, the benefit of middle-class social networks, and the personal value of knowing African American history and culture.

Unlike the older women who encouraged Chambers to improve her socioeconomic station, Cecilia constantly squelches Chambers's ambition to become a member of the Black bourgeoisie: "I didn't understand my mother at all; what had happened since the days of the movement? Wasn't this the point of it all—to give black boys and girls like me a chance to fly?. . . . Didn't she want me to have a better life?"[42] Even when Chambers was in primary school,[43] Cecilia feared her daughter's ambition: "But my mother always warned me about aiming too high. . . . I never understood how my mother could be so into the movement and at the same time, act as if we were just out of slavery days."[44] The quotes show the difficulty Cecilia has reconciling her desire for racial justice with her fear of the civil rights movement's integrationist agenda. According to Gary Peller, liberal integrationists presuppose a color-blind social order based on the concepts of personal merit and race neutrality, and they use this presupposition to delegitimize solidarities based on the identity politics of race-consciousness and cultural nationalism. Cecilia, then, represents the nationalist fear that integration will ultimately result in the "painless genocide" of Black culture, identity, and social life.[45]

Chambers's fraught relationships with her mother, father, and brother exemplify her complicated relationship with the luck egalitarianism of the liberal integrationist agenda. Carl Knight writes "that luck egalitarianism seeks to combine the traditionally radical idea of distributive equality with the traditionally conservative concern for holding people responsible for their actions."[46] Luck egalitarianism values personal accountability,[47] positing that people should not be exempt from the inequality (i.e., bad luck) that results from their poor choices.[48] As Chambers grows into herself, the ideological and class gulf between her and her family members widens; their interpersonal relationships grow evermore rancorous. At the heart of these strained relationships is Chambers's enmity for her mother and her drug-dealing brother, Malcolm. Chambers harbors outrage at the fact that her mother's sense of self-worth is dependent on whether Malcolm turns out to be a success:

> Despite all the things we have worked out, how we relate to my brother is the one thing that always makes me feel like I can't stand her. There is a saying that black women mother their sons and raise their daughters; when it comes to my mother, that saying is too true. . . . I felt sympathy and wanted to support Malcolm and all the young brothers in his situation. But unlike my mother and the black women of my childhood, I wasn't going to support a black man at the expense of myself. This realization changed everything about how I viewed Malcolm, how I viewed my mother, and how I viewed my father. It was like we were all playing this black woman-black man game and then I moved my piece right off the board. . . . So many times I've tried to explain to my mother that there is a difference between circumstance and choice. My brother and I grew up under the same circumstances, but we made a million different choices along the way. The circumstances we could not control, but the choices were ours to make.[49]

While it is surprising to see Chambers make a claim that bolsters discredited stereotypes about the pathology of Black matriarchy,[50] more notable is her flight from the "black woman-black man game," a game in which Black women are encouraged to sublimate personal ambition in order to uplift Black males. On the one hand, her flight from the game reveals her intersectional critique of patriarchy.[51] On the other hand, her choice-versus-circumstance polemic reveals her luck egalitarian stance on the neoliberal politics of personal accountability.

As the memoir concludes, Chambers painfully comes to accept that her elite education and vaulted occupation culturally separate her from her working-class mother and her drug-dealing brother. For instance, when Chambers mentions to her mother that she likes to see plays and purchase paintings, her mother affectionately calls her a buppie. Even as an adult, Chambers finds being called a buppie by her mother alienating: "Her voice says at once, 'I am proud of you—but you are now an entirely different being than I am.'"[52] Chambers, using a final ascension metaphor, sees her sudden "jump from poverty to solvency" as "a jump [she] made alone."[53] On the one hand, the metaphor simply describes the fact that the rest of her family still lives in poverty. On the other hand, her statement is morally judgmental, suggesting that her mother's fears and her brother's poor choices made them unfit for the jump. The ambiguity of the statement is aesthetically productive because it simultaneously provides and denies the sense of closure one expects to find in a bildung narrative about achieving the American Dream.

Furthermore, *Mama's Girl* privileges post-soul individualism by departing from the communal ideology of conventional African American and Latina autobiography.[54] The actual people who helped Chambers become the person and professional she became receive little to no attention in the body of the memoir. In the acknowledgments, however, Chambers thanks nearly fifty people from her community. She separately dedicates the book to her grandmothers, great-grandmothers, and all of her female ancestors. The acknowledgments and dedication support Lourdes Torres's argument that Latina autobiography eschews "the dominant and traditional autobiographical construction of the 'superior' individual who seeks to separate himself from his community."[55] The people Chambers tends to reference by name in the memoir's narrative are mostly people to whom she is immediately related. Chambers does not even name or describe the person who saved her from drowning at Simon's Rock.

The coming of age memoir, as a genre, tends to identify the people who hindered and helped the authors on their journeys from apprentice to adept. Chambers's choice not to name these people is uncharacteristic of the genre, but they may be grounded in the sense of cautious pragmatism. The ethics involved in publishing a memoir are fraught with interpersonal and legal peril.[56] Chambers may have left out the names of her friends and associates to preserve their right to privacy, to maintain personal relationships, and/or to avoid libel suits. That choice, however honorable or pragmatic, has the effect of devaluing communalism and producing an individualist narrative of heroic self-transformation, a narrative that mediates what it means to be and become Afro-Latina by aligning itself with the elitist and liberal integrationist modalities of the post-soul aesthetic.

Knowledge of Self: Raquel Cepeda, Afro-Mysticism, and Genomics

Whereas *Mama's Girl* features the Talented Tenth elitism of the integrationist agenda, Raquel Cepeda's *Bird of Paradise* features the cultural separatist theosophy of the Five Percent Nation, an investment in Afro-Caribbean religions, and a faith in the science of ancestral DNA testing. The FPN is a decentralized community of individuals bound by an Afro-Asiatic catechism derived from the NOI. Clarence Edward Smith founded the FPN in 1964, after he broke away from the NOI because of a disagreement with the teachings of Elijah Muhammad.[57] Between the mid-1960s and the 1990s, the FPN found a foothold in African American communities across urban America. Musicologist Felicia Miyakawa writes that FPN theology is "an idiosyncratic mix of black nationalist rhetoric, Kemetic (ancient Egyptian) symbolism, Gnosticism, Masonic mysticism, and esoteric numerology."[58] A significant faction of politically conscious 1990s hip hop bears the mark of the FPN's ethnocentric ideology, so it is not surprising that FPN references appear in a memoir written by Cepeda, a hip-hop journalist.[59]

   Bird of Paradise is equal parts coming-of-age story, speculative narrative, and genetic suspense tale. The memoir's title intertextually alludes to Paraíso, the neighborhood in which Cepeda's mother was raised in the Dominican Republic and in which Cepeda lived, on and off, for the first six years of her life. In a 2013 television interview with Melissa Harris-Perry, Cepeda reveals that the title also alludes to *I Know Why the Caged Bird Sings*, Maya Angelou's 1969 autobiography. In addition to Maya Angelou, Cepeda also claims another African American intellectual as a source of creative inspiration. Speaking of how genealogical research and genetic profiling came to inspire and inform *Bird of Paradise*, Cepeda tells Harris-Perry, "I saw Dr. Henry Louis Gates Jr. do his work and I thought it was really interesting. I feel like it would be interesting to do this with the Latino community."[60] Cepeda divides *Bird of Paradise* into two parts. Part I is a classic coming of age story. Part II is a genealogical narrative that focuses on the relationship between genetic testing and ethnoracial identity formation. The stylistic hybridity of *Bird of Paradise* mirrors Cepeda's ethnoracial hybridity, her claim to Spanish, Taíno, and West African ancestry. As the subtitle of her memoir suggests, Cepeda uses her eclectic genealogical profile as a case study to explore the historicity and constructiveness of Latinidad. Regarding Black nationalism, Cepeda chronicles how she uses hip-hop culture to rise above the abuse and neglect of her childhood and become a nationally acclaimed journalist, editor, documentary filmmaker, and memoir writer.

The thematic presence of hip hop in *Bird of Paradise* underscores the fact that in New York Latinos were essential to the genesis and evolution of hip-hop music and culture.[61] Although hip hop is a critical motif in *Bird of Paradise*, there are few published scholarly assessments of the role hip hop plays in ethnoracial identity formation in the memoir. A notable exception to this state of affairs is Sharina Maillo-Pozo's article, "Reconstructing Dominican *Latinidad*: Intersections between Gender, Race, and Hip-Hop." Maillo-Pozo argues that "Cepeda's memoir underscores the impact of the cultural movement of hip hop among second-generation Dominicans and its relationship to alternative narratives of a Dominican latinidad that drifts away from a largely hispanocentric rubric."[62] As Maillo-Pozo contends, Cepeda's "main objective is to challenge ethnoracial identifications through her participation in hip-hop culture."[63] I extend Maillo-Pozo's work by conducting a cultural and close textual analysis of FPN hip hop and theosophy in *Bird of Paradise*. I contend that Cepeda's affinity for antiracist and Afrocentric hip hop challenges the stereotype of Dominican "black denial" and shapes her Latinidad in ways that prime her to be sympathetic to the cultural separatist theosophy of the FPN.[64]

Cepeda's love affair with hip-hop music and culture begins in the 1980s when she is living in Manhattan with her father and her Finnish stepmother. Physically and verbally abused by her father,[65] Cepeda finds refuge from the dysfunction of her family life in hip-hop culture. Hip-hop music was Cepeda's healing balm, her sanctuary for spiritual uplift and renewal. To establish her credibility as a hip-hop connoisseur and journalist, Cepeda suffuses *Bird of Paradise* with references to various aspects of hip-hop culture: graffiti, dancing, movies, and music. For example, the list of hip-hop artists, producers, and studios she mentions includes Russell Simmons, Boogie Down Productions, LL Cool J, Run DMC, MC Lyte, Roxanne Shante, Monie Love, DJ Van,

Redhead Kingpin, Bobby Brown, NWA, Immortal Technique, Sha-Rock, Queen Latifah, Brand Nubian, Rakim, De La Soul, Freestyle Fellowship, and Public Enemy.[66] A number of these artists were associated with the FPN and its theosophy.[67] Between the ages of eleven and fifteen, incidents, literature, and music about racism draw Cepeda to the separatist pole of Black nationalism. These influential events and texts include the 1984 Bernhard Goetz subway shooting, her reading of *The Autobiography of Malcolm X*, and her love of the 1987 song "9mm Goes Bang" and of Public Enemy's 1988 album *It Takes a Nation of Millions to Hold Us Back*. Of this period, Cepeda says, "In New York City, I'm creating my own identity, one in which hip-hop culture, now in full effect, is at the core."[68] This is the same period in which the FPN begins to exert an influence on Cepeda's Latina identity formation.

The ethnocentric ideology of the FPN is the post-soul lens through which Cepeda interprets her Latinidad. There are three defining characteristics of FPN ideology: its syncretic theosophy,[69] its fetish for the trope of science,[70] and its belief in the divinity of "the Asiatic Black Man."[71] As Afro-Asiatic divinities, FPN members claim to possess an enlightened awareness of the human condition. They call this esoteric awareness "knowledge of self." The phrase is allusive of the Delphic maxim "know thyself."[72] The FPN version of the ancient adage originates from Question #2 in the NOI catechism known as Lesson No. 1: "Savage means a person that has lost the knowledge of himself and who is living a beast life."[73] The FPN maxim is further developed in Questions #14 to #16 of Lesson No. 2. The three questions divide humanity into three categories: the 85 percent, the 10 percent, and the 5 percent. The eighty-five percenters are the masses who worship mystery gods, lack knowledge of their own divinity, and sheepishly allow the ten-percenters (i.e., the wealthy and the elites) to exploit them intellectually, politically, and financially.[74] The FPN constitutes the enlightened and self-exalted five percent of humanity, "the poor, righteous teacher[s]."[75]

Analyzing the four references to "knowledge of self" in *Bird of Paradise* demonstrates how Cepeda came to develop her sense of post-soul Latinidad. Cepeda first uses the phrase in a failed attempt to build Pan-African solidarity with her friend Caridad, a "cinnamon" complexion, half-Cuban half-Puerto Rican teen who equates being called an "African queen" with being called a "nigga."[76] The politics of skin color is a perpetual challenge between Cepeda and her darker-skinned high school friends. The second expression of the phrase occurs in a scene in which Cepeda considers using FPN ideology to bridge the cultural gap between her and the Dominican immigrant students at her high school. Cepeda mockingly calls the immigrants "campesinos" and "plátanos."[77] Cepeda despises them for being uncouth and lacking racial consciousness, and they despise her for not being Dominican enough, for being too African American. The phrase appears a third time when Cepeda has a debate about the FPN with Angel, her long-distance, FPN boyfriend. The fourth expression of the phrase occurs when Cepeda describes a period in her life after she dropped out of college and worked in "a quasi-Afrocentric novelty store in Greenwich Village, selling watered-down fragrance oils and Ron G mix tapes."[78] In this period, Cepeda frequents the poetry scenes at the Nuyorican Poets Café and the Fez Under Time Café.[79] At the Fez, she dives "headlong into the deep end of the hip-hop-inspired poetry scene" after she hears Freestyle Fellowship rap about "knowledge of self" in their song "Inner City Boundaries."[80] Not long after, Cepeda becomes the poetry editor at *New Word*, which puts her on the path to being the hip-hop journalist, editor, and documentarian that she ultimately becomes.[81]

A close textual analysis of Cepeda's debate with Angel shows that Cepeda held the FPN up to ideological critique even though she was a fellow traveler. In the debate, Cepeda adopts a position that reconciles ethnocentricity with what the philosopher Tommie Shelby calls "pragmatic black nationalism," a big tent philosophy that promotes ideological diversity within African American organizations and coalitional politics between those institutions and their potential allies.[82] The debate between Cepeda and Angel occurs when Angel returns from his undergraduate studies at Temple University to visit Cepeda and his family.[83] At Temple, Angel becomes born again in the FPN, takes the name Infinite Reality, and starts dating women of unambiguous African descent. Angel's mother, Maria, tells Cepeda not to worry about Angel's new "*morena* girl phase."[84] When he returns home, Angel chastises Cepeda for working at a White-owned clothing store. Angel tells Cepeda that she should not work for those "devils" because "They don't have knowledge of self. They don't understand that we are the Nation of Gods and Earths, so they treat us like slaves."[85] Playing on Cepeda's reverence for Brand Nubian, Angel refers to their song "Wake Up" to convince Cepeda to leave her job.[86] Cepeda counters by telling Angel that she gives the money she makes to his mother, who uses it to buy things for him, and that Brand Nubian had to "work with a few devils" to make their album.[87] "We all have to work the system," she says, "to get what we need." Angel concurs, "Sometimes we have to dance with the devil if it enables us to get a greater message out there."[88]

Having lost that argument, Angel continues his provocation by focusing on Cepeda's tight jeans. He is perturbed with her sartorial choice because the

FPN expects female adherents to dress modestly: "Why are your clothes so tight? Don't you have self-respect as an Earth, a mother of civilization? Are you cheating on me when I'm in Philly? . . . Since you like Brand Nubian so much, listen to what the gods say and 'Slow Down.'"[89] The song "Slow Down" disparages promiscuous women, female drug addicts, and female sex workers.[90] Cepeda makes no effort to counter Angel, to reject the FPN's patriarchal ideology.

When Angel's mother encourages him to drop the discussion about female modesty, he shifts the topic to the European dispossession, enslavement, and genocide of Indigenous Caribbeans and Africans: "Listen, the white man is our collective oppressor all over the world. Look, even in the D.R., the Taíno and Carib Indians and the Original Asiatic Black man had to contend with those white devil Spaniards. And now look at how we embrace the Spaniard and call ourselves Spanish and white, even when most of us obviously are not."[91] Angel's rhetorical strategy invokes the Hispanic Caribbean concept of *mestizaje*, the notion that Puerto Ricans, Cubans, and Dominicans are a mixture of Indigenous, Spanish, and African peoples.[92] *Mulatez*, a concept related to *mestizaje*, describes the interracial mixing of people of African and European descent.[93] Cepeda rejects the conclusion of Angel's rhetorical detour, his use of FPN theosophy to categorically demonize White people: "You're the first Dominican I've ever met down with the Five Percent Nation, but I can see the link. . . . My only thing is that I've also met Black and Latino devils, and how about those Black cops who took part in Rodney King's beat-down?" Angel explains that the African American cops who beat King were "brainwashed" eighty-five percenters, "who live in the dark about their own and our collective identities."[94] Reaching an impasse, the debate concludes.

There are other FPN allusions in *Bird of Paradise*, but analyzing the representations of the phrase "knowledge of self" sufficiently demonstrates that Cepeda's Latinidad is deeply, though not exclusively, informed by Black nationalist conceptions of racial consciousness. Although Cepeda is an FPN fellow traveler, she is skeptical of its racial essentialism. The FPN's founder, says Cepeda, "delivered an ideal of self-determination and improvement that found an audience with a younger crowd of disenfranchised Black-Americans who found his so-called Supreme Mathematics and 120 Lessons palatable."[95] Her use of the words "so-called" and "palatable," as well as her debate with Angel, illustrates that Cepeda refuses to sacrifice her ideological integrity on the altar of racial chauvinism. Nevertheless, Cepeda's reverence for the decolonial aspects of the FPN's theosophy constitutes a post-soul detour that sets the stage for her focus on spirituality, ancestor veneration, *mestizaje*, genetics, and the Taíno revival movement in part II of her memoir.[96]

Raquel Cepeda's engagement with Afro-diasporic mysticism is not limited to her encounter with the FPN's racial theosophy and scientific sermonic rhetoric. At the same time that Cepeda becomes familiar with the FPN's concept of "knowledge of self," she comes to embrace Afro-Caribbean religions such as Santería,[97] Espiritismo,[98] and Santerismo.[99] In the US, the principal followers of these intersecting religions and spiritual practices tend to be Cubans, Puerto Ricans, Dominicans, and African Americans.[100] Cepeda's memoir suggests that Dominican Americans, like their Puerto Rican, Cuban, and Haitian counterparts held on to their Afro-Caribbean religious practices as a way to preserve and delineate their ethnic particularities in the diaspora. Arelis M. Figueroa argues that "a high percent [of Dominican Americans] practice popular religiosity, including Dominican Voodoo, Santería, or other African-based religious expressions."[101] New York City, notes Tallaj in her study of Dominican Vudú, is a "transnational space where Dominicans have come into contact with other Afro-Caribbean religious practitioners and have been freed from the historical, cultural, political, and racial dynamics of the Dominican Republic."[102] This cross-cultural exchange between Dominicans and Puerto Ricans is reciprocal. As we saw in chapter 3, Dominadora, an African spirit guide in Marta Moreno Vega's grandmother's Santerismo altar complex, is derived from Saint Martha La Dominadora, a Catholic saint venerated in Dominican Vudú.[103] Vega's grandmother, a medium, would become possessed by the spirits guides and communicate their wishes to their descendants and devotees. Like Vega, Cepeda had a caregiving adult who believed in and saw spirit guides.

In this section of the chapter, I focus on the relationship between Cepeda's childhood traumas and her belief in *la africana* and *la india*, her personal spirit guides. C. Christina Lam accepts Cepeda's claims about the material reality of spirit guides.[104] What, if anything, could be learned from reading *la africana* and *la india* against the grain? What would a skeptical, but generous, reading *la africana* and *la india* through the lens of "speculative realism" reveal? Ramón Saldívar, a Chicano studies scholar, coined the term speculative realism, defining it as "a hybrid crossing of the fictional modes of the speculative genres, naturalism, social realism, surrealism, magical realism, 'dirty' realism, and metaphysical realism."[105] Speculative realism, contends Saldívar, is a constituent element of what he calls the "postrace aesthetic" of contemporary US ethnic literature, literature which is highly associated with coming of age narratives.[106] Saldívar uses the term postrace "to refer both to the critical difference between the social and aesthetic conditions of the twentieth and twenty-first centuries, and the significance of this difference for the form of fiction in the contemporary American context."[107] The term postrace designates a conceptual shift in US racial discourse, a conceptual shift that decenters thinking about race strictly in terms of Blacks and Whites, a conceptual shift precipitated by "the profoundly shifting racial demographics of early twenty-first-century America."[108] Although Saldívar's postrace aesthetic resonates with George's musings about the comorbidities of the post-soul era,[109] Saldívar is not in conversation with the discourse of the post-soul aesthetic.[110] Despite that omission, Saldívar's speculative realism is a useful interpretive tool to apply to *Bird of Paradise*, a Latina coming of age memoir that is suffused with supernatural elements and spiritual tropes. In the spirit of intellectual diversity, exchange, and skepticism, I use speculative realism, among other conceptual tools, to offer an alternative explanation for the manifestation of the *la africana* and *la india* in Cepeda's traumatized childhood and adolescence.[111]

Before engaging in a close reading of the spirit guides in *Bird of Paradise*, it is helpful to further define how they function and are conceptualized in Afro-Caribbean religions. In Espiritismo and Santerismo, spirit guides function as the protectors of their descendants, communicating their desires through spiritual mediums. Aisha M. Beliso-De Jesus, a professor of African American religions, writes about how spirit guides correspond with their descendants' ethnic heritages: "Along with common congo (male and female) African slave spirits, there are Spanish gypsies, nuns, priests, and various forms of indigenous spirits that normally hail from the person's genealogy or ethnic makeup."[112] Representative female spirit guides in Afro-Caribbean religions include La Madama, La India, La Gitana, and La Conga. La Madama is "a Black 'mammy' type, turbaned and rotund in a gingham dress, representing the *curandera* or faith healer;" La India/o is typically "a North American Plains Indian, male and/or female, with typical headdress;" La Gitana is a gypsy "who is in touch with the future;" and La Conga/o is "a wise old African man or woman, familiar with nature, magic, and time-honored healing remedies."[113] Judith Bettelheim, a specialist in African and African Diaspora Arts, provides an extensive study of the Indian and Congo spirit guides in Espiritismo, explaining why generic images and figurines of Native Americans and Taínos are staple features in Espiritismo altars and imaginaries.[114]

Spirit guides figure prominently in the faith traditions of Cepeda's surrogate family. Cepeda's surrogate parents, Casimiro and Maria, both claim to possess supernatural powers. Casimiro claims to see spirit guides, whom he refers to as "los misterios," while his wife, Maria, claims to be able to see the future through her dreams. Anthropologist Cristina Sánchez-Carretero contends that in Dominican Vudú spirit guides are called *santos* or *misterios* and the mediums *curanderos, brujos, portadores,* or *servidores de misterios*.[115] "Casimiro," writes Cepeda, "becomes, by default or kismet, a father figure."[116] Cepeda describes Casimiro as an "uneducated raven-complected campesino, from Dajabón."[117] Cepeda's focus on Casimiro's complexion and hometown is a coded way of suggesting that Casimiro has Haitian ancestry. Dajabón, a city on the border between the Dominican Republic and Haiti, was the epicenter of the 1937 Haitian Massacre, a genocide that sought to purge Haitians from the Dominican Republic.[118] Linking Casimiro to Haiti also reinforces his connection to Afro-Caribbean religions. In addition, it recenters Haiti in the discourse of the Hispanic Caribbean.[119] Through Casimiro, Cepeda becomes intimately acquainted with an Afro-Caribbean religion that involves the worship of Ellegua, a Yoruba deity: "I let myself into the apartment—it's rarely locked—and walk by an elaborate gold-framed painting of San Miguel slaying a dragon on the right side of the wall behind the door; it hangs there for protection. On the floor directly below the painting are a coconut, candy, a cigar, and a stone head with eyes and a tiny mouth made of cowrie shells resting on a small plate. Next to the stone head Casimiro calls Ellegua is a cigar and a tiny bottle of half-drunk Bacardi rum he sprinkles on the stone head every Monday."[120] Casimiro teaches Cepeda about the Yoruba gods he worships and about the historic diversity of spiritual practice in the Dominican Republic,[121] a diversity that includes "*los misterios*" of enslaved Muslims and Africans, the animism of the Taínos, Crypto-Judaism, and Catholicism.[122] Casimiro is open to the cross-pollination of religions because he, Maria, and their son used to be followers of Hare Krishna.[123] Casimiro possesses the ability to see the spirit guides who walk with Cepeda:

> "Ay, coño, I got goose bumps," he responds [when Cepeda enters his apartment]. "When you walked in through the door, I saw one of your guides, *un indio,* walk in behind you."
>
> "What are you talking about?" I say, looking over on the left side of the bed to see if his bottle of mamajuana and shot glass are on the floor next to his stack of books.
>
> "Raquel, I saw my *madrina de santo* today and she gave me a reading *con los caracoles*. You came up. She says you will be the one."
>
> "The *one*? Like *Moíses*?" I ask.

"The one to carry on our tradition, who will communicate with others who we really are to the world," he says. "Your guides are strong enough to carry you even if you don't recognize them now."[124]

This passage is significant because Cepeda uses it not only to signal her skepticism in *los misterios*, but also to confirm, through a disinterested third party, her long-held belief that an Indian spirit has always served as one of her guardian angels. Even though Maria, Casimiro's wife, maligns Casimiro's faith in Afro-Caribbean religion as "that *brujería mierda*,"[125] she, like him, claims to possess supernatural powers. Maria encourages the people in her orbit to heed her dreams, which she believes are prescient. Cepeda also believes in the premonitory power of her own dreams. For example, when Cepeda has a dream that she and Chris, her boyfriend at the University of Pittsburgh, are gunned down in a drive-by shooting, she decides to leave Pittsburgh and go back home to New York. Cepeda interpreted her dream as a supernatural omen.[126] Cepeda attributes the power of clairvoyance not only to Casimiro, Maria, and herself, but also to her father, Eduardo.

Years later, when Cepeda repairs her relationship with her father, she learns what she believes is the source of her premonitory powers and her ability to see, sense, and speak with the spirits of the dead.[127] Cepeda's father tells her that he was born with a caul, "una corona." Cepeda explains the supernatural significance of the caul: "Many caul bearers, spanning centuries and cultures the world over, are believed to be born clairvoyant and to possess other preternatural abilities. Dad believes his caul may be the reason he was born with 'too much vision,' resulting in the capacity to see clearly at night. His night vision triggered terrible migraines that only an operation corrected years later."[128] Her father reveals three examples of his childhood supernatural powers. First, he dreamed that neighbors would be killed in a car accident. He warned them, but they ignored him and died. Second, he wandered into a wake and revealed to the congregants that the little girl in the coffin was not dead. They took her out and she woke up several hours later. Third, Eduardo believes Babalu, the *orisha* of contagious diseases in the Santería pantheon,[129] revealed himself to him as the floating apparition of a "middle-aged peasant" accompanied by "a pair of gigantic black dogs with immaculate fur." Although Eduardo shares his three preternatural stories with Cepeda, she does not reveal to him that she believes she has the same abilities.[130] Cepeda's recounting of Eduardo's revelations encourages the readers to believe that her supernatural powers were genetically inherited.

In addition to being the inheritor of supernatural powers, Cepeda comes to believe, as Casimiro foretold, that she has a divine destiny as a leader of her people. Cepeda refers to her exceptional "kismet" three times in *Bird of Paradise*. In chapter 1, "Love, American Style," she uses kismet to characterize her mother and father's "fairy tale" union.[131] As we saw in chapter 7, "Ave Maria, Morena," Cepeda uses it to describe how Casimiro became the surrogate father who declared that she had a providential role to play in Dominican history. In chapter 18, "Becoming Latina," Cepeda uses the word kismet to describe her meeting with Rabbi Rav DovBer Pinson, the leader of the IYYUN Center for Jewish Spirituality in Brooklyn. Through Rabbi Pinson she comes to learn about the Kabbalistic concepts of *tikkun olam* and *gigul neshamot*.[132] Using an FPN allusion, Cepeda calls Rabbi Pinson "the Rakim of gigul neshamot."[133] The Rakim to whom she refers is William Michael Griffin Jr., an FPN adherent and the MC of the late 1980s rap duo Eric B. and Rakim. Cepeda becomes fascinated by the concept of *gilgul neshamot*: "Part of the process of gilgul neshamot is that every single person has a specific soul purpose consistent with his or her body. The body is the vehicle, or the medium through which we achieve our perfection, our tikkun. . . . I learn that some Kabbalistic texts speak about the soul choosing to enter into a particular set of parents, family, and environment. We can even come back in clans where our children may have been our parents in a past life, and our parents, our siblings."[134] *Gilgul neshamot* reinforces the concepts of ancestor veneration and reincarnation that inform Santería, Espiritismo, and Santerismo,[135] if not in Dominican Vudú. Like Casimiro, Rabbi Pinson confirms Cepeda's special destiny in Dominican literary and cultural history: "Therefore, the fact that you were born to Dominican parents means something," Rabbi Pinson says. "There's something that you have to contribute to that culture or to articulate in some way—ignoring that would be denying a part of who you are."[136] The invocation of *gilgul neshamot* in the final chapter is nontrivial, given that it occurs in concert with Cepeda's inadvertent discovery that she is pregnant and in her third trimester.

Cepeda's belief in her messianic destiny resonates strongly with the Afrocentric divine humanism of the FPN. Cepeda, according to the doctrine of the FPN, would be divine, or partly divine, because she is partly African. The implication, in terms of kismet, is that to whom much is given, much is required. The FPN's belief in the divinity of people of African descent was designed to bolster the self-esteem of African Americans and to encourage them to be transformative personal and community advocates. Assuming that Cepeda is earnest about her kismet and in her adoration of FPN hip hop, it is not astonishing then that she characterizes Rabbi Pinson as the Rakim Allah of genetic profiling. If this were the only such characterization, one might say that her description of Pinson is merely tongue-in-cheek, but Cepeda also uses an FPN allusion to praise Jorge Estevez,[137] an advocate of the contemporary Taíno identity movement. Dominicans, according to Estevez, can claim to be linguistic, spiritual, or cultural Taínos even if they do not have any Indigenous DNA in their genetic profile.[138] Cepeda describes Estevez as "dropping science" like a rapper when he promiscuously mixes history, genetics, physiognomy, and personal anecdotes to dissuade listeners from the myth of Taíno extinction.[139] Here, again, we see Cepeda, a hip-hop expert, using FPN vernacular as the interpretive key for translating the mysteries of genetic profiling, Jewish mysticism, and Taíno ancestral heritage to her laity.

Not surprisingly, FPN theosophical concepts can be fruitfully used to analyze and evaluate Cepeda's bewitching mix of genetics and the supernatural. In "An Awakening," the fifth chapter of her memoir, Cepeda reveals that the spirits of two female ancestors appeared to her in childhood during times of physical and emotional crisis. Cepeda calls these ancestors *la india* and *la africana*. In FPN terms, *la india* and *la africana* represent a supernatural "knowledge of self." They are two components of a uniquely Hispanic Caribbean conception of ethnic, racial, and national identity. Many people in the Hispanophone Caribbean Basin believe that their ethnoracial ambiguity is a result of the initial genetic and cultural mixing between Spaniards, Indigenous Americans, and enslaved Africans.

Cepeda devotes the second half of *Bird of Paradise* to clarifying the historical construction of her ethnoracial ambiguity and confirming the authenticity of her spirit guides by combining traditional genealogical research with the science of genetic profiling. She writes, "Maria taught me to believe in the power dreams, and Casimiro in spiritual guides and destiny, when I was still a teenager. And today, my spiritual self still identifies with the mythos, the transcendent qualities found in Jewish Kabbalah, Sufi Islam, Indigenous and West African mysticism and religion. My rational self is drawn by the potential of ancestral DNA testing—the logos—to work in tandem with the incorporeal to help us make sense of our whole selves."[140]

Cepeda's impulse to become her family's genealogist casts her in the role of what sociologist Alondra Nelson calls a "kinkeeper," a family member, typically a woman, who devotes herself "to the work of connecting past and present kin with purposeful narrative."[141] In the early 2000s, genetic profiling became cheap and accessible to the public, providing kinkeepers with a powerful tool for conducting their research. Genetic profiling companies like Family Tree DNA (2000), African Ancestry (2003), 23andMe (2006), and AfricanDNA (2009) emerged and capitalized on the public interest in personal ancestry and ethnoracial origins. In 2012, the PBS show "Finding Your Roots with Henry Louis Gates Jr." provided a further boost to the industry by combining genetic profiling with traditional genealogical research.

When Cepeda decides to discover her ethnoracial roots, she turns to Bennett Greenspan and his company Family Tree DNA, a company that presently shares its customers' genetic data with law enforcement.[142] Cepeda seeks out Greenspan years before sociologists, scientists, physicians, legal scholars, and privacy advocates began regularly sounding a note of caution about the imprecision of genetic genealogy and its fraught relationship with consumer privacy and property rights.[143] Greenspan introduces Cepeda to the esoterica of genetic profiling and becomes her interpreter of its arcana. Like FPN theosophy and Santerismo, genetic profiling is a hermetic form of "knowledge of self" in which Cepeda places a substantial amount of faith. Cepeda uses the results of Greenspan's genetic testing of her and her family members to, in FPN parlance, "show and prove" her conviction that modern day Hispanic Caribbean Latinas, like herself, are the descendants of Indigenous Caribbeans and enslaved Africans.

Cepeda spends a great deal of time focusing on the African component of her Family Tree DNA results. The DNA evidence suggests that Cepeda's father's paternal grandfather is likely descended from either the Amazigh (Berbers) of North Africa or "Neolithic farmers who migrated west to Northern Africa from Iraq until they reached Spain."[144] The maternal ancestry of Cepeda's father's paternal grandmother points to Central Africa. However, he has a "direct maternal ancestry that points to pre-Columbian indios" of Hispaniola.[145] Cepeda equates this ancient ancestor with *la india*. *La india* first appears to Cepeda a few weeks before Rocío decides to move to San Francisco with Pascal, the Haitian boyfriend who beats her: "I first saw her, a tall handsome woman with long black hair, sitting at the edge of my bed weeks before we left Seaman Avenue. She told me she belonged to me and promised to appear whenever I was scared or in danger."[146] When Pascal would beat Rocío, Cepeda would hide in the bathroom and pray to *la india* for deliverance. *La india* helped Cepeda cope with the abuse and neglect of the caregivers in her life.

The mitochondrial DNA evidence on Cepeda's maternal side suggests that her ancient maternal ancestor originated from the region in sub-Saharan Africa currently known as Guinea-Bissau. Cepeda syncretizes this ancient ancestor with *la africana*:

When I find out that our Supreme Matriarch is West African, things begin to make perfect sense. A chill runs down my spine. I will never meet this woman Rocío and I descend from in this world, but I've already encountered her in my dreams. She is *la africana*, who in different scenarios has jumped in to save me like a guardian angel. She is the same *africana* whose face I've never seen but whose body—thick legs, a tall frame, and large healing breasts, sometimes dressed like a pauper and other times in elegant long multicolored ruffled dresses—I've known since I was a little girl.[147]

La africana first appears to Cepeda in a recurring dream in which Woody Woodpecker attacks Cepeda's face and *la africana* heals the wounds by nestling Cepeda's face in her magic cleavage.[148] In subsequent chapters, Cepeda reaffirms that she encountered *la africana* only in dreams and only in childhood in times of trauma.[149] Cepeda's abusive childhood suggests that it makes sense to at least consider a psychosocial genesis for the manifestation of *la africana*, which I will come to shortly.

Cepeda attempts to validate the spiritual manifestation of *la africana* through the science of genetic profiling. Cepeda's L3d haplogroup indicates that the real *la africana* was a sub-Saharan African woman from Guinea-Bissau. The DNA results cannot determine how *la africana*'s descendants specifically arrived in the Americas. That is left up to Cepeda's active but historically grounded imagination. Was *la africana* a Christianized Black ladino brought to the New World from Spain and enslaved in Santo Domingo, Cepeda rhetorically asks? "Perhaps L3d, la africana, was one of them," she conjectures; "Or she may have migrated to the island from present-day Haiti."[150] Cepeda's blending of history, fiction, and autobiography is emblematic of the genre blending that characterizes the speculative realism of post-race ethnic writers.[151] Cepeda uses genetic profiling to confirm that the conventional divide between the scientific and the sacred is a social construct rather than a natural fact. Instead of using science to discredit "magical beliefs" and "magical behavior,"[152] Cepeda uses it to "show and prove" the reality of *la africana* and *la india*, the female ancestors who contributed to her mixed ethnicity, her Hispanic Caribbean *mestizaje*.

Cepeda finds spiritual succor in the bosoms of *la africana* and *la india*. She places more faith in her supernatural ancestors than she does in the Judeo-Christian God whom she was taught to revere in Catholic school.[153] Although Cepeda venerates *la africana*, she also associates her with the matrilineal *fukú* that plagues the women in her family.[154] The curse condemns the women to abusive romantic relationships and dysfunctional mother-daughter ones. Regarding the African origin of the curse, Cepeda says, "I imagine the woman we descend from is someone who had a *fukú* put on her by a jilted lover, a jealous woman or a diviner to whom she may not have paid a debt. I can see it clearly, how this curse between mothers and their firstborn daughters may have started with her. I broke that *maldición* by breaking away from my own mother and unloading the baggage I would have otherwise inherited."[155] For Cepeda, the *fukú* could have occurred at any number of places and times in the early modern era: "in a marketplace in pre-colonial Guinea-Bissau," or "during the Portuguese invasion" of Guinea-Bissau, or "on a cobblestone street in the colonial district of Santo Domingo."[156] In a recurring dream, Cepeda hears the voice of the "archaic hater" who cursed *la africana*: "From this day on, the women in your family, living and not yet born, will break from one another in total repulsion."[157] Cepeda's equally plausible theories of who the hater was suggest that magical powers are a generic characteristic of people of African descent, hailing the Magical Negro trope. In a 2001 lecture at Yale, Spike Lee used the phrase "magical, mystical Negro" to describe a caricature in US popular culture that depicts people of African descent as being inherently imbued with mystical wisdom and powers.[158] Lee took issue with Magical Negro characters in early twenty-first-century films because, more often than not, those characters used their powers to aid whites rather than liberate African Americans. The trouble with the Magical Negro trope, in its nonsatirical variations, is that it romanticizes people of African descent in the same fashion that the noble savage conceit romanticizes Native Americans as people who are mystically and morally exceptional. A conviction in African and Native American guardian angels and ancestors has psychological benefits, but the danger in this conviction is its potential to encourage reliance on supernatural intervention rather than on collective action against the epistemic and physical violence of racism and patriarchy.

Cepeda claims that she manages to break the African curse when she becomes a mother. In the spring of 1996, when she is twenty-three years old and working as a music publicist, Cepeda discovers that she is pregnant. When she gives birth to her first child, her daughter Djali, she is in an emotionally dysfunctional relationship with Djali's father, Monk, and suffering from postpartum depression.[159] Eduardo helps extricate Cepeda and Djali from that situation, allowing Cepeda to consciously focus on being the nurturing parent she never had. However, because she had been estranged from her mother, the *fukú* still has its grip on Cepeda when she is doing the genetic DNA testing for and writing the draft of *Bird of Paradise*. The *fukú* is finally broken, Cepeda writes, when she reaches out to Rocío to interview her for the memoir. Cepeda flies down to Orlando to deliver the news of their West African ancestry to her mother. She wonders if Rocío will "live up to the hyped-up stereotype that all of us Dominicans, here and on the island, vehemently reject and deny, deny, deny . . . our Blackness."[160]

Rocío's putative "black denial" stands in contradistinction to Cepeda's Pan-African pride. In an interview about the production of her documentary *Bling*, Cepeda says she included Puerto Rican reggaeton performer Tego Calderón in the film because he, like her, is a "Pan-Africanist who really embraced that side of their Latino heritage. Because, you know, growing up we're not taught to embrace that; we're taught to repel that. So I thought as a Latina, as a Dominican, he would be a good representative for that, for the people I want to speak to in my community."[161] As a child and young adult in the US, it was not easy for Cepeda to cultivate and sustain Pan-Africanist pride and sensibilities. Cepeda's White-passing father and Catholic school education attempted to encourage Cepeda to disparage Africa and Africanity. However, Cepeda demonstrates her commitment to Pan-Africanism not only by embracing hip hop and FPN theosophy, but also by giving considerable thematic attention to *la africana*, the initial victim of the *fukú* that generates the series of dysfunctional mother/daughter relationships in Cepeda's family tree.

As suggested above, one of many ways to interpret *la africana* and *la india* is to interpret them as psychological symptoms of childhood abuse and neglect rather than as actual supernatural entities. Recall that there is a genealogy of troubled caregiving in Cepeda's maternal and paternal lines of descent. As a child, Rocío, Cepeda's mother, had an unhealthy relationship with her own mother, Doña Dolores. Eduardo, Cepeda's father, was abused and neglected as a child, which partly explains why he physically abused Cepeda when she came to live with him in New York. As noted above, Cepeda interprets the matrilineal genealogy of dysfunctional relationships in her family as the result of a supernatural curse. Given Cepeda's reverence for science and her skepticism in the existence of supernatural entities such as God,[162] it is interesting to consider a scientific explanation for the manifestation of *la india* and *la africana*. Studies in psychology find that troubled and erratic caregiving in a child's life can result in certain forms of attachment disorder. According to the ISSD Task Force on Children and Adolescents, having a childhood imaginary friend can be one of the many symptomatic responses of children who manifest "impaired parent-child attachment patterns," patterns that originate from a history of parental neglect; however, the taskforce is careful to point out that "there is no consensus yet on the exact etiological pathway for the development of dissociative symptomatology."[163]

The dysfunctional parenting of Rocío and Eduardo makes a strong, though speculative, case for reading the childhood spirit guides in *Bird of Paradise* as symptoms of attachment disorder. For example, *la india* first appears to Cepeda not in a dream but as an apparition sitting on the edge of her bed. Attachment theory allows one to interpret *la india* as a psychological coping mechanism rather than as a manifestation of the supernatural. Because Cepeda does not blame her spirit guides for her own behavior and choices, ISSD would not consider them to be pathological symptoms. Read through the lens of attachment theory, *la india* and *la africana*, become surrogate mothers who compensate not only for the parental shortcomings of Cepeda's biological mother, Rocío, but also for those of her stepmother Alice.

A recent study on postpartum depression suggests that it may be a genetically heritable disease.[164] Given Cepeda's acknowledgement of postpartum depression, it is interesting to interpret the matrilineal *fukú* in Cepeda's family through the lens of postpartum depression.[165] What can be gained by suggesting rational explanations for the spirit guides and *fukús* in *Bird of Paradise*? Spiritual practices like prayer and meditation have tangible mental and physical benefits,[166] but relying solely on spiritual traditions to remedy illnesses and hardships has the potential to encourage a certain segment of the religious to delay or forego primary care and psychosocial support. Interpreting *la africana* and *la india* as scientifically explainable apparitions could encourage young people in unhealthy family situations and mothers suffering from postpartum depression to complement their religious faiths with clinical interventions. Interrogating magical beliefs and behavior in *Bird of Paradise* through the lens of speculative realism acknowledges the value of Afro-Caribbean spiritual practices.[167] This line of inquiry, however, also urges the faithful to seek the affordable primary and mental healthcare they deserve, prompting them to be agents of their own destinies rather than objects of supernatural forces that surpass their understanding and control.

Conclusion: The Copiousness of Latinidad and Latino Studies

Cepeda's acknowledgment of Maya Angelou and Henry Louis Gates Jr. as sources of creative inspiration and Chambers's claiming of W. E. B. Du Bois, Ann Petry, and Zora Neale Hurston as cultural ancestors bind them to the

African American literary and autobiographical tradition. This commonality is one of the many features that warrants putting these two post-soul memoirists in dialogue with each other, but there are meaningful differences between Cepeda and Chambers's post-soul Latinidad. The proliferation of FPN ideology and Afro-Caribbean religions in *Bird of Paradise* reveals that Raquel Cepeda finds an ideological home in a separatist form of Black nationalism and in a decolonial reverence for Afro-Caribbean spiritualism. In contrast, the civil rights and luck egalitarian tropes in *Mama's Girl* reveal that Veronica Chambers is drawn to integrationist and neoliberal forms of Black nationalism. Despite their differences, Chambers and Cepeda share an intersectional critique of racial essentialism, of the notion that there is only one way to be authentically Black in the US. Their intercultural affinities for Black nationalism engage elitist, demotic, *mestizaje*, and *mulatez* modalities of ethnoracial identity formation, constituting a post-soul Latinidad that alternately embraces and rejects the "cultural mulatto" trope as the defining signifier of the post-soul condition.[168] Ultimately, Chambers and Cepeda's post-soul engagements with the antipodes of Black nationalism complicate and expand what it means to be and become Latina, underscoring the copiousness of Latinidad and the commensurability between Latino and African American studies.

Coda

Literary Nationalism, Postrace Aesthetics, and Comparative Latino Literary Studies

What fascinates me about Latino, Afro-Latino, and African American studies right now are the similarities and differences in how they have responded to the multicultural, multiracial, decolonial, transnational, postrace, and post-soul turns.[1] During the first decades of the twenty-first century, scholars and cultural critics in African American studies have been preoccupied with the post-soul/post-black condition, questioning what it means to be African American in an America transformed by desegregation and the fourth great migration.[2] With the interrogation of African American social life came the questioning of the existence of African American literature and how African American literary history should be conducted.[3] Over the course of the same period, scholars in Latino literary and cultural studies published a host of anthologies on Latino literature and the Latino condition.[4] They produced studies that compared Latino authors to non-Latino writers,[5] studies that explored hegemonic conceptions of the Latino body in American literature,[6] and studies that compared Latino authors to other Latino authors of the same and of differing ethnonational backgrounds.[7] Although cultural studies on Latinidad, and its ethnonational varieties, are abundant,[8] scholars are increasingly turning their attention to Afro-Latino history, literature, and culture. A coterie of scholars have produced monographs affirming the African contribution to Hispanic Caribbean Latinidades and forthrightly addressing the anti-Black racism in their disciplines and communities.[9] Latino cultural studies witnessed the publication of monographs exclusively devoted to Afro-Latino and African American relations,[10] whereas Latino literary studies witnessed the publication of monographs focused on US Afro-Latino literature as well as the literature of the Afro-Hispanic Atlantic.[11] *The Afro-Latino Memoir* is my contribution to the Afroethnic turn in Latino studies.

What can an African American cultural studies framework reveal about Afro-Latino life writing? What can we learn about Afro-Latinidad by studying its African American influences? How does the Afro-Latino memoir articulate the relationship between Black nationalism and Latinidad? Is the Afro-Latino memoir transcanonical? Does it destabilize the notion of Latino and African American literature as separate but equal canons? Do the ethnoracial particularities, transnational cultural elements, and liberal individualist tropes of the Afro-Latino memoir challenge or promote the American Dream? These are questions I sought to answer in this study by focusing on literary interculturalism in contemporary Afro-Latino coming-of-age memoirs. As I have shown, Afro-Latinos use African American narrative strategies, cultural tropes, and political ideologies to write themselves into the archive of US literary history in ways that require us to expand and redefine conventional notions of Latino and African American subjectivity. In becoming connoisseurs of our shared history of literary interculturalism, Latinos and African Americans can increase our chances of improving civic engagement, social cohesion, and intercultural solidarity in and between our two communities.

What is the Afro-Latino memoir's relationship to American literary nationalism, the postrace aesthetic, and the interethnic trend in comparative Latino literary studies? Concerns about US literature's cohesiveness and about the moral legitimacy of nationalism as a critical category of social analysis and belonging coalesce in long-standing debates about the merits of American literary nationalism. Historians of American literature observe that detractors of literary nationalism seek to liberate US literature and literary theory from the parochial specter of provincialism through interpretive heuristics that promote either universalism or transnationalism.[12] These concerns are not new. Harry Hayden Clark, in 1933, argued that the proponents of universalism, paradoxically, demonstrate their loyalty to and security in American literary nationalism in their efforts to transcend it.[13] Lawrence Buell, defending transnationalism in 2013, reaches a similar conclusion, suggesting "for the Americanist field-imaginary to continue to question the coherence and distinctiveness of national culture and national literary history and to continue to concentrate more of its energies on the connecting links between national culture and the rest of the world seems fruitful, pragmatic, proper—and also, one might add, safe."[14] Despite the intellectual merits and professional exigencies of interrogating American literary nationalism, Andrew Delbanco reminds us that "the work of redefining, and thereby sustaining, American literature has always been mainly carried on by writers who aspire to become part of it, not by professors who dismiss its validity or doubt its existence."[15] That the Afro-Latino memoir writers in this study take the existence of US literature and the sociopolitical utility of cultural nationalism for granted is evidenced in their acknowledgment of the constitutive aesthetic and political influence that African

American literature and Black nationalism had on their development as writers, activists, and community organizers.[16]

African American influences in Latino literary and cultural history are more common than we often imagine. During the long New Negro Renaissance, Arthur A. Schomburg developed deep relationships with John Edward Bruce, Alain Locke, and African American cultural institutions and fraternal organizations.[17] In the 1930s, Nicolás Guillén developed a relationship with Langston Hughes.[18] These relationships are well-known, but other equally compelling intercultural relationships and intertextual influences were unstudied, especially in the case of Afro-Latina memoirists. Recognizing autobiography as both a mode and a genre,[19] I chose to investigate these influences in the Afro-Latino bildung memoir because of its ostensible commitment to historical fact and veracity. Scholars in Latino studies acknowledge the preeminence of autobiographical narratives and the obsession with life writing in Latino literature. Silvio Torres-Saillant contends that autobiography is "the most important form in Latino literature" because it best captures the separate but equal multiculturalist impulse that constitutes the Latino condition.[20] David J. Vázquez finds Latino writers to be "almost obsessive" in their preoccupation with "autobiographical forms" and the trope of the self.[21] The obsessive focus on the construction and emergence of the self draws Latino authors to the bildungsroman, a narrative genre/mode that is defined by its concern with self-fashioning and identity formation.[22] Chicano studies scholar Ramón Saldívar contends that the bildungsroman is a constituent element of "historical fantasy" and "speculative realism," the narrative genres and modes that typify the "postrace" social poetics of contemporary ethnic American literature.[23] Despite life writing's plenitude and pride of place in Latino literature, a critical and exclusive study of the Afro-Latino memoir had yet to be written.

Changing the lens on a microscope, or changing the type of microscope one uses, can help one understand one's object of study in new ways. The same is true of the conceptual tools in literary and cultural studies. Applying an African American cultural studies lens to Afro-Latino memoirs yields new and significant insights about Afro-Latino identity formation and about the intersections of Latino and African American literary history and political mobilization. The Black Arts Movement, for example, had an indelible influence on Chicano and Nuyorican literary nationalism. In his cultural history of the Black Arts Movement, James Smethurst verifies that Black cultural nationalism "strongly inflected" Nuyorican literature and "left an enormous mark on the framing and forms of Chicano movement literature."[24] Like Torres-Saillant, Smethurst maintains that the desire to be simultaneously a part of and a part from the American cultural imaginary typifies Latino literary nationalism.[25] Regarding the relationship between Latino literary nationalism and the trope of the self, Smethurst notes that the autobiographical impulse shapes the prison and street life focused poetry of Nuyorican and Chicano poets, the former more so than the latter.[26] Piri Thomas notwithstanding, the racial uplift, political activist, and upward social mobility narratives in *The Afro-Latino Memoir* diversify the portrait of the Latino autobiographical tradition. Afro-Latino memoirs are productive sites for the comparative analysis of African American and Latino literary interculturalism because they deal with the shared pleasures and paradigmatic pains of being racialized as Black in the US. However, a combination of racial, ethnic, and disciplinary chauvinism in Latino, African American, and life writing studies has, to date, undeservedly marginalized the Afro-Latino memoir. This is the gap I addressed by putting Piri Thomas's critically acclaimed, best-selling, and oft-anthologized *Down These Mean Streets* in conversation with lesser-known, but equally compelling, contemporary Afro-Latino memoirs.

The contemporary Afro-Latino memoir is a rich archive of Latino and African American literary interculturalism because of its relationship to American literary nationalism, the transnational imaginary, and the postrace aesthetic. Buell sees a synergy between American literary nationalism and the US ethnic bildungsroman. Mindful of Bakhtin's definition of the bildungsroman as a biographical or autobiographical novel of "emergence," Buell argues that contemporary American literature owes its exceptional charisma to its cultivation of the emergence trope in its ethnic bildungsromans. In his discussion of the constitutive relationship between transnationalism, ethnic American literature, and American exceptionalism, Buell writes that the American Dream "may tilt either toward the materialistic or the idealistic, with different weightings attached to character and luck, or to self-generated initiative as against luck and collaboration, to untrammeled individual autonomy as goal as against communal participation as goal."[27] Oscillating between these two antipodes, the Afro-Latino memoir, with its preoccupation with self-determination, liberal individualism, cultural assimilation, community accountability, upward social mobility, and intraracial interculturalism, is a paradigmatic avatar of the American Dream.

Life writing, Latino, and African American studies must pay more attention to the Afro-Latino memoir, if one believes, as does Buell, that the sheer existence of the US ethnic bildungsroman not only reproduces but also critiques the American Dream. This tension between critique and promotion speaks to Saldívar's contention that a "postrace aesthetic" and "transnational imaginary" characterize the contemporary US ethnic novel, which is often written as a bildungsroman. Saldívar began making a case for the postrace aesthetic and the transnational imaginary in 2011, two years into Barack Obama's presidency and two years before the advent of the Black Lives Matter movement. As Saldívar reminds us, his use of the term postrace does not signify that racism in the post-civil rights US ended because America elected its first Black president. Like the proponents of critical race theory, Saldívar concedes that racism is structural, if not permanent. Saldívar uses postrace "under erasure and with full ironic force" to signify that race, in our multiracial/multiethnic contemporary moment, is understood less as a biological quality than it is as a social process and construction. Race, he contends, is "a complex set of personal and social actions, a structure of *doing*, by which race is enacted and racial injustice perpetuated."[28] Four principles constitute Saldívar's postrace aesthetic: (1) a postmodernist investment in formal and stylistic experimentation that defies literary convention and classification, (2) a commitment to the mixing of genres and a social awareness of their historicity, (3) a predilection for "speculative realism," defined as "a hybrid crossing of the fictional modes of the speculative genres, naturalism, social realism, surrealism, magical realism, 'dirty' realism, and metaphysical realism," and (4) a critically informed focus on the meanings of race in a contemporary America that is increasingly multiracial and multiethnic.[29] To make his case for the postrace aesthetic, Saldívar performs a close reading of Colson Whitehead's zombie apocalypse novel *Zone One*, classifying it as an ironically parabasic "memoir of a future America in ruins." Whitehead, Saldívar contends, "proposes that it may well be necessary first to imagine the end of the world before we may imagine the historical end of racialization and racism."[30] The COVID-19 pandemic has undermined the old sci-fi trope that a global catastrophe can be the harbinger of, or the habitus for, a postracial reality.

Although Saldívar's transnational imaginary is a borderlands concept that he originated in his Chicano studies scholarship,[31] he applies it to Oscar de León, the first-generation, Dominican-American protagonist of *The Brief Wondrous Life of Oscar Wao*, the Afro-Latino bildungsroman by Junot Díaz. One must understand Saldívar's concept of the "Postrace Generation" to understand the transnational imaginary's relationship to Afro-Latino bildung narratives. Saldívar defines "postrace, postblack, postethnic writers" as ethnic minority authors who were "born for the most part in the post-civil rights era."[32] Although Saldívar includes African American authors "Colson Whitehead, Percival Everett, Darieck Scott, and Touré" in his list of postracial writers,[33] it is essential to note that the term postrace, for Saldívar, explicitly means that discussions of US race relations are no longer reducible to a Du Boisian Black/White racial dualism.[34] The postrace turn includes literature by Asian, Native, and Latino Americans, as well as other ethnic minority groups. Buell, by and large, concurs. Focusing on the international success of the American bildungsroman as his object of study, Buell argues that the contemporary ethnic minority coming of age narrative is more distinctive of "the national cultural imaginary" than Benjamin Franklin's autobiography because its narrative of personal agency and social recognition renders the possibility and the fulfillment of social change.[35] In short, the contemporary ethnic bildungsroman tends to promote American literary nationalism even as it interrogates and indicts America's dispossession and subordination of non-White ethnic minorities.

Wanting to move beyond "restrictive nationalisms," postrace authors, argues Saldívar, are preoccupied with exploring the "new versions of the self," "new forms of identify," and "new cultural and political worlds."[36] Because they come from communities whose histories and cultures have been marginalized, distorted, or erased by and in the American popular imagination, postrace writers, contends Saldívar, gravitate toward "historical fantasy," of which the bildungsroman is a constituent element. Postrace writers, "in order to remain true to ethnic literature's utopian allegiance to social justice," says Saldívar, link history, fantasy, and the "transnational imaginary" in their social poetics.[37] The transnational imaginary is a way of, a context for, and a framework for interpreting Latino expressive culture through a hemispheric lens that is historically and intersectionally attuned to the "dialectics of political, racial, and gender forms on the border."[38] Beyond the border, the transnational imaginary is the social, cultural, and political matrix that emerges from the contact of "multinational populations across nation-states."[39] Given its concern with heroic self-transformation, it makes sense that postrace writers turn to the bildungsroman when exploring desires for, access to, or denial of the American Dream. In terms of periodization and ideological opposition to restrictive forms of cultural nationalism, Saldívar's concept of postrace aesthetics overlaps with the literary nationalism of the New Black Aesthetic, an archive of literary and cultural analysis with which Latino studies tends not to engage.

As mentioned in the introduction, the New Black Aesthetic emerged as a critical category of analysis and aesthetic ideology in the late 1980s, styling itself as a socially progressive corrective to those elements of the Black Aesthetic that placed the most restrictions on liberal individualism. Using the "cultural mulatto" as his master trope, Trey Ellis coined the term New Black Aesthetic to describe the social and ideological hybridity that defines the nature and goal of Black expressive culture in the postsegregation era.[40] The New Black Aesthetic emerged at the same time that Gloria Anzaldúa introduced the "new mestiza" concept to Chicano and Latino studies.[41] Ellis and Anzaldúa value hybridity's capacity to render hegemonic concepts of cultural purity, quiddity, and haecceity inert. The post-soul/post-black aesthetic, the name under which the New Black Aesthetic currently travels,[42] overlaps with Salídvar's postrace transnational imaginary because of their shared investment in cultural *mestizaje* as a desideratum. In his explication of Oscar de León's transnationality, Saldívar argues that Junot Díaz configures *mestizaje* as the reification of fantasy and the fantastic. As an avatar of the fantastic, *mestizaje* comes to signify the transcendence of convention, restraint, and reality, holding out the subaltern's potential to redeem, if not destroy, hegemonic moral and social hierarchies.[43]

As a scholar of African American and Ugandan descent who holds an MFA in Creative Writing, I am sympathetic to the implicit and explicit liberal individualist arguments that postrace and post-soul/post-black advocates make in defending the case for ideological freedom and aesthetic autonomy. However, as a scholar who is committed to the perpetuation of Africana studies and the demise of White supremacy's agenda of cultural, political, and socioeconomic hegemony, I am, equally, if not more, sympathetic to what Vázquez calls the "socially embedded subjectivities" of "community efficacy,"[44] by which he means the political activism and community organizing of the "aggrieved." Vázquez insists that Latino life writing contests "liberal individualist notions of identity and their accompanying racial formations" as well as "dichotomous categorical identity."[45] Weary of the risk of essentializing Latino life writing, Vázquez, acknowledges that "many Latina/o authors align themselves with doctrines of assimilation and liberal individualism"; he, however, chooses to exclusively focus on texts that "affirm the communal as a basic aspect of discursive resistance."[46] The Afro-Latino memoir, in all of its formal, stylistic, and political heterogeneity, is often a significant site of what Vázquez calls "insurgent nationalism," forms of Latino cultural nationalism that oppose the state rather than support it.[47] There is great value in investigating texts that are sociopolitically homogeneous, and there is equal value in examining the ideological continuities and ruptures in the diversity of political commitments in Afro-Latino life writing.

I concur with Vázquez that in embracing the transnational turn in literary and cultural studies we need not abandon cultural nationalism, especially given the formative role it plays in politically mobilizing and shaping the collective identities of aggrieved Afroethnic communities in the US and the hemisphere. It is important to recall that Arthur A. Schomburg and Nicolás Guillén embodied the entanglement of Puerto Rican and Cuban nationalism with Black cultural nationalism in the US. As Agustin Laó-Montez, Juan Flores, Miriam Jiménez Román, Jesse Hoffnung-Garskof, Vanessa Valdés, and Yomaira Figueroa-Vásquez, among others, have shown, transnationalism and cultural nationalism have never been mutually exclusive for Afro-Latinidad.[48] As I have demonstrated in this study, this is no less true of Piri Thomas, Marta Moreno Vega, and Raquel Cepeda. It is vital to recall that in their extraliterary lives Thomas, Vega, and Cepeda were transnationally engaged with Latino and Afro-descendant communities in the US, the Caribbean, and Africa. When Thomas was composing *Down These Mean Streets*, he spent two of those five years in Rio Piedras, Puerto Rico working as an assistant in a drug rehabilitation program run by Dr. Efrén Ramírez in the Hospital of Psychiatry.[49] Thomas and Ramírez hosted, *The Voice of a New Race*, a weekly radio show to address drug addiction among youth on the island.[50] Marta Moreno Vega founded the Frank H. Williams Caribbean Cultural Center African Diaspora Institute, codirected the Global Initiative of Afro Latin and Caribbean Organizations (GALCI), planned and conducted the first International Conference on Orisha Tradition and Culture in Ife, Nigeria, and trained as an Afrocentrist scholar under the direction of Dr. Molefe Kete Asante in the Africology and African American Studies program at Temple University.[51] Raquel Cepeda's work as a documentary filmmaker took her to Sierra Leone to expose US hip-hop artists to the history behind blood diamonds, and it took her to the Dominican Republic to examine how combining ancestral DNA profiling and cultural heritage tourism might prevent suicide in teenage Latinas from the Bronx.[52] Carlos Moore's entire memoir is a portrait of his life as an insurgent activist in the US, the Caribbean, Europe, Africa, and Latin America. The decolonial intersection of insurgent nationalism and hemispheric Black nationalisms in Afro-Latino life writing deserves much more attention than it has currently received from scholars in Latino and African American studies.

In her award-winning book *Chicana/o and Latina/o Fiction: The New Memory of Latinidad*, Ylce Irizarry issues a call for more comparative research on the internal complexities of the disparate ethnoracial groups which constitute the US Hispanic-descended population. Unlike Saldívar's postrace focus on comparing the relationships between contemporary Chicano, Latino, and Anglo-American literature,[53] Irizarry, like Vázquez and Yolanda Martínez-San-Miguel, finds value in comparative Latino literary studies.[54] I concur with Irizarry's claim that comparative literary studies of the cultural, social, and political convergences and divergences within and among writers from disparate Latino communities best illuminate how and why they use Latinidad, insurgent nationalism, mestiza/border consciousness, and other strategies of refusal to respond to liberal multiculturalism's "illusory promises of ethnic integration."[55] They use these strategies, writes Irizarry, to reject "the Crèvecoeurian melting pot . . . rhetoric of arrival."[56] I agree with Irizarry that for postwar Latinos "arrival means success without losing cultural specificity. It means being recognized not only as American but also as Chicana/o or Latina/o."[57] To examine the relationship between arrival, ethnonationalism, and intersectionality in contemporary Chicano and Latino literature, Irizarry developed a trope that she calls the "narrative of fracture." The narrative of fracture is the conceptual tool Irizarry uses to analyze "resistance to gender, race, and class hierarchy."[58] She uses narrative fracture to examine colorism, essentialist ethnonational identity formations, and representations of the Civil Rights movement and the American Dream in Latino literature. Narrative fracture speaks to why and how individuals reject fixed conceptions of ethnic identity and ideologically restrictive notions of panethnic solidarity.[59] The memoirs in this study perform Irizarry's conceptualization of arrival and illustrate her narrative of fracture trope.

The Afro-Latino Memoir, in bringing together memoirists who have ethnonational roots in Cuba, Puerto Rico, Panama, and the Dominican Republic, answers Irizarry's call "to contribute to the growing corpus of comparative Latina/o literary studies,"[60] but it does so by focusing on marginalized Afro-Latino writers. The Afro-Latino Memoir examines the complexities of Afro-Latinidad as represented by authors from different ethnonational groups, different age cohorts, and different ideological persuasions. Although it comparatively examines Afro-Latinidad among Latinos and Afro-Latinos, it offers the additional benefit of examining the intraracial ties that bind Afro-Latinos and African Americans in entangled solidarities of insurgent and Black nationalism. By revealing the literary histories and intercultural influences between African Americans and Afro-Latinos, The Afro-Latino Memoir builds interdisciplinary bridges between African American and Latino studies and contributes new and significant insights about the African American influences in Latino literary and cultural history.

Notes

Introduction

1. Ramirez and de la Cruz, "The Hispanic Population in the United States: March 2002"; McKinnon, "The Black Population in the United States: March 2002." The historical actor categories for ethnicity and race in the US change over time and vary within and among the communities and institutions that employ them. For consistency, I tend to use the terms Hispanic, Latino, Afro-Latino, Black, African American, and White as the US Census Bureau and the Pew Research Center use them. I use the term Latino to denote people of Latin American and/or Hispanic Caribbean descent living outside of Latin America and/or the Hispanic Caribbean. My use of the terms Hispanic, Latino, and their orthographic variants is equally informed by the self-identification practices of the authors in my study, the etymological history of the concepts, usage trends, and orthographic debates in the Hispanophone and Anglophone worlds, and scholarly theories concerning the utility and efficacy of the terms as panethnic categories of cultural analysis. For more on these histories, theories, practices, usage trends, and orthographic debates, see, Mignolo, *The Idea of Latin America*; Gutiérrez, "What's in a Name: The History and Politics of Hispanic and Latino Panethnicities"; Padilla, *Latino Ethnic Consciousness*; Flores, "'Qué Assimilated, Brother, Yo Soy Asimilao': The Structuring of Puerto Rican Identity in the U.S."; Noriega and López, *The Ethnic Eye Latino Media Arts*; Oboler, *Ethnic Labels, Latino Lives*; Luis, *Dance between Two Cultures*; Dávila, "Culture in the Battlefront"; Oboler and Dzidzienyo, *Neither Enemies Nor Friends*; Caminero-Santangelo, *On Latinidad*; Martinez, "Identity (Latino/a vs. Hispanic)"; Dávila, *Latinos, Inc.*; Oboler, "Disposable Strangers: Mexican Americans, Latinxs, and the Ethnic Label 'Hispanic' in the Twenty-First Century"; Cohn, "Census History"; Brown, "The Changing Categories the U.S. Census Has Used to Measure Race"; Hernández, "Latino Anti-Black Bias and the Census Categorization of Latinos: Race, Ethnicity, or Other?"; US Census Bureau, "Hispanic Origin"; US Census Bureau, "Why We Ask about . . . Hispanic or Latino Origin"; Noe-Bustamante, Mora, and Lopez, "About One-in-Four U.S. Hispanics Have Heard of Latinx, but Just 3% Use It"; Guerra and Orbea, "The Argument against the Use of the Term 'Latinx'"; Scharrón-del Río and Aja, "The Case FOR 'Latinx'"; Almo, "The X-Ing of Language"; Allatson, "From 'Latinidad' to 'Latinid@des'"; Milian, "Extremely Latin, XOXO"; Hernandez, "The Case against 'Latinx'"; Torres, "Latinx?"; Cantaño, "The RAE Has Made Its Decision about Latinx and Latine in Its First Style Manual"; Vidal-Ortiz and Martínez, "Latinx Thoughts"; Trujillo-Pagán, "Crossed Out by LatinX"; Morales, *Latinx*; de León, "Another Hot Take on the Term 'Latinx'"; "Latinx"; "'Latinx' and Gender Inclusivity"; "Latine"; "Latinx, n. and Adj."; Milian, "LatinX Studies"; McWhorter, "Why Latinx Can't Catch On"; Mochkofsky, "Who Are You Calling Latinx?"; Meraji,

"'Hispanic,' 'Latino,' Or 'Latinx'?"; Paz, "Another Problem for Latinx"; "Why Latinx/e?"; afrolatin@forum, "Why Does the Afrolatin@ Forum Use the '@' Symbol in Its Name?"; Zamora, "Transnational Renderings of Negro/a/x/*"; López Oro, "Garifunizando Ambas Américas"; Figueroa-Vásquez, Decolonizing Diasporas; López Oro, "Refashioning Afro-Latinidad: Garifuna New Yorkers in Diaspora."

2. US Census Bureau, "Race and Ethnicity in the United States." I use the terms Black and African American to denote descendants of Africans enslaved in the US as well as US immigrants of African descent and their descendants. When it is necessary to qualify the ethnonational roots of specific groups of Blacks/African Americans, I do so as the contextual need arises. For more on the history of African American panethnic labels and ethnic diversity, see "Leaders Say Blacks Want To Be Called 'African-Americans'"; Wilkerson, "'African-American' Favored by Many of America's Blacks"; Rustin, "Blacks?"; Martin, "From Negro to Black to African American"; Bennett Jr., "What's in a Name?: Negro vs. Afro-American vs. Black"; Gates Jr. and Burton, "The Question of Naming"; Gates Jr. and Burton, "The Question of Naming: Redux"; Saad, "Gallup Vault: Black Americans' Preferred Racial Label"; Tamir, "The Growing Diversity of Black America"; Tamir, "Key Findings About Black America"; Tamir et al., "Facts about the U.S. Black Population."

3. George, Post-Soul Nation; George, Buppies, B-Boys, Baps & Bohos.

4. I provide a detailed history and definition of the post-soul concept in the fourth section of the Introduction. I revisit the concept in chapter 3, chapter 4, and the Coda.

5. "Smart Black People."

6. López and Gonzalez-Barrera, "Afro-Latino."

7. Tamir, "The Growing Diversity of Black America."

8. Jones-Correa, "Commonalities, Competition, and Linked Fate"; Freer and Sandoval Lopez, "Black, Brown, Young, and Together"; Jones, "Blackness, Latinidad, and Minority Linked Fate."

9. I use the term Afro-Latino to denote Latin American and/or Hispanic Caribbean people of African descent living outside of Latin America and/or the Hispanic Caribbean. Scholars coined the term Afro-Latino to recognize the social and historical specificity of Afro-Latino culture within the larger concept of Latinidad, see Flores, "Triple Consciousness? Afro-Latinos on the Color Line"; Flores, "Triple Consciousness?"; Laó-Montes, "Afro-Latinidades and the Diasporic Imaginary"; Oboler and Dzidzienyo, Neither Enemies nor Friends; Laó-Montes, "Afro-Latinidades: Bridging Blackness and Latinidad"; Laó-Montes, "Decolonial Moves: Trans-Locating African Diaspora Spaces"; Flores and Jiménez Román, "Triple-Consciousness?," November 2009; Jiménez Román and Flores, The Afro-Latin@ Reader; Torres-Saillant, "Afro-Latinas/os and the Racial Wall"; Latorre, "Afro-Latino/a Identities"; Luis, "Afro-Latino/a Literature and Identity"; Rivera-Rideau, Jones, and Paschel, "Introduction"; Rivera-Rideau, Jones, and Paschel, Afro-Latin@s in Movement. Although the term "blacktino," and its variants, describes (1) Afro-Latinos, (2) people of mixed Latino and African American heritage, and (3) the histories of social, cultural, and political intimacies between Latinos and African Americans, I do not use the term because it can blur meaningful distinctions between the three categories it seeks to define, see Johnson and Rivera-Servera, Blacktino Queer Performance, 3–5.

10. Although Latinidad is a Spanish language term, I choose not to italicize it or produce it in lowercase. I use the term Latinidad, and its variants, to denote the cultural features, social practices, and geopolitical histories that distinguish Latin America from North America and Latinos from other US ethnic groups. For more on the theory of this concept, see Padilla, *Latino Ethnic Consciousness*; Noriega and López, *The Ethnic Eye Latino Media Arts*; Aparicio and Chávez-Silverman, *Tropicalizations*; Caminero-Santangelo, *On Latinidad*; Mignolo, *The Idea of Latin America*; Caminero-Santangelo, "Latinidad"; Allatson, "From 'Latinidad' to 'Latinid@des'"; Jones, "Blackness, Latinidad, and Minority Linked Fate."

11. Jiménez Román and Flores, *The Afro-Latin@ Reader*, 6.

12. Mirabal, "The Afro-Cuban Community in Ybor City and Tampa, 1886–1910"; Greenbaum, *More than Black*; Mirabal, "Diasporas." I use the term Caribbean to denote the geo-cultural area, which is comprised of (1) the islands within and adjacent to the Caribbean Basin and (2) the Central and South American coastal regions of the Caribbean Basin. In other words, my use of the term Caribbean is equivalent to the term Circum-Caribbean. For more on the conventional understandings of the Circum-Caribbean, see Torres-Saillant, *An Intellectual History of the Caribbean*, 12; Palmié and Scarano, *The Caribbean*, 2 and 26; Foote, *The Caribbean History Reader*, x. I use the term Hispanic Caribbean to denote the Hispanophone territories, countries, and cultural areas in the Caribbean that formerly belonged to Spain. For more on the concept of the Hispanic Caribbean, see Pérez-Rosario, "On the Hispanophone Caribbean Question"; Torres-Saillant, "The Hispanic Caribbean Question"; Ferrer, "History and the Idea of Hispanic Caribbean Studies"; Lomas, "Translation and Transculturation in the New York–Hispanic Caribbean Borderlands"; Duany, *Blurred Borders*. For work that centers Haiti's constitutive role in the idea of the Hispanic Caribbean, see Suárez, *The Tears of Hispaniola*; Myers, *Mapping Hispaniola*; Valdés, *Racialized Visions*.

13. Mirabal, *Suspect Freedoms*, 14–15 and 58.

14. Mirabal, *Suspect Freedoms*; Hoffnung-Garskof, *Racial Migrations*.

15. Duany, *Blurred Borders*.

16. In 1970, in the middle of the Black Power Movement, *Negro Digest* changed its name to *Black World*. For a complete history of this transformation, see Fenderson, *Building the Black Arts Movement*, 1–5.

17. Maeroff, "Book Ban Splits a Queens School District"; "Book Ban Is Eased by Queens Board"; *Presidents Council v. Community School Board*, 457 F.2d; "Long Island School Board Bans Three Black Books"; *Pico v. Island Trees*, 474 F. Supp.; *Pico v. Island Trees*, 638 F.2d; *Island Trees v. Pico*, 638 F.2d.

18. I use Gerard Genette's definition of intertextuality as opposed to Julia Kristeva's, see Genette, *Palimpsests*, 1–3 and Kristeva, *Desire in Language*, 15 and 36–38.

19. Rivera-Rideau, Jones, and Paschel, "Introduction," 5.

20. Rivera-Rideau, Jones, and Paschel, 14.

21. On Schomburg, see Helton and Zafar, "Arturo Alfonso Schomburg in The Twenty-First Century: A Special Issue"; Hoffnung-Garskof, *Racial Migrations*; Valdés, *Diasporic Blackness*; James, "The Peculiarities of Afro-Hispanic Radicalism in the United States: The Political Trajectories of Arturo Schomburg and Jesus Colon"; Sinnette,

Arthur Alfonso Schomburg, Black Bibliophile & Collector. On Guillén, see Ellis, *Cuba's Nicolás Guillén*; Ellis, "Images of Black People in the Poetry of Nicolás Guillén"; Ellis, "Nicolás Guillén and Langston Hughes: Convergences and Divergences"; Williams, *Self and Society in the Poetry of Nicolás Guillén*; Smart, *Nicolás Guillén, Popular Poet of the Caribbean*; Kutzinski, "Re-Reading Nicolás Guillén"; Kutzinski, *Against the American Grain*; Kutzinski, "Fearful Asymmetries"; Kutzinski, *The Worlds of Langston Hughes*. On Thomas, see Sandin, *Killing Spanish*; López, *Unbecoming Blackness: The Diaspora Cultures of Afro-Cuban America*; Vázquez, *Triangulations*; Caminero-Santangelo, *On Latinidad*; Sánchez, *"Shakin' Up" Race and Gender*, 2005; Gonzalez, *Boricua Literature*; Mohr, *The Nuyorican Experience*. On Grillo, see Milian, *Latining America*; López, *Unbecoming Blackness*; Guridy, *Forging Diaspora*; Dzidzienyo, "Coming to Terms with the African Connection in Latino Studies."

22. Noticeably absent from this list is Evelio Grillo, author of the memoir *Black Cuban, Black American* (2000). Initially, I intended the first chapter of this study to be a chapter on Grillo's memoir. To properly tell the story I want to tell about *Black Cuban, Black American*, I had hoped to visit some archives and access Grillo's privately held papers, but the COVID-19 pandemic limited my capacity to do some of the archival research I had hoped to conduct for this project in general.

23. Stepto, *From Behind the Veil*, 66–68 and 167–68.

24. Stepto, 66 and 167–68.

25. Stepto, 167.

26. Berlin, *The Making of African America*; Greer, *Black Ethnics Race, Immigration, and the Pursuit of the American Dream*; Smith, *Black Mosaic*.

27. Berlin, "Global Passages."

28. Crawford, *What Is African American Literature?*; Warren, *What Was African American Literature?*; Jarrett, *Representing the Race*; Ernest, *Chaotic Justice Rethinking African American Literary History*; Stepto, *From Behind the Veil*.

29. Shelby, *We Who Are Dark*; Van Deburg, *Modern Black Nationalism*; Moses, *The Golden Age of Black Nationalism, 1850–1925*; Bracey Jr., Meier, and Rudwick, *Black Nationalism in America*.

30. Smethurst, *The Black Arts Movement*. In addition to Smethurst, I am also indebted to the following scholars and their works: Collins and Crawford, *New Thoughts on the Black Arts Movement*; Avilez, *Radical Aesthetics and Modern Black Nationalism*; Moten, *In the Break*; Gayle, *The Black Aesthetic*.

31. Tate, "Cult-Nats Meet Freaky-Deke: The Return of the Black Aesthetic"; Ellis, "The New Black Aesthetic"; Ellis, "Response to NBA Critiques"; George, *Buppies, B-Boys, Baps & Bohos*; Golden, "Post . . ."; Neal, *Soul Babies*; George, *Post-Soul Nation*; Dickerson, *The End of Blackness*; Golden, *Thelma Golden by Glen Ligon*; Ashe, "Theorizing the Post-Soul Aesthetic"; Taylor, "Post-Black, Old Black"; Womack, *Post Black*; Touré, *Who's Afraid of Post-Blackness?*; Maus and Donahue, *Post-Soul Satire*; Baker and Simmons, *The Trouble with Post-Blackness*; Murray, *Queering Post-Black Art*; Crawford, *Black Post-Blackness*; Ashe and Saal, "Introduction"; Lordi, "From Soul to Post-Soul: A Literary and Musical History."

32. Hoffnung-Garskof, *Racial Migrations*; Valdés, *Diasporic Blackness*; Mirabal, *Suspect Freedoms*; Milian, *Latining America*; López, *Unbecoming Blackness*; Guridy,

Forging Diaspora; Mirabal and Lao-Montes, *Technofuturos*; Laó-Montes, "Afro-Latinidades: Bridging Blackness and Latinidad"; Laó-Montes, "Afro-Latinidades and the Diasporic Imaginary"; Sánchez, *"Shakin' Up" Race and Gender*, 2005; Oboler and Dzidzienyo, *Neither Enemies nor Friends*; Flores, *From Bomba to Hip-Hop*; Brock and Castañeda Fuertes, *Between Race and Empire*; Flores, *Divided Borders*.

33. Ortiz, *Latinx Literature Now*; Roguez, *Latinx Literature Unbound*; Richardson, *The Afro-Latin@ Experience in Contemporary American Literature and Culture*; Irizarry, *Chicana/o and Latina/o Fiction*; Machado Sáez, *Market Aesthetics*; Vázquez, *Triangulations*; Caminero-Santangelo, *On Latinidad*; Dalleo and Machado Sáez, *The Latino/a Canon and the Emergence of Post-Sixties Literature*; Sánchez, *"Shakin' Up" Race and Gender*, 2005; Nwankwo, "Reading U. S. Latina Writers"; Gonzalez, *Boricua Literature*; Jackson, *Black Writers and Latin America*; Luis, *Dance between Two Cultures*; Stavans, *Growing Up Latino: Memoirs and Stories*; Mohr, *The Nuyorican Experience*.

34. Couser, *Memoir*; Yagoda, *Memoir*; Smith and Watson, *Reading Autobiography*; Eakin, *Living Autobiographically*; Couser, *Vulnerable Subjects*; Eakin, *The Ethics of Life Writing*; Gilmore, *The Limits of Autobiography*; Olney, *Memory and Narrative*; Lejeune, *On Autobiography*.

35. Cantú, "Memoir, Autobiography, Testimonio"; Torres-Saillant, "The Latino Authobiography"; Torres, "The Construction of the Self in U.S. Latina Autobiographies"; Mostern, *Autobiography and Black Identity Politics*; Andrews, *African-American Autobiography*; Dudley, *My Father's Shadow*; Braxton, *Black Women Writing Autobiography*; Andrews, *To Tell a Free Story*; Butterfield, *Black Autobiography in America*.

36. Latinez, *Developments: Encounters of Formation in the Latin American and Hispanic/Latino Bildungsroman.*; Bolaki, *Unsettling the Bildungsroman*; Japtok, *Growing Up Ethnic*; Jeffers, *Apprenticeships the Bildungsroman from Goethe to Santayana*; Kester, *Writing the Subject*; LeSeur, *Ten Is the Age of Darkness*.

37. Lejeune, *On Autobiography*.

38. Yagoda, *Memoir*; Couser, *Memoir*; Smith and Watson, *Reading Autobiography*; Couser, *Vulnerable Subjects*; Eakin, *The Ethics of Life Writing*.

39. Torres-Saillant, "The Latino Authobiography," 64 and 61.

40. Stavans, *Growing Up Latino: Memoirs and Stories*; Torres, "The Construction of the Self in U.S. Latina Autobiographies"; Torres-Saillant, "The Latino Autobiography"; Cantú, "Memoir, Autobiography, Testimonio"; Dúran, "Latina/o Life Writing"; Borland, "Memoirs."

41. Couser, *Memoir*, 15.

42. Couser, 15.

43. Couser, 17.

44. Couser, 16.

45. Redfield, *Phantom Formations: Aesthetic Ideology and the "Bildungsroman."*

46. Alden, *Social Mobility in the English Bildungsroman*, 1.

47. Jeffers, *Apprenticeships: The Bildungsroman from Goethe to Santayana*, 2.

48. Kester, *Writing the Subject*, 8.

49. Bolaki, *Unsettling the Bildungsroman*, 21.

50. Kester, *Writing the Subject*, 7–8.

51. Jeffers, *Apprenticeships: The Bildungsroman from Goethe to Santayana*, 4.

52. Bolaki, *Unsettling the Bildungsroman*, 12.

53. Cocalis, "The Transformation of 'Bildung' from an Image to an Ideal," 400.

54. Cocalis, 400.

55. Cocalis, 400.

56. Cocalis, 401.

57. Cocalis, 401.

58. Cocalis, 402.

59. Slaughter, "Clef à Roman: Some Uses of Hu."

60. Jeffers, *Apprenticeships: The Bildungsroman from Goethe to Santayana*, 2.

61. Kester, *Writing the Subject*, 51.

62. Jeffers, *Apprenticeships: The Bildungsroman from Goethe to Santayana*, 7.

63. "They either don't have fathers alive or they have fathers who are tyrannical or feckless. In any case, the boys don't have fathers able to show them, with authority, the way to manhood, and in consequence they are driven now to depend on their mothers, a symbiosis finally less mutualistic than parasitic, and now reach out to older males who might stand in for the absent, or absently present, fathers," see Jeffers, 188.

64. "There are studies available on the Latino/Latina, the Asian American, the African American, the cross-culturally female, and the so forth *Bildungsroman*, and my own purposes have seemed ambitious enough without trying to compass those occasionally heuristic though often overspecialized and hyphenated subsets. And in any event, youthful white males have come to seem like the segment of our society that one needs to worry about, and precisely because they constitute a large segment that—often fatherless, guilt-heaped, and feeling undervalued—tests lower, goes to college less often, and gets into legal trouble more than white females do," see Jeffers, 7.

65. LeSeur, *Ten Is the Age of Darkness*, 5.

66. Bolaki, *Unsettling the Bildungsroman*, 23.

67. Bolaki, 23.

68. Bolaki, 25.

69. Bolaki, 24.

70. Bolaki, 23.

71. Here I am thinking specifically of Evelio Grillo's memoir *Black Cuban, Black American*.

72. "For the writers I study here, autobiography's project—to tell the story of one's life—appears to constrain self-representation through its almost legalistic definition of truth telling, its anxiety about invention, and its preference for the literal and verifiable, even in the presence of some ambiguity about those criteria. . . . Yet conventions about truth telling, salutary as they are, can be inimical to the ways in which some writers bring trauma stories into language. . . . When the contest is over who can tell the truth, the risk of being accused of lying (or malingering, or inflating, or whining) threatens the writer into continued silence. . . . These departures offer an opportunity to calibrate our attention to the range of demands made by autobiography and the silencing or shaming effects they impose," see Gilmore, *The Limits of Autobiography*, 3. For a more recent account on the relationship between public scrutiny, veracity, and the autobiographical genre of *testimonio*, see Ortiz, *Latinx Literature Now*.

73. Gilmore, *The Limits of Autobiography*, 4.

74. Bolaki, *Unsettling the Bildungsroman*, 11.

75. Bolaki, 13.

76. Jeffers, *Apprenticeships: The Bildungsroman from Goethe to Santayana*, 6.

77. Mostern, *Autobiography and Black Identity Politics*, 10.

78. Mostern, 11.

79. Kester, *Writing the Subject*, 16.

80. Kester, 47.

81. Latinez, *Developments: Encounters of Formation in the Latin American and Hispanic/Latino Bildungsroman*, 11.

82. Latinez, 2.

83. Latinez, 3.

84. Pérez, *Cuba in the American Imagination Metaphor and the Imperial Ethos*.

85. "Development remains intriguing and puzzling for its permanent presence in Latin American and in the Hispanic/Latino literatures and cultures; it defines an essential characteristic of these works as narratives of *becoming*. In the stories, the condition of becoming does not allow a closure of the process of 'bild'; it seals the narratives with open endings. If the growth toward maturity implies a final stage of becoming a citizen of a modern nation, the permanence of uncertainties and anxieties about identity and national goals indicates that the Latin American and Hispanic/Latino narrative of formation challenges the outcome of the process, see Latinez, *Developments: Encounters of Formation in the Latin American and Hispanic/Latino Bildungsroman*, 82–83.

86. Couser, *Memoir*, 41.

87. "Depicting the journey from youth to maturity, a classic Bildungsroman concentrates on a protagonist striving to reconcile individual aspirations with the demands of social conformity. The narrative offers privileged access to the psychological development of a central character whose sense of self is in flux, paralleling personal concerns with prevailing values. The Bildungsroman's ability to explore the relationship between self and society accounts for its lasting global appeal," see Graham, *A History of the Bildungsroman*, 1.

88. Bakhtin, "The Bildungsroman and Its Significance in the History of Realism (Toward a Historical Typology of the Novel)," 19.

89. Bakhtin, 22.

90. Bakhtin, 23.

91. Bakhtin, 21 and 25.

92. Graham, *A History of the Bildungsroman*, 117.

93. Graham, 6.

94. Jauss, "Literary History as a Challenge to Literary Theory," 12; Jauss, *Aesthetic Experience and Literary Hermeneutics*; Jauss, *Toward an Aesthetic of Reception*.

95. Lejeune, *On Autobiography*.

96. Gramsci, "Justification of Autobiography," 132.

97. Flores, "'Qué Assimilated, Brother, Yo Soy Asimilao': The Structuring of Puerto Rican Identity in the U.S.," 187–88.

98. Flores, 189.

99. Cohn, "Census History."

100. Gutiérrez, "What's in a Name: The History and Politics of Hispanic and Latino Panethnicities," 34.

101. In terms of italics, capitalization, hyphenation, and suffixes, my orthographic choices for these ethnoracial identifiers are situational, see note 1.

102. "Afro-Latin-American, Adj."; "Afro-Latin, Adj." It is interesting to note that in a 1927 letter to Alain Locke, Jane Nardal of Martinique used the term Afro-Latin to describe herself, troubling contemporary notions of Latin as an exclusively Hispano-phone category, see Edwards, *The Practice of Diaspora*, 16.

103. "Cuban intellectual Fernando Ortiz wrote about an Afrocuban culture in 1904 and by the 1930s was one of the founders of the *Asociacion de Estudios Afrocubanos*. In Mexico an *Instituto de Estudios Afroramericanos* was organized in the early 1940s and published a short-lived magazine called *Afroamerica*," see Laó-Montes, "Decolonial Moves: Trans-Locating African Diaspora Spaces," 322.

104. Luis, "Editor's Note," 5.

105. Dzidzienyo, "Activity and Inactivity in the Politics of Afro-Latin America"; Fontaine, "Research in the Political Economy of Afro-Latin America."

106. Torres-Saillant, "Inventing the Race"; Hernández, "'Too Black to Be Latino/a'"; Dzidzienyo, "Coming to Terms with the African Connection in Latino Studies"; Laó-Montes, "Afro-Latinidades and the Diasporic Imaginary"; Laó-Montes, "Afro-Latinidades: Bridging Blackness and Latinidad"; Laó-Montes, "Decolonial Moves: Trans-Locating African Diaspora Spaces."

107. Caminero-Santangelo, *On Latinidad*, 1–35. Recent studies on what constitutes Latinidad and Latino literature turn to the philosophy of literature, the philosophy of history, and genre theory to answer these questions, see Ortiz, *Latinx Literature Now*; Rodriquez, *Latinx Literature Unbound*.

108. Laó-Montes, "Afro-Latinidades and the Diasporic Imaginary"; Laó-Montes, "Afro-Latinidades: Bridging Blackness and Latinidad."

109. Laó-Montes, "Afro-Latinidades: Bridging Blackness and Latinidad," 125–26. For more recent scholarship that explores Afro-Latinidad's marginalization in Africana critical theory, see Rivera-Rideau, "If I Were You"; Figueroa-Vásquez, *Decolonizing Diasporas*.

110. Flores and Jiménez Román, "Triple-Consciousness?," 320.

111. Torres-Saillant, "The Tribulations of Blackness," 1102–9. For formal definitions of *mestizaje, mulatez, mulataje*, and *mulatería*, see Pérez-Torres, "Mestizaje"; Allatson, "Mestizo/a, Mestizaje"; Ortega-Aponte, "Mulatez"; Allatson, "Mulato/a, Mulatez"; Asociación de Academias de la Lengua Española, "mulataje"; Asociación de Academias de la Lengua Española, "mulatería"; Buscaglia-Salgado, *Undoing Empire*.

112. Torres-Saillant, "Afro-Latinas/os and the Racial Wall," 365.

113. Flores and Jiménez Román, "Triple-Consciousness?"

114. Jiménez Román and Flores, *The Afro-Latin@ Reader*, 1.

115. Luis, "Afro-Latino/a Literature and Identity," 34.

116. Gates Jr. and Burton, "The Question of Naming," 86–87. For additional discussion of this topic, see Gates Jr. and Burton, "The Question of Naming: Redux."

117. Power-Greene, *Against Wind and Tide*.

118. Domingo, "What Are We, Negroes or Colored People?"; Bennett Jr., "What's in a Name?: Negro vs. Afro-American vs. Black"; Rustin, "Blacks?"; Hanchard, "Identity, Meaning and the African-American."

119. Domingo, "What Are We, Negroes or Colored People?"; Moore, *The Name "Negro"*; Appiah, "The Case for Capitalizing the 'B' in Black"; Cooperman, "Capitalizing 'Black'"; Craven, "What It Means That the Associated Press Is Capitalizing 'Black'"; Izadi, "Why Hundreds of American Newsrooms Have Started Capitalizing the 'b' in 'Black'"; Sun-Times Staff, "To Our Readers."

120. On the virtues and vices of pan-ethnic terminology and categories, see Bennett Jr., "What's in a Name?: Negro vs. Afro-American vs. Black"; Caminero-Santangelo, *On Latinidad*, 1–35; Milian, "Extremely Latin, XOXO."

121. Berlin, *The Making of African America*.

122. Greer, *Black Ethnics Race, Immigration, and the Pursuit of the American Dream*, 43.

123. Greer, 7.

124. Greer, 43.

125. Greer, 52.

126. Zamora, "Transnational Renderings of *Negro/a/x/*"; Figueroa-Vásquez, *Decolonizing Diasporas*; Rivera-Rideau, "If I Were You."

127. Jiménez Román, "Real Unity for Afro-Latinos and African Americans."

128. Kutzinski, "Afro-Hispanic American Literature."

129. Luis, "Latin American (Hispanic Caribbean) Literature Written in the United States," 526.

130. Luis, 526 and 527.

131. For recent theories about the conceptual utility and scope of the Hispanic Caribbean, see Pérez-Rosario, "On the Hispanophone Caribbean Question"; Torres-Saillant, "The Hispanic Caribbean Question"; Valdés, *Racialized Visions*.

132. Luis, "Latin American (Hispanic Caribbean) Literature Written in the United States," 527.

133. Hernández, "Louis Reyes Rivera," 131.

134. Esdaille, "Same Trip, Different Ships."

135. Milian, *Latining America*, 1.

136. Milian, 2 and 1.

137. Ernest, *Chaotic Justice Rethinking African American Literary History*, 2 and 10.

138. Ernest, 28.

139. Ernest, 5 and 4–5.

140. Jarrett, *Representing the Race*, 14.

141. Warren, *What Was African American Literature?*, 5.

142. Warren, 2.

143. Warren, 8.

144. Crawford, *What Is African American Literature?*, 8.

145. Crawford, 19 and 20.

146. Crawford, 22.

147. Crawford, 2, 5, and 13.

148. Crawford, 103.

149. Crawford, 104.

150. Chude-Sokei, "Foreign Negro Flash Agents: Eric Walrond and the Discrepancies of Diaspora"; Davis, *Eric Walrond*; Walrond, *In Search of Asylum*.

151. Luis, "Latin American (Hispanic Caribbean) Literature Written in the United States," 532.

152. Gates and Smith, 913.

153. Gates and Smith, 914.

154. Gates and Smith, 914 and 915.

155. Gates and Smith, 923.

156. Melamed, *Represent and Destroy*; Antonsich et al., "Interculturalism versus Multiculturalism: The Cantle-Modood Debate"; Bouchard, "What Is Interculturalism?"; Cantle, "National Identity, Plurality and Interculturalism"; Cantle, *Interculturalism*; Raab and Greiffenstern, *Interculturalism in North America*; Sexton, *Amalgamation Schemes*.

157. Golden, "Post . . ."; Golden, Thelma Golden by Glen Ligon.

158. Ashe and Saal, "Introduction," 7.

159. Golden, "Post . . ."; Neal, *Soul Babies*, 2002; George, *Post-Soul Nation*; Grant, *Post-Soul Black Cinema*; Dickerson, *The End of Blackness*; Mukherjee, *The Racial Order of Things*; Ashe, "Theorizing the Post-Soul Aesthetic," January 12, 2007; Taylor, "Post-Black, Old Black"; Haggins, *Laughing Mad the Black Comic Persona in Post-Soul America*; Womack, *Post Black*; Touré, *Who's Afraid of Post-Blackness?*; Kennedy, "The Fallacy of Touré's Post-Blackness Theory"; Royster, *Sounding Like a No-No?*; Maus and Donahue, *Post-Soul Satire*; Robinson, *This Ain't Chicago*; Baker and Simmons, *The Trouble with Post-Blackness*; Lieber, "Being Afraid of 'Post-Blackness': What's Neoliberalism Got to Do with It?"; Murray, *Queering Post-Black Art*; Crawford, *Black Post-Blackness*; Lordi, "From Soul to Post-Soul: A Literary and Musical History."

160. Ellis, "The New Black Aesthetic"; Ashe, "Theorizing the Post-Soul Aesthetic"; Ashe, "These Are the 'Breaks': A Roundtable Discussion on Teaching the Post-Soul Aesthetic"; Touré, *Who's Afraid of Post-Blackness?*; Murray, *Queering Post-Black Art*.

161. Tate, "Cult-Nats Meet Freaky-Deke: The Return of the Black Aesthetic"; Ellis, "The New Black Aesthetic"; Neal, *Soul Babies*, 2002; George, *Post-Soul Nation*; Touré, *Who's Afraid of Post-Blackness?*

162. Ashe, "Theorizing the Post-Soul Aesthetic"; Ashe, "These Are the 'Breaks': A Roundtable Discussion on Teaching the Post-Soul Aesthetic"; Maus and Donahue, *Post-Soul Satire*; Ashe and Saal, "Introduction."

163. Dickerson, introduction to *The End of Blackness*, 3–26; Womack, introduction to *Post Black*, 1–28.

164. Kennedy, "The Fallacy of Touré's Post-Blackness Theory."

165. Simmons, introduction to *The Trouble with Post-Blackness*, 1–20.

166. Crawford, *Black Post-Blackness*.

167. Lordi, "From Soul to Post-Soul: A Literary and Musical History," 38 and 42.

168. Tate, "Cult-Nats Meet Freaky-Deke: The Return of the Black Aesthetic"; Ellis, "The New Black Aesthetic"; Ellis, "Response to NBA Critiques"; Ashe, "Theorizing the Post-Soul Aesthetic"; Royster, *Sounding Like a No-No?*

169. Lordi, "From Soul to Post-Soul: A Literary and Musical History," 41.

170. Dickerson, *The End of Blackness*, 259.

171. Vásquez, "Television Satire in the Black Americas: Transnational Border Crossings in Chappelle's Show and The Ity and Fancy Cat Show."

172. Royster, *Sounding Like a No-No?*

173. "Smart Black People."

174. Hereafter, I refer to Vega's memoir as *WSDM*.

175. Vega's concept, though essentialist, is similar to Gilroy's concept of the Black Atlantic and Figueroa-Vasquez's concept of the Afro-Atlantic, see Gilroy, *The Black Atlantic*; Figueroa-Vásquez, *Decolonizing Diasporas*.

Chapter One

1. The symbolic geography of Thomas being born in Harlem Hospital is rich because the hospital is situated across the street from the Schomburg Center for Research in Black Culture.

2. The neighborhood known as Spanish Harlem acquired that name at the end of World War I. After the wave of Puerto Rican migration spurred by Operation Bootstrap in 1947, Spanish Harlem increasingly became known as El Barrio. For an overview of the history, character, and boundaries of Spanish Harlem, see Federal Writers' Project, "Spanish Harlem."

3. *Manchild in the Promised Land* (Claude Brown, 1965), *The Autobiography of Malcolm X* (1965), *Soul on Ice* (Eldridge Cleaver, 1968), *Coming of Age in Mississippi* (Anne Moody, 1968), *Die, Nigger Die!* (H. Rap Brown, 1969), *I Know Why the Caged Bird Sings* (Maya Angelou, 1970), and *Angela Davis* (1974).

4. Aldich, "Inside the Skin"; Maddox, "The Knuckle-Hard Code of the Barrio"; Jackson, "Culture or Color? The Moyetos of San Juan and New York"; Shockley, "Two Books with Soul"; Stern, "In the Arms of Lady Snow"; Cordasco, "Down These Mean Streets"; Killens, "On El Barrio and Piri Thomas"; Taylor, "Thomas, Piri."

5. Thomas, "An Interview with Piri Thomas," 72.

6. Dudley, "Piri Thomas," 728.

7. Dudley, "Piri Thomas," 728.

8. Dudley to Masiki, "Piri Thomas Entry in the Oxford Companion to African American Literature," October 16, 2019.

9. Andrews to Masiki, "Piri Thomas Entry in the Oxford Companion to African American Literature," November 13, 2019.

10. Luis, "Editor's Note."

11. Exceptions to this silence include a book review, two articles, and a reprint of one of the two articles, see Shockley, "Two Books with Soul"; Reid-Pharr, "Tearing the Goat's Flesh"; Blake, "What Does It Mean to Be Black?: Gendered Redefinitions of Interethnic Solidarity in Piri Thomas's *Down These Mean Streets*."

12. Blake, "What Does It Mean to Be Black"; Martínez-San Miguel, "Ethnic Specularities"; Martínez-San Miguel, "Négropolitains and Nuyorícans: Metropolitan Racialization in Frantz Fanon and Piri Thomas"; López, *Unbecoming Blackness*; Cruz-Malavé, "The Antifoundational Foundational Fiction of Piri Thomas (1928–2011)"; Caminero-Santangelo, *On Latinidad*.

13. Luis, *Dance between Two Cultures*; Sánchez González, *Boricua Literature*; Vázquez, *Triangulations*; Martínez-San Miguel, "Ethnic Specularities."

14. Ellison, *Shadow and Act*, 140 and 162.

15. Luis, *Dance Between Two Cultures*, 139.

16. Thomas, "An Interview with Piri Thomas"; Thomas, "'They Have Forced Us to Be Universal': Interview with Piri Thomas"; Thomas, "Race and Mercy." In prison, Thomas also read Ralph Ellison's *Invisible Man*, see Thomas, "Piri Thomas." Thomas erroneously claims to have read Killens's *And Then We Heard the Thunder* (1962) and *Black Man's Burden* (1965) while he was in prison, see Thomas, "A Conversation with Piri Thomas." In the same way that it did for Malcolm X, Etheridge Knight, and Chester Himes, prison became a site of education for Thomas, a site of reading and writing, see Malcolm X, *The Autobiography of Malcolm X*; Collins, *Understanding Etheridge Knight*, 6, 8, 22; Anaporte-Easton, "Etheridge Knight," 942; Rowell and Knight, "An Interview with Etheridge Knight," 977; Jackson, *Chester B. Himes*, 92; Margolies, *The Several Lives of Chester Himes*, 35–36. Although *Youngblood* is a novel and *Down These Mean Streets* is a memoir, future source studies research on these two texts should consider the stark contrast between Killen's heroic representations of women and Thomas's misogynistic treatment of the real women in his autobiography. Additionally, future research could explore how Killen's addressed the topic of gender and sexuality in his conception of the Black Aesthetic.

17. Thomas, "Race and Mercy," 350.

18. Thomas, "Piri Thomas on Writing: Excerpts from an Interview," 547.

19. Thomas, "An Interview with Piri Thomas," 71.

20. Thomas, "A Talk with Piri Thomas," 46; Thomas, "An Interview with Piri Thomas," 71.

21. Thomas, "An Interview with Piri Thomas," 71; Thomas, "They Have Forced Us to Be Universal"; Thomas, "Piri Thomas," 80.

22. Rabinowitz, *Unrepentant Leftist*, 164.

23. Thomas, "A Talk with Piri Thomas"; Rabinowitz, *Unrepentant Leftist*, 164. Thomas tells the story of how he used the money to buy a silver-blue Chevy and wrote the memoir in the car, see Thomas, "Piri Thomas on Writing: Excerpts from an Interview," 547.

24. Thomas, "Piri Thomas on Writing: Excerpts from an Interview"; Thomas, "An Interview with Piri Thomas."

25. Hatch and Shine, "Lonne Elder III (1931–)"; Frye, "Elder, Lonne, III."

26. Thomas, "An Interview with Piri Thomas," 73; Thomas, "A Conversation with Piri Thomas," 180.

27. Thomas, "An Interview with Piri Thomas," 73.

28. Thomas, 74; Hernández, "Louis Reyes Rivera," 131.

29. Thomas, "A Conversation with Piri Thomas," 180.

30. Thomas, 180.

31. *The Black Arts Movement*, 129.

32. Smethurst, 26.

33. Dolinar, *The Black Cultural Front*, 63.

34. Caldwell, "Leading the Protest."

35. Smethurst, *The Black Arts Movement*, 26–29 and 36–38.

36. Gilyard, *John Oliver Killens*, 231.

37. Killens, "On El Barrio and Piri Thomas."

38. Baker, "The American Society of African Culture"; McLymont, "The American Society of African Culture"; Wilford, "The American Society of African Culture: The CIA and Transnational Networks of African Diaspora Intellectuals in the Cold War"; Geerlings, "Performances in the Theatre of the Cold War."

39. Wilder, *The French Imperial Nation-State*; Rabaka, *Africana Critical Theory*; Rabaka, *The Negritude Movement*.

40. U.S. Department of Education, "What Is an HBCU?"

41. "Ideology in the Writers' Conferences" in *Liberation Memories*.

42. Gilyard, *John Oliver Killens*, 238–39.

43. "TV Highlights"; "Day's Highlights"; Gould, "TV Review."

44. *The World of Piri Thomas*.

45. Gilyard, *John Oliver Killens*, 240.

46. For biographies of the poet Nikki Giovanni, see Fowler, *Nikki Giovanni*, 2013; Fowler, *Nikki Giovanni*, 1992.

47. Gilyard, *John Oliver Killens*, 246.

48. See the description on the Kislak Center Banks Collection's online finding aid, "The National Conference of Afro-American Writers."

49. "Ideology in the Writers' Conferences" in *Liberation Memories*.

50. Cuban students began attending Tuskegee in 1898 while Puerto Ricans began attending in 1901. Cuban students began attending Hampton at least as early as 1907, if not before, see Guridy, *Forging Diaspora*.

51. Stanley Cyrus, Henry Richards, and Ian Smart founded the journal *Afro-Hispanic Review* at Howard in 1982, see Luis, "Editor's Note." The late Miriam DeCosta Willis, one of the key figures in the development of Afro-Hispanic literary studies, was an associate editor of *Afro-Hispanic Review*. DeCosta Willis, editor of *Blacks in Hispanic Literature: Critical Essays* (1977), taught Spanish at Howard from 1970 to 1976, serving as chair of the Spanish Department from 1974 to 1976, see "Miriam DeCosta-Willis."

52. Parks, "On Images and Control: The National Black Writers Convention."

53. Thomas is featured or mentioned in *The Crisis* ten times between 1968 and 1980 and seven times in *Negro Digest/Black World* between 1968 and 1976. In 1970, in the middle of the Black Power Movement, *Negro Digest* changed its name to *Black World*, reflecting the intense ideological debates over nomenclature, over the transition from Negro, to Black, and eventually to African American. For more on the history of the journal's name change, see Fenderson, *Building the Black Arts Movement*, 1–5. Thomas is featured three times in *Jet*: once in connection with Ossie Davis's film company and twice about the censorship of his book in New York. Thomas is featured six times in *Ebony*: five times in advertisements for *Streets* in 1968 and once in 1978 in an article on how to escape the ghetto.

54. *Presidents Council v. Community School Board*, 457 F.2d; "Minarcini v. Strongville"; *Pico v. Island Trees*, 474 F. Supp.; *Pico v. Island Trees*, 638 F.2d; *Island Trees v. Pico*, 638 F.2d.

55. Riordan, "Scriptotherapy"; Henke, *Shattered Subjects*; Bolton et al., *Writing Cures*; Hunsaker Hawkins, "Writing about Illness: Therapy? Or Testimony?"; Chidiac, "On Writing Therapy. From Finding Forrester to Imre Kertész."

56. Henke, *Shattered Subjects*, xii.

57. Hunsaker Hawkins, "Writing about Illness," 124.

58. Thomas, "They Have Forced Us to Be Universal."

59. Thomas, "They Have Forced Us to Be Universal."

60. Thomas.

61. Thomas, "Race and Mercy," 353.

62. Herman, *Trauma and Recovery*, 62.

63. Hunsaker Hawkins, "Writing about Illness," 123.

64. Hunsaker Hawkins, 127.

65. Gilmore, *The Limits of Autobiography*, 49; Couser, *Memoir*, 83.

66. Thomas, "Piri Thomas," 82–83 and 85.

67. Riolli and Savicki, "Coping Effectiveness and Coping Diversity under Traumatic Stress"; Garrick, "The Humor of Trauma Survivors: Its Application in a Therapeutic Milieu"; Lipman, *Laughter in Hell*, 19–21.

68. Thomas, *Down These Mean Streets*, 110, 121, 128, and 133. Thomas mentions his use of the dozens in his interview with Hernández, see Thomas, "They Have Forced Us to Be Universal."

69. Chimezie, "The Dozens," 401.

70. Jordan, "Social Construction as Tradition"; Lefever, "Playing the Dozens"; Abrahams, "Playing the Dozens."

71. Mitchell-Kernan, "Signifying and Marking: Two Afro-Americans Speech Acts," 152. For additional definitions of signifying, see Gates, *The Signifying Monkey*; Watkins, *On the Real Side*, 64; Tucker, *Furiously Funny*, 258.

72. Thomas, *Down These Mean Streets*, 189.

73. In 2014, I presented this argument in a paper at the 28th Annual MELUS Conference. For discussions of the African American tropes in *Down These Mean Streets*, see Caminero-Santangelo, *On Latinidad*; Carpio, "Now Check It: Junot Diaz's Wondrous Spanglish"; Perez, "Racial Spills and Disfigured Faces in Piri Thomas's *Down These Mean Streets* and Junot Diaz's 'Ysrael'"; Sánchez; and Vázquez, *Triangulations*. For a comparison of Junot Díaz to Piri Thomas, see Carpio, "Now Check It: Junot Diaz's Wondrous Spanglish"; Perez, "Racial Spills and Disfigured Faces in Piri Thomas's *Down These Mean Streets* and Junot Diaz's 'Ysrael'"; and Torres-Saillant.

74. Stepto, *From Behind the Veil*, 66–67.

75. Moyeto is a corrupt spelling of the Puerto Rican slang term "molleto," which is a "black person or anyone with very dark skin, generally not muscular," see Stephens, 158.

76. Stephens, "Indio Claro"; Stephens, "Indio Oscuro"; Wing, "Indio Claro o Oscuro?"; Howard, *Coloring the Nation*; Robles, "Black Denial"; Simmons, *Reconstructing Racial Identity and the African Past in the Dominican Republic*.

77. Thomas, *Down These Mean Streets*, 144.

78. Thomas, 145.

79. The original Indigenous peoples of Puerto Rico were the Taínos.

80. Thomas, *Down These Mean Streets*, 145.

81. Caminero-Santangelo, *On Latinidad*, 60–61. Although this whitening strategy appears in the memoirs of Afro-Puerto Rican and Afro-Cuban writers like Piri Thomas and Carlos Moore, it is also associated with the racial discourse of the Dominican Republic, where the terms *indio claro* and *indio oscuro* were used as euphemisms for Afro-Dominicans, see Stephens, "Indio Claro"; Stephens, "Indio Oscuro"; Wing, "Indio Claro o Oscuro?"; Robles, "Black Denial."

82. Flores and Jiménez Román, "Triple-Consciousness?," 82.

83. López, *Unbecoming Blackness*, 145.

84. Thomas, *Down These Mean Streets*, 120.

85. Thomas, 120.

86. Thomas, 123.

87. On the Hegelian notion of "national character," see Eze, *Race and the Enlightenment*, 110–12.

88. Pickering, *Stereotyping*, 94 and 95–96.

89. Litwack, *Trouble in Mind*, 9.

90. Litwack, 10 and 9.

91. "Baldwin v. Buckley Debate."

92. Sánchez, *"Shakin' Up" Race and Gender*, 42.

93. Thomas, *Down These Mean Streets*, 170.

94. Thomas, 170.

95. Thomas, 173–74.

96. Thomas, 177.

97. Caminero-Santangelo, *On Latinidad*, 54.

98. Caminero-Santangelo, 59.

99. See Elkin's *Slavery: A Problem in American Institutional and Intellectual Life*.

100. Genovese and Fox-Genovese, *Fatal Self-Deception*, 145.

101. Thomas, *Down These Mean Streets*, 126.

102. Thomas, 122.

103. Cha-Jua, "Beyond the Rape Myth: Black Resistance to Lynching, 1867–1930."

104. Thomas, *Down These Mean Streets*, 122.

105. Thomas, 124.

106. Thomas, 126.

107. Thomas, 126.

108. Thomas, 126.

109. Davies, "Ethnic Jokes, Moral Values and Social Boundaries," 384.

110. Thomas, *Down These Mean Streets*, 133.

111. Thomas, "Piri Thomas," 83.

112. Weaver, "The 'Other' Laughs Back," 39.

113. Weaver, "Jokes, Rhetoric and Embodied Racism," 414.

114. *The Game of Humor*, 84. Gruner goes on to write, "Davies suggests that black cowardice jokes may have been begun by southern whites to make fun of the blacks who had to remain at their most humble and meek around white folks who would otherwise lynch them or burn them out of their meager homes. He also implies that a large number of "black cowardice" jokes that came into being shortly after World War I

were prompted by the perception of some that black soldiers in the war showed less courage than did whites (which the evidence does not widely support); and that the high percentage of blacks assigned to 'work' or 'service' units (as opposed to combat units such as rifle companies) compared to that of whites may have been a partial cause. At any rate, there exist many jokes featuring the fearful black man, ready to run at the slightest glimmer of physical danger. For years this comic script was exercised and reinforced in American films by the antics of the black character actor 'Stepin' Fetchit'" (85).

115. Rappoport, *Punchlines*, xiii.

116. Rahman, "An Ay for and Ah," 89.

117. Rappoport, *Punchlines*, 2.

118. Rappoport, 7.

119. Norrick, "Issues in Conversational Joking"; Norrick, *Conversational Joking*, 148–50.

120. Thomas, *Down These Mean Streets*, 127.

121. I rely on Pratt's definition of black humor: "Black humor involves the humorous treatment of what is grotesque, morbid, or terrifying. And while it bitterly ridicules institutions, value systems, and traditions, black humor offers neither explicit nor implicit proposals for improving, reforming, or changing the painful realities on which it focuses," see Pratt, *Black Humor*, xix.

122. Thomas, *Down These Mean Streets*, 187.

123. Thomas, 187.

124. Thomas, 188.

125. Thomas, 188.

126. Thomas, 188.

127. Thomas, 189.

128. Sánchez, *"Shakin' Up" Race and Gender*, 42.

129. *Down These Mean Streets*, 188.

130. Thomas, "An Interview with Piri Thomas," 68.

131. Wiggins, "Black Folktales in the Novels of John O. Killens," 52.

132. Killens, *Youngblood*, 239.

133. Killens, 239.

134. Thomas, *Down These Mean Streets*, 183.

135. Thomas, 184.

136. Thomas, 184–85.

137. Aparicio and Chávez-Silverman, *Tropicalizations*, 8.

138. Shelby, *We Who Are Dark*.

Chapter Two

1. On Afro-Cuban's support for the Batista regime, see Andrews, *Afro-Latin America, 1800–2000*, 161–62.

2. Though not covered in this chapter, it is important to mention that Moore clandestinely escapes from Cuba in November 1963, fleeing racial oppression and political persecution.

3. "Pichón: Race and Revolution in Castro's Cuba: A Memoir," September 1, 2008; "Pichón: Revolution and Racism in Castro's Cuba: A Memoir, September 1, 2008"; "Pichón: Race and Revolution in Castro's Cuba: A Memoir," November 1, 2008; "Pichón: Race and Revolution in Castro's Cuba: A Memoir," February 2009; "Pichón: Race and Revolution in Castro's Cuba: A Memoir," April 2009. Jelly-Schapiro, "An Empire of Vice"; According to Moore, the word *pichón* denotes black vultures, but it is used as a racial slur for people of African descent.

4. Mišković, Fischer-Tiné, and Boškovska Leimgruber, *The Non-Aligned Movement and the Cold War*.

5. The Supreme Court case Brown v. Board of Education was decided in 1954.

6. The first African country to win independence in the postwar era was Eritrea, in 1947. Libya won independence in 1951, Sudan in 1956, Tunisia in 1956, Morocco in 1956, and Ghana in 1957.

7. On the nature of the SWP, see Gosse, *Rethinking the New Left*, 25. On the nature of the FPCC, see Gosse, 59–61; Gosse, "The Cuban Revolution and the New Left"; Gosse, *Where the Boys Are*. On the nature of the OGFF, see Smethurst, *The Black Arts Movement*, 118–19.

8. Moore, *Pichón*, 143–48.

9. Moore, 135.

10. Moore, 153.

11. Fraser, "Lewis Michaux," 92, Dies; Ran Bookstore in Harlem"; "Michaux, Lewis H."

12. A *piolo* is Cuban term for a Black person who only associates with White people. A *jorocón* is a "street fighter with the biggest balls," see Moore, *Pichón*, 115 and 17.

13. Angelou, "foreword to *Pichón*," ix.

14. "Riot in Gallery Halts U.N. Debate."

15. Smethurst, *The Black Arts Movement*, 118.

16. Smethurst, 118; Caldwell, "Leading the Protest."

17. Angelou, *The Heart of a Woman*, 168.

18. *The Black Arts Movement*, 118.

19. Angelou, *The Heart of a Woman*, 168–77.

20. Moore confirms Angelou's account, saying he repeatedly used his U.N. pass to get demonstrators, in batches of ten, inside the U.N., see Moore, *Pichón*, 153.

21. Angelou, *The Heart of a Woman*, 190 and 182.

22. Moore, *Pichón*, 155.

23. Srivastava, *Secularism in the Postcolonial Indian Novel*, 175.

24. Johansen, "Imagining the Global and the Rural: Rural Cosmopolitanism in Sharon Butala's The Garden of Eden and Amitav Ghosh's The Hungry Tide," 2 and 3.

25. Moore, *Pichón*, 120.

26. Ortiz, *Cuban Counterpoint*.

27. García-Peña, *Translating Blackness*, 4.

28. García-Peña, 5 and 225. For an African American studies definition and view of hegemonic blackness, see Crawford, *What Is African American Literature?*, 112.

29. Moore, "Frozen Fear," chapter 27; "Roots (Biography of Carlos Moore)"; "Carlos Moore Biography."

30. García-Peña, *Translating Blackness*, 5, 19, 23, and 26.

31. García-Peña, 2.

32. Figueroa-Vásquez, *Decolonizing Diasporas*, 2.

33. Glissant, *Poetics of Relation*, 29–30 and 159.

34. Crawford, *What Is African American Literature?*, 104.

35. Glissant, *Poetics of Relation*, 159.

36. Crawford, *What Is African American Literature?*, 104.

37. Gilroy, *The Black Atlantic*, 4–5.

38. Crawford, *What Is African American Literature?*, 112.

39. Gilroy, *The Black Atlantic*, ix.

40. Van Deburg, *Modern Black Nationalism*, 15.

41. Shepperson, "Pan-Africanism and 'Pan-Africanism,'" 346. On Pan-Africanism's role in the African diaspora and its relationship to communism, see Walters, *Pan Africanism in the African Diaspora*; Adi, *Pan-Africanism and Communism*. For a sober history of W. E. B. Du Bois's role in the Pan-African Congresses, see Lewis, *W. E. B. Du Bois, 1868–1919*. On the chain of influence between Pan-Africanism, Du Boisian thought, and Negritude movement, see Rabaka, *The Negritude Movement*.

42. Moses, *The Golden Age of Black Nationalism, 1850–1925*, 19.

43. Moore, *Pichón*, 120.

44. Hartman, *Scenes of Subjection*, 81 and 4.

45. Hartman, 11.

46. Gilroy, *The Black Atlantic*, 55.

47. Gilroy, 40.

48. Van Deburg, *Modern Black Nationalism*, 15.

49. Tracy, *Hot Music, Ragmentation, and the Bluing of American Literature*, 337.

50. Tracy, 338.

51. Tracy, 338.

52. Lordi, *Black Resonance Iconic Women Singers and African American Literature*, 67.

53. *Black Resonance Iconic Women Singers and African American Literature*, 71; emphasis added.

54. Lordi, 67.

55. Lordi, 69.

56. Moore, *Pichón*, 95.

57. Asukile, "Joel Augustus Rogers"; Asukile, "J.A. Rogers."

58. Fraser, "Lewis Michaux, 92, Dies; Ran Bookstore in Harlem"; "Michaux, Lewis H. (1885–1976), Bookseller and Black Nationalist."

59. Hicks, Calvin Hicks.

60. Baraka, *The Autobiography of LeRoi Jones*.

61. Cruse is the author of *The Crisis of the Negro Intellectual*, a major work in African American studies, see Cruse, *The Crisis of the Negro Intellectual*.

62. Angelou, *The Heart of a Woman*.

63. Terry, "Abbey Lincoln and Max Roach"; "Abbey Lincoln."

64. Terry, "Abbey Lincoln and Max Roach."

65. Moore, *Pichón*, 112.

66. Moore, 104–105.

67. This was the first political lecture that Moore ever attended.

68. The books could have included the following titles: *100 Amazing Facts About the Negro with Complete Proof* (1934), *World's Great Men of Color* (1946–47), *Sex and Race* (1941, 1942, and 1944), and *Nature Knows No Color Line* (1952).

69. Moore, *Pichón*, 79.

70. "Rallying Point," 267.

71. Moore, *Pichón*, 100.

72. *Moore*, 99 and 101.

73. *Moore*, 99.

74. Moore, 112.

75. Werner, *A Change Is Gonna Come*, 68–71.

76. Hubbard, *The Sermon and the African American Literary Imagination*, 6.

77. Hubbard, 14.

78. Hubbard, 23.

79. Lordi, *Black Resonance Iconic Women Singers and African American Literature*.

80. Lordi.

81. Shelby, *We Who Are Dark*.

82. Helen is one of the many older women, all White, whom Moore meets and dates in the Village.

83. Moore, *Pichón*, 116.

84. Moore, 116.

85. Moore, 115.

86. Moore, 115.

87. Moore, 97.

88. Moore, 109.

89. Moore, 110–11. Moore's recollection of the album covers may not be accurate. Makeba's hair is natural on her 1960 album cover, and so is Odetta's on her 1959 and 1960 album covers, but this is not true of any of Simone's pre-1967 album covers.

90. Moore, 96 and 117–18.

91. Moore, 32 and 320.

92. The beatings stopped in 1952, the year when Victor and Winifred separated. When Victor was bedridden with tuberculosis, Winifred moved to Havana to make money to pay for his medication and treatment. After Victor's health improved, he discovered letters between Winifred and another man who lived in Havana. Victor may have been right about Winifred's new infidelity, but he did not have the moral high ground. For years, he had an open affair in town with a married woman named Mable Cross. When Victor confronted Winifred about the letters, they got into a fight; she attempted to stab him with a pair of scissors. She moved to Havana permanently after the altercation, see 34 and 51.

93. Moore, *Pichón*, 31.

94. Moore, 111.

95. Moore, 112.

96. Shea, *Spiritual Autobiography in Early America*, xi.

97. Moore, *Pichón*, 113.

98. Moore, 115 and 118.

99. Moore, 73.

100. Moore, 117.

101. Moore, 118.

102. Moore, 119.

103. Gilroy, *The Black Atlantic*, 40.

104. Van Deburg, *Modern Black Nationalism*, 15.

105. Moore, *Pichón*, 123.

106. Moore, 123.

107. Moore, 124.

108. Hartman, *Scenes of Subjection*, 80–81.

109. Moore, *Pichón*, 124–25.

110. Moore, 125.

111. Moore, 125.

112. Hartman, *Scenes of Subjection*, 4.

113. Moore, *Pichón*, 126.

114. It is not clear which lectures Moore attended, but it seems that they may have occurred between May and July. According to the NYS Division of Military and Naval Affairs, the site did not take this name until 1961. From 1940 to 1961 it was known as the 369th Coast Artillery Regiment.

115. Moore, *Pichón*, 132–33.

116. Moore, 134.

117. Kerina worked as a lobbyist for the South West Africa People's Organisation, promoting its cause to the United Nations Committee on Decolonization. Through Kerina, Moore comes into contact with other African diplomats in the UN, see Moore, 133–34.

118. Moore, 134.

119. Moore, 132 and 133.

120. King James Version, *The Holy Bible*, Acts 9:18.

121. See my discussion of the pietistic origins of the bildungsroman in the Introduction.

122. Payne, *The Self and the Sacred*, 7.

123. Payne, 16 and 41.

124. Caldwell, *The Puritan Conversion Narrative*, 120.

125. Moore, *Pichón*, 58.

126. Robert Stepto, a scholar of African American literature, coined the terms ascent and immersion narrative, see Stepto, *From Behind the Veil*. For my discussion of how these concepts arise in and apply to the Afro-Latino memoir, see my Introduction.

127. Crawford, *What Is African American Literature?*, 104.

128. García-Peña, *Translating Blackness*.

Chapter Three

1. For a review of the public debates about Obama's Blackness, see Graham, "A Short History of Whether Obama Is Black Enough, Featuring Rupert Murdoch."

2. George, *Post-Soul Nation*, ix.

3. Dickerson, *The End of Blackness*, 49–50 and 257–58.

4. Hereafter referred to as *Altar*.

5. Vega, *The Altar of My Soul*, 215 and 243.

6. Temple University is the home of the nation's first doctoral program in African American Studies, see Reid-Merritt, "Temple University's African American Studies PhD Program @ 30." Temple is sometimes mistakenly considered to be an HBCU, see Owens, "Temple Students, Let That HBCU Comparison Die"; Russ and Wellington, "HBCU-ish? Some Say Temple T-Shirts Ignore the Significance of Actual Historically Black Colleges." On the federal definition of an HBCU, see U.S. Department of Education, "What Is an HBCU?"

7. Asante, *The Afrocentric Idea*, Revised and Expanded Edition; Asante and Mazama, "Afrocentricity."

8. Smith, *Black Mosaic*; Greer, *Black Ethnics Race, Immigration, and the Pursuit of the American Dream*; Berlin, *The Making of African America*.

9. Jackson, *Black Writers and Latin America*; Brock and Castañeda Fuertes, *Between Race and Empire*; Sánchez, *"Shakin' Up" Race and Gender*; Guridy, *Forging Diaspora*; López, *Unbecoming Blackness*; Milian, *Latining America*; García-Peña, *Translating Blackness*.

10. George, *Post-Soul Nation*, 230. Recall that African Americans lost their demographic primacy to Latinos, see Ramirez and de la Cruz, "The Hispanic Population in the United States: March 2002"; Clemetson, "Hispanics Now Largest Minority, Census Shows"; Vries, "Hispanics Now Largest U.S. Minority."

11. Taylor, "Post-Black, Old Black"; Womack, *Post Black*; Touré, *Who's Afraid of Post-Blackness?*; Murray, *Queering Post-Black Art*; Crawford, *Black Post-Blackness*; Ashe and Saal, *Slavery and the Post-Black Imagination*. Although Taylor used the term in 2007, it increased in popularity among cultural critics and scholars after Barack H. Obama won the 2008 presidential election.

12. Ashe and Saal, *Slavery and the Post-Black Imagination*, 7.

13. Ashe and Saal, 5.

14. Ashe and Saal, 6.

15. Ashe, "Theorizing the Post-Soul Aesthetic," 614.

16. Ashe and Saal, *Slavery and the Post-Black Imagination*, 6.

17. De La Torre, "Rethinking Mulatez"; Allatson, "Mulato/a, Mulatez"; Ortega-Aponte, "Mulatez"; Gillman, "Latina/o Mestizaje/Mulatez"; Asociación de Academias de la Lengua Española, "mulataje"; Buscaglia-Salgado, "Circumventing Racialism through Mulataje."

18. Ashe and Saal, *Slavery and the Post-Black Imagination*, 14–15.

19. Shelby, *We Who Are Dark*.

20. Womack, *Post Black*, 1 and 23–24.

21. Touré, *Who's Afraid of Post-Blackness?*, 12.

22. Murray, *Queering Post-Black Art*.

23. Kennedy, "The Fallacy of Touré's Post-Blackness Theory."

24. Baker and Simmons, *The Trouble with Post-Blackness*, 3.

25. Crawford, *Black Post-Blackness*, 15.

26. Crawford, 12.

27. Crawford, 2.

28. Crawford, 4.

29. Crawford, 12.

30. Mason, *Living Santería*; Cros Sandoval, *Worldview, the Orichas, and Santería*; Boaz, *Banning Black Gods*.

31. Babalawo is the Yoruba word for priest.

32. Pinn, "Ashe!: Santería, Orisha-Voodoo, and Oyotunji African Village," 85; Brandon, *Santeria from Africa to the New World*, 106.

33. Hucks, *Yoruba Traditions and African American Religious Nationalism*, chap. 2; Brandon, *Santeria from Africa to the New World*, 107 and 114–20; Hunt, "Oyotunji Village: The Yoruba Movement in America," 2 and 12–13.

34. Brandon, *Santeria from Africa to the New World*, 107.

35. De La Torre, "Kardecism," 172.

36. Otero, "Espiritismo"; Santo, *Developing the Dead*; Ballard, "Espiritismo"; Fernández Olmos and Paravisini-Gebert, "Espiritismo: Creole Spiritism in Cuba, Puerto Rico, and the United States"; Edmonds and Gonzalez, "Creole African Traditions: Santería, Palo Monte, Abakuá, Vodou, and Espiritismo"; De La Torre, "Espiritismo"; Clark, "Espiritismo"; Bettelheim, "Caribbean Espiritismo (Spiritist) Altars"; Torres Rivera, "Espiritismo"; Vega, "Espiritismo in the Puerto Rican Community: A New World Recreation with the Elements of Kongo Ancestor Worship."

37. Fernández Olmos and Paravisini-Gebert, *Creole Religions of the Caribbean*, 194–98; Brandon, *Santeria from Africa to the New World*, 107–14. Brandon, "Hierarchy Without a Head."

38. *Santeria from Africa to the New World*, 113.

39. *Santeria from Africa to the New World*, 113.

40. Fernández Olmos and Paravisini-Gebert, *Creole Religions of the Caribbean*, 189.

41. In her essays on Espiritismo and the Black Global Aesthetic, Vega cites the following sources: Herskovits, *The Myth of the Negro Past*; Herskovits, *The New World Negro*; Metraux, *Voodoo in Haiti*; Fernández Olmos and Paravisini-Gebert, *Sacred Possessions*; Jahn, *Muntu*; Bastide, *The African Religions of Brazil*; Abiodun, "Understanding Yoruba Art and Aesthetics: The Concept of Àse."

42. Vega, "The Yoruba Orisha Tradition Comes to New York City"; Vega, "Espiritismo in the Puerto Rican Community: A New World Recreation with the Elements of Kongo Ancestor Worship"; Vega, "The Ancestral Sacred Creative Impulse of Africa and the African Diaspora"; Vega, "Interlocking African Diaspora Cultures in the Work of Fernando Ortiz."

43. Vega, "The Ancestral Sacred Creative Impulse of Africa and the African Diaspora," 45.

44. Abiodun, "Understanding Yoruba Art and Aesthetics: The Concept of Àse," 71.

45. Vega, 45 and 46.

46. Vega, 56.

47. Vega, 45.

48. Vega, 48.

49. Vega, "The Ancestral Sacred Creative Impulse of Africa and the African Diaspora," 51 and 53.

50. Vega, "The Yoruba Orisha Tradition Comes to New York City," note #2 on 205; Vega, "Yoruba Philosophy."

51. Vega, "The Yoruba Orisha Tradition Comes to New York City," 201.

52. Vega, "The Ancestral Sacred Creative Impulse of Africa and the African Diaspora," 53–54.

53. Vega, "The Yoruba Orisha Tradition Comes to New York City," 202–3; Washburne, "'El Tema Del Apollo'"; Jacques, "CuBop!: Afro-Cuban Music and Mid-Twentieth-Century American Culture."

54. "The Ancestral Sacred Creative Impulse of Africa and the African Diaspora," 54.

55. Vega, "Yoruba Philosophy," 164.

56. Vega, "The Ancestral Sacred Creative Impulse of Africa and the African Diaspora," 55.

57. Neal, "Some Reflections on the Black Aesthetic."

58. They were most likely initiated in Yoruba Temple in Harlem, Vega, "Yoruba Philosophy," 166.

59. Vega, "The Ancestral Sacred Creative Impulse of Africa and the African Diaspora," 56.

60. Vega, 55.

61. Vega, When the Spirits Dance Mambo, 3.

62. Vega, 13.

63. Vega, 3.

64. Mongelli, "True Colors: Intellectual Latina Has Made the Study of Races Her Life."

65. Vega, When the Spirits Dance Mambo, 2.

66. Vega, 9.

67. Vega, 20 and 21.

68. Vega, 16–17.

69. Olmos and Paravisini-Gebert, Creole Religions of the Caribbean, 195.

70. Vega, When the Spirits Dance Mambo, 262.

71. Gitana, is one of Vega's three personal spirit guides. Vega's personal Gitana is a "gypsy of two waters . . . a daughter of las dos aguas—of sweet and salt water." Vega's other two personal spirits are Nacer and María de la O. Nacer, an Arab spirit who controls Vega's thoughts, is a messenger of the orisha Obatalá, and he values the concepts of truth and justice. María de la O, the Conga, is a warrior spirit, a fugitive slave woman who adopts the name of Vega's great-great-grandmother, see Vega, 193 and 194.

72. Vega, 194.

73. The fact that she is a spirit of two waters suggests that she is fusion of Ochún and Yemaya, see Vega, 193, 241, 262, 264, and 265.

74. Davis, "Vodú of the Dominican Republic: Devotion to 'La Veintiuna División,'" 84; Ricourt, "Criollismo Religioso."

75. Davis suspects that Dominadora is of East Indian origin, but she does not provide support for her conjecture, see Davis, "Diasporal Dimensions of Dominican Folk Religion and Music," 162.

76. Vega, *When the Spirits Dance Mambo*, 82; Original Products Botanica, "Martha The Dominator"; The Fat Feminist Witch, "The Nine Tuesdays of Saint Martha the Dominator."

77. Daas, "From Holy Hostess to Dragon Tamer"; de Voragine, "Saint Martha."

78. Vega, *When the Spirits Dance Mambo*, 82, 83, and 262.

79. Vega, 82–83.

80. Heredia, "Marta Moreno Vega's When the Spirits Dance Mambo," 74.

81. Delgadillo, *Spiritual Mestizaje*, 1–4.

82. Vega, "The Ancestral Sacred Creative Impulse of Africa and the African Diaspora," 51.

83. Clark and Johnson, *Kaiso!*, 131–32.

84. Vega, "The Ancestral Sacred Creative Impulse of Africa and the African Diaspora," 51.

85. Vega, 51.

86. Vega, 53.

87. Vega, 53–54.

88. Delgadillo, "African, Latina, Feminist, and Decolonial," 160.

89. Delgadillo, 161.

90. Genette and Macksey, *Paratexts*, 5.

91. On Alfaro's relationship with Dunham and Celia Cruz, see Fernandez, *From Afro-Cuban Rhythms to Latin Jazz*, 120 and 147. Fleming, "A Concert of Cuba."

92. Cantor-Navas, "Cuban Country Queen Celina Gonzalez Dead at 85"; World Music Central News, "Celina González, Queen of Cuban Punto Dies at 86."

93. Aparicio, "The Blackness of Sugar"; Cruz and Reymundo, *Celia*.

94. Austerlitz, "Machito and Mario Bauza Latin Jazz in the U.S. Mainstream"; Washburne, "'El Tema Del Apollo'"; Ratliff, "Graciela Per'ez-Gutierrez, 94, Afro-Cuban Singer"; Contreras, "Before Celia Cruz Or J.Lo, There Was Graciela"; "Remember Graciela Pérez Gutiérrez of Machito & His Afro-Cubans!"; "Remember Machito and His Afro-Cubans Who Defined Latin Jazz"; Tamargo, "Obituario: Graciela (La Habana, 1915-Nueva York, 2010)."

95. Vega, *When the Spirits Dance Mambo*, 73.

96. Heredia, "Marta Moreno Vega's When the Spirits Dance Mambo," 76.

97. Heredia, 75.

98. Eliot, "Hamlet and His Problems," 58.

99. Hoffnung-Garskof, "The World of Arturo Schomburg," 77.

100. Hoffnung-Garskof, *Racial Migrations*, 108, 109 and 273.

101. Rich, *The Post-Racial Society Is Here*.

102. Foster, *White Race Discourse*; Kamaloni, "Introduction."

103. Powell, "The Rhetorical Allure of Post-Racial Process Discourse and the Democratic Myth"; Cho, "Post-Racialism Critical Race Theory Speaker Series—CRT 20"; Dawson and Bobo, "One Year Late and the Myth of a Post-Racial Society"; Boyce and Chunnu, "Toward a Post-Racial Society, or a 'Rebirth' of a Nation?"; Kaplan, *The Myth of Post-Racial America*.

104. Da Costa, "Thinking 'Post-Racial' Ideology Transnationally," 477.

105. Taylor, "Interculturalism or Multiculturalism?"; Meer and Modood, "How Does Interculturalism Contrast with Multiculturalism?"; Modood, "Multiculturalism, Interculturalisms and the Majority"; Antonsich et al., "Interculturalism versus Multiculturalism: The Cantle-Modood Debate"; Modood, "Must Interculturalists Misrepresent Multiculturalism?"

106. Da Costa, "Thinking 'Post-Racial' Ideology Transnationally," 482.

107. Meer and Modood, "How Does Interculturalism Contrast with Multiculturalism?"

108. Bouchard, "What Is Interculturalism?"

109. Joppke, "War of Words"; Levrau and Loobuyck, "Introduction"; Zapata-Barrero, "Interculturalism in the Post-Multicultural Debate"; Antonsich et al., "Interculturalism versus Multiculturalism: The Cantle-Modood Debate"; Zapata-Barrero, "Introduction"; Zapata-Barrero, "Interculturalism"; Cantle, "National Identity, Plurality and Interculturalism."

110. Perlmann and Waters, "Intermarriage and Multiple Identities."

111. Perlmann, "Reflecting the Changing Face of America: Multiracials, Racial Classification, and American Intermarriage."

112. Pascoe, *What Comes Naturally*.

113. Telles and Project, *Pigmentocracies*; Middleton IV, "Institutions, Inculcation, and Black Racial Identity"; Lynn, "Pigmentocracy: Racial Hierarchies in the Caribbean and Latin America"; Jim Sidanius, Yesilernis Peña, and Mark Sawyer, "Inclusionary Discrimination."

114. Monk Jr., "Colorism and Physical Health"; Reece, "The Gender of Colorism"; Oh, Lincoln, and Waldman, "Perceived Colorism and Lifetime Psychiatric Disorders among Black American Adults"; Caraballo-Cueto and Godreau, "Colorism and Health Disparities in Home Countries"; Bell, "Confronting Colorism"; Monroe and Hall, "Colorism and U.S. Immigration"; Dhillon-Jamerson, "Euro-Americans Favoring People of Color"; Hernández, *Multiracials and Civil Rights*; Wassink, Perreira, and Harris, "Beyond Race/Ethnicity"; Tharps, *Same Family, Different Colors*; Aja, "Anyone but Blacks."

115. Da Costa, "Thinking 'Post-Racial' Ideology Transnationally," 480.

116. Hernández, *Multiracials and Civil Rights*; Da Costa, "Thinking 'Post-Racial' Ideology Transnationally"; Pérez-Torres, "Mestizaje"; Aja, "Anyone But Blacks"; Miller, *Rise and Fall of the Cosmic Race*.

117. Chavez-Dueñas, Adames, and Organista, "Skin-Color Prejudice and Within-Group Racial Discrimination"; Wade, "Afterword: Race and Nation in Modern Latin America: An Anthropological View"; Montalvo and Codina, "Skin Color and Latinos in the United States."

118. Sexton, *Amalgamation Schemes*, 1.

119. Vega, *When the Spirits Dance Mambo*, 131.

120. Vega, 131.

121. Heredia, "Marta Moreno Vega's When the Spirits Dance Mambo," 71.

122. Vega, *When the Spirits Dance Mambo*, 131 and 132.

123. Vega, 133.

124. Vega, 161.

125. Vega, 154.

126. Huck, "Machismo, Marianismo, and Malinchismo"; De La Torre, "Marianismo"; Allatson, "Marianismo."

127. Vega, *When the Spirits Dance Mambo*, 158.

128. Vega, 159.

129. Vega, 162.

130. Vega, 165.

131. Vega, 210.

132. Vega, 212.

133. Lee, *Building a Latino Civil Rights Movement*, 27.

134. Ortiz, *An African American and Latinx History of the United States*, 7.

135. Lee, *Building a Latino Civil Rights Movement*, 28.

136. The Center for the Study of White American Culture, "The Multiracial Movement: Part I, A History."

137. Hochschild, "Multiple Racial Identifiers in the 2000 Census, and Then What?"

138. Frey, *Diversity Explosion*, 205.

139. Perlmann, "Reflecting the Changing Face of America: Multiracials, Racial Classification, and American Intermarriage."

140. Williams, *Mark One or More*, 42.

141. Hernández, *Multiracials and Civil Rights*, 4.

142. Ramirez and de la Cruz, "The Hispanic Population in the United States: March 2002."

143. Dickerson, *The End of Blackness: Returning the Souls of Black Folk to Their Rightful Owners*, 259.

144. Dickerson, 284.

145. Dickerson, 137.

146. On the complexities of Latino ethnoracial identity formation and "black denial," see Oboler, *Ethnic Labels, Latino Lives*; Dávila, *Latino Spin*; Parker et al., "Hispanic Racial Identity"; Duany, *Blurred Borders*; Flores, *The Diaspora Strikes Back Caribeño Tales of Learning and Turning*; Jiménez Román, "Looking at That Middle Ground: Racial Mixing as Panacea?"; Robles, "Black Denial"; Howard, *Coloring the Nation*; Candelario, *Black behind the Ears*.

147. Simmons, *Reconstructing Racial Identity and the African Past in the Dominican Republic*; Chetty and Rodríguez, "Introduction."

148. Dickerson, *The End of Blackness*, 151.

149. Dickerson, 151.

150. Tate, "Cult-Nats Meet Freaky-Deke: The Return of the Black Aesthetic"; Ellis, "The New Black Aesthetic"; Neal, *Soul Babies: Black Popular Culture and the Post-Soul Aesthetic*; Ashe, "Theorizing the Post-Soul Aesthetic"; Ashe, "Theorizing the Post-Soul Aesthetic: An Introduction"; Ashe, "Post-Soul President: Dreams from My Father and the Post-Soul Aesthetic."

151. George, *Post-Soul Nation*; Dickerson, *The End of Blackness: Returning the Souls of Black Folk to Their Rightful Owners*; Womack, *Post Black*.

152. Vega, "Yoruba Philosophy"; Vega, "The Yoruba Orisha Tradition Comes to New York City"; Vega, "Espiritismo in the Puerto Rican Community: A New World

Recreation with the Elements of Kongo Ancestor Worship"; Vega, "Interlocking African Diaspora Cultures in the Work of Fernando Ortiz"; Vega, *The Altar of My Soul*; Torres-Saillant, "The Tribulations of Blackness"; Torres-Saillant, "Inventing the Race"; Luis, "Latin American (Hispanic Caribbean) Literature Written in the United States"; Luis, *Dance between Two Cultures*; Flores, "Making the Strong Survive"; Flores, *From Bomba to Hip-Hop*; Flores, "Triple Consciousness? Afro-Latinos on the Color Line"; Flores, "Triple Consciousness?"; DeCosta-Willis, "Can(n)on Fodder"; Laó-Montes, "Afro-Latinidades and the Diasporic Imaginary"; Laó-Montes, "Afro-Latinidades: Bridging Blackness and Latinidad"; Kutzinski, "Afro-Hispanic American Literature."

153. Although Dunham served as an ideological role model for Vega, as far as I know, she was not, like Maya Angelou was to Carlos Moore, a personal mentor to Vega. The major contact between Dunham and Vega seems to have been Dunham's secretary who, with Dunham's permission, sent Vega excerpts from Dunham's unpublished autobiography, see Vega, "Yoruba Philosophy," 65.

154. Heredia, "Marta Moreno Vega's When the Spirits Dance Mambo," 72.

Chapter Four

1. Nwankwo, "Reading U. S. Latina Writers"; Sánchez, *"Shakin' Up" Race and Gender*; Caminero-Santangelo, *On Latinidad*; Guridy, *Forging Diaspora*; Vázquez, *Triangulations*; López, *Unbecoming Blackness*; Milian, *Latining America*; Maillo-Pozo, "Reconstructing Dominican Latinidad"; Blake, "What Does It Mean to Be Black?: Gendered Redefinitions of Interethnic Solidarity in Piri Thomas's *Down These Mean Streets*"; Delgadillo, "African, Latina, Feminist, and Decolonial"; Myers, *Mapping Hispaniola*.

2. Chambers and Cepeda are part of a growing set of Latina memoirists who celebrate or acknowledge their African heritage: Esmeralda Santiago, Marta Moreno Vega, Sonia Manzano, Rosie Perez, Daisy Hernández, and Sonny Hostin.

3. For a definition and history of the post-soul aesthetic, see the "Latinities, African American Literature, and the Post-Soul Aesthetic" section of this book's Introduction.

4. It is unclear whether Chambers is partly Dominican. In *Mama's Girl*, she says her father was born in the Dominican Republic and moved to the US in 1962 when he was twelve, see Chambers, *Mama's Girl*, 12. In "Secret Latina at Large," she writes, "I was born in Panama to black Panamanian parents. My father's parents came from Costa Rica and Jamaica. My mother's family came from Martinique. I left Panama when I was two years old, we lived in England for three years, and I came to the U.S. when I was five," see Chambers, "Secret Latina at Large," 21. She repeats this genealogy in "The Secret Latina," see Chambers, "The Secret Latina," 102.

5. Before moving to Inwood with her father, Cepeda lived briefly in California and the Dominican Republic with her mother.

6. The Five Percent Nation is hereafter referred to as FPN. The FPN is also known as the Nation of Gods and Earths because they refer to their female members as Earths, Moons, and Queens and their male members as Suns and Gods, see Allen, Jr., "Making the Strong Survive," 166. The Nation of Islam is hereafter referred to as the NOI. In *Down These Mean Streets*, Thomas discusses his engagement with NOI when he was incarcerated. Thomas and Cepeda's engagement with the NOI and FPN are part of a

long history of Latino engagement with African American Islamic sects, see Bowen, "U.S. Latina/o Muslims Since 1920"; Salgado, "Stories of Some of the Early 'Latino' Muslims"; Aidi, "'Verily, There Is Only One Hip-hop Umma.'" For a definition of decolonial, see Maldonado-Torres, "The Decolonial Turn."

7. Milian, *Latining America*, 1.

8. Milian, 2 and 1.

9. Jiménez Román and Flores, *The Afro-Latin@ Reader*; Guridy, *Forging Diaspora*; Vega, Alba, and Modestin, *Women Warriors of the Afro-Latina Diaspora*; López, *Unbecoming Blackness: The Diaspora Cultures of Afro-Cuban America*; Milian, *Latining America*; Richardson, *The Afro-Latin@ Experience in Contemporary American Literature and Culture*; Valdés, *Diasporic Blackness*; Ortiz, *An African American and Latinx History of the United States*; Hoffnung-Garskof, *Racial Migrations*; Myers, *Mapping Hispaniola*; Figueroa-Vásquez, *Decolonizing Diasporas*.

10. Oboler, *Ethnic Labels, Latino Lives*, 1995; Gruesz, *Ambassadors of Culture*; Laó-Montes and Dávila, *Mambo Montage: The Latinization of New York*; Dávila, *Latinos, Inc.*; Duany, *The Puerto Rican Nation on the Move*; Dávila, *Barrio Dreams*; Dávila, *Latino Spin*; Oboler, *Latinos and Citizenship the Dilemma of Belonging*; Caminero-Santangelo, *On Latinidad*; Beltran, *The Trouble with Unity*; Milian, *Latining America*; Gutiérrez, "What's in a Name: The History and Politics of Hispanic and Latino Panethnicities"; Ortíz, *Latinx Literature Now*.

11. Milian, *Latining America*; Laó-Montes, "Afro-Latinidades: Bridging Blackness and Latinidad"; Luis, "Afro-Latino/a Literature and Identity"; Jiménez Román and Flores, *The Afro-Latin@ Reader*; Torres-Saillant, "Afro-Latinas/os and the Racial Wall."

12. Torres-Saillant, "The Latino Autobiography"; Stavans, *Growing Up Latino: Memoirs and Stories*; Torres, "The Construction of the Self in U.S. Latina Autobiographies"; Cantú, "Memoir, Autobiography, Testimonio"; Dúran, "Latina/o Life Writing"; Borland, "Memoirs."

13. Yagoda, *Memoir*; Couser, *Memoir*; Smith and Watson, *Reading Autobiography*; Couser, *Vulnerable Subjects*; Eakin, *The Ethics of Life Writing*.

14. Lejeune, *On Autobiography*.

15. Melamed, *Represent and Destroy*, 92.

16. Melamed, xix–xx.

17. Huggan, *The Postcolonial Exotic*, 28.

18. Head, *The State of the Novel*, 97–98.

19. Machado Sáez, *Market Aesthetics*, 2.

20. Machado Sáez, 1.

21. Japtok, *Growing Up Ethnic*, 11 and 19.

22. Riverhead-Penguin published Chambers and Díaz's first books in 1996. Chambers and Danticat are coauthors of an *Essence Magazine* article that promotes their books *Mama's Girl* and *Krick? Krack!*, see Danticat, Chambers, and Jackson, "Three Young Voices."

23. For a history of the 1990s memoir boom, see Rak, *Boom!*

24. On the model minority myth as it applies to Afro-Caribbean and African immigrants, see Ukpokodu, "African Immigrants, the 'New Model Minority'"; Ifatunji, "A Test of the Afro Caribbean Model Minority Hypothesis"; Lindsay, "Beyond 'Model

Minority,' 'Superwoman,' and 'Endangered Species'"; Morrison, "Are Black Immigrants a Model Minority?"; Rogers, *Afro-Caribbean Immigrants and the Politics of Incorporation*.

25. Nwankwo, "Reading U. S. Latina Writers," 26.

26. Wallace, *Black Macho and the Myth of the Superwoman*.

27. Danticat, Chambers, and Jackson, "Three Young Voices," 103–4.

28. Chambers, "Secret Latina at Large"; Chambers, "The Secret Latina."

29. Chambers, "Veronica Chambers '87: Writer and Editor."

30. Chambers, "Veronica Chambers '87: Writer and Editor."

31. Du Bois's essay focuses on the educational development of Black men and genders the Black race as male, Du Bois, "The Talented Tenth," 231.

32. Flores, "Triple Consciousness?"; Flores and Jiménez Román, "Triple-Consciousness?"; Torres-Saillant, "Afro-Latinas/os and the Racial Wall"; Candelario, "Color Matters: Latina/o Racial Identities and Life Chances"; Luis, "Afro-Latino/a Literature and Identity."

33. Ellison, *Shadow and Act*, 140 and 162.

34. Five reviews describe Chambers as African American, see Seaman, "Mama's Girl"; Kraft, "Adult Book for Young Adults"; Cassel, "Book Reviews"; Rochman, "Mama's Girl"; Kirkus Reviews, "Mama's Girl." Three reviews, however, correctly acknowledged *Mama's Girl* as an Afro-Latino and/or Caribbean text, see Stuttaford, "Mama's Girl"; Harlan, "Mama's Girl"; Huneven, "MAMA'S GIRL." Other reviews simply identify Chambers as "black," of Panamanian heritage, or do not mention her race at all, see McHugh, "Mama's Girl"; Petty, "Mama's Girl"; Booklist, "Mama's Girl."

35. Chambers, *Mama's Girl*, 12–13.

36. Chambers, 13.

37. Chambers, 52.

38. Hurston, "Dust Tracks," 572.

39. Chambers, *Mama's Girl*, 91.

40. Chambers, 53.

41. George, *Buppies, B-Boys, BAPs, and Bohos*, 2.

42. Chambers, *Mama's Girl*, 91.

43. This is the school in which Chambers learned about African American history, about how women like Charlayne Hunter-Gault integrated white colleges, see Chambers, 53.

44. Chambers, 53.

45. Peller, "Race-Consciousness," 135.

46. Knight, *Luck Egalitarianism*, 1.

47. Segall, *Why Inequality Matters*; Lippert-Rasmussen, *Luck Egalitarianism*; Tan, "Defending Luck Egalitarianism."

48. Knight, *Luck Egalitarianism*, 1.

49. Chambers, *Mama's Girl*, 181–82.

50. Chambers's jeremiad parallels the Moynihan Report's conclusion that matrifocal Black families are to blame for the crisis of Black masculinity, see Moynihan, "The Negro Family—The Case for National Action"; Geary, *Beyond Civil Rights*, chap. 5.

51. Hill Collins and Bilge, *Intersectionality*.

52. Chambers, *Mama's Girl*, 186.

53. Chambers, 187.

54. Butterfield, *Black Autobiography in America*; Braxton, *Black Women Writing Autobiography*; Andrews, *African-American Autobiography*; Mostern, *Autobiography and Black Identity Politics*; Torres, "The Construction of the Self in U.S. Latina Autobiographies."

55. Torres, "The Construction of the Self in U.S. Latina Autobiographies," 278.

56. Couser, *Vulnerable Subjects*; Eakin, *The Ethics of Life Writing*.

57. Smith, known as Clarence 13X, was a congregant of Malcolm X's Temple No. 7, see Knight, *The Five Percenters*, chaps. 1 and 3; Allen, Jr., "Making the Strong Survive."

58. Miyakawa, *Five Percenter Rap*, 23.

59. Raquel Cepeda's memoir is her most compelling work to date. Her first book and film deal with the history, nature, and politics of hip hop. She published *And It Don't Stop* in 2004, and she released her documentary *Bling* in 2007. Cepeda explores ethnoracial identity formation in her second documentary, *Some Girls* (2017).

60. "Melissa Harris-Perry."

61. For a review of the Latino origins of and contributions to hip-hop music and culture, see Rose, *Black Noise*, 59; Guevara, "Droppin' Science"; Del Barco, "Droppin' Science"; Flores, "Droppin' Science"; Verán, "Breaking It All Down: The Rise and Fall and Rise of the B-Boy Kingdom"; Flores, *From Bomba to Hip-Hop*; Rivera, "Hip Hop, Puerto Ricans, and Ethnoracial Identities in New York"; Rivera, "Hip Hop and New York Puerto Ricans"; Rivera, *New York Ricans from the Hip Hop Zone*; Rivera, "Between Blackness and Latinidad in the Hip Hop Zone"; Rivera, Marshall, and Hernandez, *Reggaeton*, 138, 145, 147–48, 157; Rivera, "Ghettocentricity, Blackness, and Pan-Latinidad."

62. Maillo-Pozo, "Reconstructing Dominican Latinidad," 86.

63. Maillo-Pozo, 95.

64. On the subjects of Dominican immigration, Dominican "black denial" and racial identity formation, and the significance of autobiography in Dominican and Haitian American literature and life writing, see Duany, *Blurred Borders*; Duany, "Transnational Migration from the Dominican Republic: The Cultural Redefinition of Racial Identity"; Duany, "Reconstructing Racial Identity"; Torres-Saillant, "The Tribulations of Blackness"; Itzigsohn and Dore-Cabral, "Competing Identities? Race, Ethnicity and Panethnicity among Dominicans in the United States"; Torres-Saillant, "Inventing the Race"; Candelario, "Color Matters: Latina/o Racial Identities and Life Chances"; Robles, "Black Denial"; Jiménez Román, "Looking at That Middle Ground: Racial Mixing as Panacea?"; Torres-Saillant, "Afro-Latinas/os and the Racial Wall"; Howard, *Coloring the Nation*; Candelario, *Black behind the Ears*; Simmons, *Reconstructing Racial Identity and the African Past in the Dominican Republic*; Torres-Saillant, *Introduction to Dominican Blackness*; Mayes, *Mulatto Republic*; García-Peña, *The Borders of Dominicanidad*; Ramírez, *Colonial Phantoms*; Myers, *Mapping Hispaniola*; Maillo-Pozo, "Resisting Colonial Ghosts"; Suárez, *The Tears of Hispaniola*.

65. Cepeda's father's violence and his expectation of Cepeda to be socially respectable and sexually virtuous exemplifies the discourse of machismo and *marianismo*,

see Huck, "Machismo, Marianismo, and Malinchismo"; De La Torre, "Marianismo." New studies are focusing on the changing nature of machismo, exploring how feminist consciousness mediates contemporary representations and understanding of machismo in high-achieving Latino men, see Hurtado and Sinha, *Beyond Machismo*. For the representation of machismo in Latino-Caribbean narrative, see Cortés, *Macho Ethics*. Although a sustained treatment of machismo and *marianismo* is beyond the scope of this chapter, future studies could, on the basis of first-person narration, compare representations of machismo and *marianismo* in *Bird of Paradise* and the novel *The Brief and Wonderous Life of Oscar Wao*. It might also be fruitful to use Ramon Saldívar's concept of speculative realism to compare Cepeda and Díaz's respective representations of *fukú*.

66. Cepeda also mentions Shannon and Joyce Simms, African American freestyle singers, see Cepeda, *Bird of Paradise*, 72.

67. For sources on the FPN's influence on hip hop, see Ahearn, "The Five Percent Solution"; Miyakawa, "The Duty of the Civilized Is to Civilize the Uncivilized: Tropes of Black Nationalism in the Messages of Five Percent Rappers"; Miyakawa, *Five Percenter Rap*; Knight, *The Five Percenters*; Mohaiemen, "Fear of a Muslim Planet: Hip-Hop's Hidden History"; Bassil, "The Prestige, The Five Percenters, and Why Jay Electronica Hasn't Released His Debut Album."

68. Cepeda, *Bird of Paradise*, 68.

69. Miyakawa, *Five Percenter Rap*, 23.

70. Nuruddin, "The Five Percenters: A Teenage Nation of Gods and Earths," 112 and 123; Allen, Jr., "Making the Strong Survive," 9; Allen, Jr., "Identity and Destiny."

71. Like the NOI, the FPN teaches the following: "The original man is the Asiatic Black Man, Owner, Maker, cream of the planet Earth, God of the Universe and Father of Civilization," see Federal Bureau of Investigation, "Nation of Islam: Part 1 of 3," 73. For the Moorish Science Temple origins of the Asiatic Black Man concept, see Deutsch, "The Asiatic Black Man," 196.

72. Pausanias, *Description of Greece*, 506–7.

73. Federal Bureau of Investigation, "Nation of Islam: Part 2 of 3," 72.

74. For scholars in African American studies, the concept of the ten-percenters resonates with the trope of the Talented Tenth.

75. Federal Bureau of Investigation, "Nation of Islam: Part 2 of 3," 79.

76. Cepeda, *Bird of Paradise*, 71.

77. Cepeda, 107.

78. Cepeda, 131. For Ron G's biography, see DJ Ron G, "About Us."

79. For a history and analysis of the significance of Nuyorican Poets Café, its Black Aesthetic allies, and its relationship to hip hop, see Zapf, "Slammin' in Transnational Heterotopia: Words Being Spoken at the Nuyorican Poets Cafe"; Algarín and Holman, *Aloud*, 3–28; Cortes, Falcon, and Flores, "The Cultural Expression of Puerto Ricans in New York."

80. Cepeda, *Bird of Paradise*, 131. For a biography of Freestyle Fellowship, see Proefrock, "Freestyle Fellowship Biography."

81. Cepeda, 131.

82. Shelby, *We Who Are Dark*, 137–38.

83. See note 6 in chapter 3 for Temple University's role in the history of the development of African American Studies in higher education.

84. Cepeda, *Bird of Paradise*, 112.

85. Cepeda, 108–9.

86. "Wake Up" sets to lyrics the essential doctrine of the FPN catechism, and the video for the single prominently features an FPN temple and the movement's seven-point star badge/logo, see, Brand Nubian, *Wake Up (Reprise in the Sunshine)*; *Wake Up (Official Video)*.

87. Cepeda, *Bird of Paradise*, 109 and 110.

88. Cepeda, 110.

89. Cepeda, 111.

90. Brand Nubian, *Slow Down*.

91. Cepeda, *Bird of Paradise*, 111.

92. Pérez-Torres, "Mestizaje."

93. Ortega-Aponte, "Mulatez"; Allatson, "Mulato/a, Mulatez."

94. Cepeda, *Bird of Paradise*, 111.

95. Cepeda, 110.

96. On the Neo Taíno identity movement, see Haslip-Viera, "The Taíno Identity Movement among Caribbean Latinas/os in the United States"; Haslip-Viera, "Amerindian MtDNA Does Not Matter"; Haslip-Viera, "The 'Indigenous' or 'Neo-Taíno' Movement in The Spanish-Speaking Caribbean and Its Diaspora and the Return of The Old Anglo Neo-Imperialist Scholarship?"; Poole, "What Became of the Taíno?"; González, "A Piece Not the Puzzle," June 2015; University of Cambridge, "Ancient Genome Study Identifies Traces of Indigenous 'Taíno' in Present-Day Caribbean Populations"; Wade, "Genes of 'Extinct' Caribbean Islanders Found in Living People"; Estevez, "Meet the Survivors of a 'Paper Genocide.'"

97. Brandon, *Santeria from Africa to the New World*; Mason, *Living Santería*; Cros Sandoval, *Worldview, the Orichas, and Santería*; Pinn, "Ashe!: Santería, Orisha-Voodoo, and Oyotunji African Village"; Thomas, "Santería"; Boaz, *Banning Black Gods*.

98. Ballard, "Espiritismo"; Santo, *Developing the Dead*; Paravisini-Gebert, Fernández Olmos, and Murphy, "Espiritismo Creole Spiritism in Cuba, Puerto Rico, and the United States"; De La Torre, "Espiritismo"; Clark, "Espiritismo"; Bettelheim, "Caribbean Espiritismo (Spiritist) Altars"; Vega, "Espiritismo in the Puerto Rican Community: A New World Recreation with the Elements of Kongo Ancestor Worship"; Brandon, *Santeria from Africa to the New World*, 85–90.

99. Brandon, *Santeria from Africa to the New World*; Brandon, "Hierarchy Without a Head"; Fernández Olmos and Paravisini-Gebert, *Creole Religions of the Caribbean*.

100. Edmonds and Gonzalez, "Creole African Traditions: Santería, Palo Monte, Abakuá, Vodou, and Espiritismo," 102.

101. Figueroa, "Dominican Americans," 207.

102. Tallaj, "Religion on the Dance Floor," 96.

103. Sanchez Carretero, "Santos y Misterios as Channels of Communication in the Diaspora," 317.

104. Lam, "Bearing Witness: Alternate Archives of Latinx Identity in Raquel Cepeda's Bird of Paradise: How I Became Latina."

105. Saldívar, "The Second Elevation of the Novel," 5. For Saldívar's, initial definition of speculative realism, see Saldívar, "Historical Fantasy, Speculative Realism, and Postrace Aesthetics in Contemporary American Fiction," 585.

106. Saldívar, "Historical Fantasy, Speculative Realism, and Postrace Aesthetics in Contemporary American Fiction," 585.

107. Saldívar, 575.

108. Saldívar, 575.

109. George, Post-Soul Nation.

110. For a more substantive discussion of the conceptual and historical links between the post-soul aesthetic and Saldívar's postrace aesthetic, see this book's Coda.

111. I presented my research on Cepeda's memoir at the 2018 Latino Studies Association Biennial Conference, the 2019 MELUS conference, the 2019 Global Dominicanidades: New Approaches to Dominican Studies in the Twenty-First Century conference, and the 2019 American Studies Association conference, discussing these issues with friends and colleagues.

112. Beliso-De Jesús, Electric Santería, 69.

113. Fernández Olmos and Paravisini-Gebert, Creole Religions of the Caribbean, 195.

114. Bettelheim, "Caribbean Espiritismo (Spiritist) Altars."

115. Sanchez Carretero, "Santos y Misterios as Channels of Communication in the Diaspora," 322.

116. Cepeda, Bird of Paradise, 89.

117. Cepeda, 93.

118. Turits, "A World Destroyed, A Nation Imposed"; Moya Pons, The Dominican Republic, 367–70; Roorda, Derby, and Gonzalez, "The Haitian Massacre."

119. Valdés, Racialized Visions.

120. Cepeda, Bird of Paradise, 91.

121. For an analysis of prevalence and value of these practices in the Dominican Republic," see Davis, "Vodú of the Dominican Republic- Devotion to La Veintiuna División."

122. Cepeda, Bird of Paradise, 91.

123. Cepeda, 91. Founded in New York City in 1966, Hare Krishna is a religious movement that promotes vegetarianism and that venerates the Hindu god Krishna, see Rochford, Hare Krishna Transformed.

124. Cepeda, Bird of Paradise, 93.

125. Cepeda, 112.

126. Cepeda, 125.

127. In chapter 6 "Jesus Christ and the Freakazoid," Cepeda has a dream about her friend Priscilla going to a funeral. Two weeks later Priscilla's grandmother dies and Priscilla calls Cepeda a "bruja." Cepeda's paternal grandmother, Ercilia, visits her in a dream to say goodbye. A week later, Cepeda learns that the dream happened around the time that Ercilia died. Because she can see the dead, fifteen-year-old Cepeda comes to think of herself as a "freakazoid," see Cepeda, 78–79. In chapter 8, "God Bodies and Indios," Cepeda interprets an inexplicable wintertime cold spot in her dorm room as a ghost. See Cepeda, 121.

128. Cepeda, *Bird of Paradise*, 165.

129. Tsang, "The Art of Sweeping Sickness and Catching Death"; Murrell, *Afro-Caribbean Religions*, 112–13; Cros Sandoval, chap. 18 "Shopono/Babalú Ayé: God of Diseases and Plagues," in *Worldview, the Orichas, and Santería*, 259–68; De La Torre, "Babalú-Ayé: Ruler over Illness," *Santería*, 70–72; O'Brien, *Animal Sacrifice and Religious Freedom*; González-Wippler, "Babalú-Ayé," *Santería*, 53–54.

130. Cepeda, *Bird of Paradise*, 166–67.

131. Cepeda, 4.

132. Greenspan was the first person to introduce Cepeda to the concept of *gilgul neshamot*, see Cepeda, 267.

133. Cepeda, 267.

134. Cepeda, 268.

135. Fernández Olmos and Paravisini-Gebert, *Creole Religions of the Caribbean*, 76, 206, and 207; Pichardo, "Santería," 507.

136. Cepeda, *Bird of Paradise*, 268.

137. Estevez, "Meet the Survivors of a 'Paper Genocide'"; Gibbens, "Ancient Islanders Visited by Columbus Not 'Extinct,' Study Finds."

138. There are intense debates about Taíno heritage being used as a vehicle for "black denial," see Haslip-Viera, "The 'Indigenous' or 'Neo-Taíno' Movement in The Spanish-Speaking Caribbean and Its Diaspora and the Return of The Old Anglo Neo-Imperialist Scholarship?"; Haslip-Viera, "Amerindian MtDNA Does Not Matter"; Haslip-Viera, "The Taíno Identity Movement among Caribbean Latinas/os in the United States"; González, "A Piece Not the Puzzle"; Wade, "Genes of 'Extinct' Caribbean Islanders Found in Living People"; Estevez, "Meet the Survivors of a 'Paper Genocide'"; "Exploring Taino Traditions." See also, TallBear, *Native American DNA*.

139. Cepeda, *Bird of Paradise*, 262; University of Cambridge, "Ancient Genome Study Identifies Traces of Indigenous 'Taíno' in Present-Day Caribbean Populations."

140. Cepeda, *Bird of Paradise*, 156.

141. Nelson, *The Social Life of DNA*, 2016, 71.

142. Hesman Saey, "What FamilyTreeDNA Sharing Genetic Data with Police Means for You."

143. Nelson, *The Social Life of DNA*, 2016; Wailoo, Nelson, and Lee, *Genetics and the Unsettled Past*; Nelson, "The Social Life of DNA," 2018; Watson, "Forensic DNA Analysis, the Fourth Amendment, and Personal Privacy"; Annas, *Genomic Messages*; Murphy, *Inside the Cell*; Gutmann and Wagner, "Found Your DNA on the Web"; May, "Sociogenetic Risks—Ancestry DNA Testing, Third-Party Identity, and Protection of Privacy"; Moran, "Damned by DNA—Balancing Personal Privacy with Public Safety."

144. Cepeda, *Bird of Paradise*, 161.

145. Cepeda, 227.

146. Cepeda, 31.

147. Cepeda, 191–92.

148. Cepeda, 64–65.

149. Cepeda, 156.

150. Cepeda, 192.

151. Saldívar, "Historical Fantasy, Speculative Realism, and Postrace Aesthetics in Contemporary American Fiction"; Saldívar, "Imagining Cultures"; Saldívar, "Imagining Cultures: The Transnational Imaginary in Postrace America."

152. Subbotsky, "The Belief in Magic in the Age of Science"; Subbotsky, "Magical Reality."

153. Unlike *la india* and *la africana*, God never directly reveals himself to Cepeda. God's unwillingness to show Himself to her causes Cepeda to doubt not only His existence but also His supposed male gender. Consequently, she develops, like her father, a skepticism in the existence of God, see Cepeda, 64.

154. In the Dominican Republic, *fukú* is the African-derived term for bad luck, ill omens, and supernatural curses, whereas the interjection *¡zafa!* is a counter spell that rebukes and wards off a *fukú*, see Christensen and Christensen, *The Discovery of America & Other Myths*, xxvii; Foley and Jermyn, "The Curse of Columbus"; Asociación de Academias de la Lengua Española, "fucú"; Asociación de Academias de la Lengua Española, "¡zafa!"

155. Cepeda, *Bird of Paradise*, 192.

156. Cepeda, 192 and 193.

157. Cepeda, 193.

158. Lee may have popularized the term, but the concept was in the popular media three months before he delivered his Yale lecture Gonzalez, "Director Spike Lee Slams 'same Old' Black Stereotypes in Today's Films." Coining the term "Magical African-American Friend," Christopher John Farley addressed the issue in his Time Magazine article, "That Old Black Magic: Hollywood Is Still Bamboozled When It Comes to Race."

159. Cepeda, *Bird of Paradise*, 139.

160. Cepeda, 196.

161. Cepeda, Raquel Cepeda—Interview Pt. 2.

162. Cepeda writes, "Like Papi, I'm not sure God exists. He—I'm told God is a He—never visits me," see Cepeda, *Bird of Paradise*, 64.

163. ISSD Task Force on Children and Adolescents, "Dissociative Symptoms in Children and Adolescents," 123.

164. Viktorin et al., "Heritability of Perinatal Depression and Genetic Overlap With Nonperinatal Depression."

165. Zagorski, "Is Postpartum Depression a Unique Psychiatric Disorder?"; Fox et al., "A Longitudinal Study of Women's Depression Symptom Profiles during and after the Postpartum Phase."

166. Under the category of prayer, one might also include "brujxing," a form Afro-Latino political activism involving the casting of spells and hexes, see Beliso-De Jesús, "Brujx: An Afro-Latinx Queer Gesture."

167. For an analysis of the prevalence and value of these practices in the Dominican Republic," see Davis, "Vodú of the Dominican Republic- Devotion to La Veintiuna División."

168. Ellis, "The New Black Aesthetic"; Ellis, "Response to NBA Critiques"; Ashe, "Theorizing the Post-Soul Aesthetic: An Introduction"; Ashe, "These Are the 'Breaks': A Roundtable Discussion on Teaching the Post-Soul Aesthetic"; Ashe and Saal, "Introduction."

Coda

1. Melamed, *Represent and Destroy*; Goldberg, *Multiculturalism*; Perlmann and Waters, *The New Race Question*; Sexton, *Amalgamation Schemes*; Hernández, *Multiracials and Civil Rights*; Boyce Davies, *Decolonizing the Academy*; Laó-Montes, "Decolonial Moves: Trans-Locating African Diaspora Spaces"; Maldonado-Torres, "The Decolonial Turn"; Bieger, Saldívar, and Voelz, *The Imaginary and Its Worlds American Studies after the Transnational Turn*; Saldívar, "Historical Fantasy, Speculative Realism, and Postrace Aesthetics in Contemporary American Fiction"; George, *Post-Soul Nation*; Ashe, "Theorizing the Post-Soul Aesthetic: An Introduction"; Baker and Simmons, *The Trouble with Post-Blackness*; Crawford, *Black Post-Blackness*; Lordi, *The Meaning of Soul*.

2. Berlin, *The Making of African America*; Greer, *Black Ethnics Race, Immigration, and the Pursuit of the American Dream*; Smith, *Black Mosaic*.

3. Ernest, *Chaotic Justice Rethinking African American Literary History*; Warren, *What Was African American Literature?*; Warren, "Does African-American Literature Exist?"; Jarrett, *Representing the Race*; Crawford, *Black Post-Blackness*; Crawford, *What Is African American Literature?*

4. Luis, *Dance between Two Cultures*; West-Durán, *Latino and Latina Writers*, 2009; West-Durán, *Latino and Latina Writers*, 2009; Caulfield and Davis, *A Companion to US Latino Literatures*; Stavans and Acosta-Belén, *The Norton Anthology of Latino literature*; Bost and Aparicio, *The Routledge Companion to Latino/a Literature*; Aldama, *The Routledge Concise History of Latino/a Literature*. Delgado and Stefanic, *The Latino/a Condition*. Flores and Rosaldo, *A Companion to Latina/o Studies*.

5. Sánchez, *"Shakin' Up" Race and Gender*; Martínez-San Miguel, *Coloniality of Diasporas*.

6. Lima, *The Latino Body*.

7. Calderón and Saldívar, *Criticism in the Borderlands*; Sánchez González, *Boricua Literature*; Alvarez Borland and Bosch, *Cuban-American Literature and Art*; González, *Border Renaissance: The Texas Centennial and the Emergence of Mexican American Literature*; López, *Chicano Nations: The Hemispheric Origins of Mexican American Literature*; Cutler, *Ends of Assimilation*; García, *Literature As History*; Myers, *Mapping Hispaniola*. Irizarry, *Chicana/o and Latina/o Fiction*.

8. Mohr, *The Nuyorican Experience*; Flores, *Divided Borders*; Oboler, *Ethnic Labels, Latino Lives*; Flores, *From Bomba to Hip-Hop*; Stavans, *The Hispanic Condition*; Laó-Montes and Dávila, *Mambo Montage: The Latinization of New York*; Habell-Pallan and Romero, *Latino/a Popular Culture*; Dávila, *Barrio Dreams*; Oboler, *Latinos and Citizenship the Dilemma of Belonging*; Mirabal and Lao-Montes, *Technofuturos*; Ortíz, *Cultural Erotics in Cuban America*; Dávila, *Latino Spin*; Flores, *The Diaspora Strikes Back: Caribeño Tales of Learning and Turning*; Dávila, *Latinos, Inc.: The Marketing and Making of a People*; Pérez Firmat, *Life on the Hyphen the Cuban-American Way*; García-Peña, *The Borders of Dominicanidad*.

9. Brock and Castañeda Fuertes, *Between Race and Empire*; Greenbaum, *More Than Black*; Candelario, *Black behind the Ears*; Candelario, "Color Matters: Latina/o Racial Identities and Life Chances"; Guridy, *Forging Diaspora: Afro-Cubans and African Americans in a World of Empire and Jim Crow*; Jiménez Román and Flores, *The Afro-Latin@ Reader*; López, *Unbecoming Blackness: The Diaspora Cultures of Afro-Cuban America*; Milian, *Latining America*; Hoffnung-Garskof, *Racial Migrations*.

10. Oboler and Dzidzienyo, *Neither Enemies nor Friends*; Lee, *Building a Latino Civil Rights Movement*; Valdés, *Diasporic Blackness*; Ortiz, *An African American and Latinx History of the United States*.

11. Jackson, *Black Writers and Latin America*; Richardson, *The Afro-Latin@ Experience in Contemporary American Literature and Culture*; Figueroa-Vásquez, *Decolonizing Diasporas*.

12. Clark, "Nationalism in American Literature"; Frederick, "American Literary Nationalism"; Delbanco, "American Literature"; Levine, *Dislocating Race and Nation*; Kennedy, *Strange Nation*.

13. Clark, "Nationalism in American Literature," 518–19.

14. Buell, "The Necessary Fragmentation of the (U.S.) Literary-Cultural Imaginary," 37–38.

15. Delbanco, "American Literature," 34–37.

16. For my understanding of Black Nationalism, see Bracey Jr., Meier, and Rudwick, *Black Nationalism in America*; Moses, *The Golden Age of Black Nationalism, 1850–1925*; Moses, *Classical Black Nationalism*; Van Deburg, *Modern Black Nationalism*.

17. Valdés, *Diasporic Blackness*; Meehan, "Vested in the Anonymous Thousands: Arthur A. Schomburg as Decolonizing Historian"; Crowder, *John Edward Bruce*; Seraile, *Bruce Grit*; James, "The Peculiarities of Afro-Hispanic Radicalism in the United States: The Political Trajectories of Arturo Schomburg and Jesus Colon"; Sinnette, *Arthur Alfonso Schomburg, Black Bibliophile & Collector*.

18. Roszak, "Intersectional Feminism, Black Love, and the Transnational Turn"; John Patrick Leary, "Havana Reads the Harlem Renaissance"; Kutzinski, "Fearful Asymmetries"; Ellis, "Nicolás Guillén and Langston Hughes: Convergences and Divergences."

19. Lejeune, *On Autobiography*; de Man, "Autobiography as De-Facement."

20. Torres-Saillant, "The Latino Autobiography," 64–65.

21. Vázquez, *Triangulations*, 189.

22. Bakhtin, "The Bildungsroman and Its Significance in the History of Realism (Toward a Historical Typology of the Novel)"; LeSeur, *Ten Is the Age of Darkness*; Redfield, *Phantom Formations Aesthetic Ideology and the "Bildungsroman"*; Jeffers, *Apprenticeships the Bildungsroman from Goethe to Santayana*; Japtok, *Growing up Ethnic Nationalism and the Bildungsroman in African American and Jewish American Fiction*; Bolaki, *Unsettling the Bildungsroman*; Latinez, *Developments Encounters of Formation in the Latin American and Hispanic/Latino Bildungsroman*; Graham, *A History of the Bildungsroman*.

23. Saldívar, "Historical Fantasy, Speculative Realism, and Postrace Aesthetics in Contemporary American Fiction," 585 and 590; Saldívar, "Imagining Cultures: The Transnational Imaginary in Postrace America," 5 and 9.

24. Smethurst, *The Black Arts Movement*, 172 and 313.

25. Smethurst, 313–14.

26. Smethurst, 174.

27. Buell, "The Necessary Fragmentation of the (U.S.) Literary-Cultural Imaginary," 31.

28. Saldívar, "The Second Elevation of the Novel," 2.

29. Saldívar, 4–6.

30. Saldívar, "The Second Elevation of the Novel," 13.

31. Saldívar, *The Borderlands of Culture*.

32. Saldívar, "Imagining Cultures: The Transnational Imaginary in Postrace America," 4.

33. Saldívar, 4.

34. Saldívar, 3.

35. Buell, "The Necessary Fragmentation of the (U.S.) Literary-Cultural Imaginary," 36.

36. Saldívar, "Imagining Cultures: The Transnational Imaginary in Postrace America," 10.

37. Saldívar, 15.

38. Saldívar, *The Borderlands of Culture*, 15.

39. Saldívar, "Imagining Cultures: The Transnational Imaginary in Postrace America," 9.

40. Ellis, "The New Black Aesthetic"; Ellis, "Response to NBA Critiques."

41. Anzaldúa, *Borderlands/La Frontera: The New Mestiza*.

42. George, *Buppies, B-Boys, Baps & Bohos*; Neal, *Soul Babies: Black Popular Culture and the Post-Soul Aesthetic*; George, *Post-Soul Nation*; Dickerson, *The End of Blackness: Returning the Souls of Black Folk to Their Rightful Owners*; Ashe, "Theorizing the Post-Soul Aesthetic: An Introduction"; Taylor, "Post-Black, Old Black"; Womack, *Post Black*; Maus and Donahue, *Post-Soul Satire*; Murray, *Queering Post-Black Art*; Crawford, *Black Post-Blackness*.

43. Saldívar, "Imagining Cultures: The Transnational Imaginary in Postrace America," 5–6.

44. Vázquez, *Triangulations*, 23–24.

45. Vázquez, 2 and 17.

46. Vázquez, 13.

47. Vázquez, 33.

48. Laó-Montes, "Afro-Latinidades and the Diasporic Imaginary"; Laó-Montes, "Afro-Latinidades: Bridging Blackness and Latinidad"; Jiménez Román and Flores, *The Afro-Latin@ Reader*; Valdés, *Diasporic Blackness*; Hoffnung-Garskof, *Racial Migrations*; Figueroa-Vásquez, *Decolonizing Diasporas*.

49. Morris, "Piri Thomas: Author's New Book"; Thomas, "An Interview with Piri Thomas," 72.

50. Thomas, "They Have Forced Us to Be Universal."

51. "Marta Moreno Vega," January 8, 2006; "Marta Moreno Vega," September 7, 2007; Vega, *The Altar of My Soul*, 258–59 and 261.

52. *Bling: A Planet Rock*; *Some Girls*.

53. Irizarry, *Chicana/o and Latina/o Fiction*, 11.

54. Irizarry, 27.
55. Irizarry, 7.
56. Irizarry, 14.
57. Irizarry, 14.
58. Irizarry, 7.
59. Irizarry, 110.
60. Irizarry, 27.

Bibliography

Primary Sources: Memoirs

Cepeda, Raquel. *Bird of Paradise: How I Became Latina*. New York: Atria Paperback, 2014.

Chambers, Veronica. *Mama's Girl*. Paperback Edition. New York: Riverhead Books, 1997.

Moore, Carlos. *Pichón: A Memoir: Race and Revolution in Castro's Cuba*. Chicago, IL: Lawrence Hill Books, 2008.

Thomas, Piri. *Down These Mean Streets*. 30th Anniversary Edition. New York: Vintage Books, 1997.

Vega, Marta Moreno. *The Altar of My Soul: The Living Traditions of Santería*. New York: One World-Ballantine Books, 2000.

———. *When the Spirits Dance Mambo: Growing Up Nuyorican in El Barrio*. New York: Three Rivers Press, 2004.

Website Materials and Email Correspondence

afrolatin@forum. "Why Does the Afrolatin@ Forum Use the '@' Symbol in Its Name?" afrolatin@forum. Accessed December 20, 2021. https://www .afrolatinoforum.org/faq.

Andrews, William L. Email to Trent Masiki. "Piri Thomas Entry in the Oxford Companion to African American Literature." November 13, 2019.

Borland, Isabel Alvarez. "Memoirs." Oxford Bibliographies Online in Latino Studies. https://www.oxfordbibliographies.com/view/document/obo-9780199913701/obo -9780199913701-0041.xml.

Brand Nubian. "Slow Down." *One For All*. Elektra, 1990. https://genius.com/Brand -nubian-slow-down-lyrics.

———. "Wake Up (Reprise in the Sunshine)." *One For All*. Elektra, 1990. https:// genius.com/Brand-nubian-wake-up-reprise-in-the-sunshine-lyrics.

"Carlos Moore Biography." April 17, 2019. https://web.archive.org/web /20190417021053/http://bunchecenter.ucla.edu/carlos-moore-collection -overview-2/carlos-moore-biography/.

The Center for the Study of White American Culture. "The Multiracial Movement: Part I, A History." May 2, 2019. https://cswac.org/the-multiracial-movement-a -history/.

———. "The Multiracial Movement: Part 2 Retrospective Analysis." May 16, 2019. https://cswac.org/the-multiracial-movement-retrospective-analysis/.

———. "The Multiracial Movement: Part 3 Lessons Learned." May 30, 2019. https://cswac.org/the-multiracial-movement-lessons-learned/.

El Centro. "Why Latinx/e?" Accessed September 5, 2020. https://elcentro.colostate
.edu/about/why-latinx/.

Cha-Jua, Sundiata Keita. "Beyond the Rape Myth: Black Resistance to Lynching,
1867–1930." Conference paper abstract for the 35th annual National Council for
Black Studies, March 16, 2011. http://citation.allacademic.com/meta/p_mla_apa
_research_citation/4/9/7/0/0/p497008_index.html.

Chambers, Veronica. "Veronica Chambers '87 to Discuss the Meaning of Michelle."
August 20, 2017. https://simons-rock.edu/news/veronica-chambers-meaning-of
-michelle.php.

———. "Veronica Chambers '87: Writer and Editor," 2019. https://simons-rock.edu
/giving/donor-stories/veronica-chambers.php.

Columbia College Chicago. "Exploring Taino Traditions: Jorge Estevez." Accessed
October 14, 2019. https://events.colum.edu/event/exploring_taino_traditions
_jorge_estevez.

Dudley, David L. Email to Trent Masiki. "Piri Thomas Entry in the Oxford
Companion to African American Literature." October 16, 2019.

Jiménez Román, Miriam. "Real Unity for Afro-Latinos and African Americans."
Accessed December 12, 2021. https://www.afrolatinoforum.org/real-unity-for
-afrolatin.

Meraji, Shereen Marisol. "'Hispanic,' 'Latino,' Or 'Latinx'? Survey Says . . ." *Code
Switch*, August 11, 2020, sec. Hispanic Heritage Month. https://www.npr.org
/sections/codeswitch/2020/08/11/901398248/hispanic-latino-or-latinx-survey-says.

"The National Conference of Afro-American Writers." n.d. https://franklin.library
.upenn.edu/catalog/FRANKLIN_9977579546203681.

Original Products Botanica. "Martha the Dominator." *Original Botanica* (blog),
July 7, 2015. https://www.originalbotanica.com/blog/martha-dominator-marta
-dominadora/.

"Roots (Biography of Carlos Moore)," 2016. http://moorecarlos.com/roots.asp.

The Fat Feminist Witch. "The Nine Tuesdays of Saint Martha the Dominator." *The
Fat Feminist Witch Podcast* (blog), September 15, 2020. https://thefatfeministwitch
.com/2020/09/15/the-nine-tuesdays-of-saint-martha-the-dominator/.

University of Cambridge. "Ancient Genome Study Identifies Traces of Indigenous
'Taíno' in Present-Day Caribbean Populations." University of Cambridge,
February 19, 2018. https://www.cam.ac.uk/research/news/ancient-genome-study
-identifies-traces-of-indigenous-taino-in-present-day-caribbean-populations.

Secondary Sources: Books, Chapters, Essays, Articles, Dissertations,
Documents, Documentaries, Films, Videos, Conference Abstracts
and Papers, Dictionary and Encyclopedia Entries, Radio Broadcasts,
and Reports

"Abbey Lincoln: The Power of Voice." NPR, August 17, 2010. https://www.npr.org
/2010/08/17/129255992/abbey-lincoln-the-power-of-voice.

Abiodun, Rowland. "Understanding Yoruba Art and Aesthetics: The Concept of
Àse." *African Arts* 27, no. 3 (1994): 68–102.

Abrahams, Roger D. "Playing the Dozens." *Journal of American Folklore* 75, no. 297 (September 1962): 209–20.

Adi, Hakim. *Pan-Africanism and Communism: The Communist International, Africa and the Diaspora, 1919–1939.* Trenton, NJ: Africa World Press, 2013.

"Afro-Latin, Adj." In *OED Online*, n.d. Boston University. Accessed December 3, 2021.

"Afro-Latin-American, Adj." In *OED Online*, n.d. Boston University. Accessed December 3, 2021.

Ahearn, Charlie. "The Five Percent Solution." *Spin*, February 1991. Google Books.

Aidi, Hisham. "'Verily, There Is Only One Hip-Hop Umma': Islam, Cultural Protest and Urban Marginality." *Socialism and Democracy* 18, no. 2 (July 2004): 107–26. https://doi.org/10.1080/08854300408428402.

Aja, Alan A. "Anyone But Blacks." *Souls: A Critical Journal of Black Politics, Culture & Society* 14, no. 1/2 (January 2012): 88–116.

Aldama, Frederick Luis. *The Routledge Concise History of Latino/a Literature.* Routledge Concise Histories of Literature Series. New York: Routledge, 2013.

Aldich, Nelson. "Inside the Skin." In *"Piri Thomas" in Contemporary Literary Criticism*, 17:497. Detroit, MI: Gale, 1981. Originally published in "Book Week" in *World Journal Tribune*, May 21, 1967, 4.

Algarín, Miguel, and Bob Holman, eds. *Aloud: Voices from the Nuyorican Poets Cafe.* New York: H. Holt, 1994.

Allatson, Paul. "From 'Latinidad' to 'Latinid@des': Imagining the Twenty-First Century." In *The Cambridge Companion to Latina/o American Literature*, edited by John Morán González, 128–44. Cambridge: Cambridge University Press, 2016. https://doi.org/10.1017/CBO9781107045385.010.

———. "Marianismo." In *Key Terms in Latino/a Literary and Cultural Studies*, 153–55. Malden, MA: Blackwell Publishing, 2007.

———. "Mestizo/a, Mestizaje." In *Key Terms in Latino/a Literary and Cultural Studies*, 158–59. Malden, MA: Blackwell Publishing, 2007.

———. "Mulato/a, Mulatez." In *Key Terms in Latino/a Literary and Cultural Studies*, 166–67. Malden, MA: Blackwell Publishing, 2007.

Allen, Earnest, Jr. "Identity and Destiny: The Formative Views of the Moorish Science Temple and the Nation of Islam." In *Muslims of the Americanization Path*, 163–214. New York: Oxford University Press, 1998.

———. "Making the Strong Survive: The Contours and Contradictions of Message Rap." In *Droppin' Science: Critical Essays on Rap Music and Hip Hop Culture*, edited by William Eric Perkins, 159–91. Philadelphia, PA: Temple University Press, 1996.

Almo, Hector Luis. "The Xing of Language: The Case AGAINST 'Latinx.'" *Latino Rebels* (blog), December 12, 2015. https://www.latinorebels.com/2015/12/12/the-x-ing-of-language-the-case-against-latinix/.

Alvarez Borland, Isabel, and Lynette M. F. Bosch, eds. *Cuban-American Literature and Art: Negotiating Identities.* Albany: State University of New York Press, 2009.

Anaporte-Easton, Jean. "Etheridge Knight: Poet and Prisoner. An Introduction." *Callaloo* 19, no. 4 (1996): 941–46.

Andrews, George Reid. *Afro-Latin America, 1800–2000.* Oxford: Oxford University Press, 2004.

Andrews, William L. *African-American Autobiography: A Collection of Critical Essays*. Englewood Cliffs, NJ: Pearson, 1992.

———. *To Tell a Free Story: The First Century of Afro-American Autobiography, 1760–1865*. Urbana: University of Illinois Press, 1986.

Angelou, Maya. "Foreword." In *Pichón: A Memoir: Race and Revolution in Castro's Cuba*, ix. Chicago: Lawrence Hill Books, 2008.

———. *The Heart of a Woman*. New York: Random House, 1981. Kindle.

Annas, George J., and Sherman Elias. *Genomic Messages: How the Evolving Science of Genetics Affects Our Health, Families, and Future*. New York: HarperOne, 2015.

Antonsich, Marco, Ted Cantle, Tariq Modood, and Raffaele Iacovino. "Interculturalism versus Multiculturalism: The Cantle-Modood Debate." *Ethnicities* 16, no. 3 (2016): 470–93. https://doi.org/10.1177/1468796815604558.

Anzaldúa, Gloria. *Borderlands/La Frontera: The New Mestiza*. 25 Anniversary 4th Edition. San Francisco, CA: Ann Lute Books, 2012.

Aparicio, Frances R. "The Blackness of Sugar: Celia Cruz and the Performance of (Trans)Nationalism." *Cultural Studies* 13, no. 2 (April 1999): 223–36. https://doi.org/10.1080/095023899335257.

Aparicio, Frances R., and Susana Chávez-Silverman, eds. *Tropicalizations: Transcultural Representations of Latinidad*. Hanover, NH: University Press of New England, 1997.

Appiah, Kwame Anthony. "The Case for Capitalizing the 'B' in Black." *Atlantic*, June 18, 2020. https://www.theatlantic.com/ideas/archive/2020/06/time-to-capitalize-blackand-white/613159/.

Asante, Molefi. *The Afrocentric Idea*. Revised and Expanded Edition. Philadelphia, PA: Temple University Press, 1998.

Asante, Molefi Kete, and Mambo Ama Mazama, eds. "Afrocentricity." In *Encyclopedia of Black Studies*, 72–74. Thousand Oaks, CA: SAGE Publications, Inc., 2004.

Ashe, Bertram D., ed. "Post-Soul Aesthetic Special Issue: Essays on Contemporary African American Art." *African American Review* 41, no. 4 (January 12, 2007). https://doi.org/10.2307/25426980.

———. "Post-Soul President: Dreams from My Father and the Post-Soul Aesthetic." In *The Obama Effect: Multidisciplinary Renderings of the 2008 Campaign*, 103–15. New York: SUNY Press, 2010.

———. "Theorizing the Post-Soul Aesthetic: An Introduction." *African American Review* 41, no. 4 (Winter 2007): 609–23.

Ashe, Bertram D., Crystal Anderson, Mark Anthony Neal, Evie Shockley, and Alexander Weheliye. "These—Are—The 'Breaks': A Roundtable Discussion on Teaching the Post-Soul Aesthetic." *African American Review* 41, no. 4 (December 1, 2007): 787. https://doi.org/10.2307/25426990.

Ashe, Bertram D., and Ilka Saal. "Introduction." In *Slavery and the Post-Black Imagination*, 3–20. Seattle: University of Washington Press, 2020.

Asociación de Academias de la Lengua Española. "fucú." In *Diccionario de americanismos*, 1007. Barcelona: Penguin-Random House, 2015. https://www.asale.org/damer/fucú.

———. "mulataje." In *Diccionario de americanismos*, 1480. Barcelona: Penguin-Random House, 2015. https://www.asale.org/damer/mulataje.

———. "¡zafa!" In *Diccionario de americanismos*, 2200. Barcelona: Penguin-Random House, 2015. https://www.asale.org/damer/¡zafa!.

Asukile, Thabiti. "Joel Augustus Rogers: Black International Journalism, Archival Research, and Black Print Culture." *Journal of African American History* 95, no. 3–4 (July 1, 2010): 322–47. https://doi.org/10.5323/jafriamerhist.95.3-4.0322.

Atlantic Records. *Brand Nubian — All For One (Video Version)*, 2009. https://www.youtube.com/watch?v=8auuY4fvLyY.

Austerlitz, Paul. "Machito and Mario Bauza Latin Jazz in the U.S. Mainstream." In *Jazz Consciousness: Music, Race, and Humanity*, 42–97. Music/Culture. Middletown, CT: Wesleyan University Press, 2005.

Avilez, GerShun. *Radical Aesthetics and Modern Black Nationalism*. Urbana: University of Illinois Press, 2016.

Baker, Houston A., and K. Merinda Simmons, eds. *The Trouble with Post-Blackness*. New York: Columbia University Press, 2015.

Baker, James K. "The American Society of African Culture." *Journal of Modern African Studies* 4, no. 3 (November 1966): 367–69.

Bakhtin, M. M. "The Bildungsroman and Its Significance in the History of Realism (Toward a Historical Typology of the Novel)." In *Speech Genres and Other Late Essays*, edited by Caryl Emerson and Michael Holquist, translated by Vern W. McGee, 10–59. Austin: University of Texas Press, 1987.

Ballard, Eoghan Craig. "Espiritismo." In *The Voodoo Encyclopedia: Magic, Ritual, and Religion*. Santa Barbara, CA: ABC-CLIO, 2015.

Baraka, Amiri. *The Autobiography of LeRoi Jones*. Chicago: Lawrence Hill Books-Chicago Review Press, 1997.

Bassil, Ryan. "The Prestige, The Five Percenters, and Why Jay Electronica Hasn't Released His Debut Album." *Vice*, October 23, 2013. https://www.vice.com/en_uk/article/6ed3xk/the-prestige-the-five-percenters-and-why-jay-electronica-hasnt-released-his-debut-album.

Beliso-De Jesús, Aisha. "Brujx: An Afro-Latinx Queer Gesture." In *Critical Dialogues in Latinx Studies: A Reader*, 528–38. New York: New York University Press, 2021.

———. *Electric Santería: Racial and Sexual Assemblages of Transnational Religion*. Gender, Theory, and Religion. New York: Columbia University Press, 2015.

Bell, John Frederick. "Confronting Colorism: Interracial Abolition and the Consequences of Complexion." *Journal of the Early Republic* 39, no. 2 (Summer 2019): 239–65. https://doi.org/10.1353/jer.2019.0027.

Beltran, Cristina. *The Trouble with Unity: Latino Politics and the Creation of Identity*. Oxford: Oxford University Press, 2010.

Bennett, Lerone, Jr. "What's In a Name?: Negro vs. Afro-American vs. Black." *Ebony Magazine*, November 1967. Google Books.

Berlin, Ira. "Global Passages." In *The Making of African America: The Four Great Migrations*. New York: Viking, 2010. Kindle.

———. *The Making of African America: The Four Great Migrations*. New York: Viking, 2010. Kindle.

Bettelheim, Judith. "Caribbean Espiritismo (Spiritist) Altars: The Indian and the Congo." *Art Bulletin* 87, no. 2 (June 2005): 312–30. https://doi.org/10.1080/00043079.2005.10786241.

Bieger, Laura, Ramón Saldívar, and Johannes Voelz, eds. *The Imaginary and Its Worlds American Studies after the Transnational Turn*. Re-Mapping the Transnational: A Dartmouth Series in American Studies. Hanover, NH: Dartmouth College Press, 2013.

Blake, Felice. "What Does It Mean to Be Black?: Gendered Redefinitions of Interethnic Solidarity in Piri Thomas's *Down These Mean Streets*." *African American Review* 51, no. 2 (Summer 2018): 95–110.

Board of Education, Island Trees Union Free School District 26 v. Pico et al, 638 F.2d 404 (1982).

Boaz, Danielle N. *Banning Black Gods: Law and Religions of the African Diaspora*. University Park: Penn State University Press, 2021. https://doi.org/10.5325/j.ctv1hcg066.

Bolaki, Stella. *Unsettling the Bildungsroman: Reading Contemporary Ethnic American Women's Fiction*. Amsterdam: Rodopi, 2011.

Bolton, Gillie, Stephanie Howlett, Colin Lago, and Jeannie K. Wright, eds. *Writing Cures: An Introductory Handbook of Writing in Counselling and Therapy*. Abingdon, UK: Taylor & Francis Group, 2004.

"Book Ban Is Eased by Queens Board." *New York Times*, June 3, 1971, sec. Archives. https://www.nytimes.com/1971/06/03/archives/book-ban-is-eased-by-queens-board-copies-of-mean-streets-to-be.html.

Booklist. "Mama's Girl." *Booklist*, January 1997.

———. "Mama's Girl." *Booklist*, April 1997.

Bost, Suzanne, and Frances R. Aparicio, eds. *The Routledge Companion to Latino/a Literature*. London: Routledge, 2013. Kindle.

Bouchard, Gerard. "What Is Interculturalism?" *McGill Law Journal* 56, no. 2 (2011 2010): 435–70.

Bowen, Patrick D. "U.S. Latina/o Muslims Since 1920: From 'Moors' to 'Latino Muslims.'" *Journal of Religious History* 37, no. 2 (2013): 165–84. https://doi.org/10.1111/1467-9809.12026.

Boyce Davies, Carole. *Decolonizing the Academy: African Diaspora Studies*. Trenton, NJ: Africa World Press, 2003.

Boyce, Travis D., and Winsome M. Chunnu. "Toward a Post-Racial Society, or a 'Rebirth' of a Nation?: White Anxiety and Fear of Black Equality in the United States." In *Historicizing Fear: Ignorance, Vilification, and Othering*, 122–53. Boulder: University Press of Colorado, 2020.

Bracey, John H., Jr., August Meier, and Elliott M. Rudwick. *Black Nationalism in America*. American Heritage Series Indianapolis, IN: Bobbs-Merrill Co., 1970.

Brammer, John Paul. "Digging into the Messy History of 'Latinx' Helped Me Embrace My Complex Identity." *Mother Jones* (blog), June 2019. https://www.motherjones.com/media/2019/06/digging-into-the-messy-history-of-latinx-helped-me-embrace-my-complex-identity/.

Brand Nubian. "Slow Down." *One For All*. Elektra, 1990. https://genius.com/Brand-nubian-slow-down-lyrics.

———. "Wake Up (Reprise in the Sunshine)." *One For All*. Elektra, 1990. https://genius.com/Brand-nubian-wake-up-reprise-in-the-sunshine-lyrics.

Brandon, George. "Hierarchy Without a Head: Observations on Changes in the Social Organization of Some Afroamerican Religions in the United States, 1959–1999 with Special Reference to Santeria." *Archives de Sciences Sociales Des Religions*, no. 117 (January 1, 2002): 151–74. https://doi.org/10.4000/assr.2491.

———. *Santeria from Africa to the New World: The Dead Sell Memories*. Bloomington: Indiana University Press, 1993.

Braxton, Joanne M. *Black Women Writing Autobiography: A Tradition within a Tradition*. Philadelphia: Temple University Press, 1989.

Brock, Lisa, and Digna Castañeda Fuertes, eds. *Between Race and Empire: African-Americans and Cubans before the Cuban Revolution*. Philadelphia: Temple University Press, 1998.

Brown, Anna. "The Changing Categories the U.S. Census Has Used to Measure Race." *Pew Research Center* (blog), February 25, 2020. https://www.pewresearch.org/fact-tank/2020/02/25/the-changing-categories-the-u-s-has-used-to-measure-race/.

Brunsma, David L., ed. *Mixed Messages: Multiracial Identities in the "Color-Blind" Era*. Boulder, CO: Lynne Rienner Publishers, 2006.

Buell, Lawrence. "The Necessary Fragmentation of the (U.S.) Literary-Cultural Imaginary." In *The Imaginary and Its Worlds: American Studies after the Transnational Turn*, edited by Laura Bieger, Ramón Saldívar, and Johannes Voelz., 23–41. Re-Mapping the Transnational: A Dartmouth Series in American Studies. Hanover, NH: Dartmouth College Press, 2013.

Buscaglia-Salgado, José F. "Circumventing Racialism through Mulataje." In *Oxford Research Encyclopedia of Literature*, May 24, 2018. https://doi.org/10.1093/acrefore/9780190201098.013.395.

———. *Undoing Empire: Race and Nation in the Mulatto Caribbean*. Minneapolis: University of Minnesota Press, 2003.

Butterfield, Stephen. *Black Autobiography in America*. Amherst: University of Massachusetts Press, 1974.

Calderón, Héctor, and José David Saldívar, eds. *Criticism in the Borderlands: Studies in Chicano Literature, Culture, and Ideology*. Post-Contemporary Interventions. Durham, NC: Duke University Press, 1991.

Caldwell, Katrina Myers. "Leading the Protest." *Footsteps* 7, no. 2 (March/April 2005). General OneFile.

Caldwell, Patricia. *The Puritan Conversion Narrative: The Beginnings of American Expression*. Cambridge: Cambridge University Press, 1983.

Caminero-Santangelo, Marta. "Latinidad." In *The Routledge Companion to Latino/a Literature*, edited by Suzanne Bost and Frances R. Aparicio, 13–24. London: Routledge, 2013. Kindle.

———. *On Latinidad: U.S. Latino Literature and the Construction of Ethnicity*. Gainesville: University Press of Florida, 2007.

Candelario, Ginetta E. B. *Black Behind the Ears: Dominican Racial Identity from Museums to Beauty Shops*. Durham, NC: Duke University Press Books, 2007.

————. "Color Matters: Latina/o Racial Identities and Life Chances." In *A Companion to Latina/o Studies*, edited by Juan Flores and Renato Rosaldo, 337–50. Malden, MA: Blackwell Publishing, 2007.

Cantaño, Adriana. "The RAE Has Made Its Decision About Latinx and Latine in Its First Style Manual." *Remezcla* (blog), November 28, 2018. https://remezcla.com /culture/rae-style-manual/.

Cantle, Ted. *Interculturalism: The New Era of Cohesion and Diversity*. Basingstoke, UK: Palgrave Macmillan, 2012.

————. "National Identity, Plurality and Interculturalism." *Political Quarterly* 85, no. 3 (July 2014): 312–19. https://doi.org/10.1111/1467-923X.12101.

Cantor-Navas, Judy. "Cuban Country Queen Celina Gonzalez Dead at 85." *Billboard* (blog), February 5, 2015. https://www.billboard.com/music/music-news/celina -gonzalez-dead-85-cuban-country-queen-6458543/.

Cantú, Norma E. "Memoir, Autobiography, Testimonio." In *Routledge Companion to Latino/a Literature*, edited by Suzanne Bost and Frances R. Aparicio, 310–22. London: Routledge, 2013.

Caraballo, Ecleen Luzmila. "This Comic Breaks Down Latinx vs. Latine for Those Who Want to Be Gender-Inclusive." *Remezcla* (blog), October 24, 2019. https:// remezcla.com/culture/latinx-latine-comic/.

Caraballo-Cueto, Jose, and Isar P. Godreau. "Colorism and Health Disparities in Home Countries: The Case of Puerto Rico." *Journal of Immigrant and Minority Health* 23, no. 5 (October 2021): 926–35. https://doi.org/10.1007/s10903-021 -01222-7.

"Carlos Moore Biography," April 17, 2019. https://web.archive.org/web /20190417021053/http://bunchecenter.ucla.edu/carlos-moore-collection -overview-2/carlos-moore-biography/.

Carpio, Glenda R. "Now Check It: Junot Diaz's Wondrous Spanglish." In *Junot Diaz and the Decolonial Imagination*, edited by Monica Hanna, Jennifer Harford Vargas, and José David Saldívar, Durham, NC: Duke University Press, 2016. Kindle.

Cassel, Jeris. "Mama's Girl." *Library Journal* 121, no. 12 (7/1/1996 1996): 126.

Caulfield, Carlota, and Darién J. Davis, eds. *A Companion to US Latino Literatures*. Woodbridge, UK: Tamesis, 2010.

Cepeda, Raquel. *Bling: A Planet Rock*. Image Entertainment, 2010.

————. Raquel Cepeda—Interview Pt. 2, 2008. https://www.youtube.com/watch?v =ulN6eQHYF9M.

————. *Some Girls*. San Francisco, CA: Saboteur Media, 2017. https://nhfpl.kanopy .com/node/3467650.

Cha-Jua, Sundiata Keita. "Beyond the Rape Myth Black Resistance to Lynching, 1867–1930." March 16, 2011. http://citation.allacademic.com/meta/p_mla_apa _research_citation/4/9/7/0/0/p497008_index.html.

Chambers, Veronica. "Secret Latina at Large." In *Becoming American: Personal Essays by First Generation Immigrant Women*, 21–28. New York: Hyperion, 2000.

————. "The Secret Latina." *Essence* 31, no. 3 (July 2000): 102 and 152.

———. "Veronica Chambers '87 to Discuss the Meaning of Michelle." August 20, 2017. https://simons-rock.edu/news/veronica-chambers-meaning-of-michelle.php.

———. "Veronica Chambers '87: Writer and Editor," 2019. https://simons-rock.edu/giving/donor-stories/veronica-chambers.php.

Chavez-Dueñas, Nayeli Y., Hector Y. Adames, and Kurt C. Organista. "Skin-Color Prejudice and Within-Group Racial Discrimination: Historical and Current Impact on Latino/a Populations." *Hispanic Journal of Behavioral Sciences* 36, no. 1 (February 2014): 3–26. https://doi.org/10.1177/0739986313511306.

Chetty, Raj, and Amaury Rodríguez. "Introduction." *Black Scholar* 45, no. 2 (2015): 1–9. https://doi.org/10.1080/00064246.2015.1012990.

Chidiac, Nayla. "On Writing Therapy. From Finding Forrester to Imre Kertész." *Annales Médico-Psychologiques, Revue Psychiatrique* 177, no. 5 (May 2019): 394–403. https://doi.org/10.1016/j.amp.2019.02.006.

Chimezie, Amuzie. "The Dozens: An African-Heritage Theory." *Journal of Black Studies* 6, no. 4 (1976): 401–20.

Cho, Sumi. "Post-Racialism." *Iowa Law Review* 94, no. 5 (2009 2008): 1589–650.

Christensen, Thomas, and Carol Christensen, eds. *The Discovery of America & Other Myths: A New World Reader*. San Francisco, CA: Chronicle Books, 1992.

Chude-Sokei, Louis. "Foreign Negro Flash Agents: Eric Walrond and the Discrepancies of Diaspora." In *Eric Walrond: The Critical Heritage*, edited by Louis J. Parascandola and Carl A. Wade, 72–99. Jamaica: University of West Indies Press, 2012.

Clark, Harry Hayden. "Nationalism in American Literature." *University of Toronto Quarterly* 2, no. 4 (1933): 492–519. https://doi.org/10.3138/utq.2.4.492.

Clark, Mary Ann. "Espiritismo." In *African American Religious Cultures*, edited by Anthony B. Pinn, 181–83. Santa Barbara, CA: ABC-CLIO, 2009.

Clark, Veve A., and Sara E. Johnson, eds. *Kaiso!: Writings by and about Katherine Dunham*. Madison: University of Wisconsin Press, 2006.

Claudia, Mitchell-Kernan. "Signifying and Marking: Two Afro-Americans Speech Acts." In *Linguistic Anthropology: A Reader*, edited by Alessandro Duranti, 151–64. Malden, MA: Blackwell Publishing, 2001. http://doi.wiley.com/10.1525/aa.2002.104.2.677.

Clemetson, Lynette. "Hispanics Now Largest Minority, Census Shows." *New York Times*, January 22, 2003.

Cocalis, Susan L. "The Transformation of 'Bildung' from an Image to an Ideal." *Monatshefte* 70, no. 4 (Winter 1978): 399–414.

Cohn, D'vera. "Census History: Counting Hispanics." *Pew Research Center's Social & Demographic Trends Project* (blog), March 3, 2010. https://www.pewresearch.org/social-trends/2010/03/03/census-history-counting-hispanics-2/.

Collins, Lisa Gail, and Margo Natalie Crawford. *New Thoughts on the Black Arts Movement*. New Brunswick, NJ: Rutgers University Press, 2006.

Collins, Michael S. *Understanding Etheridge Knight*. Understanding Contemporary American Literature. Columbia: University of South Carolina Press, 2012.

Contreras, Felix. "Before Celia Cruz or J.Lo, There Was Graciela." *NPR*, April 8, 2010. https://www.npr.org/sections/ablogsupreme/2010/04/before_celia_or_j_lo_there_was_graciela.html.

Cooperman, Jeannette. "Capitalizing 'Black.'" *Common Reader: A Journal of the Essay*, July 14, 2020. https://commonreader.wustl.edu/capitalizing-black/.

Cordasco, F. Review of *Down These Mean Streets*, by Thomas Piri. *International Migration Review* 2, no. 3 (1968): 89–89. https://doi.org/10.2307/3002635.

Cortes, Felix, Angel Falcon, and Juan Flores. "The Cultural Expression of Puerto Ricans in New York: A Theoretical Perspective and Critical Review." *Latin American Perspectives* 3, no. 3 (1976): 117–52.

Cortés, Jason. *Macho Ethics: Masculinity and Self-Representation in Latino-Caribbean Narrative*. Lewisburg, PA: Bucknell University Press, 2015.

Couser, G. Thomas. *Memoir: An Introduction*. Oxford: Oxford University Press, 2011.

———. *Vulnerable Subjects: Ethics and Life Writing*. Ithaca, NY: Cornell University Press, 2004.

Craven, Julia. "A Sudden Shift of Recognition: The Associated Press Joins the Movement to Capitalize 'Black.'" *Slate Magazine*, June 22, 2020. https://slate.com/news-and-politics/2020/06/ap-capitalizing-black.html.

Crawford, Margo Natalie. *Black Post-Blackness: The Black Arts Movement and Twenty-First-Century Aesthetics*. New Black Studies Series. Urbana: University of Illinois Press, 2017.

———. *What Is African American Literature?* Hoboken, NJ: Wiley-Blackwell, 2021.

Cros Sandoval, Mercedes. *Worldview, The Orichas, and Santería: Africa to Cuba and Beyond*. Gainesville: University Press of Florida, 2006.

Crowder, Ralph. *John Edward Bruce: Politician, Journalist, and Self-Trained Historian of the African Diaspora*. New York: New York University Press, 2004.

Cruse, Harold. *The Crisis of the Negro Intellectual*. New York: New York Review Book, 1967.

Cruz, Celia, and Ana Cristina Reymundo. *Celia: My Life*. New York: Rayo, 2004.

Cruz-Malavé, Arnaldo. "The Antifoundational Foundational Fiction of Piri Thomas (1928–2011)." *Centro Journal* 24, no. 1 (Spring 2012): 4–19.

Cutler, John Alba. *Ends of Assimilation: The Formation of Chicano Literature*. New York: Oxford University Press, 2014.

Da Costa, Alexandre Emboaba. "Thinking 'Post-Racial' Ideology Transnationally: The Contemporary Politics of Race and Indigeneity in the Americas." *Critical Sociology* 42, no. 4–5 (July 2016): 475–90. https://doi.org/10.1177/0896920515591175.

Daas, Martha M. "From Holy Hostess to Dragon Tamer: The Anomaly of Saint Martha." *Literature & Theology* 22, no. 1 (March 2008): 1–15. https://doi.org/10.1093/litthe/frm050.

Dalleo, R., and Elena Machado Sáez. *The Latino/a Canon and the Emergence of Post-Sixties Literature*. Paperback Edition. New York: Palgrave Macmillan, 2013.

Danticat, Edwidge, Veronica Chambers, and Sheneska Jackson. "Three Young Voices." *Essence* 27, no. 1 (May 1996): 101–2, 104, 164, and 166.

Davies, Christie. "Ethnic Jokes, Moral Values and Social Boundaries." *British Journal of Sociology* 33, no. 3 (1982): 383–403. https://doi.org/10.2307/589483.

Dávila, Arlene. *Barrio Dreams: Puerto Ricans, Latinos, and the Neoliberal City.* Berkeley: University of California Press, 2004.

———. "Culture in the Battlefront: From Nationalist to Pan-Latina Projects." In *Mambo Montage*, edited by Agustín Laó-Montes, 159–82. Columbia University Press, 2001. https://doi.org/10.7312/lao-11274-007.

———. *Latino Spin: Public Image and the Whitewashing of Race.* New York: New York University Press, 2008.

———. *Latinos, Inc.: The Marketing and Making of a People.* Berkeley: University of California Press, 2012.

Davis, James. *Eric Walrond: A Life in the Harlem Renaissance and the Transatlantic Caribbean.* New York: Columbia University Press, 2015.

Davis, Martha Ellen. "Diasporal Dimensions of Dominican Folk Religion and Music." *Black Music Research Journal* 32, no. 1 (2012): 161–91. https://doi.org/10.5406/blacmusiresej.32.1.0161.

———. "Vodú of the Dominican Republic: Devotion to 'La Veintiuna División.'" *Afro-Hispanic Review* 26, no. 1 (2007): 75–90.

Dawson, Michael C., and Lawrence D. Bobo. "One Year Late and the Myth of a Post-Racial Society." *Du Bois Review: Social Science Research on Race* 6, no. 2 (2009): 247–49. https://doi.org/10.1017/S1742058X09990282.

"Day's Highlights." *Chicago Tribune*, November 18, 1968, sec. 1A.

De La Torre, Miguel A. "Espiritismo." In *Hispanic American Religious Cultures*, 220–24. American Religious Cultures. Santa Barbara, CA: ABC-CLIO, 2009.

———. "Kardecism." In *Santería: The Beliefs and Rituals of a Growing Religion in America*, 172–74. Grand Rapids, MI: William B. Eerdmans Pub. Co., 2004.

———. "Marianismo." In *Hispanic American Religious Cultures*, 1:346–48. American Religious Cultures. Santa Barbara, CA: ABC-CLIO, 2009.

———. "Rethinking Mulatez." In *Rethinking Latino(a) Religion & Identity*, edited by Gaston Espinosa, 158–75. Cleveland: Pilgrim Press, 2006.

———. *Santería: The Beliefs and Rituals of a Growing Religion in America.* Grand Rapids, MI: William B. Eerdmans, 2004.

"Debate: Baldwin vs. Buckley." British Broadcasting Corporation. American Archive of Public Broadcasting (GBH and the Library of Congress). Accessed January 17, 2022. http://americanarchive.org/catalog/cpb-aacip-151-sn00z71m54.

DeCosta-Willis, Miriam. "Can(n)on Fodder: Afro-Hispanic Literature, Heretical Texts, and the Polemics of Canon-Formation." *Afro-Hispanic Review* 19, no. 2 (2000): 30–39.

Del Barco, Mandalit. "Rap's Latin Sabor." In *Droppin' Science: Critical Essays on Rap Music and Hip Hop Culture*, edited by William Eric Perkins, 63–84. Philadelphia: Temple University Press, 1996.

Delbanco, Andrew. "American Literature: A Vanishing Subject?" *Daedalus* 135, no. 2 (2006): 22–37. https://doi.org/10.1162/daed.2006.135.2.22.

Delgadillo, Theresa. "African, Latina, Feminist, and Decolonial: Marta Moreno Vega's Remembrance of Life in El Barrio in the 1950s." In *Theories of the Flesh:*

Latinx and Latin American Feminisms, Transformation, and Resistance, edited by
Andrea J. Pitts, Mariana Ortega, and José Medina, 157–170. Oxford: Oxford
University Press, 2019. https://doi.org/10.1093/oso/9780190062965.003.0010.

———. *Spiritual Mestizaje: Religion, Gender, Race, and Nation in Contemporary
Chicana Narrative*. Durham, NC: Duke University Press, 2011.

———. "Spirituality." In *The Routledge Companion to Latino/a Literature*, edited by
Suzanne Bost and Frances R. Aparicio, 240–50. London: Routledge, 2013.
Kindle.

Delgado, Richard, and Jean Stefanic, eds. *The Latino/a Condition: A Critical Reader*.
2nd ed. New York: NYU Press, 2011.

Deutsch, Nathaniel. "'The Asiatic Black Man': An African American Orientalism?"
Journal of Asian American Studies 4, no. 3 (2001): 193–208. https://doi.org/10.1353
/jaas.2001.0029.

Dhillon-Jamerson, Komal K. "Euro-Americans Favoring People of Color: Covert
Racism and Economies of White Colorism." *American Behavioral Scientist* 62,
no. 14 (December 2018): 2087–100. https://doi.org/10.1177/0002764218810754.

Dickerson, Debra J. *The End of Blackness: Returning the Souls of Black Folk to Their
Rightful Owners*. New York: Anchor Books, 2005. Kindle.

DJ Ron G. "About Us." Legendary DJ Ron G. Accessed June 18, 2018. https://
legendarydjrong.com/bio-%26-press.

Dolinar, Brian. *The Black Cultural Front: Black Writers and Artists of the Depression
Generation*. Jackson: University Press of Mississippi, 2012. Kindle.

Domingo, Wilfred A. "What Are We, Negroes or Colored People?" *The Messenger*,
June 1919.

Du Bois, W. E. B. "The Talented Tenth." In *Call and Response: Key Debates in African
American Studies*, 230–41. New York: Norton, 2011.

Duany, Jorge. *Blurred Borders: Transnational Migration between the Hispanic Caribbean
and the United States*. Chapel Hill: The University of North Carolina Press, 2011.

———. "Reconstructing Racial Identity: Ethnicity, Color, and Class among
Dominicans in the United States and Puerto Rico." *Latin American Perspectives* 25,
no. 3 (May 1998): 147–72. https://doi.org/10.1177/0094582X9802500308.

———. *The Puerto Rican Nation on the Move: Identities on the Island and in the United
States*. First Edition. Chapel Hill: The University of North Carolina Press, 2002.

———. "Transnational Migration from the Dominican Republic: The Cultural
Redefinition of Racial Identity." *Caribbean Studies* 29, no. 2 (1996): 253–82.

Dudley, David L. *My Father's Shadow: Intergenerational Conflict in African American
Men's Autobiography*. Philadelphia: University of Pennsylvania Press, 1991.

———. "Piri Thomas." In *The Oxford Companion to African American Literature*,
edited by William L. Andrews, Frances Smith Foster, and Trudier Harris, 728.
New York: Oxford University Press, 1997.

Dumanescu, Luminiţa, Daniela Mârza, Marius Eppel, Carmen-Veronica Borbely,
and Carmen Albert, eds. *Intermarriage Throughout History*. Newcastle upon Tyne,
England: Cambridge Scholars Publishing, 2014.

Dúran, Isabel. "Latina/o Life Writing: Autobiography, Memoir, Testimonio." In
The Cambridge Companion to Latina/o American Literature, edited by John Morán

González, 161–77. Cambridge: Cambridge University Press, 2016. https://doi.org
/10.1017/CBO9781107045385.012.

Dzidzienyo, Anani. "Activity and Inactivity in the Politics of Afro-Latin America."
Secolas Annals 9 (November 1978): 48–61.

———. "Coming to Terms with the African Connection in Latino Studies." *Latino
Studies* 1, no. 1 (March 2003): 160–67. https://doi.org/10.1057/palgrave.lst
.8600003.

Eakin, Paul John. *Living Autobiographically: How We Create Identity in Narrative.*
Ithaca, NY: Cornell University Press, 2008.

———. *The Ethics of Life Writing.* Ithaca, NY: Cornell University Press, 2004.

Edmonds, Ennis B., and Michelle A. Gonzalez. "Creole African Traditions: Santería,
Palo Monte, Abakuá, Vodou, and Espiritismo." In *Caribbean Religious History: An
Introduction.* New York: New York University Press, 2010.

Edwards, Brent Hayes. *The Practice of Diaspora: Literature, Translation, and the Rise of
Black Internationalism.* Cambridge, MA: Harvard University Press, 2009.

Eliot, T. S. "Hamlet and His Problems." In *The Sacred Wood and Major Early Essays,*
55–59. Mineola, NY: Dover Publications, 1998. Google Books.

Ellis, Keith. *Cuba's Nicolás Guillén: Poetry and Ideology.* University of Toronto
Romance Series: 47. Toronto: University of Toronto Press, 1983.

———. "Images of Black People in the Poetry of Nicolás Guillén." *Afro-Hispanic
Review* 7, no. 1/2/3 (September 1988): 19–22.

———. "Nicolás Guillén and Langston Hughes: Convergences and Divergences." In
Between Race and Empire: African-Americans and Cubans before the Cuban Revolution,
edited by Lisa Brock and Digna Castañeda Fuertes, 129–67. Philadelphia, PA:
Temple University Press, 1998.

Ellis, Trey. "Response to NBA Critiques." *Callaloo*, no. 38 (1989): 250–51. https://doi
.org/10.2307/2931160.

———. "The New Black Aesthetic." *Callaloo* 38 (Winter 1989): 233–43.

Ellison, Ralph. *Shadow and Act.* New York: Vintage Books-Random House, 1972.

Emblidge, David. "Rallying Point: Lewis Michaux's National Memorial African
Bookstore." *Publishing Research Quarterly* 24, no. 4 (July 25, 2008): 267–76.
https://doi.org/10.1007/s12109-008-9075-x.

Ernest, John. *Chaotic Justice Rethinking African American Literary History.* Chapel Hill:
The University of North Carolina Press, 2009.

Esdaille, Milca. "Same Trip, Different Ships." *Black Issues Book Review*, April 2001.

Estevez, Jorge Baracutei. "Meet the Survivors of a 'Paper Genocide.'" October 14,
2019. https://www.nationalgeographic.com/history/2019/10/meet-survivors
-taino-tribe-paper-genocide/.

"Exploring Taino Traditions: Jorge Estevez." Columbia College Chicago. Accessed
October 14, 2019. https://events.colum.edu/event/exploring_taino_traditions
_jorge_estevez.

Eze, Emmanuel Chukwudi, ed. *Race and the Enlightenment: A Reader.* Malden, MA:
Wiley-Blackwell, 1997.

Farley, Christopher John. "That Old Black Magic: Hollywood Is Still Bamboozled
When It Comes to Race." *TIME Magazine*, November 27, 2000.

Federal Bureau of Investigation. "Nation of Islam: Part 1 of 3." Accessed July 27, 2016. https://vault.fbi.gov/Nation%20of%20Islam/Nation%20of%20Islam%20Part%201%20of%203.

———. "Nation of Islam: Part 2 of 3." Accessed July 27, 2016. https://vault.fbi.gov/Nation%20of%20Islam/Nation%20of%20Islam%20Part%202%20of%203.

Federal Writers' Project. "Spanish Harlem." In *New York City Guide; a Comprehensive Guide to the Five Boroughs of the Metropolis: Manhattan, Brooklyn, the Bronx, Queens, and Richmond*, 265–68. New York: Random House, 1939. http://archive.org/details/newyorkcityguide00federich.

Fenderson, Jonathan. *Building the Black Arts Movement: Hoyt Fuller and the Cultural Politics of the 1960s*. Urbana: University of Illinois Press, 2019.

Fernández Olmos, Margarite, and Lizabeth Paravisini-Gebert. *Creole Religions of the Caribbean: An Introduction from Vodou and Santería to Obeah and Espiritismo*. 2nd ed. New York: New York University Press, 2011.

———. "Espiritismo: Creole Spiritism in Cuba, Puerto Rico, and the United States." In *Creole Religions of the Caribbean: An Introduction from Vodou and Santeria to Obeah and Espiritismo*, 2nd ed., 203–49. New York: New York University Press, 2011.

Fernandez, Raul A. *From Afro-Cuban Rhythms to Latin Jazz*. Berkeley: University of California Press, 2006.

Ferrer, Ada. "History and the Idea of Hispanic Caribbean Studies." *Small Axe* 20, no. 3 (2016): 49–64.

Figueroa, Arelis M. "Dominican Americans." In *Hispanic American Religious Cultures*, edited by Miguel A. De La Torre, 205–8. American Religious Cultures. Santa Barbara, CA: ABC-CLIO, 2009.

Figueroa-Vásquez, Yomaira C. *Decolonizing Diasporas: Radical Mappings of Afro-Atlantic Literature*. Evanston, IL: Northwestern University Press, 2020.

Fleming, John. "A Concert of Cuba." *St. Petersburg Times*. May 31, 2007.

Flores, Juan. *Divided Borders: Essays on Puerto Rican Identity*. 2nd ed. Houston, TX: Arte Público Press, 1993.

———. *From Bomba to Hip-Hop: Puerto Rican Culture and Latino Identity*. New York: Columbia University Press, 2000.

———. "Puerto Rocks: New York Ricans Stake Their Claim." In *Droppin' Science: Critical Essays on Rap Music and Hip Hop Culture*, edited by William Eric Perkins, 85–116. Philadelphia, PA: Temple University Press, 1996.

———. "'Qué Assimilated, Brother, Yo Soy Asimilao': The Structuring of Puerto Rican Identity in the U.S." In *Divided Borders: Essays on Puerto Rican Identity*, 2nd ed, 182–97. Houston, TX: Arte Público Press, 1993.

———. *The Diaspora Strikes Back Caribeño Tales of Learning and Turning*. Cultural Spaces Series. New York: Routledge, 2009. Kindle.

———. "Triple Consciousness? Afro-Latinos on the Color Line." *Wadabagei: A Journal of the Caribbean and Its Diaspora* 8, no. 1 (Winter 2005): 80–85.

Flores, Juan, and Miriam Jiménez Román. "Triple-Consciousness? Approaches to Afro-Latino Culture in the United States." *Latin American and Caribbean Ethnic Studies* 4, no. 3 (November 2009): 319–28. https://doi.org/10.1080/17442220903331662.

Foley, Erin, and Leslie Jermyn. "The Curse of Columbus." In *Cultures of the World: Dominican Republic*, 92. New York: Marshall Cavendish, 2005. Google Books.

Fontaine, Pierre-Michel. "Research in the Political Economy of Afro-Latin America." *Latin American Research Review* 15, no. 2 (1980): 111–41.

Foote, Nicola, ed. *The Caribbean History Reader*. New York: Routledge, 2012.

Foster, John. *White Race Discourse: Preserving Racial Privilege in a Post-Racial Society*. Lanham, MD: Lexington Books, 2013.

Fowler, Virginia C. *Nikki Giovanni*. Twayne's United States Authors Series. New York: Maxwell Macmillan International, 1992.

———. *Nikki Giovanni: A Literary Biography*. Women Writers of Color. Santa Barbara, CA: Praeger, 2013.

Fox, Molly, Curt A. Sandman, Elysia Poggi Davis, and Laura M. Glynn. "A Longitudinal Study of Women's Depression Symptom Profiles during and after the Postpartum Phase." *Depression and Anxiety* 35, no. 4 (2018): 292–304. https://doi.org/10.1002/da.22719.

Fraser, C. Gerald. "Lewis Michaux, 92, Dies; Ran Bookstore in Harlem." *New York Times*, August 27, 1976, sec. Archives. https://www.nytimes.com/1976/08/27/archives/lewis-michaux-92-dies-ran-bookstore-in-harlem.html.

Frederick, John T. "American Literary Nationalism: The Process of Definition, 1825–1850." *Review of Politics* 21, no. 1 (1959): 224–38.

Freer, Regina M., and Claudia Sandoval Lopez. "Black, Brown, Young, and Together." In *Just Neighbors?: Research on African American and Latino Relations in the US*, edited by Edward Eric Telles, Mark Q. Sawyer, and Gaspar Rivera-Salgado, 267–98. New York: Russell Sage Foundation, 2011.

Frey, William H. *Diversity Explosion: How New Racial Demographics Are Remaking America*. Revised edition. Washington, DC: Brookings Institution Press, 2018.

Frye, Karla Y. E. "Elder, Lonne, III." In *The Oxford Companion to African American Literature*, edited by William L. Andrews, Frances Smith Foster, and Trudier Harris, 250–51. New York: Oxford University Press, 1997.

Frye Jacobson, Matthew. "Hyphen Nation: Ethnicity in American Intellectual and Political Life." In *A Companion to Post-1945 America*, edited by Jean-Christophe Agnew and Roy Rosenzweig., 175–210. Williston, UK: John Wiley & Sons, 2002.

García, Mario T. *Literature As History: Autobiography, Testimonio, and the Novel in the Chicano and Latino Experience*. Tucson: University of Arizona Press, 2016.

García-Peña, Lorgia. *The Borders of Dominicanidad: Race, Nation, and Archives of Contradiction*. Durham: Duke University Press, 2016.

———. *Translating Blackness: Latinx Colonialities in Global Perspective*. Durham, NC: Duke University Press, 2022.

Garrick, Jacqueline. "The Humor of Trauma Survivors: Its Application in a Therapeutic Milieu." In *Trauma Treatment Techniques: Innovative Trends*, edited by Jacqueline Garrick and Mary Beth Williams, 169–82. Binghamton, NY: Haworth, 2006. https://doi.org/10.4324/9781315864518.

Gates, Henry Louis. *The Signifying Monkey: A Theory of Afro-American Literary Criticism*. New York: Oxford University Press, 1988.

Gates, Henry Louis, and Valerie Smith, eds. *The Norton Anthology of African American Literature*. 3rd ed. Volume 2. New York: W.W. Norton, 2014.

Gates, Henry Louis, Jr., and Jennifer Burton, eds. "The Question of Naming." In *Call and Response: Key Debates in African American Studies*, 86–87. New York: W. W. Norton, 2008.

———. "The Question of Naming: Redux." In *Call and Response: Key Debates in African American Studies*, 867–73. New York: W. W. Norton, 2008.

Gayle, Addison. *The Black Aesthetic*. Garden City, NY: Doubleday, 1972.

Geary, Daniel. *Beyond Civil Rights: The Moynihan Report and Its Legacy*. Philadelphia: University of Pennsylvania Press, 2015.

Geerlings, Lonneke. "Performances in the Theatre of the Cold War: The American Society of African Culture and the 1961 Lagos Festival." *Journal of Transatlantic Studies (Springer Nature)* 16, no. 1 (March 2018): 1–19. https://doi.org/10.1080/14794012.2018.1423601.

Genette, Gerard. *Palimpsests: Literature in the Second Degree*. Lincoln: University of Nebraska Press, 1997. Google Books.

———. *Paratexts: Thresholds of Interpretation*. Translated by Jane E. Lewin. Cambridge: Cambridge University Press, 1997.

Genovese, Eugene D., and Elizabeth Fox-Genovese. *Fatal Self-Deception: Slaveholding Paternalism in the Old South*. Cambridge: Cambridge University Press, 2011.

George, Nelson. *Buppies, B-Boys, Baps & Bohos: Notes on Post-Soul Black Culture*. New York: De Capo Press, 2001.

———. "Nelson George: 'Smart Black People.'" Interview by Ed Gordon. News and Notes on NPR, July 19, 2005. http://www.npr.org/templates/story/story.php?storyId=4760378.

———. *Post-Soul Nation: The Explosive, Contradictory, Triumphant, and Tragic 1980s as Experienced by African Americans (Previously Known as Blacks and before That Negroes)*. New York: Viking, 2004.

Gibbens, Sarah. "Ancient Islanders Visited by Columbus Not 'Extinct,' Study Finds." National Geographic News, February 20, 2018. https://www.nationalgeographic.com/news/2018/02/taino-caribbean-indigenous-groups-ancient-dna-spd/.

Gillman, Laura. "Latina/o Mestizaje/Mulatez: Vexed Histories, Ambivalent Symbolisms, and Radical Revisions." In *Unassimilable Feminisms: Reappraising Feminist, Womanist, and Mestiza Identity Politics*, 133–61. Breaking Feminist Waves. New York: Palgrave Macmillan US, 2010. https://doi.org/10.1057/9780230109926_5.

Gilmore, Leigh. *The Limits of Autobiography: Trauma and Testimony*. Ithaca, NY: Cornell University Press, 2000.

Gilroy, Paul. *The Black Atlantic: Modernity and Double-Consciousness*. Cambridge, MA: Harvard University Press, 1993.

Gilyard, Keith. *John Oliver Killens: A Life of Black Literary Activism*. Athens: University of Georgia Press, 2010.

———. *Liberation Memories: The Rhetoric and Poetics of John Oliver Killens*. Detroit, MI: Wayne State University Press, 2003. Kindle.

Glissant, Édouard. *Poetics of Relation*. Translated by Betsy Wing. Ann Arbor: University of Michigan Press, 1997.

Goldberg, David Theo, ed. *Multiculturalism: A Critical Reader*. Cambridge, MA: Blackwell Publishers, 1994.

Golden, Thelma. "Post . . ." In *Freestyle*, 14–15. New York: The Studio Museum in Harlem, 2001.

———. "Thelma Golden by Glen Ligon." Interview by Betsy Sussler. *Bomb Magazine*, April 4, 2004. https://bombmagazine.org/articles/thelma-golden/.

González, Christina. "A Piece Not the Puzzle: Genetics and Affirmations of Taíno Identity Among Puerto Ricans." *GeneWatch* 28, no. 2 (June 2015): 14–17.

González, John Morán. *Border Renaissance: The Texas Centennial and the Emergence of Mexican American Literature*. CMAS History, Culture, & Society Series. Austin: University of Texas Press, 2009.

Gonzalez, Susan. "Director Spike Lee Slams 'Same Old' Black Stereotypes in Today's Films." *Yale Bulletin and Calendar* 29, no. 21 (March 2, 2001). https://web.archive.org /web/20160912154112/http://www.yale.edu:80/opa/arc-ybc/v29.n21/story3.html.

González-Wippler, Migene. *Santería: The Religion. A Legacy of Faith, Rites, and Magic*. 2nd edition. Llewellyn's World Religion & Magic Series. St. Paul, MN: Llewellyn, 1994.

Gosse, Van. "A Movement of Movements: The Definition and Periodization of the New Left." In *A Companion to Post-1945 America*, edited by Jean-Christophe Agnew and Roy Rosenzweig, 277–302. Williston, UK: John Wiley & Sons, 2002.

———. *Rethinking the New Left: An Interpretative History*. New York: Palgrave Macmillan, 2005.

———. "The Cuban Revolution and the New Left." In *The Cuba Reader: History, Culture, Politics*, edited by Aviva Chomsky, Barry Carr, and Pamela Maria Smorkaloff, 526–29. Durham, NC: Duke University Press Books, 2004.

———. *Where the Boys Are: Cuba, Cold War and the Making of a New Left*. London: Verso, 1993.

Gould, Jack. "TV Review: Life in Spanish Harlem: A Cry for Dignity." *New York Times*, November 20, 1968.

Graham, David A. "A Short History of Whether Obama Is Black Enough, Featuring Rupert Murdoch." *Atlantic*, October 8, 2015. https://www.theatlantic.com/politics /archive/2015/10/a-short-history-of-whether-obama-is-black-enough-featuring -rupert-murdoch/409642/.

Graham, Sarah, ed. *A History of the Bildungsroman*. Cambridge: Cambridge University Press, 2019.

Gramsci, Antonio. "Justification of Autobiography." In *Selections from Cultural Writings*, 132–33. Cambridge, MA: Harvard University Press, 1985. http://archive .org/details/selectionsfromcu0000gram.

Grant, W. R. *Post-Soul Black Cinema: Discontinuities, Innovations, and Breakpoints, 1970–1995*. Studies in African American History and Culture. New York: Routledge, 2004.

Greenbaum, Susan D. *More Than Black: Afro-Cubans in Tampa*. Gainesville: University Press of Florida, 2002.

Greer, Christina M. *Black Ethnics: Race, Immigration, and the Pursuit of the American Dream*. Oxford: Oxford University Press, 2013.

Gruesz, Kirsten Silva. *Ambassadors of Culture: The Transamerican Origins of Latino Writing*. Princeton, NJ: Princeton University Press, 2001.

Gruner, Charles R. *The Game of Humor: A Comprehensive Theory of Why We Laugh*. New Brunswick, NJ: Transaction Publishers, 1997.

Guerra, Gilbert, and Gilbert Orbea. "The Argument against the Use of the Term 'Latinx.'" *Phoenix*. November 19, 2015, sec. Op-Eds. https://swarthmorephoenix .com/2015/11/19/the-argument-against-the-use-of-the-term-latinx/.

Guevara, Nancy. "Women Writin' Rappin' Breakin'." In *Droppin' Science: Critical Essays on Rap Music and Hip Hop Culture*, edited by William Eric Perkins, 49–62. Philadelphia: Temple University Press, 1996.

Guridy, Frank A. *Forging Diaspora: Afro-Cubans and African Americans in a World of Empire and Jim Crow*. Chapel Hill: University of North Carolina Press, 2010.

Gutiérrez, Ramón A. "What's in a Name: The History and Politics of Hispanic and Latino Panethnicities." In *The New Latino Studies Reader: A Twenty-First-Century Perspective*, 19–53. Oakland: University of California Press, 2016. Kindle.

Gutmann, Amy, and James W. Wagner. "Found Your DNA on the Web: *Reconciling Privacy and Progress*." *Hastings Center Report* 43, no. 3 (May 2013): 15–18. https:// doi.org/10.1002/hast.162.

Habell-Pallán, Michelle, and Mary Romero, eds. *Latino/a Popular Culture*. New York: New York University Press, 2002.

Haggins, Bambi. *Laughing Mad: The Black Comic Persona in Post-Soul America*. ACLS Humanities E-Book. New Brunswick, NJ: Rutgers University Press, 2007.

Hanchard, Michael. "Identity, Meaning and the African-American." *Social Text*, no. 24 (1990): 31–42. https://doi.org/10.2307/827825.

Harlan, Megan. "Mama's Girl." *Entertainment Weekly*, no. 340 (1996), 56.

Hartman, Saidiya. "Venus in Two Acts." *Small Axe* 12, no. 2 (July 17, 2008): 1–14.

———. *Scenes of Subjection: Terror, Slavery, and Self-Making in Nineteenth-Century America*. Race and American Culture. New York: Oxford University Press, 1997.

Haslip-Viera, Gabriel. "Amerindian MtDNA Does Not Matter: A Reply to Jorge Estevez and the Privileging of Taíno Identity in the Spanish-Speaking Caribbean." *Centro Journal* 20, no. 2 (Fall 2008): 228–37.

———. "The 'Indigenous' or 'Neo-Taíno' Movement in The Spanish-Speaking Caribbean and Its Diaspora and the Return of The Old Anglo Neo-Imperialist Scholarship?" *National Institute for Latino Policy*, February 8, 2015. https://www .academia.edu/11598013.

———. "The Taíno Identity Movement Among Caribbean Latinas/os in the United States." In *A Companion to Latina/o Studies*, edited by Juan Flores and Renato Rosaldo, 417–426. Malden, MA: Blackwell Publishing, 2007.

Hatch, James Vernon, and Ted Shine, eds. "Lonne Elder III (1931–)." In *Black Theatre USA: Plays by African Americans*, 555–56. New York: Free Press, 1996. http://archive .org/details/blacktheatreusa00.

Head, Dominic. *The State of the Novel: Britain and Beyond*. Malden, MA: Wiley-Blackwell, 2009.

Helton, Laura E., and Rafia Zafar, eds. "Arturo Alfonso Schomburg in The Twenty-First Century: A Special Issue." *African American Review* 54, no. 1–2 (Spring/Summer 2021).

Henke, Suzette A. *Shattered Subjects: Trauma and Testimony in Women's Life-Writing.* New York: St. Martin's Press, 1998.

Heredia, Juanita. "Marta Moreno Vega's When the Spirits Dance Mambo: Growing Up Nuyorican in El Barrio (2004): The Diasporic Formation of an Afro-Latina Identity." In *Transnational Latina Narratives in the Twenty-First Century*, by Juanita Heredia, 61–84. New York: Palgrave Macmillan US, 2009. https://doi.org/10.1057/9780230623255_4.

Herman, Judith L. *Trauma and Recovery: The Aftermath of Violence—From Domestic Abuse to Political Terror.* New York: Basic Books, 2015.

Hernández, Carmen Dolores. "Louis Reyes Rivera." In *Puerto Rican Voices in English: Interviews with Writers*, 118–35. Westport, CT: Praeger, 1997.

Hernandez, Daniel. "The Case against 'Latinx.'" *Los Angeles Times*, December 17, 2017, sec. Opinion. https://www.latimes.com/opinion/op-ed/la-oe-hernandez-the-case-against-latinx-20171217-story.html.

Hernández, Tanya Katerí. *Multiracials and Civil Rights: Mixed-Race Stories of Discrimination.* New York: New York University Press, 2018.

———. "'Too Black to Be Latino/a': Blackness and Blacks as Foreigners in Latino Studies." *Latino Studies* 1, no. 1 (March 2003): 152–59. https://doi.org/10.1057/palgrave.lst.8600011.

Hesman Saey, Tina. "What FamilyTree DNA Sharing Genetic Data with Police Means for You." *Science News*, February 6, 2019. https://www.sciencenews.org/article/family-tree-dna-sharing-genetic-data-police-privacy.

Hicks, Calvin. Calvin Hicks. Interview by Robert Hayden and Scott Stearns. HistoryMakers Video Oral History, 2016.

Hill Collins, Patricia, and Sirma Bilge. *Intersectionality.* 2nd edition. Cambridge: Polity, 2020.

Hochschild, Jennifer. "Multiple Racial Identifiers in the 2000 Census, and Then What?" In *The New Race Question: How the Census Counts Multiracial Individuals*, edited by Joel Perlmann and Mary C. Waters, 340–53. New York: Russell Sage Foundation, 2002.

Hoffnung-Garskof, Jesse. *Racial Migrations: New York City and the Revolutionary Politics of the Spanish Caribbean.* Princeton, NJ: Princeton University Press, 2019.

———. "The World of Arturo Schomburg." In *The Afro-Latin@ Reader: History and Culture in the United States*, edited by Miriam Jiménez Román and Juan Flores, 70–91. Durham, NC: Duke University Press, 2010.

Howard, David. *Coloring the Nation: Race and Ethnicity in the Dominican Republic.* Boulder, CO: Lynne Rienner Publishers, 2001.

Hubbard, Dolan. *The Sermon and the African American Literary Imagination.* Columbia: University of Missouri Press, 1996.

Huck, James D., Jr. "Machismo, Marianismo, and Malinchismo." In *Modern Mexico*, 156–58. Santa Barbara, CA: ABC-CLIO, 2017.

Hucks, Tracey E. *Yoruba Traditions and African American Religious Nationalism*. Religions of the Americas. Albuquerque: University of New Mexico Press, 2012.

Huggan, Graham. *The Postcolonial Exotic: Marketing the Margins*. London: Routledge, 2001.

Huneven, Michelle. "MAMA'S GIRL." *Los Angeles Times*, August 26, 1996, 3.

Hunsaker Hawkins, Anne. "Writing About Illness: Therapy? Or Testimony?" In *Unfitting Stories: Narrative Approaches to Disease, Disability, and Trauma*, edited by Valerie Raoul, Connie Canam, Angela D. Henderson, and Carla Paterson, 113–27. Waterloo, Ontario, Canada: Wilfrid Laurier University Press, 2007.

Hunt, Carl Monroe. "Oyotunji Village: The Yoruba Movement in America." PhD diss., West Virginia University, 1977. ProQuest (Order No. 7808734).

Hurston, Zora Neale. "Dust Tracks on a Road." In *Zora Neale Hurston: Folklore, Memoirs, and Other Writings: Mules and Men, Tell My Horse, Dust Tracks on a Road, Selected Articles*, edited by Cheryl Wall, 557–808. New York: Library of America, 1995.

Hurtado, Aída, and Mrinal Sinha. *Beyond Machismo: Intersectional Latino Masculinities*. Austin: University of Texas Press, 2016.

Ifatunji, Mosi Adesina. "A Test of the Afro Caribbean Model Minority Hypothesis." *Du Bois Review; Cambridge* 13, no. 1 (Spring 2016): 109–38.

Irizarry, Ylce. *Chicana/o and Latina/o Fiction: The New Memory of Latinidad*. Urbana: University of Illinois Press, 2016.

ISSD Task Force on Children and Adolescents. "Dissociative Symptoms in Children and Adolescents." *Journal of Trauma & Dissociation* 5, no. 3 (2004): 119–50.

Itzigsohn, Jose, and Carlos Dore-Cabral. "Competing Identities? Race, Ethnicity and Panethnicity among Dominicans in the United States." *Sociological Forum* 15, no. 2 (2000): 225–47.

Izadi, Elahe. "Why Hundreds of American Newsrooms Have Started Capitalizing the 'b' in 'Black.'" *Washington Post*, June 18, 2020. https://www.washingtonpost .com/lifestyle/media/why-hundreds-of-american-newsrooms-have-started -capitalizing-the-b-in-black/2020/06/18/7687a7a8-b16e-11ea-8f56-63f38c990077 _story.html.

Jackson, Lawrence Patrick. *Chester B. Himes: A Biography*. New York: W. W. Norton & Company, 2017. Kindle.

Jackson, Luther P. "Culture or Color? The Moyetos of San Juan and New York." *The Crisis* 75, no. 6 (July 1968).

Jackson, Richard L. *Black Writers and Latin America: Cross-Cultural Affinities*. Washington, DC: Howard University Press, 1998.

Jacques, Geoffrey. "CuBop!: Afro-Cuban Music and Mid-Twentieth-Century American Culture." In *Between Race and Empire: African-Americans and Cubans before the Cuban Revolution*, edited by Lisa Brock and Digna Castañeda Fuertes, 249–65. Philadelphia, PA: Temple University Press, 1998.

James, Winston. *Holding Aloft the Banner of Ethiopia: Caribbean Radicalism in Early Twentieth Century America*. London: Verso, 1998.

———. "The Peculiarities of Afro-Hispanic Radicalism in the United States: The Political Trajectories of Arturo Schomburg and Jesus Colon." In *Holding Aloft the Banner of Ethiopia: Caribbean Radicalism in Early Twentieth-Century America*, 195–231. London: Verso, 1998.

Japtok, Martin. *Growing Up Ethnic Nationalism and the Bildungsroman in African American and Jewish American Fiction*. Iowa City: University of Iowa Press, 2005.

Jarrett, Gene Andrew. *Representing the Race: A New Political History of African American Literature*. New York: New York University Press, 2011.

Jauss, Hans Robert. *Aesthetic Experience and Literary Hermeneutics*. Volume 3. Theory and History of Literature. Minneapolis: University of Minnesota Press, 1982.

———. "Literary History as a Challenge to Literary Theory." Translated by Elizabeth Benzinger. *New Literary History* 2, no. 1 (1970): 7–37. https://doi.org/10 .2307/468585.

———. *Toward an Aesthetic of Reception*. Volume 2. Theory and History of Literature. Minneapolis: University of Minnesota Press, 1982.

Jeffers, Thomas L. *Apprenticeships: The Bildungsroman from Goethe to Santayana*. New York: Palgrave Macmillan, 2005.

Jelly-Schapiro, Joshua. "An Empire of Vice." *Nation* 288, no. 25 (June 29, 2009): 27–28.

Jiménez Román, Miriam. "Looking at That Middle Ground: Racial Mixing as Panacea?" In *A Companion to Latina/o Studies*, edited by Juan Flores and Renato Rosaldo, 325–36. Malden, MA: Blackwell Publishing, 2007.

———. "Real Unity for Afro-Latinos and African Americans." Accessed December 12, 2021. https://www.afrolatinoforum.org/real-unity-for-afrolatin.

Jiménez Román, Miriam, and Juan Flores, eds. *The Afro-Latin@ Reader: History and Culture in the United States*. Durham, NC: Duke University Press, 2010.

Johansen, Emily. "Imagining the Global and the Rural: Rural Cosmopolitanism in Sharon Butala's The Garden of Eden and Amitav Ghosh's The Hungry Tide." Postcolonial Text 4, no. 3 (2008): 18.

John Patrick Leary. "Havana Reads the Harlem Renaissance: Langston Hughes, Nicolás Guillén, and the Dialectics of Transnational American Literature." *Comparative Literature Studies* 47, no. 2 (2010): 133–58. https://doi.org/10.1353/cls .2010.0007.

Johnson, E. Patrick, and Ramón H. Rivera-Servera, eds. *Blacktino Queer Performance*. Durham, NC: Duke University Press Books, 2016.

Jones, Jennifer A. "Blackness, Latinidad, and Minority Linked Fate." In *Critical Dialogues in Latinx Studies: A Reader*, 425–37. New York: New York University Press, 2021.

Jones-Correa, Michael. "Commonalities, Competition, and Linked Fate." In *Just Neighbors?: Research on African American and Latino Relations in the US*, edited by Edward Eric Telles, Mark Q. Sawyer, and Gaspar Rivera-Salgado, 63–95. New York: Russell Sage Foundation, 2011.

Joppke, Christian. "War of Words: Interculturalism v. Multiculturalism." *Comparative Migration Studies* 6, no. 1 (May 17, 2018): 11. https://doi.org/10.1186 /s40878-018-0079-1.

Jordan, Larry E. "Social Construction as Tradition: A Review and Reconceptualization of the Dozens." *Review of Research in Education* 10 (1983): 79. https://doi.org/10.2307/1167136.

Kamaloni, Sunshine. "Introduction." In *Understanding Racism in a Post-Racial World: Visible Invisibilities*, 1–24. Cham, Switzerland: Springer International Publishing, 2019. https://doi.org/10.1007/978-3-030-10985-1_1.

Kaplan, H. Roy. *The Myth of Post-Racial America: Searching for Equality in the Age of Materialism*. Lanham, MD: Rowman & Littlefield Education, 2011.

Kennedy, J. Gerald. *Strange Nation: Literary Nationalism and Cultural Conflict in the Age of Poe*. New York: Oxford University Press, 2016.

Kennedy, Randall. "The Fallacy of Touré's Post-Blackness Theory." *The Root*, August 8, 2011. https://www.theroot.com/the-fallacy-of-toures-post-blackness -theory-1790865279.

Kester, Gunilla Theander. *Writing the Subject: Bildung and the African American Text*. New York: Peter Lang Publishing, 1995.

Killens, John Oliver. "On El Barrio and Piri Thomas." *Negro Digest*, January 1968. Google Books.

———. *Youngblood*. Athens: University of Georgia Press, 1982.

Kirkus Reviews. "Mama's Girl." *Kirkus Reviews*, no. 9 (May 1, 1996). https://www .kirkusreviews.com/book-reviews/veronica-chambers/mamas-girl/.

Knight, Carl. *Luck Egalitarianism: Equality, Responsibility, and Justice*. Edinburgh, Scotland: Edinburgh University Press, 2009.

Knight, Michael Muhammad. *The Five Percenters: Islam, Hip-Hop, and the Gods of New York*. London: Oneworld Publications, 2013. Kindle.

Kraft, Dottie. "Adult Book for Young Adults: Nonfiction." *School Library Journal* 42, no. 7 (July 1996): 109.

Kristeva, Julia. *Desire in Language: A Semiotic Approach to Literature and Art*. Edited by Leon S. Roudiez. Translated by Thomas Gora and Alice Jardine. European Perspectives. New York: Columbia University Press, 1980.

Kutzinski, Vera M. "Afro-Hispanic American Literature." In *The Cambridge History of Latin American Literature*, edited by Roberto González Echevarría and Enrique Pupo-Walker, 164–94. Cambridge: Cambridge University Press, 1996.

———. *Against the American Grain: Myth and History in William Carlos Williams, Jay Wright, and Nicolás Guillén*. Baltimore: Johns Hopkins University Press, 1987.

———. "Fearful Asymmetries: Langston Hughes, Nicolás Guillén, and 'Cuba Libre.'" *Diacritics* 34, no. ¾ (2004): 112–42.

———. "Re-Reading Nicolás Guillén: An Introduction." *Callaloo*, no. 31 (1987): 161–67. https://doi.org/10.2307/2930729.

———. *The Worlds of Langston Hughes: Modernism and Translation in the Americas*. Ithaca, NY: Cornell University Press, 2012.

Kymlicka, Will. *Politics in the Vernacular: Nationalism, Multiculturalism, and Citizenship*. Oxford: Oxford University Press, 2001.

Kymlicka, Will, and Keith G. Banting, eds. *Multiculturalism and the Welfare State Recognition and Redistribution in Contemporary Democracies*. Oxford: Oxford University Press, 2006.

Lam, C. Christina. "Bearing Witness: Alternate Archives of Latinx Identity in Raquel Cepeda's Bird of Paradise: How I Became Latina." *Studies in American Culture* 43 (2020): 26–34.

Laó-Montes, Agustín. "Afro-Latinidades and the Diasporic Imaginary." *Iberoamericana (2001–)* 5, no. 17 (2005): 117–30.

———. "Afro-Latinidades: Bridging Blackness and Latinidad." In *Technofuturos: Critical Interventions in Latina/o Studies*, edited by Nancy Raquel Mirabal and Agustín Laó-Montes, 117–40. Lanham, MD: Lexington Books, 2007.

———. "Decolonial Moves: Trans-Locating African Diaspora Spaces." *Cultural Studies* 21, no. 2/3 (March 2007): 309–38. https://doi.org/10.1080 /09502380601164361.

Laó-Montes, Agustín, and Arlene Dávila. *Mambo Montage: The Latinization of New York*. New York: Columbia University Press, 2001.

"Latine." In *Merriam-Webster.Com Dictionary*. Accessed August 24, 2022. https:// www.merriam-webster.com/dictionary/Latine.

Latinez, Alejandro. *Developments: Encounters of Formation in the Latin American and Hispanic/Latino Bildungsroman*. New York: Peter Lang Publishing, 2014.

"Latinx." In *Merriam-Webster.Com Dictionary*. Accessed August 24, 2022. https:// www.merriam-webster.com/dictionary/Latinx.

"'Latinx' and Gender Inclusivity." In *Merriam-Webster.Com Dictionary*. Accessed August 20, 2022. https://www.merriam-webster.com/words-at-play/word-history -latinx.

"Latinx, n. and Adj." In *OED Online*. Oxford University Press. Accessed August 21, 2022. http://www.oed.com/view/Entry/79123233.

Latorre, Sobeira. "Afro-Latino/a Identities: Challenges, History, and Perspectives." *Anthurium: A Caribbean Studies Journal* 9, no. 1 (April 20, 2012): 5. https://doi.org /10.33596/anth.212.

"Leaders Say Blacks Want To Be Called 'African-Americans.'" AP NEWS, December 21, 1988. https://apnews.com/article/5ef3f6b9a4efe1c47c7e0bbecc746149.

Lee, Sonia Song-Ha. *Building a Latino Civil Rights Movement: Puerto Ricans, African Americans, and the Pursuit of Racial Justice in New York City*. Chapel Hill: University of North Carolina Press, 2016.

Lefever, Harry G. "'Playing the Dozens': A Mechanism for Social Control." *Phylon (1960–)* 42, no. 1 (1981): 73. https://doi.org/10.2307/274886.

Lejeune, Philippe. *On Autobiography*. Edited by Paul John Eakin. Translated by Katherine Leary. Minneapolis: University of Minnesota Press, 1989.

León, Concepción de. "Another Hot Take on the Term 'Latinx.'" *New York Times* (online). November 21, 2018.

LeSeur, Geta J. *Ten Is the Age of Darkness: The Black Bildungsroman*. Columbia: University of Missouri Press, 1995.

Levine, Robert S. *Dislocating Race and Nation: Episodes in Nineteenth-Century American Literary Nationalism*. Chapel Hill: The University of North Carolina Press, 2008.

Levrau, François, and Patrick Loobuyck. "Introduction: Mapping the Multiculturalism-Interculturalism Debate." *Comparative Migration Studies* 6, no. 1 (May 17, 2018): 13. https://doi.org/10.1186/s40878-018-0080-8.

Lewis, David Levering. *W. E. B. Du Bois, 1868–1919: Biography of a Race*. New York: Henry Holt and Co., 1993.

Lieber, Marlon. "Being Afraid of 'Post-Blackness': What's Neoliberalism Got to Do with It?" In *African American Culture and Society after Rodney King: Provocations and Protests, Progression and "Post-Racialism,"* edited by Josephine Metcalf and Carina Spalding, 269–82. Surrey, UK: Ashgate, 2015.

Lima, Lazaro. *The Latino Body: Crisis Identities in American Literary and Cultural Memory*. New York: New York University Press, 2007.

Lind, Nancy S., and Erik Rankin, eds. *Privacy in the Digital Age: 21st-Century Challenges to the Fourth Amendment*. Santa Barbara, CA: Praeger, 2015.

Lindsay, Keisha. "Beyond 'Model Minority,' 'Superwoman,' and 'Endangered Species': Theorizing Intersectional Coalitions among Black Immigrants, African American Women, and African American Men." *Journal of African American Studies* 19, no. 1 (March 1, 2015): 18–35. https://doi.org/10.1007/s12111-014-9286-5.

Lipman, Steve. *Laughter in Hell: Use of Humor during the Holocaust*. Northvale, NJ: Jason Aronson Inc., 1995.

Lippert-Rasmussen, Kasper. *Luck Egalitarianism*. Bloomsbury Ethics Series. London: Bloomsbury Academic, 2016.

Litwack, Leon F. *Trouble in Mind: Black Southerners in the Age of Jim Crow*. New York: Vintage Books-Random House, 1998.

Lomas, Laura. "Translation and Transculturation in the New York–Hispanic Caribbean Borderlands." *Small Axe* 20, no. 3 (2016): 147–62.

"Long Island School Board Bans Three Black Books." *Jet*, August 19, 1976.

López, Antonio M. *Unbecoming Blackness the Diaspora Cultures of Afro-Cuban America*. New York: NYU Press, 2012.

López, Gustavo, and Ana Gonzalez-Barrera. "Afro-Latino: A Deeply Rooted Identity among U.S. Hispanics." *Pew Research Center* (blog), March 1, 2016. https://www.pewresearch.org/fact-tank/2016/03/01/afro-latino-a-deeply-rooted-identity-among-u-s-hispanics/.

López, Marissa K. *Chicano Nations: The Hemispheric Origins of Mexican American Literature*. American Literatures Initiative 4. New York: University Press, 2011.

López Oro, Paul Joseph. "Garifunizando Ambas Américas: Hemispheric Entanglements of Blackness/Indigeneity/AfroLatinidad." *Postmodern Culture* 31, no. 1 & 2 (2020). https://doi.org/10.1353/pmc.2020.0025.

———. "Refashioning Afro-Latinidad: Garifuna New Yorkers in Diaspora." In *Critical Dialogues in Latinx Studies: A Reader*, 223–38. New York: New York University Press, 2021.

Lordi, Emily J. *Black Resonance Iconic Women Singers and African American Literature*. New Brunswick, NJ: Rutgers University Press, 2013. Kindle.

———. "From Soul to Post-Soul: A Literary and Musical History." In *The Meaning of Soul: Black Music and Resilience since the 1960s*, 19–45. Refiguring American Music. Durham, NC: Duke University Press, 2020.

———. *The Meaning of Soul: Black Music and Resilience since the 1960s*. Refiguring American Music. Durham, NC: Duke University Press, 2020.

Luis, William. "Afro-Latino/a Literature and Identity." In *The Routledge Companion to Latino/a Literature*, edited by Suzanne Bost and Frances R. Aparicio, 34–45. London: Routledge, 2013. Kindle.

——. *Dance Between Two Cultures: Latino Caribbean Literature Written in the United States*. Nashville, TN: Vanderbilt University Press, 1997.

——. "Editor's Note." *Afro-Hispanic Review* 34, no. 1 (Spring 2015): 5–8.

——. "Latin American (Hispanic Caribbean) Literature Written in the United States." In *The Cambridge History of Latin American Literature*, edited by Roberto Gonzalez Echevarría and Enrique Pupo-Walker, 2:526–56. Cambridge: Cambridge University Press, 1996.

Lynn, Richard. "Pigmentocracy: Racial Hierarchies in the Caribbean and Latin America." *The Occidental Quarterly* 8, no. 2 (2008): 25–44.

Machado Sáez, Elena. *Market Aesthetics: The Purchase of the Past in Caribbean Diasporic Fiction*. New World Studies. Charlottesville: University of Virginia Press, 2015.

Mack, Kenneth Walter, and Guy-Uriel E. Charles, eds. *The New Black: What Has Changed and What Has Not with Race in America*. New York: New Press, 2013.

Maddox, Melvin. "The Knuckle-Hard Code of the Barrio." *Life*, June 9, 1967.

Maeroff, Gene I. "Book Ban Splits a Queens School District." *New York Times*, May 9, 1971, sec. Archives. https://www.nytimes.com/1971/05/09/archives/book-ban -splits-a-queens-school-district-ban-on-book-splits-a.html.

Maillo-Pozo, Sharina. "Reconstructing Dominican Latinidad: Intersections between Gender, Race, and Hip-Hop." *Small Axe* 22, no. 2 (August 14, 2018): 85–98.

——. "Resisting Colonial Ghosts." *Small Axe: A Caribbean Journal of Criticism* 23, no. 2 (July 1, 2019): 132–41. https://doi.org/10.1215/07990537-7703368.

Malcolm X. *The Autobiography of Malcolm X*. Ballantine Books, 2015. Kindle.

Maldonado-Torres, Nelson. "The Decolonial Turn." In *New Approaches to Latin American Studies: Culture and Power*, 111–27. London: Routledge, 2017.

"Mama's Girl." In *Reading Group Choices*, 48–49. Nashville, TN: Paz and Associates, 1997.

Man, Paul de. "Autobiography as De-Facement." *MLN* 94, no. 5 (December 1979): 919. https://doi.org/10.2307/2906560.

Margolies, Edward. *The Several Lives of Chester Himes*. Jackson: University Press of Mississippi, 1997.

"Marta Moreno Vega." In *Gale Biography Online Collection*. Detroit, MI: Gale, January 8, 2006. Gale In Context: Biography.

"Marta Moreno Vega." In *Contemporary Black Biography*. Vol. 61. Detroit, MI: Gale, September 7, 2007. Gale In Context: Biography.

Martin, Ben L. "From Negro to Black to African American: The Power of Names and Naming." *Political Science Quarterly* 106, no. 1 (1991): 83–107. https://doi.org/10 .2307/2152175.

Martinez, Juan Francisco. "Identity (Latino/a vs. Hispanic)." In *Hispanic American Religious Cultures*, edited by Miguel A. De La Torre, 289–94. Santa Barbara, CA: ABC-CLIO, 2009. Google Books.

Martínez-San Miguel, Yolanda. "Ethnic Specularities: Exploring the Caribbean and Latino Dimensions of *Down These Mean Streets*." *Latino Studies* 13, no. 3 (Autumn 2015): 358–75. https://doi.org/10.1057/lst.2015.31

——. "Négropolitains and Nuyorícans: Metropolitan Racialization in Frantz Fanon and Piri Thomas." In *Coloniality of Diasporas: Rethinking Intra-Colonial Migrations in a Pan-Caribbean Context*, 99–123. New York: Palgrave Macmillan, 2014. Kindle.

Mason, Michael Atwood. *Living Santería: Rituals and Experiences in an Afro-Cuban Religion*. Washington, DC: Smithsonian Institution Press, 2002.

Maus, Derek C, and James J. Donahue, eds. *Post-Soul Satire: Black Identity after Civil Rights*. Jackson: University Press of Mississippi, 2014. Kindle.

May, Thomas. "Sociogenetic Risks—Ancestry DNA Testing, Third-Party Identity, and Protection of Privacy." *New England Journal of Medicine* 379, no. 5 (August 2, 2018): 410–12. https://doi.org/10.1056/NEJMp1805870.

Mayes, April J. *Mulatto Republic: Class, Race, and Dominican National Identity*. Gainesville: University Press of Florida, 2014.

McHugh, Clare. "Review of *Mama's Girl*." *People Weekly* 46, no. 1 (July 1, 1996).

McKinnon, Jesse. "The Black Population in the United States: March 2002." United States Census Bureau, April 1, 2003.

McLymont, Rosalind. "The American Society of African Culture." *Network Journal* 19, no. 1 (February 2012): 24.

McWhorter, John. "Why Latinx Can't Catch On." *The Atlantic*, December 23, 2019.

Meehan, Kevin. *People Get Ready: African American and Caribbean Cultural Exchange*. Jackson: University Press of Mississippi, 2009.

——. "Vested in the Anonymous Thousands: Arthur A. Schomburg as Decolonizing Historian." In *People Get Ready: African American and Caribbean Cultural Exchange*, 52–75. Jackson: University Press of Mississippi, 2009.

Meer, Nasar, and Tariq Modood. "How Does Interculturalism Contrast with Multiculturalism?" *Journal of Intercultural Studies* 33, no. 2 (April 2012): 175–96. https://doi.org/10.1080/07256868.2011.618266.

Melamed, Jodi. *Represent and Destroy: Rationalizing Violence in the New Racial Capitalism*. Minneapolis: University of Minnesota Press, 2011.

Meraji, Shereen Marisol. "'Hispanic,' 'Latino,' Or 'Latinx'? Survey Says . . ." *Code Switch*, August 11, 2020, sec. Hispanic Heritage Month. https://www.npr.org/sections/codeswitch/2020/08/11/901398248/hispanic-latino-or-latinx-survey-says.

Middleton IV, Richard T. "Institutions, Inculcation, and Black Racial Identity: Pigmentocracy vs. The Rule of Hypodescent." *Social Identities* 14, no. 5 (September 2008): 567–85. https://doi.org/10.1080/13504630802343390.

Mignolo, Walter D. *The Idea of Latin America*. Malden, MA: Blackwell Publishing, 2005. Kindle.

Milian, Claudia. "Extremely Latin, XOXO: Notes on LatinX." *Cultural Dynamics* 29, no. 3 (August 2017): 121–40. https://doi.org/10.1177/0921374017727850.

——. *Latining America: Black-Brown Passages and the Coloring of Latino/a Studies*, 2013.

——. "LatinX Studies: Variations and Velocities." *Cultural Dynamics* 31, no. 1–2 (February 1, 2019): 3–15. https://doi.org/10.1177/0921374019826196.

Miller, Marilyn Grace. *Rise and Fall of the Cosmic Race*. Austin: University of Texas Press, 2004. http://muse.jhu.edu/book/3020.

"Minarcini v. Strongsville City School District, 384 F. Supp. 698 (N.D. Ohio 1974)." August 9, 1974. https://law.justia.com/cases/federal/district-courts/FSupp/384 /698/1370485/.

Mirabal, Nancy Raquel. "Diasporas: Afro-Cubans in the Diaspora." In *Cuba*, edited by Alan West-Durán, 1:152–55. Detroit: Charles Scribner's Sons, 2012.

——. *Suspect Freedoms: The Racial and Sexual Politics of Cubanidad in New York, 1823–1957*. Reprint edition. New York: New York University Press, 2017.

——. "The Afro-Cuban Community in Ybor City and Tampa, 1886–1910." *OAH Magazine of History* 7, no. 4 (Summer 1993): 19–22.

Mirabal, Nancy Raquel, and Agustín Lao-Montes, eds. *Technofuturos: Critical Interventions in Latina/o Studies*. Lanham, MD: Lexington Books, 2007.

"Miriam DeCosta-Willis." In *Contemporary Authors*. Farmington Hills, MI: Gale, 2007. Gale In Context: Biography.

Mišković, Nataša, Harald Fischer-Tiné, and Nada Boškovska Leimgruber, eds. *The Non-Aligned Movement and the Cold War: Delhi-Bandung-Belgrade*. Routledge Studies in the Modern History of Asia 96. Abingdon, Oxon: Routledge, 2014.

Mitchell-Kernan, Claudia. "Signifying and Marking: Two Afro-Americans Speech Acts." In *Linguistic Anthropology: A Reader*, edited by Alessandro Duranti., 151–64. Blackwell Anthologies in Social and Cultural Anthropology. Malden, MA: Blackwell Publishing, 2001.

Miyakawa, Felicia M. *Five Percenter Rap: God Hop's Music, Message, and Black Muslim Mission*. Bloomington: Indiana University Press, 2005.

——. "The Duty of the Civilized Is to Civilize the Uncivilized: Tropes of Black Nationalism in the Messages of Five Percent Rappers." In *Understanding African American Rhetoric: Classical Origins to Contemporary Innovations*, edited by Elaine B. Richardson, 171–86. London: Routledge, 2003.

Mochkofsky, Graciela. "Who Are You Calling Latinx?" *New Yorker*, September 5, 2020. https://www.newyorker.com/news/daily-comment/who-are-you-calling -latinx.

Modood, Tariq. "Multiculturalism, Interculturalisms and the Majority." *Journal of Moral Education* 43, no. 3 (September 2014): 302–15. https://doi.org/10.1080 /03057240.2014.920308.

——. "Must Interculturalists Misrepresent Multiculturalism?" *Comparative Migration Studies* 5, no. 1 (September 8, 2017): 1–17. https://doi.org/10.1186 /s40878-017-0058-y.

Mohaiemen, Naeem. "Fear of a Muslim Planet: Hip-Hop's Hidden History." *Daily Star*, June 2008. http://archive.thedailystar.net/forum/2008/june/fear.htm.

Mohr, Eugene V. *The Nuyorican Experience: Literature of the Puerto Rican Minority*. Westport, CT: Greenwood Press, 1982.

Mongelli, Lorena. "True Colors: Intellectual Latina Has Made the Study of Races Her Life." *New York Post*, June 9, 2004. https://nypost.com/2004/06/09/true-colors -intellectual-latina-has-made-the-study-of-races-her-life/.

Monk, Ellis P., Jr. "Colorism and Physical Health: Evidence from a National Survey." *Journal of Health & Social Behavior* 62, no. 1 (March 2021): 37–52. https://doi.org/10.1177/0022146520979645.

Monroe, Carla R., and Ronald E. Hall. "Colorism and U.S. Immigration: Considerations for Researchers." *American Behavioral Scientist* 62, no. 14 (December 2018): 2037–54. https://doi.org/10.1177/0002764218810753.

Montalvo, Frank F., and G. Edward Codina. "Skin Color and Latinos in the United States." *Ethnicities* 1, no. 3 (September 1, 2001): 321–41. https://doi.org/10.1177/146879680100100303.

Moore, Richard B. *The Name "Negro: Its Origin and Evil Use*. Black Classic Press, 1992. Kindle.

Morales, Ed. *Latinx: The New Force in American Politics and Culture*. London: Verso, 2018. Kindle.

Moran, Kimberlee Sue. "Damned by DNA—Balancing Personal Privacy with Public Safety." *Forensic Science International* 292 (November 2018): e3–e4. https://doi.org/10.1016/j.forsciint.2018.09.011.

Morris, John. "Piri Thomas: Author's New Book." *Sun Reporter (1968–1979)*. September 2, 1972.

Morrison, Mosi Adesina. "Are Black Immigrants A Model Minority? Race, Ethnicity and Social Mobility in the United States." PhD diss., University of Illinois at Chicago, 2011. ProQuest (Order No. 3551288).

Moses, Wilson Jeremiah, ed. *Classical Black Nationalism: From the American Revolution to Marcus Garvey*. New York: New York University Press, 1996.

———. *The Golden Age of Black Nationalism, 1850–1925*. Hamden, CT: Archon Books, 1978.

Mostern, Kenneth. *Autobiography and Black Identity Politics: Racialization in Twentieth-Century America*. Cambridge: Cambridge University Press, 1999.

Moten, Fred. *In the Break: The Aesthetics of the Black Radical Tradition*. Minneapolis: University of Minnesota Press, 2003.

Moya Pons, Frank. *The Dominican Republic: A National History*. Princeton, NJ: Markus Wiener Publishers, 2010.

Moynihan, Daniel P. "The Negro Family—The Case for National Action." Office of the Assistant Secretary for Administration and Management (OASAM)—United States Department of Labor, Web 2018–31 1965. https://web.archive.org/web/20181231013539/https://www.dol.gov/oasam/programs/history/webid-meynihan.htm.

Mukherjee, Roopali. *The Racial Order of Things: Cultural Imaginaries of the Post-Soul Era*. Minneapolis: University of Minnesota Press, 2006.

Murphy, Erin E. *Inside the Cell: The Dark Side of Forensic DNA*. New York: Nation Books, 2015.

Murray, Derek Conrad. *Queering Post-Black Art: Artists Transforming African-American Identity after Civil Rights*. International Library of Modern and Contemporary Art 30. London: I.B. Tauris, 2016.

Murrell, Nathaniel Samuel. *Afro-Caribbean Religions: An Introduction to Their Historical, Cultural, and Sacred Traditions*. Philadelphia: Temple University Press, 2010.

Myers, Megan Jeanette. *Mapping Hispaniola: Third Space in Dominican and Haitian Literature*. Charlottesville: University of Virginia Press, 2019.

———. "Raquel Cepeda's Digital and Literary Publics: Twitter and Bird of Paradise." *Chiricú Journal: Latina/o Literatures, Arts, and Cultures* 2, no. 1 (December 28, 2017): 40–57.

Neal, Larry. "Some Reflections on the Black Aesthetic." In *The Black Aesthetic*, edited by Addison Gayle Jr., 12–15. Garden City, NY: Anchor Books, 1972.

Neal, Mark Anthony. *Soul Babies: Black Popular Culture and the Post-Soul Aesthetic*. New York: Routledge, 2002.

Nelson, Alondra. *The Social Life of DNA: Race, Reparations, and Reconciliation after the Genome*. Boston: Beacon Press, 2016.

———. "The Social Life of DNA: Racial Reconciliation and Institutional Morality after the Genome—a Response." *British Journal of Sociology* 69, no. 3 (2018): 575–79. https://doi.org/10.1111/1468-4446.12612.

"Nelson George: 'Smart Black People.'" *News and Notes*. NPR, July 19, 2005. https://www.npr.org/templates/story/story.php?storyId=4760378.

Noe-Bustamante, Luis, Lauren Mora, and Mark Hugo Lopez. "About One-in-Four U.S. Hispanics Have Heard of Latinx, but Just 3% Use It." *Pew Research Center's Hispanic Trends Project* (blog), August 11, 2020. https://www.pewresearch.org/hispanic/2020/08/11/about-one-in-four-u-s-hispanics-have-heard-of-latinx-but-just-3-use-it/

Noriega, Chon A., and Ana M. López, eds. *The Ethnic Eye Latino Media Arts*. Minneapolis: University of Minnesota Press, 1996.

Norrick, Neal R. *Conversational Joking: Humor in Everyday Talk*. Bloomington: Indiana University Press, 1993.

———. "Issues in Conversational Joking." *Journal of Pragmatics* 35, no. 9 (September 2003): 1333–59. https://doi.org/10.1016/S0378-2166(02)00180-7.

Nuruddin, Yusuf. "The Five Percenters: A Teenage Nation of Gods and Earths." In *Muslim Communities in North America*, edited by Yvonne Yazbeck Haddad and Jane Ideleman Smith, 109–132. Albany: State University of New York Press, 1994.

Nwankwo, Ifeoma C. K. "Veronica Chambers, Mama's Girl." In *Reading U. S. Latina Writers: Remapping American Literature*, 25–36. Gordonville, VA: Palgrave Macmillan, 2003.

Oboler, Suzanne. "Disposable Strangers: Mexican Americans, Latinxs, and the Ethnic Label 'Hispanic' in the Twenty-First Century." In *Critical Dialogues in Latinx Studies: A Reader*, 67–80. New York: New York University Press, 2021.

———. *Ethnic Labels, Latino Lives: Identity and the Politics of (Re) Presentation in the United States*. Minneapolis: University of Minnesota Press, 1995.

———, ed. *Latinos and Citizenship: The Dilemma of Belonging*. New York: Palgrave Macmillan, 2006.

Oboler, Suzanne, and Anani Dzidzienyo, eds. *Neither Enemies Nor Friends: Latinos, Blacks, Afro-Latinos*. New York: Palgrave Macmillan, 2005.

O'Brien, David M. *Animal Sacrifice and Religious Freedom: Church of the Lukumi Babalu Aye v. City of Hialeah*. Landmark Law Cases & American Society. Lawrence: University Press of Kansas, 2004.

Oh, Hans, Karen Lincoln, and Kyle Waldman. "Perceived Colorism and Lifetime Psychiatric Disorders among Black American Adults: Findings from the National Survey of American Life." *Social Psychiatry and Psychiatric Epidemiology: The International Journal for Research in Social and Genetic Epidemiology and Mental Health Services*, 2021, 1. https://doi.org/10.1007/s00127-021-02102-z.

Olney, James. *Memory & Narrative: The Weave of Life-Writing*. Chicago: University of Chicago Press, 1998.

Original Products Botanica. "Martha the Dominator." *Original Botanica* (blog), July 7, 2015. https://www.originalbotanica.com/blog/martha-dominator-marta-dominadora/.

Ortega-Aponte, Elias. "Mulatez." In *Hispanic American Religious Cultures* [2 vols.], edited by Miguel A. De La Torre, 385–90. American Religious Cultures. Santa Barbara, CA: ABC-CLIO, 2009.

Ortiz, Fernando. *Cuban Counterpoint: Tobacco and Sugar*. Translated by Harriet de Onís. Durham, NC: Duke University Press Books, 1995.

Ortiz, Paul. *An African American and Latinx History of the United States*. Boston: Beacon Press, 2018.

Ortíz, Ricardo L. *Cultural Erotics in Cuban America*. Minneapolis: University of Minnesota Press, 2007.

———. *Latinx Literature Now: Between Evanescence and Event*. Literatures of the Americas. Cham, Switzerland: Palgrave Macmillan, 2019.

Otero, Solimar. "Espiritismo." In *Ghosts in Popular Culture and Legend*, edited by June Michele Pulliam and Anthony J. Fonseca, 92–96. Westport, CT: ABC-CLIO, 2016.

Owens, Ernest. "Temple Students, Let That HBCU Comparison Die." *Philadelphia Magazine* (blog), October 14, 2019. https://www.phillymag.com/news/2019/10/14/temple-university-hbcu-black/.

Padilla, Felix M. *Latino Ethnic Consciousness: The Case of Mexican Americans and Puerto Ricans in Chicago*. Notre Dame, IN: University of Notre Dame Press, 1985. http://archive.org/details/latinoethnicconsoooopadi.

Palmié, Stephan, and Francisco A. Scarano, eds. *The Caribbean: A History of the Region and Its Peoples*. Chicago: University of Chicago Press, 2011.

Parker, Kim, Juliana Menasce Horowitz, Rich Morin, and Mark Hugo Lopez. "Hispanic Racial Identity: Multidimensional Issue For Latinos." *Pew Research Center's Social & Demographic Trends Project* (blog), June 11, 2015. https://www.pewresearch.org/social-trends/2015/06/11/chapter-7-the-many-dimensions-of-hispanic-racial-identity/.

Parks, Carole A. "On Images and Control: The National Black Writers Convention." *Black World/Negro Digest*, January 1975. Google Books.

Pascoe, Peggy. *What Comes Naturally: Miscegenation Law and the Making of Race in America*. Oxford: Oxford University Press, 2009.

Pausanias. *Description of Greece*. Loeb Classical Library. Accessed February 5, 2022. https://www-loebclassics-com

Payne, Rodger M. *The Self and the Sacred: Conversion and Autobiography in Early American Protestantism*. Knoxville: University of Tennessee Press, 1998.

Paz, Christian. "Another Problem for Latinx." *Atlantic*, November 23, 2021. https://
www.theatlantic.com/politics/archive/2021/11/latinx-future-progressive
-congress-latino/620764/.

Peller, Gary. "Race-Consciousness." In *Critical Race Theory: The Key Writings That
Formed the Movement*, edited by Kimberle Crenshaw, Neil Gotanda, Gary Peller,
and Kendall Thomas, 127–58. New York: New Press, 1996.

Pérez, Louis A. *Cuba in the American Imagination Metaphor and the Imperial Ethos*.
Chapel Hill: The University of North Carolina Press, 2008.

Perez, Richard. "Racial Spills and Disfigured Faces in Piri Thomas's *Down These Mean
Streets* and Junot Diaz's 'Ysrael.'" In *Contemporary U.S. Latino/a Literary Criticism*,
edited by Lyn Di Iorio Sandín and Richard Perez, 93–112. New York: Palgrave
Macmillan, 2007.

Pérez Firmat, Gustavo. *Life on the Hyphen: The Cuban-American Way*. Joe R. and
Teresa Lozano Long Series in Latin American and Latino Art and Culture. Austin:
University of Texas Press, 2012.

Pérez-Rosario, Vanessa. "On the Hispanophone Caribbean Question." *Small Axe* 20,
no. 3 (2016): 21–31.

Pérez-Torres, Rafael. "Mestizaje." In *The Routledge Companion to Latino/a Literature*,
edited by Suzanne Bost and Frances R. Aparicio, 25–33. London: Routledge, 2013.
Kindle.

Perlmann, Joel. "Reflecting the Changing Face of America: Multiracials, Racial
Classification, and American Intermarriage." In *Interracialism: Black-White
Intermarriage in American History, Literature, and Law*, edited by Werner Sollors,
506–33. Oxford: Oxford University Press, 2000.

Perlmann, Joel, and Mary C. Waters. "Intermarriage and Multiple Identities." In
The New Americans: A Guide to Immigration since 1965. Harvard University Press
Reference Library, 110-123. Cambridge, MA: Harvard University Press, 2007.

Petty, Jill L. "Mama's Girl." *Ms. Magazine*, August 1996.

Pichardo, Ernesto. "Santería." In *Hispanic American Religious Cultures*, 501–13.
American Religious Cultures. Santa Barbara, CA: ABC-CLIO, 2009.

"Pichón: Race and Revolution in Castro's Cuba: A Memoir." *Kirkus Reviews* 76, no. 17
(September 1, 2008): 931.

"Pichón: Revolution and Racism in Castro's Cuba: A Memoir." *Publishers Weekly*,
September 1, 2008. 47.

"Pichón: Race and Revolution in Castro's Cuba: A Memoir." *Kirkus Reviews* 76, no. 17
(November 1, 2008). https://www.kirkusreviews.com/book-reviews/carlos
-moore/pichon/.

"Pichón: Race and Revolution in Castro's Cuba: A Memoir." *Mother Jones* 34, no. 1
(February 2009): 67.

"Pichón: Race and Revolution in Castro's Cuba: A Memoir." *Mother Jones* 34, no. 2
(April 2009): 79.

Pickering, Michael. *Stereotyping: The Politics of Representation*. Basingstoke, UK:
Palgrave, 2001.

Pico v. Board of Ed, Island Trees Union Free Sch. Dist., 474 F. Supp. 387 (U.S.
District Court for the Eastern District of New York 1979).

Pico v. Board of Ed, Island Trees Union Free Sch. Dist., 638 F.2d 404 (U.S. Court of Appeals for the Second Circuit 1980).

Pinn, Anthony B. "Ashe!: Santería, Orisha-Voodoo, and Oyotunji African Village." In *Varieties of African American Religious Experience: Toward a Comparative Black Theology—20th Anniversary Edition*, 59–114. Minneapolis, MN: Fortress Press, 2017. https://www.jstor.org/stable/j.ctt1tm7gvn.8.

Poey, Delia. *Latino American Literature in the Classroom: The Politics of Transformation*. Gainesville: University Press of Florida, 2002.

Poole, Robert M. "What Became of the Taíno?" *Smithsonian Magazine*, October 2011. https://www.smithsonianmag.com/travel/what-became-of-the-taino-73824867/.

Powell, Cedric Merlin. "The Rhetorical Allure of Post-Racial Process Discourse and the Democratic Myth." *Utah Law Review* 2018, no. 3 (2018): 523–78.

Power-Greene, Ousmane K. *Against Wind and Tide: The African American Struggle against the Colonization Movement*. New York: New York University Press, 2014.

Pratt, Alan R. *Black Humor: Critical Essays*. New York: Garland, 1993.

Presidents Council, Dist. 25, et al v. Community School Board No. 25, et al, 457 F.2d 289 (US Court of Appeals for the Second Circuit 1972).

Proefrock, Stacia. "Freestyle Fellowship Biography." AllMusic. Accessed June 6, 2021. https://www.allmusic.com/artist/mn0000802928.

Raab, Josef, and Alexander Greiffenstern, eds. *Interculturalism in North America: Canada, the United States, Mexico, and Beyond*. Tempe, AZ: Inter-American Studies. Bilingual Press/Editorial Bilingüe, 2013.

Rabaka, Reiland. *Africana Critical Theory: Reconstructing The Black Radical Tradition, from W. E. B. Du Bois and C. L. R. James to Frantz Fanon and Amilcar Cabral*. Lanham, MD: Lexington Books, 2009.

———. *The Negritude Movement: W.E.B. Du Bois, Leon Damas, Aime Cesaire, Leopold Senghor, Frantz Fanon, and the Evolution of an Insurgent Idea*. Lanham, MD: Lexington Books, 2015.

Rabinowitz, Victor. *Unrepentant Leftist: A Lawyer's Memoir*. Urbana: University of Illinois Press, 1996.

Rahman, J. "An Ay for an Ah: Language of Survival in African American Narrative Comedy." *American Speech* 82, no. 1 (March 1, 2007): 65–96. https://doi.org/10.1215/00031283-2007-003.

Rak, Julie. *Boom!: Manufacturing Memoir for the Popular Market*. Waterloo, Ontario, Canada: Wilfrid Laurier University Press, 2013.

Ramírez, Dixa. "Against Type." *Small Axe: A Caribbean Journal of Criticism* 22, no. 2 (July 1, 2018): 144–60. https://doi.org/10.1215/07990537-6985831.

———. *Colonial Phantoms: Belonging and Refusal in the Dominican Americas, from the 19th Century to the Present*. New York: New York University Press, 2018. Kindle.

Ramirez, Roberto R., and G. Patricia de la Cruz. "The Hispanic Population in the United States: March 2002." Current Population Report. Washington, DC: U.S. Census Bureau, June 2003. https://www.census.gov/prod/2003pubs/p20-545.pdf.

Rappoport, Leon. *Punchlines: The Case for Racial, Ethnic, and Gender Humor*. Westport, CT: Praeger Publishers, 2005.

"Raquel Cepeda Interview with Melissa Harris-Perry." *Melissa Harris-Perry*, April 28, 2013. http://archive.org/details/MSNBCW_20130428_140000_Melissa_Harris-Perry.

Ratliff, Ben. "Graciela Per'ez-Gutierrez, 94, Afro-Cuban Singer." *New York Times* (1923-). April 9, 2010.

———. "Graciela, Renowned Afro-Cuban Vocalist." *Boston Globe*. April 10, 2010.

Redfield, Marc. *Phantom Formations: Aesthetic Ideology and the "Bildungsroman."* Ithaca, NY: Cornell University Press, 1996.

Reece, Robert L. "The Gender of Colorism: Understanding the Intersection of Skin Tone and Gender Inequality." *Journal of Economics, Race, and Policy* 4, no. 1 (2021): 47–55. https://doi.org/10.1007/s41996-020-00054-1.

Reid-Merritt, Patricia. "Temple University's African American Studies PhD Program @ 30: Assessing the Asante Affect." *Journal of Black Studies* 49, no. 6 (September 2018): 559–75. https://doi.org/10.1177/0021934718786221.

Reid-Pharr, Robert F. "Tearing the Goat's Flesh: Homosexuality, Abjection, and the Production of a Late Twentieth-Century Black Masculinity Production of a Late Twentieth-Century Black Masculinity." *Studies in the Novel* 28, no. 3 (1996): 372–94.

"Remember Graciela Pérez Gutiérrez of Machito & His Afro-Cubans!" *New York Latin Culture Magazine*, August 3, 2021. https://www.newyorklatinculture.com/graciela -grillo-machito-and-his-afro-cubans/.

"Remember Machito and His Afro-Cubans Who Defined Latin Jazz." *New York Latin Culture Magazine*, December 4, 2021. https://www.newyorklatinculture.com /machito-and-his-afro-cubans/.

Rich, Wilbur C. *The Post-Racial Society Is Here: Recognition, Critics and the Nation-State*. London: Taylor & Francis Group, 2013.

Richardson, Jill Toliver. *The Afro-Latin@ Experience in Contemporary American Literature and Culture: Engaging Blackness*. Cham, Switzerland: Palgrave Macmillan, 2016. Kindle.

Ricourt, Milagros. "Criollismo Religioso." In *The Dominican Racial Imaginary: Surveying the Landscape of Race and Nation in Hispaniola*, 103–34. New Brunswick, NJ: Rutgers University Press, 2020. https://doi.org/10.36019/9780813584508-006.

Riolli, Laura, and Victor Savicki. "Coping Effectiveness and Coping Diversity under Traumatic Stress." *International Journal of Stress Management* 17, no. 2 (May 2010): 97–113. https://doi.org/10.1037/a0018041.

Riordan, Richard J. "Scriptotherapy: Therapeutic Writing as a Counseling Adjunct." *Journal of Counseling & Development* 74, no. 3 (February 1, 1996): 263. https://doi .org/10.1002/j.1556-6676.1996.tb01863.x.

"Riot in Gallery Halts U.N. Debate: American Negroes Ejected after Invading Session." *New York Times*, February 16, 1961.

Rivera, Raquel Z. "Between Blackness and Latinidad in the Hip Hop Zone." In *A Companion to Latina/o Studies*, edited by Juan Flores and Renato Rosaldo, 351–62. Malden, MA: Blackwell Publishing, 2007.

———. "Ghettocentricity, Blackness, and Pan-Latinidad." In *The Afro-Latin@ Reader: History and Culture in the United States*, edited by Miriam Jiménez Román and Juan Flores, 373–86. Durham, NC: Duke University Press Books, 2010.

———. "Hip Hop and New York Puerto Ricans." In *Latino/a Popular Culture*, edited by Michelle Habell-Pallán and Mary Romero, 127–46. New York: New York University Press, 2002.

———. "Hip Hop, Puerto Ricans, and Ethnoracial Identities in New York." In *Mambo Montage: The Latinization of New York*, edited by Agustín Laó-Montes and Arlene M. Dávila, 235–62. New York: Columbia University Press, 2001.

———. *New York Ricans from the Hip Hop Zone*. New York: Palgrave Macmillan, 2003.

Rivera, Raquel Z., Wayne Marshall, and Deborah Pacini Hernandez, eds. *Reggaeton*. Durham, NC: Duke University Press Books, 2009.

Rivera-Rideau, Petra R. "'If I Were You': Tego Calderón's Diasporic Interventions." *Small Axe* 22, no. 1 (2018): 55–69.

Rivera-Rideau, Petra R., Jennifer A. Jones, and Tianna S. Paschel, eds. *Afro-Latin@s in Movement: Critical Approaches to Blackness and Transnationalism in the Americas*. Afro-Latin@ Diasporas. New York: Palgrave Macmillan, 2016.

———. "Introduction: Theorizing Afrolatinidades." In *Afro-Latin@s in Movement*, edited by Petra R. Rivera-Rideau, Jennifer A. Jones, and Tianna S. Paschel, 1–29. New York: Palgrave Macmillan US, 2016. https://doi.org/10.1057/978-1-137-59874 -5_1.

Robinson, Zandria F. *This Ain't Chicago: Race, Class, and Regional Identity in the Post-Soul South*. New Directions in Southern Studies. Chapel Hill: The University of North Carolina Press, 2014. https://doi.org/10.5149/9781469614236_robinson.

Robles, Frances. "Black Denial." *Miami Herald*, June 13, 2007. http://media .miamiherald.com/multimedia/news/afrolatin/part2/index.html.

Rochford, E. Burke, Jr. *Hare Krishna Transformed*. New York: New York University Press, 2007.

Rochman, Hazel. "Mama's Girl." *Booklist* 92, no. 17 (May 1, 1996): 1494.

Rodriquez, Ralph E. *Latinx Literature Unbound: Undoing Ethnic Expectation*. New York: Fordham University Press, 2018.

Roorda, Eric Paul, Lauren H. Derby, and Raymundo Gonzalez, eds. "The Haitian Massacre." In *The Dominican Republic Reader: History, Culture, Politics*, 281–85. Durham, NC: Duke University of Press, 2014.

"Roots (Biography of Carlos Moore)." 2016. http://moorecarlos.com/roots.asp.

Rose, Tricia. *Black Noise: Rap Music and Black Culture in Contemporary America*. Hanover, NH: University Press of New England, 1994.

Roszak, Suzanne Manizza. "Intersectional Feminism, Black Love, and the Transnational Turn: Rereading Guillén, Hughes, and Roumain." *Journal of Modern Literature* 44, no. 4 (Summer 2021): 37–56. https://doi.org/10.2979 /jmodelite.44.4.03.

Rowell, Charles H., and Etheridge Knight. "An Interview with Etheridge Knight." *Callaloo* 19, no. 4 (1996): 967–81.

Royster, Francesca T. *Sounding Like a No-No?: Queer Sounds and Eccentric Acts in the Post-Soul Era*. Ann Arbor: University of Michigan Press, 2013.

Russ, Valerie, and Elizabeth Wellington. "HBCU-ish? Some Say Temple T-Shirts Ignore the Significance of Actual Historically Black Colleges." *Philadelphia Inquirer*, October 16, 2019. http://web.archive.org/web/20191017193835/https://

www.inquirer.com/news/hbcuish-temple-university-blackish-tshirt-20191016
.html.

Rustin, Bayard. "Blacks? African-Americans?: What's in a Name?" *New York Times*,
February 1, 1989, sec. Sports Pages.

Saad, Lydia. "Gallup Vault: Black Americans' Preferred Racial Label." Gallup.com,
July 13, 2020. https://news.gallup.com/vault/315566/gallup-vault-black
-americans-preferred-racial-label.aspx.

Saldívar, Ramón. "Historical Fantasy, Speculative Realism, and Postrace Aesthetics
in Contemporary American Fiction." *American Literary History* 23, no. 3 (2011):
574–99.

———. "Imagining Cultures: The Transnational Imaginary in Postrace America."
Journal of Transnational American Studies 4, no. 2 (2012). https://doi.org/10.5070
/T842015762.

———. "Imagining Cultures: The Transnational Imaginary in Postrace America." In
The Imaginary and Its Worlds American Studies after the Transnational Turn, edited by
Laura Bieger, Ramón Saldívar, and Johannes Voelz, 3–22. Re-Mapping the
Transnational: A Dartmouth Series in American Studies. Hanover, NH:
Dartmouth College Press, 2013.

———. *The Borderlands of Culture: Américo Paredes and the Transnational Imaginary*.
New Americanists. Durham, NC: Duke University Press, 2006.

———. "The Second Elevation of the Novel: Race, Form, and the Postrace Aesthetic
in Contemporary Narrative." *Narrative* 21, no. 1 (2013): 1–18.

Salgado, Danny "Khalil." "Stories of Some of the Early 'Latino' Muslims." *Islamic
Horizons*. Plainfield, IN: Islamic Society of North America, February 2020.

Sanchez Carretero, Cristina. "Santos y Misterios as Channels of Communication in
the Diaspora: Afro-Dominican Religious Practices Abroad." *Journal of American
Folklore* 118, no. 469 (2005): 308–26. https://doi.org/10.1353/jaf.2005.0034.

Sánchez, Marta E. *"Shakin' Up" Race and Gender: Intercultural Connections in Puerto
Rican, African American, and Chicano Narratives and Culture*. Austin: University of
Texas Press, 2005.

Sánchez González, Lisa M. *Boricua Literature: A Literary History of the Puerto Rican
Diaspora*. New York: New York University Press, 2001.

———. "Decolonizing Schomburg." *African American Review* 54, no. 1–2 (2021):
129–42. https://doi.org/10.1353/afa.2021.0007.

Sandín, Lyn Di Iorio. *Killing Spanish: Literary Essays on Ambivalent U.S. Latino/a
Identity*. New York: Palgrave Macmillan, 2016.

Santo, Diana Espirito. *Developing the Dead: Mediumship and Selfhood in Cuban
Espiritismo*. Gainesville: University Press of Florida, 2015.

Scharrón-del Río, María R., and Alan A. Aja. "The Case FOR 'Latinx': Why
Intersectionality Is Not a Choice." *Latino Rebels* (blog), December 5, 2015.
https://www.latinorebels.com/2015/12/05/the-case-for-latinx-why
-intersectionality-is-not-a-choice/.

Seaman, Donna. "Mama's Girl." *Booklist*, May 1, 1996. Literature Resource Center.

Segall, Shlomi. *Why Inequality Matters: Luck Egalitarianism, Its Meaning and Value*.
Cambridge: Cambridge University Press, 2016.

Seraile, William. *Bruce Grit: The Black Nationalist Writings of John Edward Bruce*. Knoxville: University of Tennessee Press, 2003.

Sexton, Jared. *Amalgamation Schemes: Antiblackness and the Critique of Multiracialism*. Minneapolis: University of Minnesota Press, 2008.

Shea, Daniel B. *Spiritual Autobiography in Early America*. Princeton, NJ: Princeton University Press, 1968.

Shelby, Tommie. *We Who Are Dark: The Philosophical Foundations of Black Solidarity*. Cambridge, MA: Belknap Press of Harvard University Press, 2005.

Shepperson, George. "Pan-Africanism and 'Pan-Africanism': Some Historical Notes on JSTOR." *Phylon (1960-)* 23, no. 4 (1962): 346–58.

Shockley, Ann Allen. "Two Books with Soul: For Defiant Ones." *English Journal* 58, no. 3 (1969): 396–98. https://doi.org/10.2307/811796.

Sidanius, Jim, Yesilernis Peña, and Mark Sawyer. "Inclusionary Discrimination: Pigmentocracy and Patriotism in the Dominican Republic." *Political Psychology* 22, no. 4 (December 1, 2001): 827–51.

Simmons, Kimberly Eison. *Reconstructing Racial Identity and the African Past in the Dominican Republic*. New World Diasporas Series. Gainesville: University Press of Florida, 2009.

Sinnette, Elinor Des Verney. *Arthur Alfonso Schomburg, Black Bibliophile & Collector: A Biography*. Detroit, MI: Wayne State University Press, 1989. http://archive.org /details/arthuralfonsoschoosinn.

Slaughter, Joseph R. "Clef à Roman: Some Uses of Hu." *Politics and Culture*, no. 3 (2003). http://politicsandculture.org/2010/08/10/joseph-r-slaughter-clef-a-roman -some-uses-of-hu-2/.

Smart, Ian. *Nicolás Guillén, Popular Poet of the Caribbean*. Colombia: University of Missouri Press, 1990.

Smethurst, James Edward. *The Black Arts Movement: Literary Nationalism in the 1960s and 1970s*. Chapel Hill: The University of North Carolina Press, 2005.

Smith, Candis Watts. *Black Mosaic: The Politics of Black Pan-Ethnic Diversity*. New York: New York University Press, 2014.

Smith, Sidonie, and Julia Watson. *Reading Autobiography: A Guide for Interpreting Life Narratives*. Minneapolis: University of Minnesota Press, 2010.

Some Girls. San Francisco, CA: Saboteur Media, 2017. https://nhfpl.kanopy.com /node/3467650.

Srivastava, Neelam. *Secularism in the Postcolonial Indian Novel: National and Cosmopolitan Narratives in English*. London: Routledge, 2007.

Stavans, Ilan. *Growing Up Latino: Memoirs and Stories*. Edited by Harold Augenbraum. Boston, MA: Mariner Books, 1993.

———. *The Hispanic Condition: Reflections on Culture and Identity in America*. 2nd edition. New York: Rayo-Harper Collins, 2001.

Stavans, Ilan, and Edna Acosta-Belén, eds. *The Norton Anthology of Latino Literature*. New York: W. W. Norton, 2011.

Stephens, Thomas M. "Indio Claro." In *Dictionary of Latin American Racial and Ethnic Terminology*, 128. Gainesville: University of Florida Press, 1989.

———. "Indio Oscuro." In *Dictionary of Latin American Racial and Ethnic Terminology*, 130. Gainesville: University of Florida Press, 1989.

Stepto, Robert B. *From Behind the Veil: A Study of Afro-American Narrative*. Ilini Books Edition. Urbana: University of Illinois Press, 1991.

Stern, Daniel. "In the Arms of Lady Snow." *Newsweek*, May 29, 1967.

Stuttaford, Genevieve. "Mama's Girl." *Publishers Weekly*, May 6, 1996. Literature Resource Center.

Suárez, Lucía M. *The Tears of Hispaniola: Haitian and Dominican Diaspora Memory*. New World Diasporas. Gainesville: University Press of Florida, 2006.

Subbotsky, Eugene. "Magical Reality." In *Magic and the Mind: Mechanisms, Functions, and Development of Magical Thinking and Behavior*, 3–17. New York: Oxford University Press, 2010. https://doi.org/10.1093/acprof:oso/9780195393873.003.0001.

———. "The Belief in Magic in the Age of Science." *SAGE Open* 4, no. 1 (January 1, 2014): 2158244014521433. https://doi.org/10.1177/2158244014521433.

Sun-Times Staff. "To Our Readers: Why We're Now Capitalizing the 'B' in Black." *Chicago Sun-Times*, June 15, 2020. https://chicago.suntimes.com/2020/6/15/21292317/capitalzing-b-black-sun-times-african-american-latino-white-style-newsroom.

Tallaj, Angelina. "Religion on the Dance Floor: Afro-Dominican Music and Ritual from Altars to Clubs." *Civilisations*, no. 67 (August 12, 2018): 95–109. https://doi.org/10.4000/civilisations.4961.

TallBear, Kimberly. *Native American DNA: Tribal Belonging and the False Promise of Genetic Science*. Minneapolis: University of Minnesota Press, 2013.

Tamargo, Luis. "Obituario: Graciela (La Habana, 1915-Nueva York, 2010)." *Latin Beat Magazine*, May 2010. Gale OneFile: High School Edition.

Tamir, Christine. "Key Findings about Black America." *Pew Research Center* (blog), March 25, 2021. https://www.pewresearch.org/fact-tank/2021/03/25/key-findings-about-black-america/.

———. "The Growing Diversity of Black America." *Pew Research Center's Social & Demographic Trends Project* (blog), March 25, 2021. https://www.pewresearch.org/social-trends/2021/03/25/the-growing-diversity-of-black-america/.

Tamir, Christine, Abby Budiman, Luis Noe-Bustamante, and Lauren Mora. "Facts about the U.S. Black Population." *Pew Research Center's Social & Demographic Trends Project* (blog), March 25, 2021. https://www.pewresearch.org/social-trends/fact-sheet/facts-about-the-us-black-population/.

Tan, Kok-Chor. "Defending Luck Egalitarianism." In *Justice, Institutions, and Luck: The Site, Ground, and Scope of Equality*, 116–46. Oxford, England: Oxford University Press, 2012. https://doi.org/10.1093/acprof:oso/9780199588855.003.0005.

Tate, Greg. "Cult-Nats Meet Freaky-Deke: The Return of the Black Aesthetic." In *Flyboy in the Buttermilk: Essays in Contemporary America*, reprint edition, 198–210. New York: Touchstone, 1992.

Taylor, Charles. "Interculturalism or Multiculturalism?" *Philosophy & Social Criticism* 38, no. 4-5 (May 1, 2012): 413–23. https://doi.org/10.1177/0191453711435656.

Taylor, Chet. "Thomas, Piri." *Revista Interamericana* 1, no. 2 (Winter 1972): 156–57.

Taylor, Paul C. "Post-Black, Old Black." *African American Review* 41, no. 4 (Winter 2007): 625–40.

Telles, Edward Eric, and Project on Ethnicity and Race in Latin America (PERLA). *Pigmentocracies: Ethnicity, Race, and Color in Latin America*. Chapel Hill: the University of North Carolina Press, 2014.

Terry, Lilian. "Abbey Lincoln and Max Roach." In *Dizzy, Duke, Brother Ray, and Friends*, 39–58. On and off the Record with Jazz Greats. Urbana: University of Illinois Press, 2017. https://doi.org/10.5406/j.ctt1ws7vzb.6.

Tharps, Lori L. *Same Family, Different Colors: Confronting Colorism in America's Diverse Families*. Boston: Beacon Press, 2016.

The Center for the Study of White American Culture. "The Multiracial Movement: Part 2 Retrospective Analysis," May 16, 2019. https://cswac.org/the-multiracial -movement-retrospective-analysis/.

———. "The Multiracial Movement: Part 3 Lessons Learned," May 30, 2019. https://cswac.org/the-multiracial-movement-lessons-learned/.

———. "The Multiracial Movement: Part I, a History," May 2, 2019. https://cswac .org/the-multiracial-movement-a-history/.

The Fat Feminist Witch. "The Nine Tuesdays of Saint Martha the Dominator." *The Fat Feminist Witch Podcast* (blog), September 15, 2020. https://thefatfeministwitch .com/2020/09/15/the-nine-tuesdays-of-saint-martha-the-dominator/.

"The National Conference of Afro-American Writers," n.d. https://franklin.library .upenn.edu/catalog/FRANKLIN_9977579546203681.

The World of Piri Thomas. National Educational Television and Radio Center, 1968. http://archive.org/details/theworldofpirithomas.

Thomas, Douglas. "Santería." In *African Religions: Beliefs and Practices Through History*, edited by Temilola Alanamu., 222-224. Santa Barbara, CA: ABC-CLIO, 2019.

Thomas Nelson Publishers. *The Holy Bible: Old and New Testaments in the King James Version*. Giant Print Reference Edition. Nashville, TN: Thomas Nelson, 1976.

Thomas, Piri. "A Conversation with Piri Thomas." Edited by Lisa D. McGill. *Bilingual Review / La Revista Bilingüe* 25, no. 2 (2000): 179–84.

———. "A Talk with Piri Thomas." Interview by Christopher Lehmann-Haupt. *New York Times*. 1967, sec. *New York Times* Book Review.

———. "An Interview with Piri Thomas." Interview by Wolfgang Binder. *Minority Voices*, 1980.

———. Interview with Piri Thomas: Of Prisons, Wordsongs, Self-Determination and Laughter, Part 3. Interview by Nic Paget-Clarke. In Motion Magazine, January 21, 1998. https://www.inmotionmagazine.com/ptinter3.html.

———. Interview with Piri Thomas: The Inspiration to Write "Down These Mean Streets," Part 1. Interview by Nic Paget-Clarke. In Motion Magazine, January 21, 1998. https://www.inmotionmagazine.com/ptinter1.html.

———. Interview with Piri Thomas: The Inspiration to Write "Down These Mean Streets," Part 2. Interview by Nic Paget-Clarke. In Motion Magazine, January 21, 1998. https://www.inmotionmagazine.com/ptinter2.html.

———. "Piri Thomas: An Interview." Interview by Dorothee von Huene Greenberg. *MELUS* 26, no. 3 (2001): 77–99. https://doi.org/10.2307/3185558.

———. "Piri Thomas on Writing: Excerpts from an Interview." Interview by Revista/Review Interamericana. *Revista/Review Interamericana* 4, no. 4 (Winter 1974): 547–49.

———. "Race and Mercy: A Conversation with Piri Thomas." *Massachusetts Review* 37, no. 3 (Autumn 1996): 344–54.

———. "'They Have Forced Us to Be Universal': Interview with Piri Thomas." Interview by Carmen Dolores Hernandez, March 5, 1995. http://web.archive.org /web/19980509010156/www.cheverote.com/reviews/hernandezinterview.html.

Torres, Lourdes. "Latinx?" *Latino Studies* 16, no. 3 (October 2018): 283–85. https://doi .org/10.1057/s41276-018-0142-y.

———. "The Construction of the Self in U.S. Latina Autobiographies." In *Women, Autobiography, Theory: A Reader*, edited by Sidonie Smith and Julia Watson, 276–87. Madison: University of Wisconsin Press, 1998.

Torres Rivera, Edil. "Espiritismo: The Flywheel of the Puerto Rican Spiritual Traditions." *Revista Interamericana de Psicología* 39 (January 1, 2005): 295–300.

Torres-Saillant, Silvio. "Afro-Latinas/os and the Racial Wall." In *A Companion to Latina/o Studies*, edited by Juan Flores and Renato Rosaldo, 363–75. Malden, MA: Blackwell Publishing, 2007.

———. "Artistry, Ancestry, and Americanness in the Works of Junot Diaz." In *Junot Diaz and the Decolonial Imagination*, edited by Monica Hanna, Jennifer Harford Vargas, and José David Saldívar. Durham, NC: Duke University Press, 2016. Kindle.

———. "Inventing the Race: Latinos and the Ethnoracial Pentagon." *Latino Studies* 1, no. 1 (March 2003): 123–51.

———. *An Intellectual History of the Caribbean*. 2006th edition. Basingstoke, England: Palgrave Macmillan, 2006.

———. *Introduction to Dominican Blackness*. CUNY Dominican Studies Institute, 2010. https://www.ccny.cuny.edu/sites/default/files/dsi/upload/Introduction_to _Dominican_Blackness_Web.pdf.

———. "The Latino Autobiography." In *Latino and Latina Writers*, Vol. 1, edited by Alan West-Durán, 61–79. New York: Charles Scribner's Sons, 2004.

———. "The Tribulations of Blackness: Stages in Dominican Racial Identity." *Latin American Perspectives* 25, no. 3 (1998): 126–46.

Touré. *Who's Afraid of Post-Blackness?: What It Means to Be Black Now*. New York: Free Press, 2011. Kindle.

Tracy, Steven C. *Hot Music, Ragmentation, and the Bluing of American Literature*, Tuscaloosa: University of Alabama Press, 2015.

Trujillo-Pagán, Nicole. "Crossed Out by LatinX: Gender Neutrality and Genderblind Sexism." *Latino Studies* 16, no. 3 (October 2018): 396–406. https://doi.org/10.1057 /s41276-018-0138-7.

Tsang, Martin. "The Art of Sweeping Sickness and Catching Death: Babalú Aye, Materiality, and Mortality in Lukumí Religious Practice." *Journal of Africana Religions* 8, no. 2 (2020): 292–316.

Tucker, Terrence T. *Furiously Funny: Comic Rage from Ralph Ellison to Chris Rock*. Gainesville: University Press of Florida, 2018.

Turits, Richard Lee. "A World Destroyed, a Nation Imposed: The 1937 Haitian Massacre in the Dominican Republic." *Hispanic American Historical Review* 82, no. 3 (August 2002): 549.

"TV Highlights." *Chicago Daily Defender* (Daily Edition) (1960–73), November 18, 1968.

Ukpokodu, Omiunota N. "African Immigrants, the 'New Model Minority': Examining the Reality in U.S. k-12 Schools." *The Urban Review* 50, no. 1 (March 1, 2018): 69–96. https://doi.org/10.1007/s11256-017-0430-0.

University of Cambridge. "Ancient Genome Study Identifies Traces of Indigenous 'Taíno' in Present-Day Caribbean Populations." University of Cambridge, February 19, 2018. https://www.cam.ac.uk/research/news/ancient-genome-study -identifies-traces-of-indigenous-taino-in-present-day-caribbean-populations.

US Census Bureau. "Hispanic Origin." July 6, 2022. https://www.census.gov/topics /population/hispanic-origin.html.

———. "Race and Ethnicity in the United States: 2010 Census and 2020 Census." August 12, 2021. https://www.census.gov/library/visualizations/interactive/race -and-ethnicity-in-the-united-state-2010-and-2020-census.html.

———. "Why We Ask About . . . Hispanic or Latino Origin." Accessed June 15, 2021. https://www.census.gov/acs/www/about/why-we-ask-each-question /ethnicity/.

US Department of Education. "What Is an HBCU? | White House Initiative on Advancing Educational Equity, Excellence, and Economic Opportunity through Historically Black Colleges and Universities." Accessed November 23, 2021. https://sites.ed.gov/whhbcu/one-hundred-and-five-historically-black-colleges -and-universities/.

Valdés, Vanessa K. *Diasporic Blackness: The Life and Times of Arturo Alfonso Schomburg*. Albany: State University of New York Press, 2017.

———, ed. *Racialized Visions: Haiti and the Hispanic Caribbean*. Albany: State University of New York Press, 2020.

Van Deburg, William L., ed. *Modern Black Nationalism: From Marcus Garvey to Louis Farrakhan*. New York: New York University Press, 1997.

Vásquez, Sam. "Television Satire in the Black Americas: Transnational Border Crossings in Chappelle's Show and The Ity and Fancy Cat Show." In *Post-Soul Satire: Black Identity After Civil Rights*, edited by Derek C. Maus and James J. Donahue, 254–68. Jackson: University Press of Mississippi, 2014. Kindle.

Vázquez, David J. *Triangulations: Narrative Strategies for Navigating Latino Identity*. Minneapolis: University of Minnesota Press, 2011.

Vega, Marta Moreno. "Espiritismo in the Puerto Rican Community: A New World Recreation with the Elements of Kongo Ancestor Worship." *Journal of Black Studies* 29, no. 3 (1999): 325–53.

———. "Interlocking African Diaspora Cultures in the Work of Fernando Ortiz." *Journal of Black Studies* 31, no. 1 (September 2000): 39–50. https://doi.org/10.1177 /002193470003100103.

———. *The Altar of My Soul: The Living Traditions of Santeria*. New York: One World-Ballantine Books, 2000.

———. "The Ancestral Sacred Creative Impulse of Africa and the African Diaspora: Ase, the Nexus of the Black Global Aesthetic." *Lenox Avenue: A Journal of Interarts Inquiry* 5 (1999): 45. https://doi.org/10.2307/4177077.

———. "The Yoruba Orisha Tradition Comes to New York City." *African American Review* 29, no. 2 (Summer 1995): 201–6.

———. "Yoruba Philosophy: Multiple Levels of Transformation and Understanding." PhD diss., Temple University, 1995. ProQuest (Order No. 9535818).

Vega, Marta Moreno, Marinieves Alba, and Yvette Modestin, eds. *Women Warriors of the Afro-Latina Diaspora*. Houston, TX: Arte Público Press, 2012.

Verán, Cristina. "Breaking It All Down: The Rise and Fall and Rise of the B-Boy Kingdom." In *The Vibe History of Hip Hop*, edited by Alan Light, 53–59. New York: Three Rivers Press, 1999.

Vidal-Ortiz, Salvador, and Juliana Martínez. "Latinx Thoughts: Latinidad with an X." *Latino Studies* 16, no. 3 (October 2018): 384–95.

Viktorin, Alexander, Samantha Meltzer-Brody, Ralf Kuja-Halkola, Patrick F. Sullivan, Mikael Landén, Paul Lichtenstein, and Patrik K. E. Magnusson. "Heritability of Perinatal Depression and Genetic Overlap With Nonperinatal Depression." *American Journal of Psychiatry* 173, no. 2 (September 4, 2015): 158–65. https://doi.org/10.1176/appi.ajp.2015.15010085.

Voragine, Jacobus de. "Saint Martha." In *The Golden Legend: Readings on the Saints*, translated by William Granger Ryan, 409–12. Princeton, NJ: Princeton University Press, 2012.

Vries, Lloyd. "Hispanics Now Largest U.S. Minority." CBS News, January 21, 2003. https://www.cbsnews.com/news/hispanics-now-largest-us-minority/.

Wade, Lizzie. "Genes of 'Extinct' Caribbean Islanders Found in Living People." *Science*, February 19, 2018. https://www.sciencemag.org/news/2018/02/genes-extinct-caribbean-islanders-found-living-people.

Wade, Peter. "Afterword: Race and Nation in Modern Latin America: An Anthropological View." In *Race and Nation in Modern Latin America*, 263–81. Chapel Hill: The University of North Carolina Press, 2003.

Wailoo, Keith, Alondra Nelson, and Catherine Lee, eds. *Genetics and the Unsettled Past: The Collision of DNA, Race, and History*. New Brunswick, NJ: Rutgers University Press, 2012.

Wake Up (Official Video). Accessed July 24, 2016. https://www.youtube.com/watch?v=TE0J4Ewc1kA.

Wallace, Michele. *Black Macho and the Myth of the Superwoman*. London: Verso, 2015.

Walrond, Eric. *In Search of Asylum: The Later Writings of Eric Walrond*, edited by Louis J. Parascandola and Carl A. Wade. Gainesville: University Press of Florida, 2017.

Walters, Ronald W. *Pan Africanism in the African Diaspora: An Analysis of Modern Afrocentric Political Movements*. African American Life Series. Detroit, MI: Wayne State University Press, 1993.

Warren, Kenneth W. "Does African-American Literature Exist?" *Chronicle of Higher Education* 57, no. 26 (March 4, 2011): B10–B11.

———. *What Was African American Literature?* Cambridge: Harvard University Press, 2011.

Washburne, Christopher. "'El Tema Del Apollo': Latin American and Caribbean Music in Harlem." In *Latin Jazz*, 90–112. New York: Oxford University Press, 2020. https://doi.org/10.1093/oso/9780195371628.003.0005.

Wassink, Joshua, Krista M. Perreira, and Kathleen M. Harris. "Beyond Race/ Ethnicity: Skin Color and Cardiometabolic Health Among Blacks and Hispanics in the United States." *Journal of Immigrant and Minority Health* 19, no. 5 (2017): 1018. https://doi.org/10.1007/s10903-016-0495-y.

Watkins, Mel. *On the Real Side: Laughing, Lying, and Signifying: The Underground Tradition of African-American Humor That Transformed American Culture, from Slavery to Richard Pryor*. New York: Simon & Schuster, 1994.

Watson, Wendy. "Forensic DNA Analysis, the Fourth Amendment, and Personal Privacy." In *Privacy in the Digital Age: 21st-Century Challenges to the Fourth Amendment*, edited by Nancy S. Lind and Erik Rankin, 61–82. Santa Barbara, CA: ABC-CLIO, 2015.

Weaver, Simon. "Jokes, Rhetoric and Embodied Racism: A Rhetorical Discourse Analysis of the Logics of Racist Jokes on the Internet." *Ethnicities* 11, no. 4 (December 2011): 413–35. https://doi.org/10.1177/1468796811407755.

———. "The 'Other' Laughs Back: Humour and Resistance in Anti-Racist Comedy." *Sociology* 44, no. 1 (2010): 31–48.

Werner, Craig. *A Change Is Gonna Come: Music, Race & the Soul of America*. Revised edition. Ann Arbor: University of Michigan Press, 2006.

West-Durán, Alan. *Latino and Latina Writers*. Volume 1. New York: Scribner, 2009.

———. *Latino and Latina Writers*. Volume 2. New York: Scribner, 2009.

Wiggins, William H. "Black Folktales in the Novels of John O. Killens." *Black Scholar* 3, no. 3 (November 1, 1971): 50–58. https://doi.org/10.1080/00064246.1971.11431197.

Wilder, Gary. *The French Imperial Nation-State: Negritude & Colonial Humanism between the Two World Wars*. Chicago: University of Chicago Press, 2005.

Wilford, Hugh. "The American Society of African Culture: The CIA and Transnational Networks of African Diaspora Intellectuals in the Cold War." In *Transnational Anti-Communism and the Cold War: Agents, Activities, and Networks*, edited by Luc van Dongen, Stéphanie Roulin, and Giles Scott-Smith, 23–34. London: Palgrave Macmillan, 2014.

Williams, Kim M. *Mark One or More: Civil Rights in Multiracial America*. Ann Arbor: University of Michigan Press, 2006.

Wilkerson, Isabel. "'African-American' Favored by Many of America's Blacks." *New York Times*, January 31, 1989.

Williams, Lorna V. *Self and Society in the Poetry of Nicolás Guillén*. Johns Hopkins Studies in Atlantic History and Culture. Baltimore: Johns Hopkins University Press, 1982.

Wing, Bob. "Indio Claro o Oscuro? Zenaida Mendez Gives Bob Wing a Dominican Perspective on Race and Immigration." *Colorlines*. Oakland, CA: Applied Research Center, July 31, 2001.

Womack, Ytasha. *Post Black: How a New Generation Is Redefining African American Identity*. Chicago: Lawrence Hill Books, 2010.

World Music Central News. "Celina González, Queen of Cuban Punto Dies at 86 | World Music Central." February 5, 2015. https://worldmusiccentral.org/2015/02/04/celina-gonzalez-queen-of-cuban-punto-dies-at-86/.

Yagoda, Ben. *Memoir: A History*. New York: Riverhead Books, 2010.

Youel, Barbara Kraley. "Michaux, Lewis H." In *American National Biography*. https://doi.org/10.1093/anb/9780198606697.article.1602787.

Zagorski, Nick. "Is Postpartum Depression a Unique Psychiatric Disorder?" *Psychiatrics News*, May 4, 2018. https://doi.org/10.1176/appi.pn.2018.4a14.

Zamora, Omaris Z. "Transnational Renderings of *Negro/a/x/**." *Small Axe: A Caribbean Journal of Criticism* 26, no. 2 (July 1, 2022): 93–99. https://doi.org/10.1215/07990537-9901654.

Zapata-Barrero, Ricard. "Interculturalism in the Post-Multicultural Debate: A Defence." *Comparative Migration Studies* 5, no. 1 (September 4, 2017): 14. https://doi.org/10.1186/s40878-017-0057-z.

———. "Interculturalism: Main Hypothesis, Theories and Strands." In *Interculturalism in Cities: Concept, Policy, and Implementation*. Cheltenham, UK: Edward Elgar Publishing, 2015.

———. "Introduction: Framing the Intercultural Turn." In *Interculturalism in Cities: Concept, Policy, and Implementation*. Cheltenham, UK: Edward Elgar Publishing, 2015.

Zapf, Harald. "Slammin' in Transnational Heterotopia: Words Being Spoken at the Nuyorican Poets Cafe." In *Imagined Transnationalism: U.S. Latino/a Literature, Culture, and Identity*, edited by Kevin Concannon, Francisco A. Lomelí, and Marc Priewe, 117–36. New York: Palgrave Macmillan, 2009.

Index

Abiodun, Rowland, 85
accountability, personal, 111, 112
Acosta, Oscar Zeta, 36–37
African, as term, 22–23
African American, as term, 22, 23
African American and Latinx History of the United States, An (Ortiz), 7, 98
African American autobiography, 13–14
African American literature, 2, 16, 24–28, 29, 64
African American studies: background and overview of, 3–4, 25, 29; conclusions on, 130, 132, 137; global turn of, 63–64; Thomas and, 36, 47; transculturalism and, 81. *See also* Afro-Latino studies
African diaspora, 20, 26, 64, 85
Afro-American, as term, 22
Afro-Atlantic, 64, 66, 74
Afro-Caribbean, as term, 22–23
Afro-Caribbean religion. *See* religion, Afro-Caribbean
Afrocentricity: about, 80, 102–3; Cepeda and, 122; Dickerson and, 101; religion and, 84; Vega and, 32, 80, 81, 86, 103
Afro-Cubans, 2, 49. *See also specific Afro-Cubans*
Afroethnic, as term, 22
Afroethnic Renewal, 5–6, 16, 22, 29
Afro-Hispanic Atlantic, 130
Afro-Hispanic Review (*AHR*), 19, 151n51
Afro-Hispanics, as term, 21
Afro-Latin, as term, 19–20, 146n102
Afro-Latin American, as term, 19, 146n102
Afro-Latin@ Reader (Jiménez Román and Flores), 1–2, 21
Afro-Latin@s in Movement (Rivera-Rideau, Jones, and Pachel), 3

"Afro-Latindades" (Laó-Montes), 20
Afro-Latinidad: background and overview of, 1, 3, 19–21, 30, 141n10; Moore and, 65; Vega and, 80, 102–3
Afro-Latino, as term, 20–21, 140n9
"Afro-Latino/a Literature and Identity" (Luis), 21, 23–24, 27
Afro-Latino population, 1
Afro-Latino studies, 19–20, 63–64, 80–81, 82, 130. *See also* African American studies; Latino studies
Alden, Patricia, 9
Alfaro, Olympia, 92
Alfaro, Xiomara, 90, 91–93
All-Africa Peoples Conference, 64
Altar of My Soul, The (Vega), 80
Althusser, Louis, 26
Alvarez, Julia, 24
American Colonization Society (ACS), 22
American Dream, 8, 16–17, 105, 109–10, 133–34, 135, 138
American Society for African Culture, 41
Amigos del Museo del Barrio, 80
Ananias, 77
ancestors and relatives, 38, 122, 123, 124–25. *See also* literary ancestors
And It Don't Stop (Cepeda), 168n59
Andrews, William, 35, 37
Angel, 116–17
"Angelitos Negros" (Alfaro), 92
Angelou, Maya: about, 34; *Heart of a Woman*, 62; *I Know Why the Caged Bird Sings*, 113; *Miss Calypso*, 72; Moore and, 62, 67, 68, 70–73, 74, 76; Thomas and, 42; UN protest and, 62; *We Insist! Max Roach's Freedom Now Suite*, 70
anthologies on literature, 2, 26–27, 35–36, 130

Anzaldúa, Gloria, 51, 89, 136
Aparicio, Frances, 37, 59
apprenticeship, ethnoracial, 9, 14, 17–19, 31, 35, 60, 77, 78
Arnie and Nina, 67
Asante, Molefe Kete, 80, 137
ascent narratives, 5, 77–78, 158n126
àse, 85, 86
àse feminism, 86–87, 88–93
Ashe, Bertram D., 81–82
Asiatic Black Man, 115, 117, 169n71
Association of Hispanic Arts, 80
"As the Spirit Moves Mahalia" (Ellison), 66
attachment disorders, 127–28
At the Bottom of the River (Kincaid), 12–13
"Audacity of Hope, The" (Obama), 79
authenticity, Black, 79, 82, 86, 102, 129
autobiographical pact, 16, 49, 105
autobiography: African American, 35–36; background and overview of, 8, 10, 13–14, 16–17; Latino/a, 105, 112, 132–33; ritualization and, 43
Autobiography (Franklin), 10, 135
Autobiography of a Brown Buffalo, The (Acosta), 36–37
Autobiography of an Ex-Colored Man, The (Johnson), 56

Babalu, 121
"Babalú Babalú Ayé" (Valdez), 92
Bakhtin, M. M., 16, 133
Baldwin, James, 34, 35, 50
Bal Negre, 90
BAM (Black Arts Movement). See Black Arts Movement (BAM)
Baraka, Amiri, 82, 86
BARTS (Black Arts Repertory Theater/ School), 86
becoming, narratives of, 15, 16, 64, 65, 145n85
Beliso-DeJesus, Aisha M., 119
Berlin, Ira, 5–6

Bettelheim, Judith, 119
"Beyond the Rape Myth" (Cha-Jua), 53
BGA (Black Global Aesthetic), 32, 85–87, 88, 89, 93, 98, 103
bildung, as term, 10–11, 14
bildungshelds, 11–12, 15
bildungsroman genre, 8–19; celebratory and depreciatory strands of, 16, 17; conclusions on, 133–35; definitions and types of, 9–10, 16–17; development and, 15–16; didactic function of, 10–11; ethnoracial apprenticeship and, 14, 17–19; identity politics and, 13–15; Latino autobiography and, 8–9; parental crisis and, 11–13; tropes of, 71, 132. See also specific books
biological racism, 54–55
Bird of Paradise (Cepeda): Afro-Caribbean religions and, 118–19; attachment disorders and postpartum depression and, 127–28; background and overview of, 32–33, 103, 104–6, 113–14, 168n59; conclusions on, 128–29; FPN ideology and, 115–18, 123, 124; fukú and, 125–28, 173n154; genetic profiling and, 123–25; hip hop theme of, 114–15; spirit guides and, 118–21, 123, 124–26, 127–28; supernatural powers and, 121–23, 126
Black, as term, 21, 22, 100
Black Aesthetic: background and overview of, 28–29, 32; conclusions on, 136; New, 82, 101, 135–36; Thomas and, 35, 36, 37, 40–41, 42, 46; Vega and, 86
black American, as term, 22–23
Black Arts Movement (BAM): background and overview of, 2, 23, 26, 28, 31; Crawford on, 82–83; literary boom and, 36, 105; nationalism and, 132; Thomas and, 34, 36, 37, 40, 42, 60; Vega and, 85, 86, 102, 161n58
Black Arts Repertory Theater/School (BARTS), 86

Black Atlantic, 64, 65, 74

Black consciousness, 26, 31, 40, 64, 68, 82–83, 84, 86. *See also* ethnoracial consciousness

"black cowardice" jokes, 55, 153–54n114

Black Cuban, Black American (Grillo), 4, 142n22

Black denial, 101, 114, 127, 172n138

black diasporic shivers, 26, 64, 78

black ethnics, as term, 22–23

Black female blues/jazz singers, 65–66, 69–70, 76, 77

"Black Folktales in the Novels of John O. Killens" (Wiggins), 58

Black Global Aesthetic (BGA), 32, 85–87, 88, 89, 93, 98, 103

Black in Latin America (Gates), 1

Black Judgement (Giovanni), 41

Black Latinidad, as term, 63

Black matriarchy, 111–12, 167n50

"BLACK MOTHER WOMAN" (Lorde), 107

Black nationalism. *See* nationalism, Black

Blackness: background and overview of, 14, 24, 26; black post-, 82–83; Cepeda and, 127; Chambers and, 108; end of, 81–82, 100–101, 102–3; global, 63; hegemonic, 63, 64; Moore and, 71–72; post-, 28–29, 81–83, 101, 102; as term, 29–30, 100; Thomas and, 51

black post-blackness, 82–83

Black Post-Blackness (Crawford), 28–29, 82–83

Black Power movement, 19, 23, 24, 25, 29, 105

Black Resonance (Lordi), 66, 69

Black Scholar, The, 30

Black studies. *See* African American studies

black Superwoman trope, 107

blacktino, as term, 140n9

black woman–black man game, 111–12

Black World, 38, 141n16, 151n53

Bling (Cepeda), 127, 168n59

blues, the, 65–66, 69–70, 72, 75, 76

blues/jazz singers, 65–66, 69–70, 72, 76, 77

Bolaki, Stella, 10, 12–13

Brand Nubian, 116–17, 170n86

Brandon, George, 84

Brief Wondrous Life of Oscar Wao, The (Díaz), 30, 134

Brown, Claude, 34, 35, 36

Bruce, John Edward, 132

Buckley, William F., Jr., 50

Buell, Lawrence, 131, 133–34, 135

buppies, 110, 112

Buppies, B-Boys, Baps, and Bohos (George), 28

"Burst of Light, A" (Lorde), 12–13

Calderón, Tego, 127

Caldwell, Katrina Myers, 40

Caldwell, Patricia, 77

Callender, Mr., 68

Cameron, Angus, 38–39

Caminero-Santangelo, Marta, 20, 48, 51–52

Caribbean, as term, 141n12

Caribbean Cultural Center African Diaspora Institute, 79

Casimiro, 119–22, 123

Castro, Fidel, 61, 78

caul bearers, 121

CAWAH (Cultural Association for Women of African Heritage), 62

Center for the Study of White American Culture, 99

Cepeda, Eduardo, 121–22, 126, 127–28

Cepeda, Raquel: about, 4, 18, 32–33, 104, 113, 137, 165–66nn5–6, 168n59; *And It Don't Stop*, 168n59; *Bird of Paradise* (see *Bird of Paradise* (Cepeda)); *Bling*, 127, 168n59; God and, 125, 173n153; *Some Girls*, 168n59

Cepeda, Rocío, 124, 127–28

Cha-Jua, Sundiata, 53

Chambers, Cecilia, 107–8, 109, 110–11
Chambers, Malcolm X, 109, 111
Chambers, Veronica: about, 4, 32–33, 104, 109, 165n2, 165n4; Black nationalism and, 108–9, 167n34; essays of, 108; *Mama's Girl* (see *Mama's Girl*); privileging Blackness of, 108; "Three Young Voices," 108
"Changó Ta Veni" (Machito), 91
Characteristics of Men, Manners, Opinions, and Times (Shaftsbury), 11
Chávez-Silverman, Susana, 37, 59
Chetty, Raj, 101
Chicana/o Latina/o Fiction (Irizarry), 137–38
Chicano movement, 132–33
Chicano studies, 37, 134, 136, 138
Chimezie, Amuzie, 46
Choate Rosemary Hall, 110
choices, 111–12
Christianity, 77, 84
Christmas, Walter, 39, 40
Clarke, John Henrik, 39, 40, 42
civil rights movement, 19, 23, 24, 32–33, 94, 99, 108, 109–10
clairvoyance, 120, 121–22
Clark, Harry Hayden, 131
Clarke, John Henrik, 39, 40, 42
Clifton, Lucille, 24
CNA (Committee for the Negro in Arts), 40
Cocalis, Susan L., 11
Collazo, Julito, 85
collective armed defense, 53
collective armed resistance, 56
collectivity, 82
colored, as term, 22
"Colored Blues Singer" (Cullen), 65–66
colorism, 47, 87–88, 95–98, 138
coming-of-age memoirs, 2, 8, 32, 106, 112–13, 118–19, 135. *See also specific memoirs*
Committee for the Negro in Arts (CNA), 40
Communist Party USA (CPUSA), 39
comparative literary studies, 81, 131, 133, 137–38

conferences on African American literature, 41–42
Conga, 88, 119
Congo, the, 61, 68
Congo Mission to the UN, 61
consciousness: Black, 26, 31, 40, 64, 68, 82–83, 84, 86; decolonial (*see* decolonial consciousness); ethnoracial, 17–19, 21, 37, 75, 76, 87, 111, 117; triple, 48, 105, 108
conservatism, cultural, 96–97
"Contemporary Period, The," 27–28
conversion narratives, 69–70, 72, 77, 78
copiousness of Latinidad, 24, 27, 104–5, 129
Cortés, Hernán, 51
Cosby Show, The, 110
cosmopolitanism, 28, 63, 106
Couser, G. Thomas, 9, 16, 45
COVID-19 pandemic, 134
cowardice, Black, 31, 37, 52–53, 55–56, 153–54n114
CPUSA (Communist Party USA), 39
Crawford, Margo N., 6, 25–26, 28–29, 63, 64, 82–83
"Creation, The" (Johnson), 24
Crisis, The, 2, 38, 42, 151n53
crisis of maternity, 12–13
crisis of paternity, 12, 144n63
Crisis of the Negro Intellectual, The (Cruse), 40–41
critical multiculturalism, 94–95
crucifixion, 52, 53
Cruse, Harold, 40–41, 68, 156n61
Cruz, Celia, 91, 92, 93
Cruz, Victor Hernández, 27
Cuba in the American Imagination (Pérez), 15
Cuban immigrants, 2
Cubop, 85–86, 93
Cullen, Countee, 65–66
"Cult-Nats Meet Freaky Deke, The" (Tate), 28
Cultural Association for Women of African Heritage (CAWAH), 62

cultural conservatism, 96–97
cultural imaginary, 51–52, 81, 133, 135
cultural mulatto trope, 29, 81, 82, 101, 129, 136
cultural pluralism, 104
cultural racism, 54–55
cultural separatism, 104
Cunningham, James, 40
curses, 125–27, 173n154
Cyrus, Stanley, 151n51

Da Costa, Alexandre Emboaba, 94, 95
Dajabón, 120
dance, 85–86, 88, 90–92
Dandridge, Dorothy, 89
Danticat, Edwidge, 107, 108, 166n22
David Copperfield (Dickens), 12, 13
Davies, Catherine Evan, 54, 153n114
Davis, Martha Ellen, 88, 161n75
Davis, Ossie, 151n53
decolonial consciousness, 137; Cepeda and, 104, 117–18, 129; Moore and, 67, 69, 74, 155n6; Vega and, 84, 86–87, 89, 93, 103
DeCosta Willis, Miriam, 151n51
Delbanco, Andrew, 131
Delgadillo, Theresa, 87, 89, 91
demon metaphor, 42, 44
denial, black, 101, 114, 127, 172n138
detours, race and ethnic, 105, 117–18
dialect humor, 54
diasporic shivers, 26, 64, 78
Díaz, Junot, 30, 107, 134, 136, 166n22
Dickerson, Debra, 29–30, 32, 79, 80, 81, 100–102
Different World, A, 110
dignity, 57–59
DNA profiling, 33, 113–14, 123–25
Dolinar, Brian, 40
Dolores, Doña, 127
Dominadora, 88–90, 91–92, 93, 103, 161n75
Dominican Americans, 118
Dominican Republic, 2, 48, 83, 120, 153n81

Dominican Vudú, 88, 118, 120, 122
double standard, patriarchal, 96–97
Douglass, Frederick, 52
Down These Mean Streets (Thomas): background and overview of, 2, 4, 7, 31, 34, 37; bravery and cowardice and, 50–53, 55–56, 153–54n114; censorship of, 42, 151n53; conclusions on, 60, 133, 137; dignity and, 57–59; femininity and masculinity and, 49–52; humor and, 54–56, 153–54n114, 154n121; literary anthologies and, 35–36; NOI and, 165–66n6; origins and rebirth of, 38–42, 150n16; racial identity and, 47–50; Sánchez and, 36–37; therapy of writing of, 42–46
dozens, the, 46, 47, 52
Du Bois, W. E. B., 4, 51, 108–9, 167n31
Dudley, David L., 35, 37
Dunham, Katherine, 32, 85–86, 89, 90–92, 93, 103, 165n154
dysfunctional parenting, 126–28
Dzidzienyo, Anani, 19

Ebony, 38, 42, 151n53
Eckhardt, Meister, 11
eighty-five percenters, 115, 117
El Barrio, 34, 149n2
Elder, Lonne, III, 39
Elkins, Stanley, 52
Ellegua, 120
Ellis, Trey, 28, 29, 82, 101, 136
Ellison, Ralph, 38, 46, 57, 66
Emblidge, David, 68
emergence novels, 16, 133
encoding messages speech practice, 46
end of Blackness, 81–82, 100–101, 102–3
End of Blackness, The (Dickerson), 29–30, 32, 79, 80, 81, 100–102
Ernest, John, 24–25, 26
erotics of terror, 65, 74–76
Espiritismo, 33, 83, 84–85, 86, 118, 119, 122
Essence magazine, 108, 166n22
Estevez, Jorge, 123

ethnic intermarriage. *See* intermarriage, ethnic

ethnicity and race terms, 139n1, 140n2, 140–41nn9–10, 141n12. *See also* *specific terms*

ethnic joking. *See* humor

ethnocentricity, 113, 115, 116

ethnoracial ambiguity, 51, 123

ethnoracial apprenticeship, 14, 17–19, 31, 35, 60, 77, 78

ethnoracial consciousness, 17–19, 21, 37, 75, 76, 87, 111, 117. *See also* Black consciousness

exceptionalism, 52, 56–57, 98, 101, 103, 109–10, 133

Facts of Life, The, 110

Fair Play for Cuba Committee (FPCC), 61, 67

Family Tree DNA, 124

Fatal Self-Deception (Genovese and Fox-Genovese), 52

female blues/jazz singers, 65–66, 69–70, 76, 77

femininity and Blacks, 51–52

feminism: movement of, 105; Vega and, 86–87, 88–93

Fernández, Johanna, 7

Fetchit, "Stepin," 154n114

Fez Under Time Café, 116

Figueroa, Arlis M., 118

Figueroa-Vásquez, Yomaira C., 63–64, 137, 149n175

"Finding Your Roots with Henry Louis Gates Jr.," 124

Fisk University, 41, 42

five percenters, 115

Five Percent Nation (FPN), 4, 104, 113, 114–18, 122–23, 169n71, 170n86

Flores, Juan, 1–2, 17, 20–21, 48

Fontaine, Pierre-Michel, 19

fourth great migration, 6, 22, 29, 130

Fox-Genovese, Elizabeth, 52

Franklin, Benjamin, 10, 135

Freestyle Fellowship, 116

Frey, William H., 99, 100

fukú, 125–27, 128, 173n154

Fuller, Hoyt, 40

García Peña, Lorgia, 63–64

Garvey, Marcus, 36, 73

Garveyite orators, 68, 70, 73–74

Gates, Henry Louis, Jr., 1, 113, 124, 128

Geertz, Clifford, 25

genetic profiling, 33, 113–14, 123–25

Genovese, Eugene D., 52

George, Nelson, 1, 30; *Buppies, B-Boys, Baps, and Bohos*, 28; *Post-Soul Nation*, 32, 79, 80, 81, 100–101, 119

gigul nesamot, 122, 172n132

Gillespie, Dizzy, 85

Gilmore, Leigh, 13, 45, 144n72

Gilroy, Paul, 14, 64, 65, 74, 149n175

Gilyard, Keith, 41, 42

Giovanni, Nikki, 41

Gitana, 87, 88, 119, 161n71, 161n73

Glaude, Eddie S., 25

Glissant, Édouard, 26, 64

Global Afro-Latino and Caribbean Initiative, 80

global black consciousness, 26, 64

global blackness, 63

Goethe, Johann Wolfgang von, 9, 14

Goetz, Bernhard, 115

Golden, Thelma, 28, 81

González Zamora, Celina, 90, 92–93

Graham, Sarah, 16, 145n87

Gramsci, Antonio, 17

Greenspan, Bennett, 124, 172n132

Greer, Christina M., 5–6, 22–23

Griffin, William Michael, Jr., 122

Grillo, Evelio, 4, 104, 142n22

Grillo, Frank "Machito," 85, 87, 91

Gruner, Charles R, 55, 153–54n114

Guillén, Nicolás, 2, 4, 27, 132, 137

Gutiérrez, Ramón A., 19

Guy, Rosa, 39, 40, 62

hair, 71–72, 73, 76, 157n89

Haiti, 120

Haitian Massacre, 120
Hare Krishna, 120, 171n123
Harlem Writers Guild (HWG): about, 24, 31, 39–40; Thomas and, 34–35, 37, 38, 39, 40, 42; UN protest and, 62
Harris-Perry, Melissa, 113
Hart-Celler Act, of 1965, 29
Hartman, Saidiya V., 65, 74–75
Head, Dominic, 106
"heart," 52, 53
Heart of a Woman (Angelou), 62
hegemonic blackness, 63, 64
Helen, 70, 157n82
Henke, Suzette A., 42–43
Heredia, Juanita, 87, 89, 92, 96–97
Herman, Judith Lewis, 44
Hernández, Carmen Dolores, 43
Hernández, Tanya Katerí, 99–100
hierarchy, racial, 98, 138
hip-hop, 113, 114–15, 116, 137, 168n59
Hispanic, as term, 19
Hispanic Caribbean, as term, 141n12
Hispanic population, 1
historical emergence, 16
historical fantasy, 132, 135
historically Black colleges and universities (HBCUs), 41–42, 80, 151n50, 159n6. See also specific HBCUs
Hoffnung-Garskof, Jesse, 94
Holmes, Odetta, 71, 157n89
Homage to Catalonia (Orwell), 67
Hot Music, Ragmentation, and the Bluing of American Literature (Tracy), 65–66, 77
Howard University, 19, 36, 39, 42, 151n51
Hubbard, Dolan, 69, 70, 77
Huggan, Graham, 106
Hughes, Langston, 132
humanism, 9, 67–68, 69, 71, 122
humor: about, 154n121; ethnic jokes, 31, 37, 54–56, 153–54n114; protest, 31, 58; Thomas and, 37, 44–46, 54–56
Hunsaker Hawkins, Anne, 43, 44
Hurston, Zora Neale, 4, 109, 110, 128–29

HWG (Harlem Writers Guild). See Harlem Writers Guild
hybridity, racial, 67, 96, 98, 100–101, 114. See also multiracialism

I-as-We motif, 65–66, 67
idealism/materialism, 106
identity: background and overview of, 2, 5, 6, 8, 18–19; Cepeda and, 114, 115, 123, 168n59; Chambers and, 109, 110; Hispanic Caribbean religion and, 84; intermarriage and, 101–2; Latinidad and, 24, 63; liberal individualism and, 136; memoir, bildungsroman, and apprenticeship and, 8, 13–15, 16, 17, 18–19, 132, 145n85; Moore and, 63, 75, 78; multiracialism and, 99–100; naming politics and, 19–20, 23; narrative fracture and, 138; Thomas and, 34, 35, 37, 47–51, 55–57, 60
I Know Why the Caged Bird Sings (Angelou), 113
immersion narrative, 5, 47, 158n126
immigration, 2, 5–6, 21, 22–23, 29
imperial cosmopolitanism, 63
In Chaotic Justice (Ernest), 24–25, 26
Indian blood, 48, 51
Indigeneity: Afro-Caribbean religion and, 119; black denial and, 101; Cepeda and, 117, 121, 123, 124, 126; Thomas and, 47–48, 49–51, 53–54, 55–56, 152n79
Indigenous bravery, 50–51, 55
individualism, 9–11, 28–29, 82, 103, 112–13, 133, 136
individualism/communalism dialects, 106, 113
infantilization, 15, 31, 52, 57–59
"Inner City Boundaries" (Freestyle Fellowship), 116
insurgent nationalism, 136, 137, 138
integrationism: background and overview of, 1, 9, 10–11; Chambers and, 32–33, 104, 109–11, 113; interculturalism and, 95, 102

integrative practice, 66–67
interculturalism: background and overview of, 1, 2, 4, 6; conclusions on, 131, 132, 133, 138; global black consciousness and, 63–64; Moore and, 61, 64, 78; Thomas and, 36–37; Vega and, 32, 83, 87, 89–91, 93–95, 97–102, 103
intermarriage, ethnic, 93–102; identity and, 100–102; patriarchal double standard and, 96–97; post-racialism, multiracialism; multiculturalism, and interculturalism and, 81, 94–101
internationalism, 67–68, 69
interpellation, 26
interracial dating, 67, 70–71
intertextualization, 58–59, 60, 67, 82, 83, 92–93, 113
Irizarry, Ylce, 137–38
ISSD Task Force on Children and Adolescents, 127–28
It Takes a Nation of Millions to Hold Us Back (Public Enemy), 115

Jackson, Blyden, 35–36
Jackson, Mahalia, 66
Jackson, Sheneska, 108
James Clifford, 56, 58–59
Japtok, Martin, 106
Jarret, Gene Andrew, 25, 26
jazz, 32, 69, 70, 85–86, 91–92, 93
jazz singers, 65–66, 69–70, 76, 77
Jeffers, Thomas L., 9–10, 12, 13, 144n64
Jet, 38, 42, 68, 151n53
Jiménez Román, Miriam, 1–2, 20–21
Johansen, Emily, 63
Johnson, Brewster "Brew," 47, 49, 50, 51, 52–56, 59
Johnson, James Weldon, 24, 56
jokes, ethnic, 31, 37, 54–56, 153–54n114. See also humor
Jones, Jennifer A., 3
Jordon, June, 24
jorocón, 62, 155n12

"Justification for Autobiography" (Gramsci), 17

Kabbalism, 122–23
kalokagathia, 11
Karenga, Ron, 40
Karina, 70
Kennedy, Randall, 28, 82
Kerina, Mburumba, 68, 76, 158n117
Kester, Gunilla Theander, 10, 12, 14
Killens, John Oliver: about, 4, 24, 38; conferences and, 41–42; HWG and, 31, 40; Thomas and, 4, 37, 38, 39, 40–41, 46–47, 60, 150n16; Wiggins on, 58; *Youngblood*, 31, 37, 38, 58–59, 150n16
Kincaid, Jamaica, 12–13
King, Rodney, 117
King, Walter Eugene, 84, 86
King Leopold's Soliloquy (Twain), 68–69
kinkeepers, 123–24
kismet, 120, 122
Knight, Carl, 111
knowledge of self, 115–17, 123, 124
Kutzinski, Vera M., 23

la africana, 118, 119, 123, 124–26, 127–28
La Conga, 88, 119
La Dominadora, 88–90, 91–92, 93, 103, 161n75
La Gitana, 87, 88, 119, 161n71, 161n73
la india, 118, 119, 123, 124–25, 127–28
Lam, C. Christina, 118
La Madama, 87, 88, 119
La Malinche trope, 36, 37, 51
Laó-Montes, Agustin, 19, 20, 146n103
La Rosa Estrada, 90
Latinez, Alejandro, 8, 15
Latinidad: background and overview of, 7, 20, 23; Cepeda and, 105, 114, 115, 117, 129; Chambers and, 103, 105, 108, 109, 129; conclusions on, 130; copiousness of, 24, 27, 104–5, 129; detours and, 105; Thomas and, 34, 43, 59. See also Afro-Latinidad

Latinities, as term, 24, 56, 104–5
Latin jazz, 80, 85–86, 91–92, 93
Latino, as term, 19, 21, 23
Latino autobiography, 2, 8–9, 105, 133
Latino studies: background and overview of, 1, 3–4, 7, 8, 19–20, 23–24, 29; conclusions on, 130, 135–36, 137; individualism and, 82; Latinidad and, 104–5, 129; Thomas and, 36, 47. *See also* Afro-Latino studies
Laura, 68, 69, 74–76, 78
Leacock, Richard, 38–39
Lee, Sonia Song-Ha, 98
Lee, Spike, 126, 173n158
León, Oscar de, 134, 136
LeSeur, Geta, 8, 12
Lewis, Oscar, 37
liberal humanism, 67–68, 69, 71
liberal individualism, 28–29, 82, 103, 133, 136
liberal multiculturalism, 94, 105–6, 138
libertarian absolutism, 28, 82
life writing: background and overview of, 2, 3, 6, 8; Cepeda and, 105; Chambers and, 105; conclusions on, 132, 133, 136, 137; Moore and, 65, 77; Thomas and, 42, 45. *See also* autobiography; bildungsroman genre; memoir genre
Ligon, Glenn, 28, 81
Lincoln, Abbey, 62, 68, 70, 71
linked racial fate, 1, 98, 108
literary ancestors, 4, 19, 38, 60, 109, 128–29
literary boom, multiethnic, 105–7
literary influence theory, 38
literary nationalism. *See* nationalism, literary
"Literature of the Negro in the United States, The" (Wright), 69
Litwack, Leon F., 50
Locke, Alain, 132
López, Antonio, 49

Lorde, Audre, 4, 12–13, 107, 109
Lordi, Emily, 29, 66, 69, 77
Louis M. Rabinowitz Foundation, 39
Loving v. Virginia, 95
luck egalitarianism, 33, 103, 104, 111–12
Lucy (Kincaid), 12–13
Luis, William, 19, 21, 23–24, 27
Lumumba, Patrice, 61, 62, 68
lynching, 47, 52–53

machismo, 35, 52, 108, 168–69n65. *See also* masculinity
Machito, 85, 87, 91
Madama, 87, 88, 119
Magical negro trope, 125, 126, 173n158
magical powers, 84, 125, 126, 128
magical realism, 118, 134
Maillo-Pozo, Sharina, 114
Makeba, Miriam, 71, 157n89
Malcolm X, 31, 34, 70, 76–77, 78, 115
Mama's Girl (Chambers): acknowledgments for, 112–13; background and overview of, 32–33, 103, 104–6, 165n4, 166n22; Black nationalism and, 108–9; conclusions on, 128–29; integrationism and, 110–11; jump metaphor in, 110, 112; luck egalitarianism and, 111–12; mother-daughter relationship in, 107–8, 110–11
mambo, 85, 87, 88, 90–91, 93
Mambo, 89, 92
Manchild in the Promised Land (Brown), 36–37
marginalization of Afro-Latino memoirs, 3, 12, 13, 103, 106, 133
Maria, 116, 119–21, 123
María de la O. (spirit guide), 161n71
marianismo, 97, 168–69n65
market aesthetics, 49, 106, 109
Marxism, 67–68
masculinity, 34, 37, 49–51, 52, 53, 58, 60, 167n50
masking, 54, 57, 66, 76
maternity, crisis of, 12–13

matriarchy, Black, 111–12, 167n50

Meaning of Soul, The (Lordi), 29

"Measures for the Economic Development of Underdeveloped Countries" (UN), 15

Melamed, Jodi, 105–6

Memoir (Couser), 9, 16

memoir genre, 4, 8, 9; coming of age, 2, 8, 32, 106, 112–13, 118–19, 135. *See also* autobiography; bildungsroman genre

memory of slavery, 14, 65, 74–76, 78

Mendez, Julio, 90

mestizaje: about, 21, 95–96; Cepeda and, 117, 118, 125, 129; Saldívar and, 136; Thomas and, 48; Vega and, 89, 91, 93, 95–96, 98

Michaux, Lewis H., 4, 31, 62, 68–69, 73

Milian, Claudia, 24, 27, 104–5

Militant, The, 67

Miss Calypso (Angelou), 72

misterios. *See* spirit guides

Mitchell-Kernan, Claudia, 46

Miyakawa, Felicia, 113

Mohr, Nicholasa, 24

Moore, Carlos: about, 4, 31, 61–62, 71–72, 137, 154n2; Angelou and, 62, 67, 68, 70–73, 74, 76; "informal schooling" of, 63, 67–70; *Pichón* (see *Pichón*); UN protest and, 62, 155n20; Whites and, 70–71

Moore, Victor, 157n92

Moore, Willard, 39

Moore, Winifred, 71–72, 157n92

Mora, Francisco Pancho, 83–84

morenophilia, 83, 86–93, 103

morenophobia, 83, 93–102, 103

Morrison, Toni, 4, 109

Moses, Wilson Jeremiah, 7, 64

Mostern, Kenneth, 13–14

mother-daughter relationships, 13, 107–8, 126, 127

moyeto, 47–48, 152n75

Moynihan, Daniel Patrick, 37, 167n50

Muhammad, Elijah, 113

Muhammad Speaks, 76

mulatez, 21, 82, 93, 95–96, 98, 117, 129

multiculturalism: background and overview of, 28, 94–95; Chambers and, 107; Dickerson and, 101; liberal, 94, 105–6, 138; Vega and, 97, 102

multiracial identity movement, 99–100

multiracialism, 28, 96, 99–101, 134

Murillo, John, 27

Murray, Conrad, 81, 82

music: Afro-Cuban, 85–86, 90–93; blues, 65–66, 69–70, 72, 75, 76; Cepeda and, 114–15, 116; hip-hop, 113, 114–15, 116, 137, 168n59; Latin jazz, 85–86, 91, 93; Moore and, 62, 68, 71, 72, 74; Santeria and, 84–85; Vega and, 85–86, 87, 88, 90–93

musical networks, 91

My Father's Shadow (Dudley), 35

mysticism, 11, 84, 113, 118, 123, 126. *See also* spirit guides; supernatural, the

Nacer, 161n71

naming, politics of, 19–23, 27

Nardal, Jane, 146n102

narrative of fracture, 138

narratives: ascent, 5, 77–78, 158n126; bildungsroman (*see* bildungsroman genre); of Cepeda, 113, 114, 123; of Chambers, 107, 112–13; conclusions on, 131, 132, 135; conversion, 69–70, 72, 77, 78; immersion, 5, 47, 158n126; of Moore, 67, 69–70, 71, 72, 77–78; post-blackness and, 81–82; of Thomas, 37, 43, 45, 47, 60; of Vega, 86, 88, 91, 93–94, 100, 101

Nasario, Isaac, 54

national character, 49–50, 52, 55

National Conference of Afro-American Writers of 1974, 42

nationalism, Black: background and overview of, 3, 6–7, 32–33; Cepeda and, 104, 105, 106, 114, 115, 117, 129; Chambers and, 104, 105, 106, 108–9, 129, 167n34; conclusions on, 132–33;

HWG and SAC and, 40, 41; Moore and, 61, 63, 64–65, 67, 68, 70, 74; pragmatic, 60, 70, 82, 116; Thomas and, 34
nationalism, insurgent, 136, 137, 138
nationalism, literary: about, 131, 132–33, 135; Thomas and, 34, 38, 40
National Memorial African Bookstore (NMAB), 5, 62, 68–69, 157n68
National Negro Congress (NNC), 39–40
Nation of Islam (NOI), 4, 67, 76, 104, 113, 115, 165–66n6
Neal, Larry, 86
Negritude, 41
Negro, as term, 22, 96
Negro Digest, 2, 38, 40, 42, 141n16, 151n53
Nelson, Alondra, 123
neoliberalism, 1, 79, 83, 99, 103, 112
New Black Aesthetic, 82, 101, 135–36
"New Black Aesthetic, The" (Ellis), 28
new mestiza, 51, 136
New Negro movement, 26
New Word, 116
"9mm Goes Bang" (Boogie Down Productions), 115
NMAB (National Memorial African Bookstore), 5, 62, 68–69, 157n68
NNC (National Negro Congress), 39–40
NOI (Nation of Islam), 4, 67, 76, 104, 113, 115, 165–66n6
Norrick, Neal R., 55
Norton Anthology of African American Literature, 2, 26–27
Norton Anthology of Contemporary African American Poetry, 27
novels of education, 16
novels of historical emergence, 16
Nuyorican Movement, 31, 37, 60
Nuyorican Poets Café, 116
Nuyoricans, 17, 84, 132. *See also specific Nuyoricans*
Nwankwo, Ifeoma C. K., 107

Obama, Barack, 79
Obatalá, Ayáguna, 80, 161n71

Oetinger, Friedrich Christoph, 11
Oliana, Chris, 86
O'Neale, Sondra, 66
one-drop rule, 48, 49
On Latinidad (Caminero-Santangelo), 20, 48, 51–52
Operation Boot Strap, 2, 149n2
orishas, 80, 83–84, 85, 86, 90–92, 121, 161n71
Ortiz, Fernando, 63
Ortiz, Paul, 7, 98
Orwell, George, 67
Oseijeman, Oba, 84, 86
Oxford Companion to African American Literature, The, 2, 27, 35–36
Oxford English Dictionary, 19

Padmore, George, 64
Pan-African Congresses, 64
Pan-Africanism: Cepeda and, 127; Moore and, 61–62, 64, 67, 68, 69
Pan-Africanism or Communism (Padmore), 64
Panama, author in, 17–18
Panamanian–West Indian experience, 107
Pandora's box metaphor, 42, 44
parental crises, 11–13
Parker, Theodore, 52
Parks, Gordon, 41
Paschel, Tianna S., 3
passing, 8–9, 13, 47, 56–57, 59–60, 105
paternity, crisis of, 12, 144n63
pathography, 42–46
patriarchal double standard, 96–97
patriarchy, 93, 112, 117, 126
Payne, Rodger M., 77
Paz, Octavio, 37
Peller, Gary, 110–11
Pérez, Louis A., Jr., 15
Pérez Gutiérrez, Felipa "Graciela," 87, 90, 92, 93
perfection, individual, 11
periodization, 26, 27–28, 135
Perlmann, Joel, 99, 100

Petey and Johnny, 38

Petry, Ann, 108, 128

Philadelphia Negro, The (Du Bois), 51

pichón, as term, 155n3

Pichón (Moore): background and overview of, 31, 61–65; Black female blues singers and, 65–66; conclusions on, 77–78; erotics of terror and, 74–76; Garveyite Orators and, 73–74; informal schooling and, 67–70; interracial dating and, 70–71; Malcolm X and, 76–77; Moore's mother and, 71–72

Pickering, Michael, 49–50

pigmentocracy, 95

Pinson, DovBer, 122–23

piolos, 62, 70, 155n12

Plotinus, 11

poetics of relation, 64, 81

Popular Front, 31, 35, 37, 39–40, 60

population of ethnic minorities, 1

post-blackness. *See* black post-blackness; post-soul aesthetic

postcolonial exotic, 106

postpartum depression, 126, 128

postrace aesthetic, 118–19, 134, 135

Postrace Generation, 134–35

post-racialism, 79, 94, 95–96

post-soul, as term, 1, 28

post-soul aesthetic: background and overview of, 28–30, 32; Cepeda and, 104, 106, 115, 117–18, 119, 129; Chambers and, 104, 106, 110, 112–13, 129; conclusions on, 130, 133, 136; Vega and, 79, 80–83, 99, 100–101, 102–3

Post-Soul Afro-Latinidades, 30

post-soul era, 1, 4, 26, 28, 100, 103, 119

Post-Soul Nation (George), 32, 79, 80, 81, 100–101, 119

post-traumatic stress, 42, 44–45

Pozo, Chano, 85

pragmatic black nationalism, 60, 70, 82, 116

pragmatism, African American, 53, 55, 56

Pratt, Alan R., 154n121

premonitory powers, 120, 121–22

Price, Lloyd, 41

Public Enemy, 115

public scrutiny, 4, 13, 45, 105

"Qué assimilated, brother, yo soy asimilao" (Flores), 17

Quinones, Margie Baynes, 84

racial chauvinism, 80, 117, 133

racial consciousness, 17–19, 21, 37, 75, 76, 87, 111, 117. *See also* Black consciousness

racial essentialism, 28, 117, 129

racial humor. *See* humor

racial hybridity. *See* hybridity, racial

racial initiation, 47, 50

racial intermarriage, 95. *See also* intermarriage, ethnic

racial social order, 25, 47, 52–53, 57, 60

racial trauma, 13–14

racism, 14, 54–55, 79, 94, 134

Rahman, Jacquelyn, 55

Ramírez, Efrén, 137

Rappaport, Leon, 55

"Reconstructing Dominican *Latinidad*" (Maillo-Pozo), 114

reincarnation, 122

relationships, intercultural, 24, 93, 102, 132

relatives and ancestors, 38, 122, 123, 124–25. *See also* literary ancestors

relief theory, 55

religion, Afro-Caribbean, 83–86, 104, 113, 118–20, 121, 123, 128–29. *See also* specific religions

Representing the Race (Jarret), 25, 26

Richards, Henry, 151n51

Ricourt, Milagros, 88

rituals, 43–44, 46, 52, 66, 84, 90

Rivail, Hippolyte Léon Denizard, 84

Rivera, Louis Reyes, 24

Rivera-Rideau, Petra R., 3

Roach, Max, 68, 70, 71

Rock, John, 52
Rogers, J. A., 68
Royster, Francesca T., 30

Saal, Ilka, 81–82
SAC (Society of African Culture), 41
Sáez, Elena Machado, 106
Saint Martha, 88–89, 118
Saldívar, Ramón, 118–19, 132, 134–36
Sambo thesis, 52
Sánchez, Marta E., 7, 36–37, 51, 57
Sánchez-Carretero, Cristina, 120
Santamaría, Ramón "Mongo," 90
Santería, 80, 83–86, 89–90, 92, 118,
    121, 122
Santerismo, 84, 86–88, 89, 93, 118,
    119, 122
Saul of Tarsus, 77
Scenes of Subjection (Hartman), 65, 74–75
Schomburg, Arthur (Arturo) A., 4, 27,
    94, 102, 132, 137
scientific and the scared, the, 125
scriptotherapy, 42–46
"Secret Latina, The" (Chambers), 108
"Secret Latina at Large" (Chambers), 108
self-determination, 43, 84, 86, 117, 133
self-esteem enhancing function, 55
Senghor, Léopold Sédar, 41, 85
sermonic rhetoric, African American,
    69–70, 77
Seven African Powers, 84
Sexton, Jared, 96
sexual violence, 74–75
Shadow and Act (Ellison), 38, 46, 57
Shaftsbury, Earl of, 11
"Shakin' Up" Race and Gender (Sánchez),
    36–37, 51, 57
Shango, 90
Shea, Daniel B., Jr., 72–73
Shelby, Tommie, 7, 60, 70, 82, 116
Shepperson, George, 64
shivers, black diasporic, 26, 64, 78
shock of elsewhere, 26, 64, 78
signifying, 31, 37, 46, 58–60
Simmons, Kimberly Eison, 101

Simmons, K. Merinda, 7, 28, 82
Simone, Nina, 71, 157n89
sincere ambivalence, 66
Singing Gods (Dunham), 86
Singleton, Joseph "Joe," 93, 95, 97–99,
    101–2
skin color, 47–48, 87–88, 95–96, 115
Slaughter, Joseph R., 11
"Slow Down" (Brand Nubian), 117
Smart, Ian, 151n51
Smethurst, James E., 7, 39, 132–33
Smith, Candis Watts, 5–6
Smith, Clarence Edward, 113, 168n57
Socialist Workers Party (SWP), 61,
    67, 68
socially embedded subjectivities, 136
social order, 25, 47, 52–53, 57, 60, 111
Society of African Culture (SAC), 41
solidarity, 6, 7, 14, 23, 63, 84–85, 93, 138
Some Girls (Cepeda), 168n59
"Some Reflections on the Black Aes-
    thetic" (Neal), 86
sonic fusions, 91
Sounding Like a No-No? (Royster), 30
sources for this study, 6–8
Southern Negro Youth Congress, 39
spaces of sincerity, 66–67, 69–70, 72, 73,
    75–76
Spalding, Johann Joachim, 11
Spanish-American War, 2, 15
Spanish Harlem, 34, 149n2
speculative realism, 104, 118–19, 125,
    128, 132, 134, 169n65
speech practices, African American, 46
spirit guides: about, 84; Cepeda and,
    118–21, 123, 128; Vega and, 87, 88–90,
    161n71, 161n73. See also specific spirit
    guides
Spiritism. See Espiritismo
Spiritual Autobiography in Early America
    (Shea), 72–73
spiritual conversion narrative, 72, 77, 78
Srivastava, Neelam, 63
Stavans, Ilan, 44
Stepto, Robert B., 5

stereotypes, 55, 59, 114
structural racism, 14, 79, 94, 134
structures of feelings, 26
supernatural, the, 33, 84, 119–22,
    123–25, 126–28, 173n154
Superwoman trope, 107
symbolic geography, 5
sympathetic audience, 44
systemic racism, 14, 79, 94, 134

Taínos, 117, 118, 119, 120, 123, 152n79,
    172n138
"Talented Tenth" (Du Bois), 108, 167n31
Talented Tenth elitism, 33, 103, 108
Tallaj, Angelina, 118
Tate, Greg, 7, 28
Taylor, Paul, 81, 159n11
"Television Satire in the Black Americas"
    (Vásquez), 30
Temple University, 5, 159n6
ten-percenters, 115, 169n74
territorialized cosmopolitanism, 63
terror of the erotic, 74–76
theory of literary influence, 38
therapy, 42–46
Thomas, Daniela, 39
Thomas, José, 47–48
Thomas, Lorenzo, 27
Thomas, Piri, 34–60; about, 4, 18, 24,
    27, 34–35, 149n1; Down These Mean
    Streets (see Down These Mean Streets);
    identity and, 34–35, 36, 37, 47–51,
    55–57, 60; Killens and, 4, 37, 38, 39,
    40–41, 46–47, 60, 150n16; literary
    conferences and, 41–42; in maga-
    zines, 42, 151n53; in prison, 38, 43,
    150n16; "World of Piri Thomas," 41
"Three Young Voices" (Chambers,
    Danticat, and Jackson), 108
tikkun olam, 122
timbre of sincerity, 66–67
time travel metaphor, 42, 44, 45
Tomasa, María de la O., 87–88
Torres, Lourdes, 8, 112
Torres-Saillant, Silvio, 8, 21, 132

Touré, 81, 82, 135
Tracy, Stephen C., 65–66, 77
transcultural detours, 105
transculturalism, 3–4, 60, 63, 66, 81
transformational agent, 69, 77
"Transformation of the Bildung from an
    Image to an Ideal, The" (Cocalis), 11
transnational imaginary, 133–35, 136
transnationalism: background and
    overview of, 1, 3–4; conclusions on,
    131, 133, 136, 137; Vega and, 82, 83,
    86, 91
trauma, 13–14, 42–43, 44–46, 75, 125
trickster passing, 56–57, 59–60
triple consciousness, 48, 105, 108
"Triple Consciousness" (Flores and
    Jiménez Román), 20–21, 48
trope of the self, 132, 133
tropicalization, 37, 58–59
Truman, Harry, 15
Turntable, 41
Twain, Mark, 68–69

universalism, 103, 131
UN Security Council meeting protest,
    62, 155n20
US Censuses, 1, 19, 99, 100
US Hispanic Caribbean literature, 23–24

Valdez, Gilberto, 90
Valdez, Miguelito, 92
Van Deburg, William L., 7, 64
Vanderhans, Gaucho, 90
Vásquez, Sam, 30
Vàzquez, David J., 132, 136–37
Vega, Alberto "Chachito," 87, 91, 97
Vega, Flora, 96–97
Vega, Luisa, 87–88, 97
Vega, Marta Moreno: about, 79–80, 87–88,
    137; Afro diaspora religions and, 84–85;
    Altar of My Soul, 80; When the Spirits
    Dance Mambo (see When the Spirits
    Dance Mambo); Yoruba Philosophy, 80
Vega, Socorro "Chachita," 87, 93, 95,
    96–99, 101–2, 103

veneration and reincarnation, 122

verbal dueling, 46

"Veronica Chambers '87" (Chambers), 108

Visual Arts Research and Resource Center Relating to the Caribbean, 79

vodun, 86, 88, 90, 118, 120

Voice of a New Race, The, 137

von Huene Greenberg, Dorothee, 45

Vudú, 118, 120, 122

"Wake Up" (Brand Nubian), 116, 170n86

Wallace, Michele, 107

Walrond, Eric, 27, 36

Warren, Kenneth W., 6, 25, 26, 29

Weaver, Simon, 54–55

We Insist! Max Roach's Freedom Now Suite (Angelou), 70

Werner, Craig, 69

West, Gerald Andrew, 51

What Is African American Literature (Crawford), 25–26

"What's in A Name" (Gutiérrez), 19

What Was African American Literature? (Warren), 25, 26

When the Spirits Dance Mambo (Vega): background and overview of, 31–32, 79–83; colorism and, 87–88, 95–98; conclusions on, 102–3; feminism and, 86–87, 88–93; intermarriage and, 93–102; music and dance and, 89,

90–93; "Negrita Linda" chapter of, 92; religion and, 83–86; spirit guides and, 88–90, 93, 161n71, 161n73

Whitehead, Colson, 134, 135

whitening, race, 48, 98, 153n81

White supremacy, 21, 96, 99

Wieland, Christoph Martin, 11

Wiggins, William H., Jr., 58

Wilhelm Meister's Apprenticeship (Goethe), 9

Wilhelm Meister's Journeyman Years, or the Renunciants (Goethe), 9

Williams, Kim M., 99, 100

Williams, Raymond, 26, 81

Williams, Robert F., 78

Wilson, Ted, 86, 161n58

Winckelmann, Johann Joachim, 11

Womack, Ytasha L., 81, 82

"World of Piri Thomas, The" (Thomas), 41

Wright, Richard, 34, 69

Wright, Sarah, 39, 62

writing therapy, 42–46

Yoruba, 83, 85, 86, 90, 120

Yoruba Philosophy (Vega), 80

Young Lords, The (Fernández), 7

Young Lords Party, 23

Youth Development Inc., 38

Zami (Lorde), 12–13

Zone One (Whitehead), 134

Printed in the USA
CPSIA information can be obtained
at www.ICGtesting.com
LVHW040947020923
757045LV00005B/199